A HISTORY OF

Washington County

From Isolation to Destination

DOUGLAS D. ALDER
KARL F. BROOKS

First Edition 1996
Utah State Historical Society
Washington County Commission

Second Edition 2007
Zion Natural History Association

ISBN 978-0-915630-45-5
Library of Congress Catalog Card Number 96-60793
Map by Automated Geographic Reference Center – State of Utah

Cover design by Sandy Bell
Book layout for second edition by Ron Woodland
Printed in the United States of America

Zion Natural History Association
Zion National Park
Springdale, Utah 84767
www.zionpark.org

*This book is dedicated to both the old-timers
and the newcomers of WASHINGTON COUNTY*

Contents

ACKNOWLEDGEMENTS   IX

GENERAL INTRODUCTION   XIII

INTRODUCTION   XV

CHAPTER   1   The Land and Its Early Inhabitants   1

CHAPTER   2   Settlement   12

CHAPTER   3   Sinking Roots   49

CHAPTER   4   Stability and Isolation   71

CHAPTER   5   Stories and Reflections   123

CHAPTER   6   Cultural Life   154

CHAPTER   7   Water   171

CHAPTER   8   End of Isolation, 1930-1960   201

CHAPTER   9   Americanization Escalates   249

CHAPTER 10   The New Pioneers   283

CHAPTER 11   Modernization   324

CHAPTER 12   The Debate over the Future
of Washington County   350

CHAPTER 13   Growth Expectations Fulfilled, 1996-2006 . . .   359

APPENDIX A   Washington County Commissioners   409

APPENDIX B   Sheriffs of Washington County   413

APPENDIX C   Mayors of St. George   415

APPENDIX D   Irrigation Systems in Washington Co.   417

Selected Bibliography   419

Index   427

Acknowledgments

The writing of this book has involved many people. The Washington County Commission — consisting of Jerry Lewis, Gayle Aldred, and Russell Gallian at that time — appointed a supervisory committee chaired by Loren Webb to select the authors and direct the project. Webb arranged the monthly meetings over three years and invited citizens throughout the county to come and share their knowledge. J. L. Crawford, Heber Jones, Dorothy Gardner, Laura Bowler, Lyman Hafen, and Helen Gardner served on that committee. They exercised a major influence on the project, including their many hours of reading the complete Washington County News. Cuba Lyle served as archives specialist and was tireless in directing us. All, including the authors, served without remuneration and have been superior advisors.

Dixie College has been a steady supporter of this effort. We are indebted particularly to the staff of the Val A. Browning Library on the campus. Audrey Shumway, library director, Allyson Martin, archivist, and Rob Snow, academic computing, were particularly helpful. We express gratitude also to the staffs of the Harold B. Lee Library at Brigham Young University, the Marriott Library at the University of

Utah, Southern Utah University Library, the LDS Family History Library in St. George, and the Utah State Historical Society Library for help with source materials.

Kent Powell and Craig Fuller of the Utah State Historical Society have been superior organizers of the larger Utah Centennial County History project of which this book is one part. They have been valued advisors and editors of our volume. Brian Reeve was a helpful research assistant. Lowell C. Bennion and Wayne Hinton were valued outside readers.

As part of the research, we held hearings concerning several individual communities: Santa Clara, Ivins, New Harmony, Springdale, Rockville, Virgin, La Verkin, Hurricane, Gunlock, Toquerville, Pine Valley, Enterprise, Silver Reef, and the Shivwits Indian Reservation. We express gratitude to those who participated in the sessions. We also interviewed many living participants in Dixie's history. These included: John Allen, Art Anderson, Bart Anderson, Clayton Atkin, Sid Atkin, Nellie Ballard, Rhanee Ballard, Wilma Beal, Paul Beatty, Effie Beckstrom, Philip Bimstein, Lenny Brinkerhoff, Arnold Brownstein, Duane Blake, Craig Booth, Marion Bowler, Truman Bowler, Erma Bracken, Chapin Burks, Ken Campbell, Bill Clark, Ed Clark, Venese Clark, Alan Coombs, Clara Ruesch Cope, Wesley Dennett, Reva Emett, Stan Esplin, T. Lavoy Esplin, Schuyler Everett, Austen Excell, Helen Excell, Louise Excell, Lynn Excell, Norman Fawson, Emma Fife, Lang Foremaster, Floyd Fox, Sue Fraley, Douglas Garner, Dean Gardner, Larry Gardner, Duane Gentry, Eldon Gentry, Larkin Gifford, Paul Graf, Wallea Baker Grayman, Sheldon Grant, Nellie Gubler, Grant Hafen, Kelton Hafen, Dick Hammer, Joy Henderlider, Bill Hickman, Willard Hirschi, Berle Holt, Glenwood Humphries, Edna Hunt, Oscar Johnson, Royce Jones, Viola Kelsey, Robert Langston, Wes Larsen, Eric Ludlow, Cuba Lyle, Mavis Madsen, Reed Mathis, Richard Mathis, Ron McArthur, Rudger McArthur, M. K. McGregor, Maurine Miles, Arvel Milne, Jeff Morby, Joyce Mundy, Carl Nelson, Elsie Peacock, Elmer Pickett, Jon Pollei, Scott Prisbrey, Robert Ralston, Elsa Ruesch, Ed Sappington, Barnard Seegmiller, Helen Shurtliff, Kathy Simkins, Angus Snow, Brent Snow, Donnitta Snow, Dolly Big Soldier, Alice Gubler Stratton, Bruce Stucki, Clair Terry, Alma Truman, Doris Truman, Eleanor Fleming Warner, Vaughn Warner, Murray Webb, Evan

Whitehead, Yvonne Wilcox, Leonard Wilcox, Wayne Wilson, Royden Wittwer, Luwayne Wood, and Evan Woodbury.

We also express gratitude to the Washington County Historical Society, to experts Thayne Robson, Lavoid Leavitt, Ted Shumway, Charles Peterson, Wayne McConkie, Paul Crosby, Elizabeth Bruhn Wright, and to scores of people who provided use of their family and town documents. Many other people called with useful suggestions and information.

Elaine, Lin, and Nate Alder, Fern Crawford, and Dan Watson donated valuable editorial assistance, as have Bob Snyder, Brian Casey, Ronald Woodland, Susan Woodland, and Lyman Hafen. To all of the above we are deeply grateful.

General Introduction

W hen Utah was granted statehood on 4 January 1896, twenty-seven counties composed the nation's new forty-fifth state. Subsequently two counties, Duchesne in 1914 and Daggett in 1917, were created. These twenty-nine counties have been the stage on which much of the history of Utah has been played.

Recognizing the importance of Utah's counties, the Utah State Legislature established in 1991 a Centennial History Project to write and publish county histories as part of Utah's statehood centennial commemoration. The Division of State History was given the assignment to administer the project. The county commissioners or their designees were responsible for selecting the author or authors for their individual histories, and funds were provided by the state legislature to cover most research and writing costs as well as to provide each public school and library with a copy of each history. Writers worked under general guidelines provided by the Division of State History and in cooperation with county history committees. The counties also established a Utah Centennial County History Council to help develop policies for distribution of state-appropriated funds and plans for publication.

Each volume in the series reflects the scholarship and interpretation of the individual authors. The general guidelines provided by the Utah State Legislature included coverage of five broad themes encompassing the economic, religious, educational, social, and political history of the county. Authors were encouraged to cover a vast period of time stretching from geologic and prehistoric times to the present. Since Utah's statehood centennial celebration falls just four years before the arrival of the twenty-first century, authors were encouraged to give particular attention to the history of their respective counties during the twentieth century.

Still, each history is at best a brief synopsis of what has transpired within the political boundaries of each county. No history can do justice to every theme or event or individual that is part of an area's past. Readers are asked to consider these volumes as an introduction to the history of the county, for it is expected that other researchers and writers will extend beyond the limits of time, space, and detail imposed on this volume to add to the wealth of knowledge about the county and its people. In understanding the history of our counties, we come to understand better the history of our state, our nation, our world, and ourselves.

In addition to the authors, local history committee members, and county commissioners, who deserve praise for their outstanding efforts and important contributions, special recognition is given to Joseph Francis, chairman of the Morgan County Historical Society, for his role in conceiving the idea of the centennial county history project and for his energetic efforts in working with the Utah State Legislature and State of Utah officials to make the project a reality. Mr. Francis is proof that one person does make a difference.

ALLAN KENT POWELL
CRAIG FULLER
GENERAL EDITORS

Introduction

This is the story of people living in an arid land. They struggled with pervasive heat, sparse forage, and scarce water because they were living in the Mohave Desert, right where it abuts the edge of the Colorado Plateau in Utah's southwest corner. Limited water determined much of what they could do, yet their ingenuity responded to the setting, producing several civilizations over many centuries in this harsh land of exquisite beauty. This book focuses on the Anglo-Europeans who settled the area in the latter part of the nineteenth century. They present a contrast to their forerunners, the Anasazi, and the Paiutes, because these pioneers more successfully molded the land to fit their will — plowing, fencing, and irrigating.

In the 1850s the Mormons (members of the Church of Jesus Christ of Latter-day Saints) came to settle; soon after European and American explorers had made the region more well known. Initially the Paiutes welcomed the "Saints." Greatly relieved, even optimistic about their relationship with the Indians, the Mormons set up villages and a subsistence agriculture that was distinguished by its cooperative labor. Their hope for friendship with the Indians dwindled over time, but they learned much from the natives (herbal medications, trails, knowledge of other tribes) and maintained a fairly peaceful relationship with the Paiutes although less so with the Navajos.

The Latter-day Saints worked together to bring water onto the land. Though they found water to be limited, they succeeded in building canals and dams. The longer they stayed, the more ambitious the water projects became — notably the Cottonwood Canal, the Hurricane Canal, the Washington Dam, the La Verkin Canal, and the Enterprise Reservoir — substantial achievements requiring many years to construct. They created irrigated oases to sustain small arable plots, sometimes called "pocket farms." As an alternative, some farmers turned to grazing sheep and cattle on the open range where the animals had to move seasonally over vast stretches to find sufficient feed.

Mormon villages were tightly organized, often, though not always, laid out in a planned four-square pattern. Within the village, family life and society were concentrated; farm lands were outside the village boundaries. Some twenty-five communities nestled close to the Virgin River and its tributaries — Santa Clara Creek, Ash Creek, and Quail Creek in Washington County; and a few more in adjacent valleys.

For 100 years these settlers lived in relative isolation. Even though they were part of the larger endeavor of settling the whole eastern side of the Great Basin, these colonists occupied a remote corner just below its rim. It was soon nicknamed "Dixie' because it was hot, southern, and produced cotton. The name "Utah's Dixie" was an inexact term, usually referring to the lands involved in the Mormon church's Cotton Mission. Neighboring towns such as Bunkerville and Mesquite, though outside of Utah, were certainly producers of cotton and closely related to St. George, the region's capital. Melvin T. Smith offers a most expansive view: "Dixie is bounded on the east by the faulted cliffs of the Colorado Plateau; on the south by the Grand Canyon... on the west by the dry deserts of the Great Basin... and on the north by the south rim of the Great Basin, old Lake Bonneville, and the lava-covered Black Ridge."

There were frequent visitors to the remote Dixie landscape — freighters, Federal officials, religious leaders — given its position on the Salt Lake/Los Angeles corridor.

A sweep of silver miners came but left after a decade. The telegraph reached the community early, so residents knew what was happening in the larger world of America. They knew of the Civil War, for example, but were relatively untouched by it.

The railroad never arrived, nor did the merchants, bankers, and investors who would have come with it. Roads in the region were extremely hard to build over volcanic flows and sandstone washes; not until 1930 was an oiled road finished, linking Washington County to the national highway system.

The relative isolation from 1854 to 1930 was both a boon and a bane. Area residents largely were left alone to pursue their peculiar culture, but they also were left without certain comforts. The heat was oppressive. The Virgin River below the Hurricane Fault was full of sand and sulphur. The ubiquitous wind blew sand into everything. But the settlers were determined to conquer one of Utah's harshest environments.

If there was to be any culture, it had to be home grown; and it did flourish, partly as encouragement against harshness. Bands, choirs, dances, literary societies, and especially theater, with regular monthly performances, sprang up. There was a modest library, and several attempts were made to sustain newspapers. Schools also were established. Although they were basic at first and held sessions only a few months each year, still, the settlers valued learning enough to require that each ecclesiastical ward maintain a regular school.

Religion was pervasive and motivating. Many people came to Dixie in response to religious assignment, but only a portion of them stayed. Those families that persisted, some for five generations, were the sinew that made Washington County. Even those who stayed moved within the region a great deal. Mobility became the norm as people sought more land and water to sustain the next generation.

The story of Utah's Dixie is a mixture of local initiatives and outside influences. The latter came increasingly after the turn of the century. The economic depression of the 1930s was especially severe for Washington County, but the New Deal programs combatting it brought Federal investment in the county as never before. The development of Zion National Park is an example of how outside forces impinged upon the region. Founded in 1909 as Mukuntuweap National Monument, it became Zion National Park in 1919. By the 1930s and 1940s, a tourist industry developed around it as motorists came to the area to view the scenic wonders of the red cliffs and towering mountains that had so long isolated the locals from the rest of Utah and the West.

When air conditioning arrived after World War II, tourism overcame its biggest obstacle, the oppressive heat. The sunshine that had driven many settlers away suddenly became an advantage instead of a curse. Outside forces flooded into the county.

Pioneer lifestyles of austerity and frugality gradually gave way to consumerism. The automobile brought America to Dixie to enjoy its desert wonders. With it also came filmmakers to enliven the saga of the cowboy. The area became the workshop of movie stars, who in turn helped make the region almost as well-known as Palm Springs.

By the 1960s, a new set of pioneers were at work in Dixie. They were largely local entrepreneurs who dreamed of the area as a destination. They built an airport and established an airline. They promoted road building. Their enterprising skills produced golf courses, planned housing communities (Bloomington and Green Valley — largely done by newcomers), a new Dixie College campus, industrial parks, and water reclamation projects. All this was a prelude to the arrival of the interstate freeway in 1973; I-15 did for the region what the railroad had done for many other communities in the nineteenth century. It opened the world for Dixie. Washington County became virtually a crossroads, connecting Utah's Wasatch Front with southern Nevada and California much more closely than in the past.

Today's county has completed that transformation from isolation to destination. Outside capital flows freely into the economy, as do newcomers. The freeway has surpassed anything the railroad could have done in making Dixie a destination. The population today has a majority of newcomers. They have been welcomed by the fifth generation of pioneer descendants. Washington County hosts virtually every national franchise available; shopping malls have moved merchandising out of the downtown section of St. George and drawn shoppers from wide distances. The community now supports many religions. Dixie has been quite thoroughly Americanized, but its pioneer heritage is still in evidence.

Though the county shares the story of conquering the frontier with the larger movement of Americans onto western lands, the local version has a few unique twists. Some of them are tragic, including the Mountain Meadows Massacre in 1857 and the nuclear radioactive fallout that killed many residents a hundred years later. At least one is curious — the numerous polygamous marriages of the nineteenth century and the isolated replay of polygamy in the twentieth. The overarching local story of cooperation and harmony contrasts with the general individualism of the West, but conflict in the area was not unknown. How it was resolved often took unusual forms. The people of this generation are committed to their cultural values and are striving to perpetuate them into the future.

The county is still an arid place. The land, weather, water, and sunshine are always dominant features. They draw visitors and newcomers and make every day stimulating, but the desert is a jealous mistress as the Anasazis found out centuries ago. So the future most likely will still be a contest between human ingenuity and nature's limitations.

WASHINGTON COUNTY

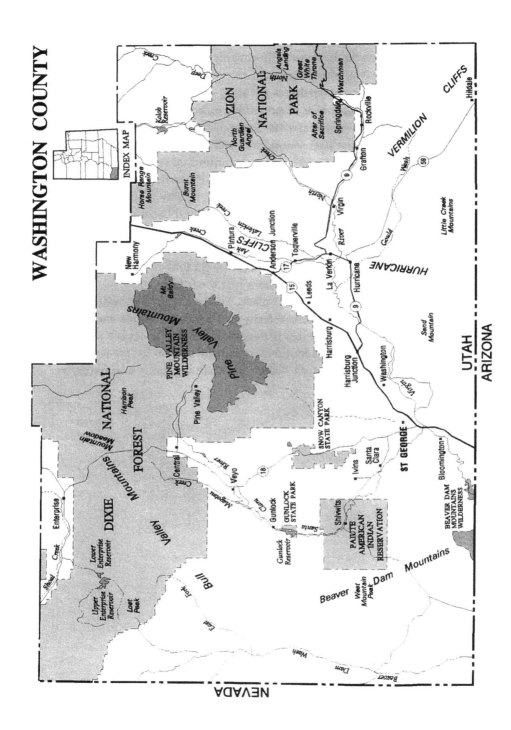

INDEX MAP

ZION NATIONAL PARK

Kolob Reservoir

North Guardian Angel

Burnt Mountain

Horse Range Mountain

Deep Creek

Angels Landing

Great White Throne

North

Watchman

Altar of Sacrifice

Springdale

Rockville

Grafton

VERMILION

Hildale

CLIFFS

Gould Wash

Little Creek Mountains

9

59

River

Virgin

HURRICANE

Hurricane

La Verkin

Leeds

Harrisburg

Harrisburg Junction

Washington

Sand Mountain

Virgin

North

Toquerville

Anderson Junction

Pintura

LaVerkin Creek

Ash Creek

CLIFFS

15

17

9

New Harmony

Mt. Baldy

PINE VALLEY MOUNTAIN WILDERNESS

Valley Mountains

Pine Valley

Pine Valley

Harrison Peak

Mountain Meadow

NATIONAL FOREST

DIXIE

Mountains

Valley

Enterprise

Shoal Creek

Lower Enterprise Reservoir

Upper Enterprise Reservoir

Lost Peak

Bull

Valley

East Fork

Central

Santa Clara River

Veyo

18

Gunlock

Gunlock Reservoir

GUNLOCK STATE PARK

Santa Clara

SNOW CANYON STATE PARK

Ivins

Santa Clara

ST GEORGE

Bloomington

BEAVER DAM MOUNTAINS WILDERNESS

Shivwits

PAIUTE AMERICAN INDIAN RESERVATION

West Mountain Peak

Beaver Dam Mountains

Wash

Beaver Dam Wash

NEVADA

UTAH

ARIZONA

1

The Land and
Its Early Inhabitants

"Show me one thing of beauty in the whole area and I'll stay." — Wilhemina Cannon

"It looks like the good Lord took everything left over from the creation, dumped it here, then set it on fire." — Juanita Brooks

"...showing no signs of water or fertility;...a wide expanse of chaotic matter presented itself, huge hills, sandy deserts, cheerless, grassless plains, perpendicular rocks, loose barren clay, dissolving beds of sandstone...lying in inconceivable confusion — in short a country in ruins, dissolved by the pelting of the storm of ages, or turned inside out, upside down by terrible convulsions in some former age..." — Parley P. Pratt

Geologic Description

The above early descriptions of Washington County reflected the feelings of many white people when they first saw the area. The geology, geography, and climate of the area all played an important role in its human activity and settlement, from the earliest inhabitants to the present; all indications are that the future will continue to be impacted by them all. A complex succession of volcanic rocks, including flows, breccia, and ignimbrites, aggregating several thousand feet in thickness, overlies the sedimentary sequence. Several laccolithic intrusive bodies in the northwest part of the county are intimately related to volcanic activity and deformation. The Pine Valley Mountains are capped by the world's largest known laccolith, its cover stripped by erosion.

Washington County, lying in the southwest corner of Utah, is more or less coincident with the area known as Utah's Dixie. It is bordered on the south by Arizona, on the west by Nevada, on the north by Iron County, and on the east by Kane County. Because of the physical barrier of the Grand Canyon, the "Arizona Strip" north of the canyon is in many practical respects more a part of Washington County than it is of Arizona. It is a region of colorful rocks, spectacular scenery, and great contrasts in rainfall, vegetation, animal life and geologic features. It has the lowest elevations and generally warmest temperatures in the state. These features have played important roles in the human activity and settlement of the area.

Washington County is divided topographically into two parts by the Hurricane Cliffs. The cliffs are the result of movement along the great Hurricane Fault, elevating the land east of the fault several hundred feet higher than that to the west. East of this escarpment are the colorful mesas and plateaus of the Zion National Park region, into which steep-walled, narrow canyons have been cut by streams of low volume and, for the most part, intermittent flow. These streams are given great erosive power by loads of abrasive silt and sand which are carried at relatively high velocities, especially during thunderstorms or periods of rapid snow melting. The plateaus and mesas, cut from horizontally layered sedimentary rocks, diminish in elevation southward in step fashion and are capped by successively older, resistant formations. West of the Hurricane Cliffs is a basin-and-range topography, reflecting a more complex geologic structure. The rock formations there are folded, faulted, and more varied.

St. George lies in a topographic basin north of which rises the dark mass of the Pine Valley Mountains. Over the eons, southwestern Utah has been subjected to great invasions of molten rock, some below the surface and some upon it. The Pine Valley Mountains are a spectacular example of the former process, now exposed by relentless erosion. Between St. George and the highest peak there is an elevation difference of more than 7,000 feet — from a low of about 2,800 feet to a high of nearly 10,000 feet at the top of the Pine Valley range. On the west, the St. George basin is bounded by the Beaver Dam Mountains, which extend below the intermountain basins into Nevada. The jumble of low, irregular hills in northwestern Washington County is the result of complex geologic forces. The lava flows along the Hurricane Cliffs, in Snow Canyon, and adjacent to St. George, ranging in age from a few thousand to several million years, are the result of outpourings of black basalt, once red hot.

Only a small northwestern portion of Washington County is part of the Great Basin, a vast region whose streamflows do not reach the ocean. The rest is drained by the Virgin River, a tributary of the Colorado River. From the high plateaus it flows southward through the depths of Zion Canyon, turns west to cut through the Hurricane Cliffs at La Verkin, crosses the St. George Basin, and then plunges into a magnificent chasm between the Beaver Dam Mountains on the north and the Virgin Mountains on the south. The Virgin River and the tributaries that feed it are subject to seasonal variation; rising sharply during thunderstorms and run-off season, they slow to a trickle in drought or by summer's end.

Rivers such as the Virgin are the creations of the topography which reflects the underlying geologic structures. Some rocks are more resistant than others to destructive weathering and erosion. Movement of crystal can cause fractures that become lines of weakness to be exploited by the streams at Bryce, Grand, and Zion Canyons. Land that is elevated — whether by uplift or the piling up of masses of igneous rocks — as in the high plateaus and at the Pine Valley Mountains, guides air movement around it. Rising air is cooled and precipitates its moisture as rain or snow. Hence, the principal sources of water, both on the surface and in the underground aquifers, are these same plateaus and mountains. The Navajo sandstone that forms the colorful cliffs in Zion and Snow canyons also contains great quantities of good water.

Within Washington County a complete structural transition takes place from the flat-lying formations of the Colorado Plateau on the east to the fault blocks of previously folded and thrust faulted rocks that define the Basin and Range geologic province. This helps account for the varied descriptions given by the early white visitors to the area mentioned at the beginning of this chapter. It is the same rugged beauty and warm climate that was a problem to the early white settlers that has been a boon to the growth and development of the county in the late twentieth century.

Native Americans

Early Native American inhabitants in Utah identified by anthropologists, archaeologists, and historians include those of the Desert Archaic, Anasazi, and Fremont cultures, as well as members of Ute, Paiute, Gosiute, Shoshoni, Navajo, and other tribes.

Evidence shows a human presence for about 10,000 years. Indian peoples had their own boundaries that separated the territory of one group from another, but they had no relationship to the present boundaries of Utah or the counties within the state. These early people generally organized themselves into small bands of several families, groups that were limited in size because of limited resources. The lack of formal organization is striking. There were no nations, no confederacies. The word "tribe" is a white man's characterization of people who spoke the same dialect and did not fight among themselves. The coming of white people made it necessary for Native Americans to band more tightly together.

Some of Utah's historic Native Americans were considered among the poorest in America. They were named "Diggers" by white intruders who watched them digging for roots and believed that they lived no better than animals. They were of the Uto-Aztecan language family, related to the modern corn-growing Pima and Hopi Indians and to the mighty Aztecs of Mexico. It was lack of corn horticulture and lack of contact that condemned them to relative stagnation. They used minimal tools yet had a great amount of knowledge about animal habits. Equipment was produced from poles and twigs, grass and bark, including the domed wickiup of poles and brush, clothing of cedar bark, and baskets, seed beaters, mush stirrers, and containers for gathering, storing, winnowing, and boiling with heated stones. They made water-tight baskets smeared inside and out with pine gum.

The quest for food kept them on the move. They grouped their brush huts and windbreaks near seed patches or pinyon trees for a few days while they harvested the yield. Then they might split up and join other families or go it alone, for there were no rules but to get food wherever and whenever possible. Without resources for further improvement

Ranger Donal J. Jolley inspects Anasazi food cache in Zion National Park. (National Park Service photo, J. L. Crawford Collection)

or stimulus from the outside, their lifestyle remained traditional. They were few in number, peaceable in disposition, and reliant on shamans or medicine men to placate the invisible forces with which their world was filled. Bows and arrows were used in hunting but rarely for warfare. Their basket-making was an art form. In the eighteenth and nineteenth centuries, their women and children were sometimes taken by raiding parties of other tribes to be sold to the Spanish and Mexicans. Though they sometimes raised corn, squash and beans, the Indians lived principally on fish, birds, wild game, wild fruits, roots, and seeds. They used the rock grinder, or metate and mano, for grinding corn, mesquite beans, and grass seeds for flour for making bread.

The largest band of Native Americans in Washington County was the Parrusits. Others in the area were Tonaquints, Paiutes, and Shivwits. At the time of the white settlement in the 1850s and 1860s there were perhaps a thousand Parrusits in the county, with their camping places near Rockville, Virgin, Toquerville, Washington Fields, and Santa Clara. These bands were held together under regular tribal control. Fatalities from white man's diseases and the diminishment of food supplies were main factors in the drastic reduction of the Indian population. Of the estimated one thousand Parrusits living along the Virgin River in the 1850s and 1860s, the last survivor, Peter Harrison, died in 1945.

Today in the 1990s there is a small community on the Shivwits reservation about ten miles west of St. George as well as several Indian families living in the cities of Washington County.

Spaniards

For white men, the Washington County area was often a place to get through as soon as possible, certainly not a place in which to live. Before the arrival of the Mormons in the mid-1850s only a few white men had ever been through it.

The most thoroughly documented evidence of early Spanish exploration of this area comes from the expedition of Fray Francisco Atanasio Dominguez and Fray Silvestre Velez de Escalante, which came through Washington County in October 1776. An early snowfall on 5 October near Milford caused them to give up the idea of going on to California. A casting of lots determined that they should return to Santa Fe.

Instead of retracing their route, they determined to attempt a short cut. They turned southeast, coming out of the desert that now bears Escalante's name a few miles west of Cedar City. The high mountains to the east forced them southward along the foot of the rough and rugged escarpment known as the Hurricane Fault. It was on this detour that they discovered the Virgin River (named by them Sulphur Creek), Ash Creek (which they called Rio de Pilar), and hot sulphur springs. They continued south to the site of subsequent Fort Pearce but repeated warnings of the Grand Canyon convinced them to change their route toward the east. A group of Parrusit Indians agreed to show them a route over the Hurricane Fault. They ended up climbing the bold face of the fault and, guided only by vague directions given by the Indians, the party left Washington County in late October.

American Explorers

After Dominguez and Escalante, the next pathbreaker of importance to enter Washington County was Jedediah Strong Smith, whose trips in 1826 and again in 1827 overlapped Escalante's trail for short distances. He was traveling southwest from the Bear Lake Valley look-ing for a route to California. On his first trip in 1826, Smith followed the Virgin River through the narrows (present route of 1-15), a hazard-ous undertaking since the steep narrow gorge is barely wide enough for the stream. This would have involved much wading of the stream over shifting quicksand, through deep holes, and around giant boulders. On his second trip, a year later, he avoided these narrows by going up the Santa Clara River, crossing over a pass to the drainage into Beaver Dam Wash, which he followed down to the Virgin. At the mouth of the Santa Clara he met a group of Paiute Indians growing corn; he called the Santa Clara "Corn Creek."

Smith's pioneering trips not only opened a new route to the Pacific coast, but reports of his travels and stories of adventure undoubtedly encouraged others to follow. One of these was George C. Yount who was with Smith in the mountains for a while. In the fall of 1830 Yount joined a party organized by William Wolfskill at Santa Fe for the pur-pose of reaching the coast. This group followed Escalante's route into Washington County, then picked up Smith's route over the Mountain Meadows and down to the Colorado River.

The story of this trip was told by Yount in his old age and the de-tails are not precise, but it appears his group must have attempted to follow Smith's trail. It is probable that these explorations had a great deal to do with the development of the Old Spanish Trail, which be-came a regular overland route crossing Washington County from Pinto through the Mountain Meadows, down the Santa Clara past Gunlock, over the divide to Beaver Dam Wash, paralleling the Virgin River across desert hills to the Muddy River, then across the desert toward Los Angeles via Las Vegas.

Jedediah Smith ignored or was unaware of Escalante's naming of the Virgin River as Sulphur Creek; he instead named it "the Adams River" (for U.S. President John Quincy Adams), which name he used in letters written on both trips of 1826 and 1827. This upsets the idea that he named it for Thomas Virgen, a member of his second party. George C. Yount told of entering the Virgin River valley on a trip in 1830, but this is no assurance that it was so named at that early date. The river bore the name of Rio Virgin in 1844 when John C. Fremont passed over the Spanish Trail and doubtless the name was given be-tween 1827 and 1844. Melvin T. Smith mentions other trapper groups of James Ohio Pattie and Thomas "Pegleg" Smith that came into the area in the late 1820s.[1]

By 1844 when Captain John C. Fremont of the U.S. Army came through Washington County from California to Utah, the Spanish Trail was a well-defined route over which annual caravans traveled back and forth from Santa Fe to the coast. Fremont gave a detailed description of the terrain as he passed through in early May of 1844, drew some rough maps, and wrote a report of his trip. His inclusion of the name "Virgin River" made its use permanent.

In mid-November 1847, Mormon leaders in Salt Lake City, eager to get seeds, cuttings, and roots from California and to open up a route for trade, called a group of sixteen men to make the journey. Among them were frontiersmen Captain Jefferson Hunt of the Mormon Battalion and Orrin Porter Rockwell. This mounted company traveled through Washington County along the Old Spanish Trail to California and returned the same way the following spring. Twenty-five returning members of the Mormon Battalion were right behind, bringing the first wagon over this route.

In October 1849 a group of "forty-niners" hired Jefferson Hunt to guide them to California; they also traveled through Washington County. Now that the southern trail was more clearly marked, Brigham Young sent Parley P. Pratt south with fifty young men for the purpose of looking for sites for future towns. Permanent settlements were soon to follow.

Definition of "Dixie"

Since the word "Dixie" is used almost synonymously with the term "Washington County" in this book, more specific explanation seems essential. Visitors from out of state are often startled to find the word "Dixie" referring to a place in Utah. People in Utah also often do not generally understand its meaning specifically, just that it is in southern Utah. Such imprecision is quickly corrected by southern Utahns from Cedar City or Beaver who do not identify themselves as being from Dixie. The word "Dixie" in Utah can be linked to the growing of cotton in the area of Washington County; it can emphasize the fact that the climate is distinctly different from that of the rest of the state, being warm in winter; it can refer to the area as of lower altitude, some 2,500 feet below the nearby rim of the Great Basin that includes much of the populated area of the state.

Not long after Mormon settlers arrived in Washington County, the area was identified as "Dixie." A newspaper was published in 1868 named *Our Dixie Times*. Pioneer George Hicks' well-known song began with these lines: "Once I lived in Cottonwood and owned a little farm, But I was called to Dixie, which did me much alarm." The first two companies to settle Washington City included people from the southern states. They were sent to raise cotton and soon began calling their new home "Utah's Dixie." The name was essentially a nickname, but it came to mean more than that — a term of endearment, of identity. The name stuck and is a point of pride as much now as it was then. Dixie College was founded in 1911 under the name "St. George Stake Academy." The students, however, painted the word "Dixie" on the "Sugar Loaf" outcropping and a block "D" on the nearby black hill, all within the first few years of the college's existence, and the name commonly used was "Dixie College."

One fairly precise way to define Utah's Dixie is to equate it with the Virgin River drainage system.[2] The match is not 100 percent but it comes close. It includes the land drained by the Virgin River and its tributaries, the Santa Clara and the other creeks draining into the Virgin — Quail Creek, Ash Creek, North Creek, East Fork, Fort Pearce Wash, Gould's Wash, La Verkin Creek, Kolob Creek, Oak Valley Creek, Three Creeks, and Shunesburg Creek.

The area from Pine Valley on the north to the Virgin River Gorge on the south and from Zion National Park to the Arizona Strip is often called "Dixie." Some areas, such as Kolob and Pine Valley, because of their higher elevation, lack the semi-tropical climate that is usually associated with Dixie, but they belong to both the drainage system and the cultural area of Dixie. Other areas lie outside the jurisdiction of Washington County, even outside of the state of Utah, but share Dixie's climate and culture. Pipe Spring in northern Arizona looks to Dixie, and for the first century Bunkerville and Mesquite (below the Gorge in Nevada) were part of Dixie. The Arizona Strip is also an area whose ranchers were (and are) tied to Washington County. Such elements of imprecision must not confuse the reality that the term Dixie remains roughly synonymous with Washington County.

Further exceptions must be noted. The Virgin River actually rises on Cedar Mountain north of Washington County. That area has never been considered part of Dixie. Also, the town of Enterprise in Washington County does not lie in the Virgin River drainage system. Politically, Enterprise belongs to Washington County, but in climate and elevation it does not.

The sphere of influence of the city of St. George is another way to define "Dixie." Officially St. George is the county seat, but it is much more than that. It was the base of Erastus Snow's apostolic territory in pioneer times. His authority was unchallenged and respected throughout the county and well beyond. The early location of the first LDS temple completed in the West increased the city's regional importance beyond the county boundaries. Now that Las Vegas has such a temple, the area of impact of the St. George temple has shrunk, but it still draws faithful Mormons from border counties, including nearby Nevada towns such as Panaca, Mesquite, and Bunkerville, as well as the Utah communities of Kanab, Cedar City, Beaver, and Panguitch.

Shopping facilities also draw people to St. George from adjacent communities and counties. The pull of the shopping malls has greatly increased this economic bond in the last decade as fewer people have found it necessary to travel to Las Vegas for their shopping needs. The Spectrum newspaper is published daily in St. George and serves Washington County as well as the nearby Nevada towns in eastern Lincoln County and the Mesquite-Bunkerville area. A separate Cedar City edition of the paper serves Iron County. Also the Dixie Regional Medical Center has helped expand St. George's sphere of influence.

The name "Dixie" does not command the loyalty of the youth as it once did, however. If they attend Hurricane or Pine View or Snow Canyon or Enterprise high schools, they do not resonate to the name "Dixie" as do those who attend Dixie High School. As long as there was only one high school in the whole county, everyone identified very closely with the word because it had so many levels of meaning. Ironically, the many newcomers, mostly older folks, who recently have come to Dixie generally are more than pleased to identify with the term "Dixie."

In the long run, the most simple definition of "Dixie" comes from a song that Roene di Fiore's students at Dixie College performed with their singing mayor, Marion Bowler, as soloist. Thousands of visitors were greeted with:

> Are you from Dixie?
> I said from Dixie.
> Where the fields of cotton beckon to me.
>
> We're glad to see ya
> To say "How be ya?"
> And the friends we're longin' to see.
>
> If you're from Santa Clara, Washington or St. George fine,
> Anywhere below the Iron County line,
> Then you're from Dixie.
> Hurray for Dixie
> 'Cause I'm from Dixie too.[3]

ENDNOTES

1. Melvin T. Smith, "Forces That Shaped Utah's Dixie," *Utah Historical Quarterly* 47 (Spring 1979): 110-25.

2. Lowell C. Bennion and Merrill K. Ridd, "Utah's Dynamic Dixie: Satellite of Salt Lake, Las Vegas, or Los Angeles?" *Utah Historical Quarterly* 47 (Spring 1979): 311-27.

3. Original music is attributed to George L. Cobb and words to Jack Yellen, with these words adapted by Dan Watson and Roene di Fiore.

2

SETTLEMENT

Parley P. Pratt was stunned when he first saw Utah's Dixie: "A wide expanse of chaotic matter presented itself, huge hills, sandy deserts, cheerless, grassless plains, perpendicular rocks, loose barren clay, dissolving beds of sandstone."[1]

Pratt's two-month journey along the western base of the Wasatch Range and Wasatch Plateau with his fifty companions in the winter of 1849 had taken them to each creek south of Provo as it exited from the mountains at about the 5,000-foot level. Those streams flowed out onto benchlands which gradually descended into broad valleys, often ten miles wide and twenty miles long. The vistas were everywhere inspiring, inviting settlement, farming, and grazing. The scouting company chose many sites for towns which later became known as Nephi, Holden, Scipio, Fillmore, Meadow, Beaver, Parowan, and Cedar City.

A smaller party from the group ventured south of Cedar City. Its members reached the southern rim of the Great Basin near present-day New Harmony; they crossed the pass and there met the foreboding lava cliffs of the Black Ridge. Descending from 5,000 to 2,800 feet down Ash Creek, they came to the Virgin River, meandering in its sandy bed. Continuing cautiously, they came to the confluence of the Virgin and the Santa Clara Creek at a place the Indians called Tonaquint. Here they visualized a small future settlement. The vista to the south was uninviting with its precipitous Virgin River Gorge and the parched Arizona Strip country. There was no foreseeable habitat for humans in this remote area, maybe to the west along the Spanish Trail to California, but not here in the parched land and blowing sand.

Turning up the Santa Clara they met Indians, many of them, and found them to be hospitable and engaged in primitive agriculture in some promising fields. This was a stunning find and the group thought these red "brethren" might be settled enough to be won to the Mormon message. The Indians invited the group to return and make a home among them. The Mormons welcomed the request and agreed to return.

Continuing up the Santa Clara, they came to the Old Spanish Trail where just two years before, their colleague, Jefferson Hunt, had returned from the Mormon Battalion trek to California. He had brought a wagon over that route to Salt Lake City and, most importantly, had discovered iron near what later became Cedar City. Pratt's group hurried back to Salt Lake City with their report of many potential settlement sites in the southern Great Basin, as well as their story of the wild landscape just below the rim of the basin.

Much of Dixie's destiny was defined right there — the potential for Indian-white compatibility, the desert isolation, the wild topography, the warm climate in the winter, the oasis type of irrigation agriculture in fields adjacent to small streams. Clearly this was a region that should be occupied before someone else did so. It lay outside the more habitable Great Basin and would presumably be of marginal importance. The streams would sustain only a few families to farm the fields, yet the Indians and the mild winter weather made it irresistible — at least for an outpost.

Village System

Parley Pratt's exploration of the area was a piece of a much larger fabric. When he and his compatriots returned to the councils in Salt Lake City, their words were welcomed. Mormon leaders were searching for scores of new settlement sites to accommodate thousands of

Brigham Young. (Lynne Clark Collection, donor — Washington County
Daughters of Utah Pioneers)

anticipated European and American converts. Between 1847 and 1849
they had already opened some two dozen settlements from Ogden to
Provo, but their vision anticipated hundreds of additional villages
where irrigation canals would "green" the dry western landscape.

Jacob Hamblin. (Lynne Clark Collection, donor — Washington County Daughters of Utah Pioneers)

The Mormon formula of cooperative labor to build those canals and erect mills for communal use would enable settlers to wrest a bare living from small, privately owned, irrigated plots of from five to thirty acres. The plan called for the faithful to live in villages wherever pos-

Erastus Snow. (Lynne Clark Collection, donor — Washington County
Daughters of Utah Pioneers)

sible. Such villages would provide protection from the Indians as well
as help to make a real community. In the villages, women and children
worked gardens, promoted schooling, manufactured home goods, kept
house, and raised large families while men worked the fields clustered
close to the community — all part of a self-sustaining economy.

It was one version of the model that had nourished European culture for centuries and would do the same in the strange, dry vastness
of Utah. Utah was not to be a Colorado, Wyoming, or Montana;
ranching and mining were not the planned Mormon mode, the former
because its people were more dispersed, the latter because they were
congregated in what Mormon leaders considered the "wrong kind"
of moral setting. Nor would 640-acre farming sections scatter the
people across the land as in the American Midwest. The Mormons

John D. Lee. (Utah State Historical Society)

intended to impose their village lifestyle on the landscape instead of adapting to the terrain; their muscle and sinew would take on the desert and attempt to bend it their way. Community was paramount; togetherness was essential.

Their vision was grandiose — an inland empire of hundreds of communities and thousands of "Saints" from many nations "gathering" to their Zion in the mountains. To Jim Bridger and others familiar

with the area, the Mormon scheme must have sounded as bizarre as
the scores of other promotional projects being huckstered around the
American West, but the Mormon vision became in great part actuality.
Some 500 villages were founded in or near the Great Basin between
1847 and 1900.

Fort Harmony

The power of Parley Pratt's first exploring trip south worked on
John D. Lee. A handsome dynamo, Lee had long been considered a
"comer." At age thirty-eight he was already a seasoned Mormon. He
had been a missionary in Tennessee, had crossed the plains after ex-
periencing the stormy expulsion from the Mormon city of Nauvoo,
Illinois, and had risen to membership in the Council of Fifty, a gov-
erning body in pioneer Salt Lake City. Called in 1850 to help found
Parowan, the first headquarters of southern Utah Mormons, Lee was
drawn farther south. Twice he led exploring groups to nearby regions.
Once he essentially retraced Pratt's route. In Dixie, Lee was particularly impressed with what would later come to be called the Washington Fields, where the Virgin River meandered across a broad flood
plain. On his second trip, he went east to Long Valley, north of Kanab,
where he met friendly Indians who helped the group avoid geologic
obstacles and find their way to the Virgin River. He reported both trips
to Brigham Young, his "adopted" father.[2]

In the spirit of individual initiative, Lee organized a group of
friends from the north including Elisha H. Graves, Charles Dalton,
and William R. Davis to join him in establishing a colony on Ash
Creek, to be called Harmony, just over the rim of the Great Basin
where the water starts to flow south. It was evident to Lee that the area
had an important future.

The territorial legislature had already designated the area below
the basin and to the Arizona border as Washington County on 3 February 1852 — before any settlements had been undertaken there. In its
original mapping, the county occupied a 36-mile-wide swath across the
territory, which then included both present-day Utah and Nevada.

Fifteen men, their families, and teams built a fort at Harmony
in the spring of 1852, according to James G. Bleak's "Annals of the
Southern Utah Mission."[3] Indian threats during the Walker War of
1853 caused them to seek refuge in Cedar City. By 1854 they returned

and built a new fort closer to the western mountains where they could control more water and till more land. This fort survived until 1862 when it was destroyed by a devastating month-long rainstorm. In Fort Harmony, John D. Lee undertook wide-ranging endeavors — farming, freighting, cattle raising, even maintaining a guest house. Enjoying the confidence of Brigham Young at the time, he was appointed local Indian agent as well as Presiding Elder of the Fort Harmony Branch of the LDS Church.

The Indian Mission

All these factors — the Pratt and Lee explorations, the establishment of a base at Harmony, the receptivity of the Indians, and the need to occupy all favorable sites before someone else did — stimulated action at Mormon headquarters. Church leaders decided to send an Indian mission to southern Utah. This was a fulfillment of rhetoric that had accompanied Mormonism since its Missouri days, an urge to bring Indians into the church's fold as foretold by the Book of Mormon.

A party of mostly young men was called to the mission at the LDS October General Conference in 1853. They prepared during the winter and twenty-one of them departed in April 1854, arriving at Harmony on 2 May. Rufus Allen, twenty-six, a friend and companion of Parley P. Pratt on several explorations, was designated captain of the group.[4]

This reinforcement contingent helped the Harmony residents clear land and build a canal, with each of the missionaries receiving an irrigation share. Their efforts to build a base camp were justified as a way to raise food, which they later used to foster their Indian relationships. To some it seemed a diversion, keeping them from their calling to be with the Indians; however, they were reconciled to the effort when they considered Harmony a refuge to fall back on.

Within two weeks of their arrival, Brigham Young and a party of 100 traveling companions visited Harmony. They had already inspected the fledgling settlements farther north, including Parowan and Cedar City. Young helped Lee choose a better site for Harmony. Young's chief concern there was the Indian mission. Thomas D. Brown recorded Brigham's revealing instructions:

> You are not sent to farm, to build nice houses and fence fine fields, not to help white men but to save red ones. Learn their languages and this you can do more effectively by living among them as well as by

writing a list of words. Go with them where they go. Live with them, and when they rest let them live with you; feed them, clothe them, and teach them in their own language. They are our brethren; we must seek after them, commit their language [to memory], get their understanding, and when they go off in parties you go with them.[5]

Harmony proved to be somewhat of a contradiction. Lee was interested in erecting the fort, clearing the land, building fences, and getting in enough crops to support the colony. Winter was coming. He welcomed the Indian missionaries as laborers. He put them to work both to support themselves and to help complete the basic elements of the community. He and his friends were there first and had a prime goal to promote and solidify their own efforts and assure a place for their families. The missionaries had another goal, however; their instructions were to devote themselves to the Indians. It did not take long for disharmony to arise in Harmony because of the conflicting goals. Some became very critical of Lee's forceful leadership, feeling that he acted arbitrarily and abused his authority.[6] Agriculture work and building structures at Harmony were not as crucial to them as being on the Santa Clara Creek with the Paiutes or scouting out other Indian groups beyond the Colorado River.

This tension finally led to a decision at church headquarters to transfer the Indian mission to Santa Clara and appoint Jacob Hamblin as its president. The differing approaches to their task — Lee as entrepreneur and Hamblin as Indian advocate — would surface on several future occasions. At Santa Clara the missionaries followed the Mormon pattern — building a fort, damming the river, digging canals, clearing land, planting crops, and sending for their families from the north.

Some fascinating twists developed in the Santa Clara story. First was the involvement of the local Indians. The Shivwits band of the Paiutes was already involved in a rude form of farming and irrigation, but it was only marginally productive. Their hunger was severe; they welcomed the missionaries, who offered to teach them better farming. The missionaries urged the natives to help build the fort, the dams and canals, promising a share in future crops. The Indians were doubtful the dams would work; they knew of seasons when the Santa Clara dried up. Hamblin promised them that they would have more water if they would help build dams, a crucial statement the Indians would later remember.

A second twist involved the weather. The missionaries were now well beyond the Great Basin and well below its accustomed elevations and temperatures. What the Mormons knew about survival was based on higher climes. They understood about limited water, but at Santa Clara water was even more tenuous. Furthermore, vegetation on the mountains in Dixie country was so thin that rainstorms often caused flash floods — floods that did not respect irrigation dams. Yet another twist was the possible crops. The warm climate permitted the cultivation of grapes, melons, and cotton in addition to the harvests the missionaries were used to.

The scorching summer heat was so oppressive that survival was an even bigger risk in Santa Clara than it was at Fort Harmony. Nonetheless, the missionaries proceeded on the premise of permanence. They went north for their families and even recruited relatives and friends. That is when more Hamblins arrived, Oscar and William, as well as others who would have a major impact, including Dudley Leavitt, a Hamblin in-law. The Indians were pleased with the sight of women, a sign of permanence and peace.[7]

The first few years of the Indian mission in Santa Clara left a rich legacy of lore, much of which is particularly revealing about the whites' perception of the Indians. Jacob Hamblin relates in his journal that shortly after their arrival an old Indian woman asked him to "practice his medicine" on her if the local medicine man's magic did not work. Hamblin and William Hennefer watched the medicine man with strained respect and waited. The Indians eventually gave up, carried her outside the camp, and left her to die. Her family urged Hamblin and Hennefer to take action. They anointed her with oil and prayed according to Mormon religious practice; she became well, which astounded the Indians. This miraculous event did not overly impress Hamblin; instead he worried about the naive faith in him which this event stimulated among the Indians. He often responded to their medicine men with respect and reportedly even welcomed their incantations in his behalf one time when he was desperately ill.

A different legend is told of Chief Agarapoots. He belittled the Indians in Santa Clara and their chief Tut-se-gab-its, trying to dissuade the Shivwits from associating with the Mormons. He occasionally stole a cow or rode into Santa Clara frightening the women and children. Then his son became very ill. His friends urged him to seek help from the Mormons. He refused. Jacob Hamblin, hearing of the illness, rode to Agarapoots's dwelling. The stubborn chief was inhospitable and grumpy. Hamblin chided him and told him to think of his child. The chief remained resistant. The next day the boy died. Agarapoots was furious and blamed Hamblin. Jacob confronted the chief and cursed him, warning that if he did not change his attitude he too would die. Only weeks later the chief did, in fact, die.

The Indians were impressed; they felt the Mormons had a power they must respect. That feeling was put to the test in the spring of 1856 when the creek's waters began to dwindle. The Indians said that they had made a deal — build the dam and get more water. They were not belligerent, however. They agreed to send a man to the mountain to pray for rain and urged the Mormons to talk to their god. Hamblin reported:

> The following morning, at daybreak, I saw the smoke of the medicine man ascending from the side of the big mountain, as the Indian called what is known now as the Pine Valley Mountain.
>
> Being among some Indians, I went aside by myself and prayed to the God of Abraham to forgive me if I had been unwise in promising the Indians water for their crops if they would plant; and that the heavens might give rain, that we might not lose the influence we had over them.
>
> The rains commenced the next day, providing sufficient water to keep the creek running. The harvest was successful. From that time they began to look upon us as having great influence with the clouds. They also believed that we could cause sickness to come upon any of them if we wished. We labored to have them understand these things in their true light, but it was difficult on account of their ignorance and superstitions.[8]

A severe test of the missionaries' toleration occurred when an adopted Indian youth picked up Thales Haskell's rifle in his cabin. The gun accidentally went off; the bullet piercing the body of Haskell's seventeen-year-old bride, Maria, through the thigh and stomach. The boy ran out of the cabin and sought Hamblin, pleading that he did not know what the gun would do. After twenty-four hours of agonizing pain, the pregnant woman died. The settlers were devastated but knew that punishing the lad was senseless.

Members of the Indian mission were accepted by the Shivwits Indians of the area. The Pieds, or Shivwits, invited Hamblin and other Mormon colonizers to settle among them. They welcomed

Many Shivwits accepted baptism at the hands of the Mormons such as David H. Cannon. (Lynne Clark Collection, donor — Rudger McArthur)

teachings to improve their farming, and even accepted some of the teachings contained in the Book of Mormon, one of the scriptures of the LDS people. Some of the Indians willingly accepted baptism into the Mormon church, but the missionaries became despondent over the Indians' practice of selling children into slavery and fighting to the death over brides, as well as by the general rampant hunger and filth that plagued the Shivwits. Initially Hamblin concluded that the missionaries should seek out other Indian groups of a "higher culture." He was particularly drawn to the Hopi, far distant across the Colorado River. Later he would gradually redefine his mission of proselyting to one of understanding, negotiating, and pacifying the Native Americans of the region.

The Mountain Meadows Massacre

The Mormons' work among the Indians was shaken to the core by one monumental event: the Mountain Meadows Massacre in 1857. Although most factors that caused it occurred outside Washington County, the actual tragedy took place within the present county boundaries.

The summer of 1857 was particularly troublesome for the people of Utah. A large U.S. Army contingent under Col. Albert Sidney Johnston was on its way to put down what government officials called "the Mormon rebellion." Everyone in the territory began preparing for war. Many of the Mormons in Utah had experienced persecution for their faith before coming to Utah; they feared that the approaching army would become another mob, legalized by the Federal government. They agreed not to run again and prepared to defend their homes, towns, and religious kingdom.

Into this emotionally charged atmosphere came the Fancher/Baker wagon train, heading to California quite unaware of the looming political confrontation. This caravan with its large number of horses, oxen, cattle, and people passed through Utah in August, having difficulty all along the way. Much of the trouble grew out of the belligerent attitude of the Mormons and their steady refusal to sell supplies to the immigrants, but some of it must be attributed to the conduct of the travelers themselves. They decided to take the southern route, despite warnings of potential Indian difficulties.

The relationship between Mormons and immigrants deteriorated as the party journeyed through Utah Territory. Insults were exchanged and accusations made. Indians became involved, and trouble intensified as the group continued south. Some of the travelers reportedly openly boasted of participation in earlier conflicts with Mormons in Missouri and even claimed a part in the killing of Mormon prophet Joseph Smith. It is also possible that they threatened to return to Utah and remove Brigham Young, although these threats remain a point of controversy.[9]

In Beaver the group was cautioned not to stop for fear of what might happen. In Parowan the company was not allowed to pass through town but was forced to break a new road around it. Evidence suggests that friction in Cedar City resulted from the refusal of the town's people to sell provisions to the immigrants. Conflict came to a head as the immigrants moved on to the Mountain Meadows.

Mountain Meadows was a regular resting point on the Old Spanish Trail. Sitting on the divide between the Great Basin and the Virgin River drainage, the mile-long meadow was a lush grassland that allowed passing trains the opportunity to rest and feed their animals before crossing the difficult Mohave Desert. While the Baker/Fancher train was there, they were attacked on 7 September 1857 by Indians and whites. A few days later, abandoning their weapons according to instructions from the Mormons and proceeding under a flag of truce, about 120 men, women, and children were murdered. Only eighteen small children were spared and later returned to relatives in Arkansas. The decision to attack was taken by local leaders.

What possibly could have provoked God-fearing Christians to this extreme is a nightmarish question. Perhaps it was revenge for treatment they had received in Missouri and Illinois, perhaps it was hysterical fear of the army that was on its way west, perhaps it was pressure from the Indians who had allied with them to fight the coming war, perhaps it was seen as a battle within that war, perhaps it was even the possibility of getting booty the immigrants were carrying. Most likely it was a combination of these and other reasons.

It is difficult to reconstruct with any degree of accuracy all the conditions. Various contributing factors and many different personalities all played a part: fervor generated by the eloquence of LDS apostle George A. Smith against the oncoming army, rehearsals of past sufferings and indignities, the imagined threat of being driven from their homes again, and repeated vows to avenge their martyred prophet had all kept fires smoldering in even the calmest hearts. It would take little to fan them into flames.

The massacre's tragic impact rippled in several directions, ruining the reputations of many residents in southern Utah, raising suspicions throughout the region and outrage in the nation, to say nothing of destroying the lives and property of the Fancher party.10 The massacre also affected the Indians. It rewarded those Indians who promoted raiding as a lifestyle instead of farming, in direct opposition to the southern Utah Indian missionaries who urged the natives to farm and to abandon looting. It was claimed that the massacre at Mountain Meadows was so rewarding to the looters that it "pulled the rug out from under the mission." Thereafter the missionaries at Santa Clara focused more on Indians in the Four Corners region to the east. Jacob Hamblin eventually moved to Kanab and many of the other missionaries scattered, leaving Santa Clara to a new group of pioneers, the Swiss settlers of 1861.

Beyond the Indian Mission

Once the outposts at Fort Harmony and Santa Clara had survived in the difficult land, other colonies were thinkable. In fairly rapid succession, between 1854 and 1858, new outposts were attempted, each clinging to a stream that watered a small meadow, enabling oasis-like agriculture in the desert. Most of the new settlers were also responding to a "call" from Brigham Young to go to what was called the Cotton Mission. After they reached Fort Harmony and passed through the Black Ridge barrier, several choices opened on the vast desert panorama before them. They could settle directly on the Virgin River or they could seek byways along several tributaries. They could also establish enclaves on the upper Santa Clara.

The resulting pattern looked something like a big twig with berries on its branches. The stem was the lower Virgin near Tonaquint. The first (left-hand) branch was the Santa Clara River with a small chain of villages: Santa Clara (1854), Pine Valley (1855), and Gunlock (1857). The main branch turned right, and settlers chose Washington (1857). Then above the Hurricane Fault they built Virgin (1858), Grafton (1859), Rockville (1861), and Springdale (1862). Tributaries Quail Creek, Ash Creek, North Creek, and the East Fork flowed into the Virgin from the north or east and provided the settlers with opportunities to build on the streams that provided river bottom or bench lands of ten to one hundred acres which could be irrigated and divided among several families.

Washington

In the spring of 1857, Mormon church leaders in Salt Lake City finally acted on the encouraging advice of John D. Lee to send people south to raise semi-tropical crops in the open fields beside the Virgin

River, next to the mesas covered by volcanic rocks. Two parties departed, one led by Samuel Adair leaving Payson on 3 March and another by Robert Covington from Salt Lake City in early April. Both groups faced their hardest traveling after they left Fort Harmony. The volcanic rock of the Black Ridge was a formidable obstacle followed by sandy stretches that exhausted their draft animals. Even traveling the last three miles challenged them as they rounded Grapevine Pass at the black mesa and could finally see their destination.

Their new home was to be called Washington, as determined in advance by Brigham Young and his counselors. Its location was also fixed — the benchland overlooking the Washington fields. The town was located near several fine springs which have favored the community above others in Dixie. The fields likewise provided a lush expanse of farmland. Washington appeared to have advantages over other communities, but this did not prove to be so. Those broad fields were formed by ancient floods; and modern floods would haunt Washington — not the town but its irrigation projects. And the springs created marshes. There, insects would spread malaria. So the Washington Saints were spared little; their plight, fighting malaria and rebuilding washed-out dams, would equal, if not surpass, the tests their neighbors encountered.

The possibility of raising cotton was a strong incentive for establishing Washington City. Successful attempts at Tonaquint and Santa Clara just a few seasons before held out the feasibility of a major cotton industry, and the warm climate seemed to ensure it. The drive for self-sufficiency was a constant theme of Brigham Young, and cotton would add greatly to such economic independence for the whole of Mormondom. John D. Lee continually extolled cotton raising as a purpose, so many of those called to the Adair expedition were from the southern states, people who had had experience raising cotton.[11]

Toquerville

Another alternative for settlement was to halt shortly below the Black Ridge on Ash Creek. Chief Toquer and a band of friendly Paiutes were settled there. They had invited Mormon explorers to come back to live. The chief was persistent, reissuing the request on a visit to Cedar City. In the spring of 1858, Isaac C. Haight, who presided in Cedar City, called Joshua T. Willis from Fort Harmony to lead a settlement on Ash Creek. The families of Wesley Willis, Josiah Reeves, John M. Higbee, Samuel Pollock, and a Mr. Brown were asked to accompany him. Charles Stapley, returning from San Bernardino, California, soon joined them.

The group was well received by Chief Toquer and began immediately to set out fields and start farming in the warm climate. They soon were raising squash, melons, grapes, figs, sweet potatoes, cotton, and alfalfa. Toquerville, as the village has since been known, has continued to this day despite its limited acreage. It still retains much of its pioneer character, particularly some wonderful old stone homes.

The spring that attracted the Indians and the earliest settlers still provides culinary water for the town as well as for its larger neighbor Hurricane.

Gunlock

Some settlements were outgrowths of the initial ones. The land was limited at Santa Clara and the young, newly arrived settlers were capable of ranging widely in search of forage and timber. Jacob Hamblin's brother William, nicknamed "Gunlock," soon found a location not unlike Santa Clara just a few miles up river, directly on the Old Spanish Trail. There in a narrow valley were small openings beside the Santa Clara Creek where crops could be planted. William Hamblin moved his family there, and his relatives Dudley and Jeremiah Leavitt and Isaac Riddle joined him.

Being upriver was a comfortable feeling, but the settlers would soon find themselves vulnerable to floods. Another threat was Indians who stole their cattle. The town, called Gunlock after its colorful founder, is an example of the individual enterprise of young families seeking land wherever they could stake their homes rather than being in a planned Mormon colony. The Leavitt and Riddle families moved there from Santa Clara, and the Holt and Hunt families later migrated from Hebron.

Pine Valley

Pine Valley is another example of a spillover settlement. Folktales claim that Isaac Riddle and William Hamblin were herding church cattle about fifteen miles north of Santa Clara in the summer of 1855. Isaac lost a cow and went in pursuit. Following up the Santa Clara River, the cow's trail eventually brought Riddle to a most beautiful and secluded, lush valley. "There stretching before me was the most beautiful sight I had ever beheld on God's green earth," he said.12 The valley floor was blanketed with thick grass, growing as high as a horse's knee; on the valley's side hills were heavy growths of pine, and quaking aspen were found on both sides of the creek. Riddle found his lost cow, peacefully grazing in the virgin meadow. As he rode after her, the heavy morning dew from the tall grass soaked his stirrups.

News of the find spread quickly, especially the availability of timber there. Robert Richey, Lorenzo Roundy, and Jehu Blackburn built a sawmill in Pine Valley in 1855. Charles Dalton asked the Washington County Court for timber and water rights in Pine Valley in September 1856. The probate court, presided over by John D. Lee, was the main civic authority at the time and took jurisdiction in legalizing land allotments. Milling continued for several years, but the initial gardening that accompanied it soon turned into real agriculture. The ample water was a great advantage even though it was offset by a short growing season. Pine Valley came to be a town of nearly 300 people as well as a favorite place to visit. Southern Utahns have always found Pine Valley's cool summer temperatures a relief. The area was especially valued in early times as a place for expectant mothers to escape from the summer heat while awaiting delivery.

Hebron

The search for water and land drew people still farther north. In 1856 Jacob Hamblin established a ranch at Mountain Meadows. Others took up ranching and settled near the Meadows. At Erastus Snow's urging, they came together and built a fort at what was called Hamblin. Richard Gibbons, Edwin R. Westover, Jacob Truman, and Simpson Emmett were among the first there.

A later group who went in the direction of Mountain Meadows was led by John and Charles Pulsipher. They were herding Mormon church stock in 1862. After grazing their animals on what they called Shoal Creek, they decided it would be a good place to locate their families. Nearby Paiute Indians encouraged them, so a community arose, focusing on ranching instead of farming, since the high altitude of 5,400 feet would limit agricultural efforts. One other difference was that their stream flowed north into the Great Basin rather than south to the Santa Clara-Virgin system. In 1868 Erastus Snow organized the seventy-five people who lived there into an ecclesiastical congregation with Dudley Leavitt as president. Snow called the town Hebron, after the biblical place.

Virgin

On the eastern side of the county a similar process occurred. With Toquerville serving as the mother colony, enterprising folks began searching for additional arable land. The Virgin River, issuing from a narrow canyon in the Hurricane Fault, presented a tantalizing challenge although the 500-foot-high fault scarp discouraged exploration. In September 1858 young Nephi Johnson, on orders from Brigham Young and with a Paiute guide, went up over the fault; he continued to the east fork of the river to the future site of Shunesburg and beyond. Back at Cedar City he reported that there were two sites suitable for settlement. He was attracted to one area in particular where the river describes a huge semicircle and is joined by North Creek. This became the site of Virgin City, which was first called Pocketville (from the Paiute word "pock-ich" meaning a cove or circular area). Johnson, along with a small group of men, built a passable road over the Hurricane Fault; by 20 September 1858, wagons were being driven over the fault below Toquerville to the Virgin River on the route known as "Johnson's Twist."[13]

The settlers knew that the Indians referred to the place as "Pockitch" but decided to call their community Virgin City to emphasize its favorable location near the river. The word "city" was added to help avoid confusion with the name of the river. Though this effort was mainly one of individual initiative, the settlers were Mormons, and they followed the regular pattern of laying out the town in square blocks, damming the river, building canals with cooperative effort, and erecting a community building to serve as church and school — most of this before starting their own homes.

John Nock Hinton, like many of his compatriots, built a home by digging a hole in a sidehill and lining it with rocks. He used cottonwood timbers and branches for a roof, which he covered with mud. On one side he built a fireplace.[14]

Farming was the lifeblood of the community, so the dam was crucial to everyone, but being flimsy structures of trees and bush, the small

The small Mormon town of Grafton near the Virgin River.
(National Park Service photo, J. L. Crawford Collection)

reservoirs had to be constantly rebuilt as floods were frequent, threatening the farms and making life along the Virgin River tenuous at best.

Grafton

In 1859 Virgin City gave forth an offspring: Grafton. Nathan Tenney led a group six miles upriver from Virgin to a broad valley beside the river. There their experience was similar to that in Virgin.

A flood literally washed the town away, requiring its relocation, and Indian troubles also plagued the settlers. Despite the uncertainty, the town achieved a degree of prosperity, even becoming county seat of Kane County for a time. As the river ate away at the available farmland, people began moving to other communities that offered more opportunities and better accessibility, Grafton being on the wrong side of the river. Final abandonment occurred in the early 1930s. Some buildings, fruit trees, and the cemetery still exist. The site is a favorite spot for ghost-town buffs, and it has also been used by movie producers as a filming location for western movies.

Rockville

Another five miles up the Virgin River is the site of present-day Rockville. In November 1862 John Langston and William R. Crawford built the first two homes there. The year before, five families led by Philip Klingonsmith had settled in Adventure just below Rockville. The floods that destroyed Grafton weren't quite as devastating to Adventure; however, subsequent flooding convinced the residents to move to higher ground which they had surveyed when the Crawford and Langston families arrived. The earliest settlers included the families of Edward Frodsham, William Scroggins, John C. Hall, George Staples, Albert Huber, Edward Huber, Thomas Hall, James McFate, Jacob Terry, Samuel Kenner, Henry Jennings, W. H. Carpenter, Hyrum Strong, Henry Stocks, Moroni Stocks, William Ashton, Daniel Q. Dennett, Thomas Flanigan, James Green, a Mr. Newman, and a Mr. Coon, in addition to Crawford and Langston.

Late in 1861, Mormon church leader Orson Pratt, instead of going to St. George, led a group up the Virgin River and after conferring with Nephi Johnson at Virgin, continued beyond Grafton. He evidently spent some time at Adventure before taking several families farther up the river to a location where the two branches of the river meet, a place which was to become known as Northrop. Here three families stayed. Others went three miles up the east fork where they established Shunesburg at the second site Nephi Johnson had picked.

Springdale/Shunesburg

Those who stopped at Northrop were James Lemmon, Isaac Behunin, and probably William Black. After the January flood, Behunin and Black moved farther up the north fork, thus becoming Springdale's first residents. Albert Petty who had first gone to Shunesburg went to Springdale in the fall of 1862 and settled near a large spring which is said to have inspired his wife to give the place its name. Other early settlers in Springdale were George Petty, Robert Brown, Newman Brown, Hardin Whitlock, Hyrum Morris, C. G. Averett, a Mr. Powell, a Mr. Davis, a Mr. Norton, and Joseph Millett and their families. Floods, malaria, and hunger continued to plague the settlers, with Indians being only a limited problem until the Blackhawk War of 1866, at which time residents of outlying towns were ordered to "fort up" in larger towns.

Shunesburg and Springdale residents moved to Rockville for the duration of the Indian menace — all except Albert Petty, who refused to leave. Petty was the only original Springdale name to be recorded when the town reemerged in 1868. Several of the new settlers moved from Shunesburg as that town continued to lose land to the hungry river. The new Springdale was located on higher ground; a new ditch was built, bringing more land under irrigation, and it was reported that malaria ceased to be a problem.

Shunesburg existed until after the turn of the century, its history being closely linked with that of Rockville, although it had its own ecclesiastical organization for three decades. Oliver DeMille and others settled there in 1862 after buying the land from the Indians. At its height (1880) there were eighty-two people in the town. Besides the DeMille rock house, which was one of the finest in its day, and a cemetery, only two or three rock chimneys remain. Today the place is held privately and has become a large commercial apple orchard.

Harrisburg/Leeds

If one line of settlements follows the Santa Clara River north and the other line of communities follows the Virgin River northeast, what about the land between? That is where the main road developed from Harmony down the Black Ridge and then on to Washington. Two communities developed at the base of the Black Ridge: Harrisburg and Leeds.

Moses Harris returned from San Bernardino, California, when that colony's members were called back to Utah in 1857 during the so-called "Utah War." He located on the Virgin River above Washington. Later settlers moved a few miles north to the junction of Quail and Cottonwood creeks. They retained the name "Harrisburg" for their settlement in honor of Moses Harris. By 1864 some sixteen families lived there, but soon it was perceived that both land and water were insufficient. Gradually the people moved three miles north to Leeds. Harrisburg became a ghost town after the 1890s, its sandstone ruins still noticeable from the 1-15 freeway. Recently, as the site of a mobile home park, it has come back to life with zest.

Leeds became a significant community even though its farmland, like Gunlock's, was limited to a narrow passageway between low mountains. One hundred and twenty acres were surveyed and the water of Quail Creek was diverted there in 1867. This took water from Harrisburg but the residents there were given land in Leeds in return for their water share in Harrisburg. Some people resisted, but gradually most moved to Leeds, making it a more stable place.

Leeds became a favorite resting spot for wagon freighters and then experienced a real boom when mining developed at Silver Reef. The products of Leeds's farms found a ready market among the miners. When the mines quit producing in the mid-1890s, the people of Leeds dismantled many buildings in Silver Reef and moved them to their village, including the Catholic church building, which they transformed into an opera house. It hosted both local talent and touring performers.

The Dixie story to this point proceeded quite naturally. Small groups of Mormons were called to open the new territory, and although they struggled against enormous odds — drought, heat, floods; nonetheless, many of them ranged throughout the area in search of land to establish permanent homes. They found small isolated meadows near streams and began to till the soil and turn the water onto their very small patches. Through intensive labor, they raised enough for a scant living as they continued to envision building their Kingdom of God. Often they sent for relatives and friends to join them. Additional Mormons from the north were encouraged by church leaders to go to the Southern Utah Mission. The population of the Virgin River area by 1860 was about 700 people, all of them struggling for a marginal existence. Sacrifice was no surprise to them. They had a great sense of history; they knew when they came south that they were pioneers. That meant survival was not assured.

St. George

On 6 October 1861, at the semi-annual general conference of the Mormon church, something dramatic occurred. Brigham Young called 300 families to go to southern Utah to establish the new community of St. George, named after his counselor, George A. Smith.[15] Smith was nominally in charge of the southern Utah colonies, and President Young asked him to select the people to be called to Dixie. Smith was also known as the "potato saint" for his generosity in giving potatoes from his farm to help people avoid scurvy. Perhaps those two facts led Brigham Young to put the words "Saint" and "George" together.

The 1861 company doubled the population of Dixie. It departed for the south in November, led by two Mormon apostles, Orson Pratt and Erastus Snow. Two members of the Seventies Quorum leadership of the church were also included, Henry Harriman and Jacob Gates. This high-profile action signaled a change for southern Utah.

Clearly things had happened in the leading councils in Salt Lake City, discussions that were substantially different from the motives that had led to the colonies of Harmony and Santa Clara. Some issues were quite obvious. First was the Utah War. When President James Buchanan ordered an army of U.S. infantry to march to Utah and install a new territorial governor in 1857, the Mormons responded with preparations for war. One aspect of those plans was to call many settlers of the most distant colonies back to the center. Leaders quickly realized that San Bernardino, California, and Las Vegas and Carson City, Nevada, were too far-flung to be defended. Those sites were abandoned, and many of their residents returned to Utah. That, in effect, left the southern flank open. The Mountain Meadows Massacre, the only real battle in the Utah War, illustrated the vulnerability of the region. Once the wider conflict was avoided, Brigham Young began thinking about the need for a new southern bastion.

Also in Young's mind was the challenge of bringing European converts to Zion. Many schemes were discussed. The railroad had not yet reached Utah, and no one knew if it would be a hostile or friendly incursion if it came. The wagon-train system across the Great Plains was hard on immigrants, many dying along the way. It did not seem like a permanent solution. A sea route was an appealing possibility. One that might conceivably develop was navigation up the Colorado River. Young followed such possibilities keenly. Certainly it would be important to have a southern entryway somewhere near Call's Landing, the northernmost point where boats could penetrate, just below the confluence of the Virgin and Colorado rivers. The Dixie Mission was the closest community to Call's Landing.

Another explanation for the call of 300 families was cotton. John D. Lee had consistently kept up his plea for reinforcements in southern Utah. He was fascinated with the idea of raising cotton on a large scale near Tonaquint or Washington. The outbreak of the Civil War in America seemed to coincide with the proposal to raise cotton extensively in Utah's Dixie. Mormon self-sufficiency would be greatly enhanced if cotton could be produced in Utah. Just like the similar hope of smelting iron near Cedar City, cotton would be a boon to all Mormons in the Great Basin. By 1861 cotton raising had become successful. Saints in Washington had grown the plants, woven the cotton, displayed it in a local fair, and sent samples to Salt Lake City.

This complex interaction of economic, demographic, and religious elements came together, convincing Brigham Young and other church leaders to launch a high-profile settlement project in the south. A most interesting element of this plan was that they did not send the 300 families to Washington or Santa Clara or any other existing settlement. Young had been on the scene. In May 1861 he visited Tonaquint, at the confluence of the Virgin and the Santa Clara, where about a dozen families were living. From there he gazed north to the broad vista with snow-capped Pine Mountain rising to 10,000 feet in the background and the two black mesas stretching south, protecting a large alluvial fan between them. He was deeply moved and prophesied, "There will yet be built, between those volcanic ridges, a city, with spires, towers and steeples, with homes containing many inhabitants."[16]

The saga of the settlement of St. George has been told in every medium — murals, books, pageants, sermons, movies, bedtime stories. It is the stuff of which legends are made. The 300 families did not likely suffer any more than the 700 people who preceded them to Dixie; in fact they were much in their debt for trails, friendships with Indians, exploration of the area, and information about struggles with the Virgin River. Nonetheless, the St. George story is pioneering in epic proportions. It is about building a Mormon regional capital in the south. If for no other reason, this was an unusual community in that it was the object of so much planning. It became the support of many other settlements, such as those on the Muddy River in Nevada, a chain of communities on the Little Colorado River in Arizona, and even several colonies in Mexico. For two decades Erastus Snow presided from St. George, traveling throughout these southern communities, exerting his remarkable pioneering leadership. St. George served as the headquarters for the whole southern strategy of the Mormons, as evidenced by the presence of church apostles there and eventually the establishment in the city of a winter residence for Brigham Young.

Of the 300 families called to St. George, 245 were listed in the census taken in the city in 1862. Whether some never came, or came and went back, or came to St. George and then moved to another Dixie community is not clear. Nonetheless, the portion that actually arrived in St. George was high, an indication of the cause's importance. Certainly all of those who moved to Washington County knew that their life in Dixie would be considerably harder than it would had they remained in the north.

Another reason the St. George story has received so much attention is that it was well recorded. James G. Bleak was appointed to keep a journal. He kept numerous notes and for four decades was the community's clerk for almost everything — church, government, business. Later in life he brought these documents together and produced a magnificent manuscript which all other writers on the subject consult. Other individuals kept journals, some of which have been published, including the masterpiece by John D. Lee. Another jewel is by Charles Lowell Walker. He gives a loyal account from the view of a follower instead of a leader. He tells that he was getting a good start in the Salt Lake Valley before his call to help settle St. George and continues, "This was the hardes[t] trial I ever had and had it not been for the gospel and those that were placed over me I should never moved a foot to go on such a trip, but then I came here not to do my will but the will of those that are over me, and I know it will all be right if I do right."[17]

From these and other records, we learn that on arriving, Erastus Snow set up several committees: one to survey a site for the town, one to set up canal plans to bring water to the fields that would support the community, another to search for timber, and finally a council to receive the reports and guide the future of the city. There was no suggestion that St. George was then a democracy. The presence of a resident apostle of the church made it clear who was in charge, but, although Erastus Snow could be very firm, his method of using authority was to involve the people in the decisions. Perhaps that is one reason his stature continued to grow over the next two decades while he presided over the ecclesiastical affairs of southern Utah as well as the Mormon colonies in Nevada, Arizona, and Mexico. His name and Dixie were intimately intertwined throughout the whole pioneer period. His colleague, Orson Pratt, remained in the area only three years before going on a mission to Europe. During his time in St. George the experience was somewhat like that in early Fort Harmony — the presence of two powerful leaders in the same place did not turn out well. Pratt was a great missionary; building communities was not as central for him as were theology, proselytizing, and contemplating the great ideas of science. He is one of Mormonism's greatest figures, but not because of his St. George experience. On the other hand, Erastus Snow is hardly remembered elsewhere than southern Utah, where he is revered. His was the tedious task of pleading with people to stay at the thankless challenge of living in the region of excessive heat and devastating floods. He articulated the vision of maintaining the kingdom's outer edges where no one wanted to be. It was a refiner's fire, and it took his compassion to help people want to stay in Dixie.[18]

Swiss Colony

Among those drawn to Dixie by the "big call" of 1861 was a group of Swiss immigrants. Daniel Bonneli was their leader and Santa Clara was designated as their destination, partly because the town was thought to be an excellent spot to raise grapes that the Swiss knew how to cultivate. In contrast to others called to the Cotton Mission, the Swiss immigrants had barely arrived in Utah and had not yet acquired the means for their trip south. Only a few even had wagons. Church leaders arranged to freight them to Santa Clara by asking each community in turn to deliver them to the next town. When they eventually arrived in St. George, church members there delivered them to Santa Clara, where they left them with their meager possessions. The group had no wagons to live in like most first-time settlers did, nor did they have food supplies to tide them over to the next harvest.

Erastus Snow and George A. Smith previously had made arrangements with the earlier settlers of Santa Clara to relinquish some of their claims to land so that the Swiss could have farms. Nellie McArthur Gubler described the arrangements:

> A survey of the new townsite was made early in December by Israel Ivins and on the twenty-second the old settlers and newly arrived Swiss met on the site which was dedicated by Elder Daniel Bonneli. Lots and vineyards were laid off and the settlers given their plots of ground in the following manner: After the lots had been platted, corresponding numbers were written on slips of paper and placed in a hat. Brother Bonneli drew the numbers from the hat and allotted them to the various families. Three different pieces were given to each family — first a piece of ground in town big enough for a home and garden (6 by 12 rods); next a piece a little farther away to

be used for vineyards and farming (1 acre); third a piece still farther
away (out past the black rocks to the east) to be used for farming
(vineyard lots). By this method each received equally. The South
Fields, or that across to the south, was left for the Indians. As soon
as this was done, people began to move away from the Fort onto
their new claims. Everyone went immediately to work and soon all
sorts of shelters sprang up among the dry, dead sunflowers and the
gray rabbit brush.[19]

From this inauspicious beginning, the Swiss worked tenaciously
in an environment alien to them, producing a permanent community
and a progeny that has influenced southern Utah most impressively.

Pioneering

Pioneering was an ever present, exacting lifestyle. Generally it
meant turning the first soil, building the first structures, creating anew
the fundamental institutions of Anglo-American society in a land that
had not hosted European civilization before. It required muscle and
sinew, spirit and character. It meant facing survival risks daily. It
was a great equalizer because all were subject to the same dangers
and discouragements. There was no aristocracy when it came to disease, flood, and scorching heat. Yet the feeling of accomplishment
was shared by all; common folk as well as their leaders knew that their
important mission would not be a brief assignment.

The harsh Dixie landscape was unrelenting; it yielded itself grudg-
ingly to these newcomers who tried to impose settled life upon its
sand and stone. Native Americans who had preceded the Mormons
by a millennium or two in this spot had demanded less of the land,
imposing fewer people for shorter seasons, impacting the land little,
gleaning instead of grazing, picking instead of plowing, drinking water instead of diverting it. The Anglo-European Mormons brought
a different mindset. The land must yield to their hands, sustain permanent villages, give of its clay, stone, and timber to fashion public
structures and permanent family dwellings. The newcomers would
change the course of streams and open the surface of the land to intensive planting of wheat, cotton, corn, lucerne, grapes, and varieties
of fruit trees.

The land balked at this change. It did not quickly yield to the
determination of the newcomers. It fought back with drought. It re-

sponded to overgrazing with flooding. The interface was not natural, and both the land and the people sustained injury. That conflict continues to this day.

The Mormons came convinced that the Lord had sent them and that the land should yield to them. They knew it would not do so spontaneously, for this was the "lone and dreary world," not the Garden of Eden. If their friends were making the desert "blossom like a rose" in the Great Basin, it was partly because those people were not really in a true desert. The pioneers in what geologists call the Basin and Range Province, along the foothills of the Wasatch Mountains, could see the deserts to the west, but they saw them from well-watered benchlands that received thunderstorms and snowstorms as clouds dropped their moisture before passing eastward over the Rocky Mountains. Those who came to the Dixie Mission knew that life would be marginal in Washington County because this was real desert, a land of red sand and merciless summer heat.

For many, pioneering was an interruption of the life they had just begun to enjoy in the north. It was an assignment, one people agreed to, but certainly under some pressure and a lot of expectation. It required soul-searching for some, and quite a few chose not to accept their call. Robert Gardner said that when he went into the office at church headquarters in Salt Lake City after being called to the Dixie Mission, George A. Smith told him he could take his name off the list if he wished.[20] Gardner did not feel that one should tamper with such calls, but there were some who hired others to fill their assignment. John Bennion, for example, equipped William Ellis Jones to take his place; however, Jones was anxious to go and initiated the idea. Others dallied in coming. Some actually volunteered, often friends and family of those assigned who, after arriving, returned north for reinforcements.

Once its members accepted the call, the 1861 company soon departed. The trek through the string of colonies south of Provo went fairly fast, often reinforced by visits with and hospitality from friends who had taken up land in emerging communities along the route — from Payson to Harmony. The 300 families of the company left Cedar City with the encouragement of all along the way; however, soon the Black Ridge imposed its terrors on the ox teams. The company could not follow the streambed because of huge boulders, so they had to drive over lava beds, carving a road as they went. They named one section "Peter's Leap" for Peter Shirts, who proposed to leap from one lava ledge to another. The company had to ease their wagons over the dangerous site by attaching ropes and holding them to brake each wagon's descent. Once they had descended to the area now called Anderson's Ranch, they met the next challenge, a stretch of deep, red sand, extending almost to Leeds. The oxen were quickly exhausted trying to pull each wagon through the sands as the wheels sank into the soft surface. By the time the pioneers reached the Virgin River, all were apprehensive. Their response to anxiety was action, particularly group action. Pioneering did not leave much time for reflection; it was a life of action.

The lives of both men and women, even of children, were dominated by work — work to clear land, work to divert water, work to build shelters, work to raise food, work to survive. In a classic understatement, Robert Gardner opened his personal memoir with the comment that nothing of much importance had transpired in his life, just hard work and a willingness to meet it and live in peace with his neighbors — these were the essential features of his life. It is fitting that he so described his life even though he was part of the decision-making core of the community. That did not relieve him from hard physical labor.

William Ellis Jones, who was very much at the other end of the social spectrum, presents another example of hard work. He never acquired more than five acres of land and, as a school teacher, he had to make frequent moves. Schools met only four or five months a year, leaving him without an income the rest of the time. He made adobes on building sites wherever he could find someone who could afford to hire him. His wife hired out as a midwife for difficult cases in which she at times had to live-in for a month at a time. Their children tended orchards. Jones was always poor but maintained an amazing attitude. For example he wrote:

> I burnt the bricks for Brother Gardner early in September my Son Hyrum brought the team up on Tuesday Sept. 8th I came home with him next day. In August last my wife was suddenly deprived of her hearing and it is with difficulty that we make her hear any thing that we say I find difficult to get things necessary for my family on account of money being so scarce and no sale for the things we raise here. Dried peaches are only worth three and a quarter cents a pound, dried grapes no sale in the stores, grain and beans no sale but

we make exchanges with our neighbors and in this way manage to
live, but notwithstanding the times are hard I feel very thankful that
we are as well off as we are we have enough to eat and are not suffering much for clothing but still we are needy and no way at present
to get the things we need but I know the Lord will open the way as
he has always done.[21]

Building dams to divert water from the Virgin or Santa Clara
rivers was a constant battle. The first dam on the Virgin, located
southeast of Washington on the north side of Shinobkiab Mountain, was washed away several times. Church leaders frequently
found the settlers discouraged, many threatening to leave the
difficult land.[22]

In contrast to irrigation in the Great Basin, the challenge of diverting water onto the land in Washington County demanded a different technology. Streams often had no set bed. The shifting sands
seldom provided a firm footing to attach posts and brush to turn the
water. Most serious of all were flash floods. The mountains had very
little vegetation. Therefore, when summer thunderstorms occurred,
and they did so regularly, the waters gushed off the hills and swelled
the otherwise placid streams, which then roared suddenly, multiplying the flow as much as tenfold. Boulders, brush, and trees, labori-
ously set in the streams to hold back the waters, were spun out of the
flood's path like flipping coins. Weeks of communal labor would
disappear in minutes. Often the roaring rivers would not only destroy
the dams but carry away farmland as they carved out new paths in the
sandy flood plains. Lizzie Ballard Isom described the floods she saw
as a young girl:

> We witnessed many awful floods in the river. One I so well re-
> member was so thick with dirt and logs that it moved so slowly
> that a person could have run across in front of it. Timber and dirt
> together made it look like the side of a log house. Father took a can
> and dipped some of what was supposed to be water and poured it
> on a log and it was so thick that it hardly reached the ground. All
> floods were not the same. One day another flood came and was
> running so swift with everything imaginable in it. There was a cow
> that had been caught in its path along with bee hives, all kinds of
> farm equipment, field and garden produce. Men tried to catch the
> cow by the horns with a lasso but the swift water filled with trees
> prevented her from getting near enough so they could get the rope

on her and she went down. The floods came so many times and claimed so much of the land that the people became discouraged and abandoned Grafton.23

Stories of the floods are legion. The flood of 1861-62 was likely the most devastating. The rains began on Christmas Day 1861, barely a month after the St. George colonists arrived. For forty days and nights the rains continued at least part of each day. Floods occurred over the whole county. In Santa Clara the fort was washed away. With miraculous fortune no lives were lost although Jacob Hamblin was twice pulled from the rushing waters with ropes as he labored to rescue others. At Fort Harmony disaster struck; the fort there caved in, killing two of John D. and Sarah Caroline Lee's children — George A. and Margaret Ann. As a result of this flooding, several towns had to be relocated to higher ground, Harmony, Santa Clara, Washington, Grafton, Virgin, and Rockville (Adventure) among them.

At least one citizen carried the remembrance of the flood with him for life. On 8 January the flood waters were rising in Grafton. The Nathan Tenney family was living in their wagon box and Nathan's wife was in labor. Tenney's neighbors helped him haul the dwelling to higher ground with the expectant mother inside. She was delivered of a healthy boy whom they named Marvelous Flood Tenney, "Marve" for short.

Irrigation water was not the only water challenge. Domestic water was also the cause of much labor, often for children. Ether Wood described how, as a young boy, he provided "dip water" for his family:

> Our water system was a fifty-gallon barrel on a sled made from two cottonwood logs, with a chain and single tree on one end to hook the horses to. I would go to the river, dip the barrel full with a bucket; coming back, we had a rocky hill to climb, which made the horse work to pull it. I would have to stop and let him rest several times. In the summer the river would get quite muddy and my mother would put milk in the water to settle the mud. When I went after another barrel of water, I would have to take the barrel off from the sled and rinse out the mud....There was also the rinse tub to fill, then I had to empty the tubs when she was through. Wash days was the days I dreaded most, for I had to haul all the water in buckets to a copper boiler on the fire, where she boiled the clothes, then to the scrubbing tub, where she scrubbed them on a board.24

Floods caused the relocation of villages after they had consumed the assiduous labor of the residents for a few seasons. That was not the only hazard to cause a move. In 1865 and 1866 Indian wars upset the whole region. Though in the long run they ended without great loss of life, Brigham Young felt that it was urgent for the Latter-day Saints in outlying settlements to move to the larger towns for the duration of the conflict. The following letter from Erastus Snow to the Saints living on the upper Virgin River captures their plight and his method of guiding them:

> We have, in council, considered your condition and thought it best to recommend Rockville as the point of concentration, unless the majority should prefer another place lower down the river. Let every one, therefore, go to without delay to carry into effect the instructions received, as fast as circumstances permit, without unnecessary waste, or destruction. Secure the growing crops, preserve the orchards and vineyards as best you can, and clear the canyons above Rockville of stock, so as to keep that range for winter.[25]

Heat and wind were other aspects of living in the desert that were terribly discouraging, particularly to women who were attempting to keep a home in something approaching the domestic style to which they were accustomed. The following account describes the problems caused by weather in Atkinville:

> A more forbidding place to build homes would be difficult to find, but it was necessary to avoid the mosquitoes of the fields and pastures. The summer sun beat relentlessly down upon the whole scene. There was no vegetation around the house, except two small tamarix trees by the front porch and small flower gardens watered by hand, for which May was chiefly responsible. She planted and tended them and kept them alive by carrying water from the barrels in buckets. Winds often blew through the gap and poured gray, sandy dust over everything. It left a layer of grit on the milk in the cellar, on the cream in the jar for churning, on the dishes in the cupboard, and over all the furniture. There was sand in the water buckets, the drinking dipper, the milk pails and pans set out to sun; on floors and window sills. It filled one's eyes and ears and gritted between one's teeth. Was it any wonder that my mother, who went to Atkinville as a bride, exclaimed during one of these windy onslaughts in sheer desperation "Nothing tries my faith so much as one of these sand storms; I feel like apostatizing."[26]

Though the Latter-day Saints in Washington County were struggling against nearly superhuman odds, they were not alone in the struggle for survival; but at times they felt alone. Other groups that commanded attention were the immigrant trains that came each summer across the plains to Utah. Brigham Young regularly requisitioned wagons, food, and drivers from the existing communities to go to Nebraska and assist the Mormons who were struggling to get to Utah. Those who traveled to help had to be gone between four and six months. Erastus Snow felt rather put upon to raise volunteers from among the Saints in Dixie for this task, since he believed that conditions there were considerably tougher than elsewhere; nonetheless, the southern Saints complied. In 1864 Snow's patience was stretched, however, and he could not help but write a questioning letter to the Presiding Bishop on the matter.

People came to Dixie out of religious duty; personal gain could have been achieved better elsewhere. Once colonies were planted, the original pioneers recruited friends and family to join them. The natural elements conspired against them, especially the sparse water and the scorching heat. The ranks were constantly thinned by disease, death, and departures. The vision of building a "Kingdom of God" was reiterated regularly by leaders and tested by personal conviction.

In contrast to the individual enterprise that was common in the settlement of much of California and Oregon and other parts of the West, Mormons settled in groups with clear local leadership linked to the central church. Cooperative use of water, organized assignments of land, and homes established in villages were key elements of the Mormon pattern. Brigham Young hoped to occupy every source of water in the region with self-sustaining communities that would host a continuing flow of immigrants. The Dixie effort was marginal, yet there was some water there and leaders felt an urgency to control the southern access to the Great Basin. About forty such communities were attempted in Dixie; twenty of them continue to exist. This area includes Washington County and adjacent areas — the Arizona Strip, Bunkerville, Mesquite, and for a time, the Muddy River settlements in Nevada.

The Dixie villages were not utopian communes. Despite their extensive cooperation, southern Utahns were private citizens with individual interests and holdings. They cleared their own land (which later became theirs even though at first they were squatters). In lieu of land deeds that would have to wait until U.S. government land offices were opened a decade later, the families drew lots and received a local surveyor's certificate as evidence of their holdings. Thus fairness ruled. Families then arranged for temporary shelter, either in a communal fort or on village lots — in dugouts, wagon boxes, reed lean-tos, or tents. To sustain their families, they established trades, farmed, herded cattle, or worked as employees for each other. They either raised their own food or bartered for it. Children worked beside their parents. Hunger, combat against the elements (especially heat and drought), the search for water and its application to uneven land, the danger of disease (especially malaria) — all these were no respecters of persons. Each day was a struggle for survival for both leaders and followers.

Like others who tried to build an empire, the Dixie enterprise required sustained leadership and devoted followers. Though there was occasional conflict, even some gnawing feuds, the settlers generally shared the vision of bringing civilization to the desert. Their muscle, creativity, and devotion sustained the effort which their leaders had articulated. The results produced a communal spirit that is still intact today — modified but clearly recognizable.

ENDNOTES

1. Juanita Brooks, "The Southern Indian Mission," in *Under the Dixie Sun*, ed. Hazel Bradshaw (Washington County Chapter Daughters of the Utah Pioneers, 1950), 23.

2. Adult adoption was an early Mormon practice wherein a person (such as John D. Lee) requested a respected figure like Brigham Young to adopt him into his eternal, not earthly, family.

3. James G. Bleak, "Annals of the Southern Utah Mission" (typescript at Dixie College Library), 16.

4. In the party were Hyrum Burgess, 17; Ira Hatch, 18; Benjamin Knell, 19; Thales Haskell, 20; Amos G. Thornton, 21; Samuel Knight, 21; Augustus P. Hardy, 23; William Henefer, 30; Lorenzo Roundy, 34; Jacob Hamblin, 35; David Lewis, 40; Elnathan Eldridge, 42; Thomas D. Brown (scribe), 46; Robert M. Dickson, 46; and Robert Richey, 47. See Brooks, "The Southern Indian Mission," 25.

5. Juanita Brooks, ed., *Diary of Thomas D. Brown, Journal of the Southern Indian Mission*, ed. Juanita Brooks (Logan: Utah State University Press, 1972), 29-30.

6. Ibid., 117-18.

7. By 1858 Santa Clara hosted Jacob Hamblin; his wife, Rachel Judd Hamblin; and their children; Oscar Hamblin and his family; Isaac Riddle and family; Richard Robinson, and family; Prime T. Colemen and family; Samuel Knight and his family; Dudley Leavitt and his wives; sisters Mary and Maria Huntsman; Zadok Judd and his wife, daughter, son, and Indian boy (Lamoni); Robert Richey and family; Thales Haskell; Thomas Eckles; Lemuel Leavitt; Jeremiah Leavitt; Wier Leavitt; Andrew S. Gibbons; Frederick Hamblin; Ira Hatch; Augustus P. Hardy; and Francis (Alsen) Hamblin.

8. Jesse A. Little, *Jacob Hamblin* (Salt Lake City: Deseret News, 1881), 39-40.

9. Larry Coates, "The Fancher/Baker Train from Salt Lake City to Mountain Meadows," unpublished manuscript, 8-11, located in Dixie College Archives.

10. See Juanita Brooks, *John D. Lee, Zealot, Pioneer Builder, Scapegoat* (Glendale, CA: Howe, 1962). See also Juanita Brooks, *The Mountain Meadows Massacre* (Stanford: Stanford University Press, 1950).

11. Bleak, "Annals of the Southern Utah Mission," 34. The heads of families listed by Bleak include: Robert D. Covington; James B. Reagan; Harrison Pearce; William R. Slade; Joseph Smith; John W. Freeman; William H. Crawford; Umpsted Rencher; James D. McCullough; George Hawley; William Hawley; John Hawley; Balus Sprouse; John Couch, Sr.; John Couch, Jr.; Alfred Johnson; Samuel Adair; John Adair; Thomas Adair; Oscar Tyler; George Spencer; J. Holden; James Richey; John Mangum; William Mangum; James B. Wilkins; Joseph Adair; Joseph Hatfield; William Dammeron; Preston Thomas; William Fream; Sims B. Matheny; Stephen Duggins; William Duggins; William J. Young; Enoch Dodge; John Price; and Robert Lloyd. Later research by Harold Cahoon of the Washington City Historical Society has added the following names to the original settler list: George W. Adair, Newton L. N. Adair, John W. Clark, Thomas W. Smith, James Nichols Mathews, Gabriel R. Coley, and John D. Lee.

12. Bessie Snow and Elizabeth Snow Beckstrom, "A History of Pine Valley," in *Under the Dixie Sun*, 178-79.

13. Angus M. Woodbury, *A History of Southern Utah and Its National Parks* (privately published, 1950), 148. Assisting in the building of the road was Nephi's brother Seth, Darius and Carl Shurtz, Anthony Stratton, James Bey, Andrew J. Workman, William Haslam, and Samuel Bradshaw. Nephi Johnson invited families from Cedar City and Fort Harmony to join them in the settlement of the upper lands. Those who responded included Joel Hills Johnson, Nephi's father; his brother Sixtus; Hugh Hilton and two sons; William A. Bebe; Moses Clawson; Charles P. Bark; Simon Anderson; Thomas Banson; Samuel B. Hardy; Augustus P. Hardy; and someone named Capson.

14. Lenora Atkin Meeks, "John Nock Hinton: The Reconstructed Life of an English Born Mormon Convert of Virgin City, Utah," (Masters thesis, Brigham Young University, 1987), 83.

15. B. H. Roberts, *Comprehensive History of the Church* (Salt Lake City: Church of Jesus Christ of Latter-day Saints, 1930) Vol. V: 123, 15. There are people who feel the name "St. George" had other origins, but the documentary evidence supports the story as found in Bleak's "Annals of the Southern Utah Mission," 77.

16. Bleak, "Annals," 75.

17. Andrew Karl Larson, ed., *Diary of Charles Lowell Walker* (Logan: Utah State University Press, 1980), I: 240-41.

18. Nels Anderson, *Desert Saints* (Chicago: University of Chicago Press, 1942, rev. 1966), 230. This book describes the relationship between Orson Pratt and Erastus Snow.

19. Nellie McArthur Gubler, "History of Santa Clara, Washington County," in *Under the Dixie Sun*, 162.

20. "Memoir of Robert Gardner," Dixie College Archives, 38.

21. "Journal of William Ellis Jones," Dixie College Archives, 42.

22. Andrew Karl Larson, *The Red Hills of November* (Salt Lake City: Deseret News Press, 1957), 77.

23. Janice Force De Mille, *Portraits of the Hurricane Pioneers* (St. George: Homestead Publishers, 1976), 142.

24. Ibid., 267.

25. History of James Monroe Ballard, 15, as cited in James T. Jones, "Old Grafton," Dixie College Archives.

26. Grace Atkin Woodbury and Angus Munn Woodbury, *The Story of Atkinville* (Salt Lake City: University of Utah Press, 1957), 13.

3

SINKING ROOTS

$\mathbf{M}$ormons were institution builders. Once their immediate survival was assured, they turned to anchoring their institutions. This was true in the Great Basin, and the Dixie pioneers implemented it without question when they arrived at the base of the Colorado Plateau. Even though their assignment took them below the Great Basin into the sandy desert, they assumed they would conquer it through irrigation, family farms, villages, churches, schools, shops, newspapers, libraries, banks, theaters, and courts, just as their co-religionists were doing in scores of other settlements at higher elevations. This institutional solution was working throughout the Mormon settled portion of the Great Basin and they intended to make it work in Dixie within the first decade.

The initial Washington County settlers accomplished the basics of laying out townsites on the grid pattern Joseph Smith had adopted for his ideal City of Zion. Settlers drew lots for a town plot and acreage in nearby fields, diverted water onto the land, and arranged temporary shelters for their families. Then they automatically turned to the next step in their minds: building civic institutions.

They employed a compressed approach to civilization — imposing several development stages at once. Within a year of set-

St. George Hall and Main Street after a rare snow storm. The Hall was used as a store after the completion of the Tabernacle — seen at the end of the street. (Lynne Clark Collection, donor — Andy Winsor)

tling St. George, a post office had been opened (it was applied for prior to their arrival), the territorial legislature had issued a charter to the city (on 18 January 1862), schools had been established, four religious congregations (wards) had been organized, dams had been built, cooperatively built canals were in place, a community bowery was erected, a city council had been elected and several committees had been organized to build irrigation canals and to find timber and build lumber mills.[1] This same, if not quite so complex, sequence had been followed in the dozen Washington County settlements that preceded St. George.

St. George Hall

Only a few days after their arrival in St. George, Erastus Snow proposed to the citizens that they build a public hall to house social and educational activities. The only way to finance it was by public subscription. He put the proposal to a vote and the people pledged to donate to the project. Historical records indicate that "a subscription list was made with contributions pledged in various amounts ranging from five to fifty dollars each, and totalling $2,074 from 120 people, not one of whom yet had a roof over his head."[2]

The building was completed in three years and became the home of numerous theatrical, musical, agricultural, civic, and educational activities. It was called the St. George Hall and was located on the west side of Main Street, just a few doors north of the church's tithing office. Dances were special favorites as were public holidays with oratory, singing, and general celebrating.

The St. George Tabernacle

Brigham Young did not wait for culture to evolve gradually after his fellow Mormons had built homes and had seen their farms producing. In the case of St. George, he called upon the residents to undertake a most ambitious civic effort first. After he visited the new settlement, some nine months following its founding, he wrote to the colony's leader, Apostle Erastus Snow, directing that they build "as speedily as possible a good, substantial, commodious well furnished meeting house, one large enough to comfortably seat at least 2,000 persons, and that will not only be useful, but also an ornament to your city, and a credit to your energy and enterprise."[3]

This request was no idle suggestion. Young had been at the site and received the plea of Snow. They both knew that the effort to establish a southern regional capital at St. George was turning out to be more of a problem than anticipated. The settlers were discouraged — northern irrigation techniques were not working in this region. Already several had abandoned their call. The need for reinforcements was urgent, but newcomers would face the same harsh realities — scorching heat, brackish water, alkaline soil, blowing sand, killing diseases, and bursting irrigation dams. It was not just a matter of character; resources had to be increased or the undertaking might fail.

Brigham Young decided on the building of a tabernacle in order to rally the colony. It was to be an heroic structure that would state categorically: "we are here to stay." This was to be the centerpiece of a capital city. Not insignificantly, its construction would provide employment for craftsmen, a subsidy to support the community for a few years while they attempted to conquer the desert. In his letter, Young went on to say: "I hereby place at your disposal, expressly to aid in the building of afore-said meeting house, the labor, molasses, vegetable and grain tithing of Cedar City and all other places south of that city. I hope you will begin the building at the earliest practicable date: and

Tithing Scrip issued by the St. George Stake Tithing Store House.
(Lynne Clark Collection)

be able with the aid thereby given, to speedily prosecute the work to completion."[4] Brigham did not often subsidize a colony, but he chose to in this case most likely because of its strategic importance and certainly because of the exceptional environment it faced.

The first task before the builders was to erect a tithing office across the street north of the tabernacle square. Erastus Snow began delivering a systematic message throughout the region to all Latter-day Saints: pay your tithes to make possible the building of the tabernacle. Obviously there was no other source of capital for civic projects than the productivity of the people. Voluntary contributions in the form of tithes were the lifeblood of all community efforts. Such donations were an indicator of one's adherence to the institution. And the tithes were paid, often after considerable exhortation and almost entirely in kind — eggs, chickens, wheat, grapes, sorghum, cattle, fruit. Much was perishable and had to be stored efficiently in the tithing office. From its stores, workmen could be paid for their labor on the limestone foundation that was soon in progress. Tithing scrip was also issued for supplies and became the de facto legal tender of local commerce.

Once the limestone foundation was completed, workmen began quarrying the distinctive red sandstone for the tabernacle's walls in a quarry where today the Red Hills Golf Course nestles into the cliffs. Edward L. Parry was the chief mason, assisted by Charles L. Walker, Joseph Worthen, David Moss, George Brooks, James G. Bleak, William G. Miles, and John Pymm, among others. Their carefully cut blocks fit on the deep, six-foot-wide limestone foundation. Today the cutters' work can be inspected to see the distinctive marks of each craftsman. Oldtimers claim they can attribute specific stones to each cutter by their distinctive tool marks. The Dixie weather and clean air have preserved the stones so that even an amateur can distinguish the markings.

Workmen were occupied from 1863 to 1875 with the demanding task. Huge timbers from Mount Trumbull were hand hewn to span the large auditorium. The lumber, milled in Pine Valley, provided a large part of the need; however, it often had to wait while mill workers produced timber for the mines in Pioche, Nevada, that had priority because the mine owners paid in cash currency. Often Erastus Snow had to reenergize the tithepayers to supply the resources for the building.

There were down times and there were also competing projects such as the cotton factory and the county courthouse. Other public subscriptions also competed for donors — the telegraph, public roads, Indian gifts, and departing missionaries, but the work proceeded gradually and safely. Orson Pratt's prayer at the tabernacle's cornerstone laying prophesied that the work would go forward without serious accident — and it did.

Inspiring incidents were told about the construction. One favorite involved the windows. The wonderful New England design style included large windows with many panes that would flood the chapel with bright light. Plans called for 2,244 small panes in the forty pairs of vertical sliding windows.[5] The glass for the windows was shipped by boat from New York to California. David H. Cannon had been assigned the task of raising $800 for the glass through yet another public subscription. This money for the final payment was to be sent with the freighters on their trip to California when they picked up the windows to bring them to St. George. Cannon optimistically set a day for the freighters' departure; however, by that time he had raised only $200. Nonetheless, he determined to depart and "depend on the Lord" to aid the endeavor.

At the same time, a Danish convert, Peter Neilsen in Washington, was anticipating his long dream of adding onto his two-room adobe home; but somehow he was uncomfortable about the expenditure of his savings. Legend has it that without knowing specifically of the needed amount, he determined to give his long-amassed funds to civic purposes. He arrived in St. George with $600 on the morning the freighters were to depart. Whether the story has been embellished with time does not matter. Its elements are sound; Nielsen's donation enabled the glass to be purchased and complete the enclosure. Many of the panes are still in place, easily distinguished.

Orpha Hunt tells of a freighting experience her father, Revilo Fuller, had while traveling to California to pick up the windowpanes. He told the story to her later, and she wrote it down:

> We had three long desert drives with no water on the way and no feed for the mules except the scanty vegetation which grew by the way.
>
> Your grandfather Elijah K. Fuller and Uncle Wid and myself with many others made many a trip to Cal. However on the trip when we brought this glass, Father and Wid's team were driven by Jim and Tom Pearce. We hired an Indian boy who we called "Josh" to go along as night herd for the teams, taking a saddle horse for him to ride.
>
> He would take the mules out to where the grazing was as good as the country afforded and at the first peep of day he would bring them back to camp. That was one trip that everything went well as far as molestation by Indians was concerned.
>
> On our arrival at the Wilmington Docks, the ship was unloading her cargo. The boxes containing glass were dumped on the dock like so many stones. I refused to accept one single box until they were opened and all broken glass thrown out. This made quite a delay but we had no broken glass to start out with.
>
> We loaded the boxes with the edge of the glass down so as to avoid breakage and it came through very well.
>
> We used to drive with one line for six or eight mules, training one of the lead mules as a "jerk mule" and it would obey the jerk to turn the team "Gee" or "Haw" as the driver desired. I tried to learn Josh how to drive, but he was scared to even touch that jerk line. You would hardly think that those little window panes cost seventy five cents a-piece, would you; at the present time you can buy all you want for ten.
>
> And this is how we got the window glass as told me by my father Revilo Fuller.[6]

Miles Romney was the general supervisor of the tabernacle's construction. His personal delight was building the two spiral staircases

The St. George Tabernacle shortly after its completion in 1876.
(Lynne Clark Collection)

that led to the balcony. Their grace depended on delicate measurements. When Brigham Young visited the project, he took exception to Romney's construction of the balcony. President Young felt that Romney had the balcony too high; it was difficult for worshipers to see the pulpit. He wanted the proportions such that the balcony bisected the windows about equally, some six feet lower than Romney had installed it. It became apparent that two strong wills were confronting each other. Romney did not intend to change his staircases, since that would ruin the proportions, but Young insisted that the balconies be lowered. Visitors today can see the result. The balcony is where Brigham wanted it, and the staircases also are in place in their original design. People must ascend to the top of the Romney staircases before taking six steps down to reach the Young balcony.

The tabernacle stands on the town square today as graceful as ever. Two major restoration projects, one on the exterior and the other on the interior, have been completed by competent restoration architects and builders at great cost (many times the original expenditure). The building reigns in the city as a masterpiece of its kind. Residents and visitors alike are fond of it, well beyond their feelings for other LDS structures. The spiritual sanctity created by the sacrifice in building it explains part of that feeling. Many hallowed events that also have occurred there add to the love felt by residents. The quality of architecture and the craftsmanship help too. But its symbolic meaning is central. It has to do with that vision the Dixie pioneers had about a kingdom of God.

Probably the most appreciative words written about the tabernacle are these by Dixie historian Andrew Karl Larson:

> The Tabernacle is beautiful; there is no other word for it. As one looks at it in the soft mellow light of early morning or late afternoon, standing there so blended with the red hills that furnished its own stones, he instinctively reacts with awe and reverence. The finely dressed stones have lost their harshness through the softening effect of the thousands of tiny short grooves cut by the crandall in the competent hands of pioneer artisans. There is no particular part that clamors for attention; what one sees is a unified structure producing a simple and satisfying harmony of purpose. It leaves no feeling of heaviness, yet neither does it convey a mood of fragility. Its numerous windows, symmetrical in their grace, draw the eyes upward to the pinnacle of the tower and back again with one easy motion. Inside and out, it carries the conviction of dignity and strength and the feeling of both solemnity and joy. Its appearance, far more than words can tell, reveals the love and infinite pains lavished upon it by those who slowly brought an architect's dream to reality. Born of suffering and travail, it imparts no sense of toil and hardship but the feeling of effortless creation that only great art can achieve. It is these things which lead the discriminating beholder to assert that the Tabernacle is the finest example of the chapel builder's art, not just in Utah, but in the whole Mormon experience.[7]

The St. George Tabernacle took on added meaning when church president Lorenzo Snow visited the city on 30 May 1899 and delivered a famous sermon on tithing.[8] It was a time when the church was facing extreme financial difficulty, partly an aftermath of the Federal government's assault on the fiscal structure of the church through the Edmunds-Tucker Act of 1887. President Snow came to St. George on a spiritual impulse and reported that he did not know why until well into his talk when he stopped and then turned to the subject of tithing.

The St. George Temple

Midway into the tabernacle building project, Brigham Young announced an even more important undertaking — a temple. The idea had been first raised by the Mormon church president in counsel with Apostles Erastus Snow and Brigham Young, Jr., on 31 January 1871. Following consultation with the other general authorities at the April general conference, Brigham sent a letter to Erastus Snow in St. George announcing the decision. He described the temple as two stories high with a basement housing a baptismal font. The structure was to be 196 feet long, 142 feet wide and 80 feet high, built of stone and plastered inside and out. Also crucial was the financing plan: all the tithing of the Latter-day Saints in Beaver and those wards south was to go to the completion of the tabernacle and the building of the temple.

Why this additional project, this continual support for the Dixie colony, this ongoing request for donated labor and contributions? Historian Heber Jones reflectively explains:

> Brigham Young was getting old. He wanted to see a temple established in the west in his lifetime. His ambitions had been frustrated in Salt Lake City by meddling Federal authorities. No significant work had been done on the Salt Lake Temple in seven years. President Young had been in and out of court or jail on several occasions and other charges were pending. He had visited St. George and knew that the people were restless and needed something to unify and sustain them when the Tabernacle was completed. It was a difficult mission in Dixie and some wanted to leave. He also knew that some of his most trusted, experienced and loyal followers were here. The place was relatively isolated and would be free from government and gentile interference. Skills, labor and materials were available. The people needed subsistence to see them through the pioneer period. The Cotton Factory was in trouble, and the natural scourges of flood, famine, and Indian fighting were competing with the sun as excuses the weak could use to question their call and go elsewhere.[9]

Brigham Young wanted his empire to be self-sufficient, and St. George was a key location for travel, supply, and defense. The colony had to be maintained.

The temple construction reinforced St. George's status as an emerging regional hub. People from southern Utah, Nevada, Arizona, and even Mexico traveled to St. George to enjoy its ordinances. The

temple was the first in Utah and clearly the one that had Brigham
Young's imprint. He selected the site, south of the city on a low hill.
(The city would later expand and surround the temple.) The architectural design by Truman O. Angell was directly influenced by Young
but, even more important, the form of the liturgy in the building would
be developed under his guidance. The economic impact was significant too; for one thing, 100 men came from Sanpete County to serve
as construction workers. They would later return home and build the
Manti LDS Temple.

On 5 November 1871 Dixie church members voted to sustain the
decision to build the temple. Four days later the groundbreaking ceremony was held. The excavation soon ran into serious water problems.
About one-fourth of the foundation rested on solid limestone (on the
north side), but the remainder of the building site was marshy. This
problem was solved by draining the ground and transporting volcanic
lava rocks from the west black mesa near where the airport is today.
A road had to be built on the hill and wagons were needed to bring the
stones to the temple site. It was tedious work to quarry the volcanic
rock, transport it to the temple site, and drive it into the ground. Today
the remnants of the road and quarry can be visited by taking a short
hike beginning at the city park near the airport.

Thousands of tons of small rocks were first placed in the marshy
soil. Workers then pounded the huge quarried volcanic blocks on top
of the small ones. Temple builders developed a piledriver by encasing
a field artillery cannon in heavy ash timbers bound by iron bands.[10]
The heavy weight was rigged to cables that pulled it into the air and
then released it to fall and pound the large squarish stones deep into
the wet soil. By this tedious and laborious method, a firm foundation
was created that has served to keep the building solid and unharmed
through a century of elements, including a major earthquake in 1992
of 5.7 magnitude on the Richter Scale. The work was slow — draining the ground and pounding each stone until the piledriver bounced
three times, indicating that the footing was solid.

Milo Andrus recorded that he was "at work on the temple, which
is progressing very well. There are over one hundred men engaged directly on the ground, over one hundred working in the quarry, and over
forty men at Mount Trumbull getting out lumber. In addition some
men are on the road for the purpose of getting wood, coal, etc. Every

St. George Temple under construction.
(Lynne Clark Collection, donor — Will Brooks)

day the President [Brigham Youngl and George A. Smith come to see
how the work is progressing."11 With as many as 240 men active in
the construction at one time, the ripple effect of this employment on
the local economy was substantial, allowing the establishment of a
bakery and several other enterprises nearby.

It took more than two years to complete the temple foundation; its
completion was the occasion of a major celebration. During that time,
volunteers had constructed a road to Mt. Trumbull on the Arizona Strip
where they built a mill to produce a million board feet of lumber.

Red sandstone was brought from the tabernacle quarry for the temple walls; that work consumed another two years. The timbers then
were placed and the interior work was begun. The baptismal room
was installed in the basement. Iron oxen were cast in Salt Lake City to
support the baptismal font. C. L. Christensen (age twenty) and several
companions traveled to the rail station in Juab County to pick up the
font and freight its parts to the temple. He recalled that his load, which
was the bottom front of the font, weighed 2,900 pounds, along with

two cast oxen, each weighing 600 pounds. Much of the travel back to St. George was done at night when it was cooler for both men and oxen. On the return trip, Christensen and other freighters frequently were forced to search for oxen that had broken away in search of water. But as Christensen relates, "The teamsters had plenty of good Dixie wine to keep them cool and we certainly enjoyed it."[12]

The entire undertaking was a construction saga. Most of the labor was performed by volunteers who were "called" to the task. They left families to come to the site, families that had to be supported by neighbors or by payments in kind from the tithing office (if the goods could be transported to them). There was a real camaraderie among the workers, many of whom learned their skills on the job. In general, the project was completed without serious accident, though John Burt fell seventy feet from the scaffolding and was not expected to live. He did, however, and was back at the building site in two weeks to visit his brethren. It was a thrill to all and an achievement — that no lives were lost during the building of either of the sacred structures.

When the baptismal room and lower floor of the temple were completed, they were dedicated by Apostle Wilford Woodruff on 1 January 1877; temple ordinances were begun on 9 January.[13] The temple was finally completed for the church's general conference on 6 April 1877. The Quorum of Twelve Apostles and First Presidency of the Mormon church gathered in St. George for the conference. It was a momentous occasion. The people of southern Utah felt it was their own achievement; and certainly all the area tithepayers had given measurably to the edifice. Wilford Woodruff was appointed president of the temple.[14]

The completion of the temple was not without its quirks. When Brigham Young saw the completed building, he was disappointed with its steeple. He felt that it was too squat, not achieving the dignity worthy of the grand structure; however, in deference to the builders, he did not require a change in its height. He had been willing to insist on a lowering of the balcony in the tabernacle because that was a matter of function, but the temple steeple was mainly decorative. Perhaps his desire to see the dedication as soon as possible overrode his disappointment with the tower; however, his displeasure about the short tower was no secret.

Brigham Young died just six months after the temple dedication. Some two years later, in a severe cloudburst, lightning struck the temple tower. It had to be replaced. The builders got the message. The new tower was twice as tall as the former.

Completion of the temple seemed to signal the end of the pioneer period in Dixie. By that time communities had been firmly established. The church's public-works projects had been a great boon to the economy. Roads, mills, and craft shops that had been created for the tabernacle and temple could be utilized in other projects without subsidy. Clearly St. George and its sister communities nearby were firmly established as the southern bastion of Mormon country. They would now become the sponsor of other new settlements including those on the Little Colorado River and in Mexico.

It should be mentioned that during the temple construction, county residents continued to improve the tabernacle. A public subscription raised funds to purchase a clock for the tower and an organ near the podium. The clock brought about change in the community, ending disputes about water turns and improving the meeting schedule and the punctuality of worshipers. It even became fashionable for young people to become engaged to be married under the clock, at the strike of a late night hour. The clock became an item of pride for the community, further evidence that civilization was taking root. The installation of the organ similarly proved that culture was significant to area residents. Choirs could perform with the support of an instrument appropriate to the stately building.

Cotton Factory

Besides the tabernacle and the temple, the most recognizable structure in Washington County is the cotton factory in Washington City. It stands today as a clear reminder that cotton was once a major element of the Dixie economy. Certainly raising cotton was a significant motive in the Mormon plan to develop communities in Washington County. John D. Lee kept up a continual lobby in the 1850s to send people to the land south of the Black Ridge to raise cotton. From his Fort Harmony colony at a high elevation he could almost see the land 3,000 feet lower; he ached to be involved in raising semitropical plants that could be grown there — cotton, grapes, figs, sugar cane. He was sure that Brother Brigham could see the natural advantages of a warm climate alternative for the Latter-day Saints.

The settlers at Santa Clara experimented successfully with cotton raising as early as 1855. Augustus Hardy obtained a quart bottle of cotton seed from Nancy Pearce Anderson in Parowan, who had brought the seeds with her from her home in South Carolina. Plants grew to maturity and did well, and farmers carefully kept seeds for the next year. Settlers in Washington brought cotton seed with them and raised cotton in the 1857 planting season. One party of Saints there, under Samuel Adair, were southerners from North Carolina, Virginia, Tennessee, and Texas who knew about cotton raising. Southerners also came south with the Covington company.

Soon cotton also was growing in Toquerville and Grafton. That success impressed Brigham Young who then sent a party of fifteen men to the confluence of the Virgin and the Santa Clara in January 1858 to experiment with raising cotton on a larger scale. Joseph Home headed the group which located where John D. Lee advised, calling the community Heberville. During the growing season, they faced the trials of heat, thirst, disease, and broken irrigation dams. Setbacks drove their costs up, but by September they were able to deliver 575 pounds of cotton to Salt Lake City at a cost of $3.40 per pound. They returned the next year with a smaller group and faced serious water and disease problems, but they delivered a load of cotton to Brigham Young at $1.90 per pound. This was still too costly to compete with cotton raised by southern states where rainfall eliminated the need for irrigation, but it suggested possible success for Mormon attempts at self-sufficiency.

With the outbreak of the Civil War in the eastern part of the United States, the idea of raising cotton in Utah's Dixie became more important. The evidence existed that cotton could be successfully raised in Washington County, and decisions had already been made to expand the mission in the south for political and geographical reasons. Therefore, one of the key instructions given to the newest Dixie missionaries was to raise cotton.

The realities of the cotton-raising enterprise were soon upon the Saints in southern Utah, however. Once they brought water to the land, overcoming the difficulties of irrigation, they faced harsh facts about their harvest. The cotton was so bulky that transporting it to either Salt Lake City or California was very costly. Brigham Young opposed selling the cotton outside the territory. If raw cotton could be

The Cotton Factory and mill race, completed in 1866. Two stories were added soon thereafter. (Cuba Lyle Collection)

woven into cloth in Utah, he felt, the Latter-day Saints would not have to buy textiles from gentiles (non-Mormons). It was good logic, but it did not face market realities. Dixie farmers could hardly give away their crop to northerners. Their grapes (as wine), dried fruit, and grain could be sold in Salt Lake City, but the cotton was a problem. That reality caused Dixie farmers to plant less cotton, not more. Within a short time, it was clear that building a cotton factory in Dixie was the only effective way to keep the farmers growing cotton.

Always pragmatic, Brigham Young realized the situation at hand. He also decided a factory had to be a business, not a religious institution. He knew the straits of the economy, so he decided to invest personally in the factory. He told the southern Mormons that if they would raise the cotton, he would build the factory. He purchased the water rights on Mill Creek and asked Erastus Snow to select a site for the factory that could use the water for power. Young determined to dismantle the underutilized woolen milling machinery in Parley's Canyon near Salt Lake City and transport it to Washington City, where the most productive cotton fields were located.

In September 1865, Young announced the cotton milling project and engaged Appleton Harmon (who had built a famous odometer

to measure mileage crossing the plains) to install the factory. The
project was pursued with haste. Elijah Averett was the major stone
mason though many others helped, several of them from the tabernacle building crew. John Peck Chidester, Hyrum Walker, and August
Mackelprang cut timber and hauled it to the site. The first floor of the
structure was completed within the year and was dedicated 24 July
1866. The dispatch with which the cotton factory was completed was
amazing, since at the same time the Saints were exerting effort to build
the tabernacle, construct dams, clear land, and build homes. They
were even sending teams to help bring new immigrants to Utah. Their
manpower was stretched to the limit.

Machinery was freighted south and installed the last few days of
1866 under the direction of a Scottish convert, James Davidson, who
had been sent to direct the project. Volunteers contributed their muscle
for building a millrace to bring the stream water to the water-wheel.
By January 1868, the factory was in operation. In 1870 the building
was enlarged by adding another story, a testimony to optimism.

During construction Erastus Snow solicited funds from the local
people to build the mill-race, and he then began a major financial project, inviting people to invest in the mill and make it a cooperative.
The idea was for Brigham Young to get the mill constructed and working, then for the local people to buy him out and take it over. This was
yet another plea for funding from people whose means were already
severely stretched. Though some people invested in the project, it was
difficult for Erastus Snow to find investors.

Courthouse

No sooner was the cotton factory completed than the community
began building a formidable courthouse. The county probate judge at
the time was James D. McCullough, who served from 1859 to 1870.
He was responsible for emphasizing the need for this significant public
building. Instead of a public subscription to raise funds, the Washington County Court proposed a tax increase of two and one-half mills.
In an election on 5 August 1867, the mill levy was approved by a large
majority. Despite their poverty, there seemed to be no end to the civic
will of the people. Yes, the building would provide some jobs and
yes, it would sink yet another root guaranteeing the permanence of the
community; nonetheless, it was another financial sacrifice for people

who were still trying to survive. It tested their mettle once more because it required a decision for the benefit of the whole instead of the individual. Once the tax was instituted, the judge authorized an expenditure of $500 to begin construction.

The workmen who were erecting the tabernacle also built the courthouse. Samuel Judd worked the lime, William Burt led the plastering, Miles Romney shaped the wood. The building was 36 by 40 feet and three stories high. It included a jail in the basement, offices on the main floor, and an assembly room on the second floor to be used as a courtroom and for many other community activities, including socials and even theater. The building featured a handsome cupola. Folklore has it that the dome was designed to be used for hanging criminals, though such a use never occurred. The building was completed in 1870, a brief three-year construction period. It is still very much in use as a community center. The St. George Chamber of Commerce occupies the main floor while the newly restored chamber on the upper floor is home to many community meetings and socials. Tourists find their way to the building in large numbers; it is often the first landing spot for people who are investigating the area for recreation or as a place to live. The Washington County Historical Society has its offices in the basement and has spearheaded the building's restoration.

These major projects — the St. George Hall, the LDS tabernacle, the LDS temple, the cotton factory and the county courthouse — were the result of an amazing decade and a half of building activity. The St. George Latter-day Saints arrived just before January 1862 and the temple was dedicated on 6 April 1877. The resources for these heroic structures were imported from throughout the region; the buildings housed institutions that were clearly respected by the people in the area, and, in the case of the temple, of the area well beyond Dixie.

Town Buildings

At the same time these major edifices were being built, almost every town in the county was in the process of building a community structure to house both church and school. Citizens throughout the county also labored on the construction of lumber mills, irrigation dams and ditches, and endless road building. Driving through these communities today, one can see many stately public buildings from the pioneer period in Toquerville, Virgin, and Pine Valley, among others.

In Washington City, a bowery was used for public meetings until 1877 (the year of the completion of the temple). After that, under bishops John Woodruff Freeman and Thomas J. Jones, residents constructed a substantial stone schoolhouse for both educational and religious uses. That building was remodeled in 1942; the original portion of the resulting building was demolished in 1961.

In 1863 a meetinghouse/school was constructed in Santa Clara and was used until it was replaced by a new one in 1902. Gunlock built an adobe school in 1881 which was used until 1912 when the school was moved into the wardhouse. Even at tiny Pinto, a small log meetinghouse was built in 1860, then replaced in 1866 with a rock edifice, 24 by 16 feet, which also served as a school.

The first meetinghouse in Pine Valley was a log building constructed in 1859. At least two schools were completed in the 1860s. In 1868 Ebenezer Bryce, an English shipbuilder, supervised the construction of the handsome Pine Valley chapel. It is built of wood, appropriate for the many sawmills that initially made the community famous. To this day it is one of the most attractive structures in the state. It was used as a school for fifty years until only a few families remained in the valley during the winter. It is still in use for religious services, being one of the oldest continuously used Mormon meetinghouses. Its structural beams are most impressive, bound together with pegs. The handsome exterior continues to grace the scenic alpine valley.

Toquerville was the site of Toquer Hall, built in 1866 and dedicated as a church by Erastus Snow. It still stands among many historic pioneer structures in that town. The community has served as the focal point for much development of the Virgin River Valley. The telegraph was located there, and the town served as the Kane County seat for several years. John C. Naegle located his extensive agricultural enterprises there, particularly wine making and horse raising. He built a fine two-story home which is now a state historical landmark. In addition to supplying Silver Reef miners with agricultural products, the community aided in the settlement of several other towns — Virgin, Rockville, Shunesburg, Grafton, Springdale, La Verkin, and Hurricane.

Virgin became independent of the Toquerville LDS Ward in 1866, the year outlying communities were advised to "fort up" as a protection against marauding Indians. The increase in population made the old log schoolhouse inadequate, and a handsome new meetinghouse, 30 by 40 feet, was built in 1866 by public subscription. In 1874-75

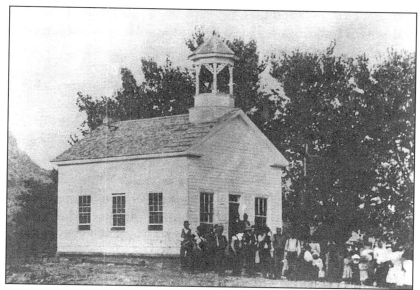

The Springdale Church and School which was destroyed by fire in 1929.
(J. L. Crawford Collection)

a two-story adobe schoolhouse was erected. It has recently been restored and serves as a city hall and museum. Other pioneer structures
also can be seen, including the old adobe church in Grafton which still
stands but has long been out of use and appears rather fragile.

Rockville and Springdale haven't been as fortunate where pioneer
buildings are concerned. The meetinghouse/schools in both communities were frame structures and both succumbed to fire — Springdale's
in 1929 and Rockville's three years later. Separate church and school
buildings replaced the old buildings in both towns. Rockville's oldest
existing pioneer structure is known as "The Rock House." Built by one
of the Huber brothers as a residence, it is still in use as such; however,
its most interesting feature is the frame building on the west end which
was one of the first telegraph offices in Utah.

Only four original homes still exist in Springdale, and all but one
have lost their pioneer identity through remodeling. A unique story
at Springdale involves the sawmill located on the east rim of Zion
Canyon and the cable system that lowered lumber to the valley floor.
This did not come until after the turn of the century, but it is a stunning
story of ingenuity and enterprise. Another element of Springdale's

St. George Tithing Office/Bishop's Store House on Main Street. Tommy Terry, Bishop James McArthur, and St. George Wells in front. (Lynne Clark Collection, donor – Nellie Gubler)

history is that of Zion Canyon becoming a national park. That, too, happened after 1900.

Funding Public Institutions

Early community building in Washington County laid a foundation for a continuing spirit of philanthropy. Though the Dixie colony benefited from financial infusions from tithing funds of neighboring colonies and from Brigham Young's personal funds, most civic endeavors had to come from the efforts of the local people. At a time when settlers needed to put great effort into building their own homes and farms, Erastus Snow appealed to them time and again to donate their labor, produce, and funds to public projects. This tradition of giving for the good of the community was well planted and has been drawn upon virtually every decade down to the present.

In St. George a tithing office was built even before the tabernacle was begun. Most county towns also built such a facility where tithing in kind could be donated, stored and distributed. In 1887 a more permanent bishop's storehouse was built at 41 North Main. Two large letters, "T&O" standing for Tithes and Offerings, hung on the front of the building. Bishop James A. McArthur managed the office and received eggs, chickens, cream, butter, cows, sheep, horses, and hay. There was a large weighing scale in front of the building to determine the amounts donated. The hay was stored in a barn two blocks away, near the opera house. Workers on the tabernacle and temple were often paid in tithing scrip which they could redeem for commodities from the storehouse. Even stores in town would accept tithing scrip, because merchants could use it to pay their tithing. Bishop McArthur's son, Andrew, reported that the storehouse was like a community center. A bulletin board next to the front door served to post notices of funerals, social events, or of items to buy, sell, or trade. The community "lost and found" area was inside, as was a place for exchanging news and current events.

This saga of community building in Washington County remains most impressive. Many structures that the early settlers built together are still in evidence. Some of them are vitally important institutions, others are historic restorations, many are but memories. Andrew McArthur recently rebuilt the St. George Tithing Office, for example. The basic story, however, is a legacy of community building by people who were undergoing most severe tests of scarcity and survival. They determined that community was as important as individuality, that culture came before profit, that group values and a sense of mission were what made individual lives significant. They achieved much of what they did by cooperation in building and sustaining institutions.

ENDNOTES

1.   Albert E. Miller, Immortal Pioneers (privately published, 1946), 34. See also Andrew Jenson, Church Chronology (Salt Lake City: Deseret News, 1886), 62.

2.   Andrew Karl Larson, *I Was Called to Dixie*, 116.

3.   James G. Bleak, "Annals," Book A, 151.

4.   Ibid., 151-52.

5.   Charles M. Brown, "The Past Restored, Historic St. George Tabernacle Reopens" (brochure distributed at 1993 reopening of the St. George Tabernacle), Dixie College Archives.

6.   This handwritten note recording Revilo Fuller's memory as told to Orpha F. Hunt was recently discovered and placed in the Dixie College Archives by Ronald McDonald.

7.   Larson, *I Was Called to Dixie*, 576.

8.   The event has been made known by a film entitled *The Windows of Heaven*, released in 1963. The movie idealized the event somewhat, causing Will Brooks to criticize it in his autobiography, *Uncle Will Tells His Story*, ed. Juanita Brooks (Salt Lake City: Taggart & Co., 1970), 62-4. Brooks said he was at the meeting and did not notice such unusual proceedings as the film depicted, however, he was writing fifty years after the fact. A thorough examination of the event was recently completed by E. Jay Bell in his article "The Windows of Heaven Revisited: The 1899 Tithing Reformation," *Journal of Mormon History* (Spring 1994): 45-83. Bell concluded that Lorenzo Snow did indeed have a revelation about tithing and that he experienced a spiritual manifestation in St. George; however, he maintains that linking the payment of tithing to the arrival of rain did not occur in that speech but was added later by folklore.

9.   Heber Jones, High Priest meeting notes, 20 March 1977, 2. In possession of Heber Jones.

10. Where did the cannon come from? The current story in vogue is that it was made in France, taken to Russia by Napoleon, abandoned in retreat, and then taken to Alaska and down the west coast to Fort Ross. It was then purchased from the Russians by John Sutter and given to members of the Mormon Battalion as a part of their pay as they left his employ in 1848. They in turn put wheels on it and took it to Salt Lake City. From Salt Lake City it was taken to Parowan and eventually to St. George. Janice DeMille, in her book on the St. George LDS Temple, attributes this version to Juanita Brooks in an article she wrote for Arizona Highways in 1947. Mrs. Brooks cites Howard R. Driggs as her source, and Driggs mentions John Bidwell and John Sutter as his sources. Some of these accounts refer to the cannon as being made of brass, which it obviously was not.

It is generally agreed that Jesse Crosby brought the cannon from California. Karl Larson in *I Was Called to Dixie*, the Daughters of the Utah Pioneers in *Under the Dixie Sun*, A. K. Hafen in *Devoted Empire Builders*, and the Crosby family all indicate that Jesse Crosby brought the cannon directly to St. George from California in the 1860s while freighting. It is believed by this group that the cannon was taken from Commodore Stockton's fleet and that it had been used to fight the Mexican War in California. It was brought to St. George to be used as an artillery piece by the local militia and thus was not the same cannon that left Sutter's Fort in 1848.

For a personal description of the rock gathering and the quarrying and foundation work see Henry G. Mathis, interviewed by Washington County Centennial History Committee, Dixie College Archives.

11. Ivan J. Barrett, *Trumpeter of God* (American Fork, UT: Covenant Communications, 1992), 271.

12. Daughters of the Utah Pioneers, *Heart Throbs of the West*, vol. IX, 3-5.

13. Jenson, *Church Chronology*, 95.

14. Thomas G. Alexander, "An Apostle in Exile: Wilford Woodruff and the St. George Connection" (Juanita Brooks Lecture, Dixie College, 1994).

4

Stability and Isolation

The Stable Core

The dedication of the St. George LDS Temple and the death of Brigham Young six months later, both in 1877, symbolized the end of the trial period for Dixie. There was no longer a question of whether the Latter-day Saints would be forced out by heat, flood, and disease. Partly because of Young's willingness to invest in the Southern Utah Mission and largely because of the ingenuity of settlers who chose to remain, the question of survival had been answered by then. Farms were yielding harvests despite the constant need to guard irrigation canals and dams against floods and silt. The pioneers had faced the difficulties of nature and won.

The victory was slim, however. Floods would yet destroy Grafton and continue to cripple Virgin. People of Harrisburg and Hebron would move to neighboring settlements — Leeds and Enterprise — where better water could be obtained. Their prized stone homes would become habitations for ghosts. Isolated communities like Bloomington and Atkinville would see their families move into towns where schools were available for the children. Settlers foresook a full dozen settlements including Dalton, Northrup, Price (Heberville), and Shunesburg.

Most dramatic was the decision to abandon much of the Muddy Mission nearby in Nevada for political as well as agricultural reasons. The plan to turn the Muddy River region into a major cotton-producing area had run into the same irrigation problems and marketing dilemmas as those along the Virgin and Santa Clara rivers. There were several small communities on the Muddy River including St. Thomas, St. Joseph, Overton, Simonsville, West Point (now Moapa), and Call's Landing; life there was so bleak that many of those called to reinforce the Muddy Mission either did not accept the call or upon arriving chose to return quickly.

Even more devastating for the settlers was the discovery in 1870, after a few years of hard work, that their towns were actually located in Nevada, not Utah. That discovery soon prompted Nevada tax collectors to show up and demand back taxes to be paid in coin. These barter-based villages had no access to currency, so, after consultations, Erastus Snow, jointly with Brigham Young and George A. Smith, released the Muddy River colonists from their mission calls on 14 December 1870, allowing them to vote on whether to stay or leave. Most moved, though settlers in Panaca remained. Nearly 200 people from the Muddy River Mission voted to move to Long Valley, founding Orderville in Kane County. A smaller contingent chose the Arizona Strip as a relatively unoccupied area open to settlement. Towns on the Muddy were abandoned as Mormon settlements, later to be taken up by gentiles. Two decades later, some of the towns were reoccupied by Mormons.

In contrast, the core colonies in Washington County took root, even deeply enough to serve as the supports of new colonizing efforts on the Little Colorado River in Arizona and in northern Mexico. St. George took on the trappings of a regional capital, despite its isolation.

Imposing structures — the tabernacle, the cotton factory, the temple, the courthouse — stood out as clear evidence that permanence was the program of the Latter-day Saints. Schoolhouses and homes in surviving communities repeated the statement of endurance — in Harmony, Santa Clara, Pine Valley, Pinto, Washington, Gunlock, Toquerville, Rockville, Springdale, Virgin, Bellevue (Pintura), St. George, and Leeds.

William Heep and Family at their cabin in Zion Canyon.
(J. L. Crawford Collection)

To Stay or Go

The initially bleak outlook for the Dixie colony caused many of the settlers to consider their personal benefit. It was a tortured decision for them. The church's need was for the experiment to succeed, but what about their families' needs for sustenance? What about their personal needs to improve their condition? How much sacrifice must they give? Charles Walker confided to his diary that his loyalty was sorely tried on a trip to Salt Lake City:

"My Father in Law want[s] me to leave my home in the south and move my family up, and as an inducement he offers me a building lot on any lot he has. But I feel like sticking to my Mission until the servants of God tell me to go, altho I could do better and get more of the comforts and luxuries of life than I can at St George. Others oft say that I am a fool to stay down in that desert country when I could do better and live easier in this place."[1]

A classic story from a woman's point of view is the account of Wilhemina Cannon. After just one season of enduring the brackish water, the blowing sand, the unbearable heat, she had had enough. She announced to her husband David that he was free to stay in Dixie but that she was determined to return north. In her exasperation she said, "There is not a single thing of beauty in this whole place." Grasping

George and Annie Isom home constructed in Virgin between 1876 and 1878. (J. L. Crawford Collection)

at a slim opportunity, David replied, "Will you stay if I find you one?" He went out into the fields and foothills until he found some sego lilies and brought them to her. She had softened during his search and she accepted his offering. They remained to become leaders and parents of a prominent family.[2]

Persistence and Mobility

Perhaps the most emphatic statement of stability was the decision of a significant portion of the settlers to remain in Dixie despite the disadvantages. Those who stayed showed great persistence. They became the core elements of the culture, but the persisters were not always the majority in most of the towns. A pioneer census gives a picture of the Virgin River settlements around 1864:

Washington 431
Harrisburg 128
Toquerville 259
Virgin 336

Duncan's Retreat.......50
Grafton....................168
Rockville..................95
Northrop..................17
Shunesburg...............45
Springdale 54
St. George 748   (in 1862)
      Total: 2,331[3]

By 1880 as tabulated by the census takers, there were 4,235 residents in Washington County, a solid increase from the 3,064 of 1870 (the count in 1860 was 691, taken before the large group was called to the Southern Utah Mission). The population figure in 1880 reflects a degree of stability that was hard won and crucial to the larger plan of the inland Mormon empire. The critical mass had been established. Though people would come and go, a core was rooted in Dixie — one sufficient to produce abiding generations.

Despite the pleadings and incentives of respected leaders, however, many people chose not to remain in such an unpromising land. Only half of those recorded in the 1870 census appeared in the census of 1880. Their persistence is what made the Dixie Mission succeed. Santa Clara, for example, in 1880 saw at least portions of twenty-one families remain from the thirty-eight listed in 1870. In 1900 forty-one of forty-nine families were represented by some of the parents or children from 1880. Although this may seem like an amazing persistence rate, 134 people out of a population of 149 from 1880 were not in the area in 1900.

Mobility was about as common as was persistence. Santa Clara had a high degree of solidarity. The ethnic nature of the town — with only four families not being Swiss — created a tight group determined to support one another. Washington City, on the other hand, saw more coming and going. Though several important families sank roots there, many others moved on. One group came there in 1857 from San Bernardino. Most of those people moved elsewhere after remaining a season or two in Washington. Some went to the Little Colorado River area as an ecclesiastical call. Others sought land elsewhere in Dixie or outside the county. Thirty-two of Washington's 84 families in 1870 persisted to 1880 — 38 percent. By that year the town had grown to 110 families; by 1910 there was a slight decrease to 105 families, but 46 of them were still there for the 1910 census taker to find — very close to half. By 1920 the population had dropped from 105 families to 76. It is clear that at least half of the people in Washington were on the move. St. George's persistence rate was 66 percent by 1910 — not as high as Toquerville's 80 percent or Hurricane's 76 percent, but still high.

The eastern side of the county saw even more moving about of its settlers. For example, Duncan's Retreat saw nine of eleven families persisting from 1870 to 1880; but in 1893 the land was almost completely washed away in a huge flood, and by 1900 only two of the original families remained. Church records indicate that the people moved either to the Arizona LDS colonies or north to Millard County.[4]

Grafton was a famous case of an unsuccessful fight with the Virgin River. In a protracted struggle, the residents of Grafton kept their town alive until 1921, but it was a constant and losing battle with the waters that repeatedly ate away at the fields and homes of the settlers. Five of seven families of Grafton remained from 1870 to 1880, and four remained until 1890. In 1907 the LDS ward was disorganized with the membership being transferred to Rockville, but a branch was maintained in Grafton until 1921.

Virgin, Rockville, and Springdale have survived to this day although nearby Shunesburg was abandoned in the mid-1890s. By 1900 seventeen of thirty-six families from the 1880 census were still living in Virgin despite serious flooding. Rockviile saw even fewer of its residents from 1880 remain. Fourteen of the forty-two families from 1880 remained in Rockville in 1900. In 1900 in Springdale, five of the same families that were there in 1880 could still be found. Overall, about 50 percent of the settlers had at least one family member who persisted in remaining for twenty years along the upper Virgin basin.[5]

A study of other towns, such as Toquerville, La Verkin, St. George, Gunlock, and Pine Valley, reveals several common elements about movement of their residents. For example, Toquerville became quite stable between 1900 and 1910. This was the period when the Hurricane Canal was opened, allowing many people to move from Virgin and other parts of the upper Virgin Valley to take up new lands on the Hurricane Bench. Although people in Toquerville were among the promoters of the Hurricane Canal, they had a good source of water and did not venture beyond the town. When Hurricane lands were opened up, 80 percent of the people of Toquerville stayed put.

Why did some people move and others stay? First, the land for farming was limited. Fields were often patches of only three to eight acres, located close to a stream. If families could subsist on such meager plots, they certainly could not divide them among heirs. Second-generation sons knew early on that they would have to seek new lands. Hebron and Enterprise were essentially safety valves for such expansion. The establishment of Hurricane was a clear case of fathers and sons trying to bring water to new lands so their sons would not have to leave Dixie. Developers of Enterprise were similarly motivated. Major water projects like the Enterprise Reservoir, the Hurricane Canal, and the La Verkin Canal encouraged people to move from villages within Dixie to new ones in the county, but not until the turn of the century.

Those who did not persist in one town very often moved to another within Dixie. For example, many people moved from Santa Clara to Gunlock, Pinto, Hamblin, or Pine Valley or even to ranches outside towns in the Santa Clara Creek drainage area. Similar movement occurred between the towns of Virgin, Toquerville, La Verkin, Rockville, Grafton, and Springdale. Interestingly, little movement took place between upper Virgin River towns and Santa Clara Creek towns. Most moves occurred within one or the other water systems.

For a short time the two regions actually were in different counties. Kane County was created in 1864, and in 1866 the upper Virgin River area was placed in Kane County with Grafton as county seat. Kanarraville was included in the county at that time but later returned to Iron County. In 1867 the county seat was moved to Rockville and then to Toquerville in 1869. In 1884 that section of the county was returned to Washington County, and St. George became the county seat of the whole.

Another factor that caused people to move was floods. Virgin City, for example, experienced severe flooding that took much of the good land with it. It survived as a community, but many people lost their land and had to move elsewhere. Duncan's Retreat and Grafton were effectively washed away. Early floods damaged Santa Clara and Washington. These disasters drove people away from their towns. Some found opportunities nearby, but others chose to move greater distances. Some people in Virgin and neighboring communities in the upper valley became attracted to Millard County, and several moved there, especially to Hinckley.

That introduces another point: people were drawn to land ventures. When they found it difficult to prosper in Dixie, many were tempted by reports of available land elsewhere. Several people moved to Wayne County although some of them, like Orson Huntsman, moved back after finding opportunities there no better.

The Mormon church itself caused some of the Dixie people to move by calling them to open new colonies. The colonizing effort along the Little Colorado River in Arizona took many from Dixie — some by call and some by choice. Miles Park Romney took his wives and family from St. George to the Little Colorado where they lived for about a decade and then, like others, moved on to northern Mexico to help found yet a new group of colonies. Henry Eyring, one-time mayor of St. George, went to Mexico from St. George, as did others. Some St. George residents were sent to settle Circleville, Marysvale, Panguitch, Hatch, Tropic, Escalante, Orderville, Glendale, and Mt. Carmel, among other places.

That brings yet another point to the fore: some people left Dixie to get away from Federal officials who were prosecuting polygamists. Escaping these officials was clearly the purpose of the establishment of the Mexican colonies. These towns were directed by Erastus Snow and, in many ways, were an extension of Dixie.[6] Some felt the Little Colorado settlements would provide protection but soon found the gentiles who had preceded them there were critical of those who moved in because of the polygamy issue. Perhaps that influenced some of them to move on after a few years.

Other Dixie settlers simply moved back to the greater comfort of the central LDS communities along the Wasatch Front. They had extended families there who could help them establish farms or other means of support. Some returned to lands they had previously worked. Others obtained a release from their mission and returned to pick up life where they left off.

Finally, a few colonists eventually dissented from the Mormon system that pervaded the county. Some merely doubted; others withdrew from activity in the faith; and a few, such as Orson Pratt, Jr., broke with the culture. Some of these people felt a necessity to leave Utah, either going farther west like Heinrich Hug, who went to Oregon, or returning to their midwestern, southern, eastern, or European origins. Orson Pratt, Jr., broke with the faith but not the region, moving to Salt Lake City.

It is likely that no more than half of those who came stayed in the same town where they began; it is also clear that there was a constant movement of people from town to town inside Dixie. The biggest factor seems to have been the shortage of tillable land, but certainly severity of the climate and floods pressed people to move. Movement within Dixie was not uncommon. William Ellis Jones, for example, reports moving among several of the communities in Santa Clara Valley as well as in and out of St. George. He came to Dixie originally in place of John Bennion, who had been called to the Muddy Mission. From there Jones tried Beaver Dam before moving to Leeds. He finally settled in Gunlock but worked some seasons in Pine Valley and Hamblin. The Nevada boundary question impacted some, and polygamy laws caused others to move, though sometimes only part of their family left. Despite all these mitigating factors, the main point remains: enough people found a way to stay, despite all the influences bearing down upon them to create permanent settlements.

Those who remained had to have a stamina and an optimism that would shout down all opposition. Paul Reeve recounts the example of A. J. Workman, one of the original settlers of Virgin. In one of his several "booster" accounts Workman said: "I have quite a family, about a dozen in all, and by the help of the Lord I live and have plenty, and raise it from four or five acres; and I believe I could live well and support my family on three acres. We do not know what we can do until we try."[7]

Were the Saints abandoning their mission call to Dixie if they moved? Perhaps, but the harsh landscape convinced some it was senseless to spend a lifetime in Dixie, so they returned north. Reeve gives two examples. Charles Burke from Virgin City decided the flooding had destroyed his opportunity. He approached the stake president and asked permission to move to Hinckley. He received the president's blessing. Joseph Black from Rockville wrote to Brigham Young and received approval to move to Millard County to buy a wheat farm.[8]

In the later period, the new towns like Enterprise, Hurricane, and La Verkin served as a population safety valve. Much of the motivation for their development was to provide new land for new generations. The Hurricane census records stimulated the tentative observation that people who moved to Hurricane after the canal was finished in 1904 came mostly from "up river." That is not surprising because people from Virgin figured significantly in developing the canal.

Census Insights

Using the methodology pioneered in Utah by Dean May and utilized by Paul Reeve, it has been possible to search the census records of Washington County for the years between 1860 and 1920. This allows us to trace people who lived in Dixie during the period, so instead of considering just the leaders or just those who kept journals or who appeared in newspapers or official documents, we can get a glimpse of almost everyone who was in the county long enough to be counted in one of the ten-year censuses.[9]

A careful study of the Federal census records of Washington County between 1860 and 1920 provides us with insights into the lives of people generally not found in diaries, newspapers, or other historical sources. For instance, generally there were hardly any unmarried men in the county between the ages of twenty and thirty. There were a few single senior men in their seventies, but most towns had only five or six single men. This suggests that marriage was a high priority in Washington County society. A stunning contrast to this trend was the gentile mining town of Silver Reef. In this thriving mining town, the 1880 census takers counted 1,013 people, of whom 459 were single men. There were more single men in Silver Reef than there were in the rest of the county combined, though Silver Reef contained people from some of the same places as other Dixie towns — sixty-seven from England, twelve from Wales, twenty-two from Scotland, twenty-nine from Germany, thirty-one from Canada, twenty-three from Scandinavia — there were at least two nationalities there unique to the county: the fifty-one people from Ireland and the fifty from China.

The census clearly shows that Santa Clara was also unique in Washington County because it became almost totally populated by Swiss immigrants. Why did the Americans and Englishmen who were originally there move? Jacob Hamblin went to Kanab to be nearer the Hopis and Navajos. Others, including Andrew Gibbons, went with him. Bishop Bunker was called to found Bunkerville in Nevada. Others moved to Gunlock and Pine Valley to find more land, but the Swiss stayed in Santa Clara. At least one immigrant, Heinrich Hug, felt that the Swiss were looked down upon by others in the county and were often the object of ethnic slurs and jokes by non-Swiss residents. Certainly it is clear that the Swiss did not let any rejection hold them back from achievement, however.

Today one can visit Santa Clara and not find anyone who still speaks German or a Swiss dialect (unless they recently went to Europe and learned the language). The Swiss Days celebration each year is of recent origin, not a continuation from the pioneer past. The families and the genes are there, but current generations have become as Americanized as people in the rest of the county.

Census records reveal not only place of birth but also marital status and nativity. Eleven of forty-three mostly Swiss families in Santa Clara in 1870 appear to have been polygamous. In 1870 Washington City had 108 family heads listed, 29 of them polygamous — about 25 percent. The city moved from being 95 percent American-born in 1860 to only 58 percent in 1870. By 1900 Washington City was 68 percent native-born. The St. George census shows about 23 percent of the people in 1870 were involved in polygamy, as were 20 percent in 1880. Foreign-born residents made up about 50 percent of the town in the same period; the native-born rate increased steadily each decade thereafter. In 1920 there were ninety-seven widows — 22 percent of the households.

In contrast to many communities, Pine Valley was settled predominantly by native-born Americans. In 1880 eight of the thirty-nine local families were headed by women with no husbands. It was possible that Pine Valley was a hideout for polygamous wives, but it also could merely have been a good place for a polygamist to station one of his families. The majority of the town was made up of regular farming and lumber mill workers' families, but the persistence rate in Pine Valley was only 13 percent in 1880; it had risen to 41 percent in 1910. Did the decline of the lumber mills cause the figure to be low in 1880, then the increase in farming see it rise by 1910? Clearly there was a higher percentage of families moving in the area than in Santa Clara and St. George.

There are a thousand details that can be gleaned from the census, but the important message is that Washington County was made up of people of many stripes — from miners to farmers, from polygamous to monogamous, from Native Americans to European immigrants, from those who moved to those who stayed, from families to singles, from young to old — all of whom made up the sinew of Dixie.[10] The land and the weather affected them all, and each had to make the decision whether to wed their lives to Washington County or seek another homeland.

Farming

The main source of sustenance was farming. In the Dixie communities, most farming was limited to small plots, under ten acres. Often farms could only be maintained near streams. In northern Utah, canals often delivered water from the streams out to broad sweeping benches, sometimes many miles from the stream. This irrigation method was attempted in the Washington Fields, south of Washington City, and much later in the Hurricane Valley and at Enterprise. There, broad valleys were watered from long canals, resulting in large acreages under cultivation. But most early farmers in the county fought silting, floods, and drought to such an extent that the water could only be coaxed a short distance, often within sight of the streams, to small plots called pockets — thus the name "pocket farming."

Dividing the land among settlers was accomplished in an orderly manner. In the beginning phases of most communities, one person surveyed the land and families drew choices from a hat for a town lot and for one or two parcels outside the town for farming. Each family's town lot was usually large enough for a corral, chicken coops, pig pens, fruit trees, and a barn, in addition to a home and a good-sized vegetable garden which was often worked by wives and children. In St. George, that lot was 0.64 of an acre. In some places, however, it was not that big because settlers in communities such as Santa Clara, Gunlock, Springdale, Rockville, and Leeds were pressed between hills.

James G. Bleak, clerk of the Southern Utah Mission, records that the settlers in St. George in late 1861 laid out the city with blocks that were 32 rods square. They made 256 town lots available at eight parcels per block. The census of the community in January 1862 showed 370 females and 378 males, clearly the largest settlement in the county even though it was only one month old.[11] Heads of households, usually males, each drew a lot, though polygamous families also had a town lot for each wife and her family.

Surveyor notes served as makeshift titles. The territorial legislature authorized the local probate courts to record the survey notes, and the settlers kept them as evidence of possession. Ideally, each family head obtained between ten and thirty acres, even though water seldom reached all lands.

Technically, county residents were squatters on the land until 1869 when the U.S. government opened a land office in Utah to implement the Homestead Act of 1862. On 2 March 1869 Congress passed "An act for the relief of the inhabitants of cities and towns upon the public lands." The intent was to accommodate people who had founded communities prior to the Federal government's actions to implement its control of the western lands. This act was of crucial importance to people throughout Washington County. By 1869 there were already some twenty communities well under way in the county so the need for legal title to land was important.

The Federal government did not rush to open land offices in Utah; there was considerable distrust of the Mormons among Federal officials, based on the complaints of territorial judges and military officials sent to the territory. Some initial Federal surveys were carried out along the Wasatch Front in 1855, but surveyor David H. Burr and the Mormons came into conflict, and he left the territory in anger. A successor, Col. Samuel C. Stambaugh, continued the surveying; but Congress had little enthusiasm for selling land to the Mormons because they were seen as potentially disloyal to the Union.[12]

During the Civil War, volunteer troops under the command of Colonel Patrick Connor were dispatched from California to Utah to protect the overland route from hostile Indians and to keep a watchful eye on the Mormons. From his newly-established military post at Fort Douglas, Connor hatched a scheme to wrest control of the territory from the Mormons. He encouraged his soldiers to prospect for precious metals. The subsequent discovery of some silver and gold encouraged many non-Mormons to pour into the territory to mine precious metals, and in some parts of the counties in the territory, they outnumbered the Mormon populace. In Washington County, for example, non-Mormons controlled Silver Reef. This new population demanded title to their mining claims which forced the Federal government to open land offices.[13] To secure their own title to lands, Mormon settlers of several decades responded quickly. Sermons from church pulpits urged the Latter-day Saints to immediately file for title on the lands they occupied.

Typically, the bishop in each village would file on a section of land, then redistribute the land to the villagers according to their existing uses.[14] This situation necessitated some delicate negotiating with the Federal government because the Homestead Act required claimants to live on their claim. In 1878 with the passage of the Desert

Land Act, the Federal government allowed completed irrigation ditches to substitute for actual residence on the land, thus adapting to the Mormon village system.

Charles Lowell Walker's journal illustrates the organized approach: "Sat December 17th [1870]... Br Geo. A Smith spoke on the importance of securing our lands according to the Laws of the U.S. Br E Snow spoke on the same subgect" [sic]. Two weeks later on 31 December, Walker reports on a session of the Mormon School of the Prophets. "Br McFarlane, R Bentley, and Pres Snow spoke on the Land Laws of the U S and urged the Brethren to secure their lands from the Government and get their deeds Patents &c."[15]

Mormon bishop's courts in each congregation were used to settle disputed land possession, thus avoiding the involvement of the Federal land offices and generally preventing claim jumping. In actuality, the Federal authorities were not averse to this quick and efficient approach. The result of the pressure by miners, including those at Silver Reef, for title to their mining claims, actually resulted in facilitating a solution that enabled Mormon farmers also to gain title to their lands.

Irrigation, Dams, Canals, and Floods

The desert heat assured that nothing could grow to a harvestable stage without water being brought to the plants regularly. The system of diverting water from streambeds into canals that worked so well north of Dixie proved undependable in the southern land. Town after town in Dixie experienced tragic failures of dams because desert rainstorms turned into quick floods that washed out even the most inventive earthen dams. Sparse undergrowth in the red hills could not hold the moisture back to run more evenly. Following major rainstorms, water poured out of the canyons as floods that swept away everything in their path.

Washington City was located just above the area called the Washington Fields. If the Mormons in Washington could construct a dam to control the Virgin River at that point, water could flow onto the most valuable agricultural land in the county. The first three dams constructed were washed out within two years. At flood tide, the Virgin River near Washington City became a torrent. Materials for dams began to get scarce; more importantly, discouragement set in. During the period from 1857 to 1865, the residents somehow rallied to rebuild

Built with trees and boulders, this dam on the Virgin River was located in what is now Zion National Park. (J. L. Crawford Collection)

and rebuild again. The workers were credited with two dollars a day for their labor, three if they were working in the water. Using such payment rates, the people of Washington City spent approximately $80,000 building dams in eight years. It was a rare year that a dam was not washed out. The story continued with similar results for the next twenty years.

George Washington Gill Averett was pressed into service as the watermaster in charge of building and repairing dams in Washington City. What was to be a temporary service soon diverted him from his trade as a gunsmith and wheelwright; the dam dominated his life. Averett had worked at damming the river near Washington for twenty years. In 1885 he once again heard the roar of the river at night after a major rainstorm. He heard the angry torrent and knew what he would find when he rode to the dam site in the morning:

> He looked at the spot where the dam had been and saw what he had known before he left his house — there was nothing left but a bit of the rock abutment where the canal left the river...He looked at the

place where the dam had been and unconsciously began to plan its replacement. He shivered involuntarily as he thought of getting into the [cold] muddy stream again to begin the job.[16]

This cycle of dam building, washouts, and rebuilding took its toll. Many people decided to give up on the Washington Fields, even though they were the most promising agricultural lands in the county. Each dam washout was a defeat. One of the most difficult was when Bishop Marcus Funk decided to leave the area in 1888. He had been mayor of Washington City, counselor to many families and chairman of the dam-building committees. In that year he was arrested for practicing polygamy and sentenced to six months in the state penitentiary. He served that term and paid his $300 fine but then asked for a release from his Dixie mission to go to the San Luis Valley in Colorado where he felt he could better support his large family. His departure was discouraging for the whole community.

Funk left during a time when the area residents decided to undertake a much more ambitious project, a pile dam. They had worked on it for three years under Funk's direction, bringing huge timbers from Pine Valley Mountain. They fashioned a huge pile-driver, cast in the town of Enoch in Iron County, to drive the timbers deep into the riverbed. The dam required great sacrifice because water was not diverted to the Washington Fields for two years. New ditches were built out into the fields. In the fall of 1888, their four years of work was completed; people took deep satisfaction in a labor they believed would last.

On the night of 7 December 1889, the largest flood in memory occurred, tearing out the dam. The headgate survived for a day, then it went too. Despondency was universal; it seemed there was no future in the Washington Fields.

Such defeat was actually the source of new determination, however, and of a new idea as well. Three men, Charles W. Seegmiller, John P. Chidester, and Isaac C. Macfarlane, developed a different strategy. They determined to go up the river, three miles higher than the pile dam, to a stone outcropping. There they decided to build a diversionary dam that would send the water into a hogback where it could be forced over the stone. This would allow them to control the water. It would thus eliminate the necessity of holding back the whole river with an earthen dam, merely using their dam to send the water into an unmovable channel of stone. The three men convinced the Wool-

The Washington Field Dam, completed in 1891.
(Lynne Clark Collection, donor – Larue Prisbrey)

ley, Lund and Judd Company which was asked to finance much of the undertaking. The St. George firm functioned as a credit source before a bank was developed in the county. The estimated cost was about $30,000. The Seegmiller-Chidester-Macfarlane proposal was accepted by the water company's board of directors. They quickly claimed 640 acres under the Desert Land Act of 1877 and filed on the water with 3,500 inches of the Virgin River at the head of the canal.

The story of building the dam is a dramatic one. There was not enough food to feed the workers because the farmers had no harvest until the dam brought them water. Mormon church leaders in Salt Lake City agreed to appropriate funds to help the farmers, who had to forego another year of planting. Those funds were utilized to feed the men. A group of railroad workers was stranded in Nevada by snow and freezing weather at their building site; and they were enlisted by Andrew Gregerson to bring their equipment to the dam site for drilling in rocks — a godsend in the eyes of the dam builders. The railroad men were destitute and willing to work for board.

Building new canals for the dam was yet another story. It involved men digging tunnels, silting gypsum stretches, adapting the Brigham

Jarvis method of eliminating the silt, and getting the water to the fields
in time for a crop in 1891. This brought the story to a gratifying conclusion. Later improvements were made on the dam, including using
cement to replace the earthen diversionary dam, so the dams at Washington City, begun in 1857, were not successful until thirty-four years
later. The result finally guaranteed farming on Dixie's best land at that
time. (Hurricane and Enterprise would be developed a decade later.)

Cotton and the Cotton Factory

With the cessation of hostilities in the U.S. Civil War, the production of cotton in the southern states rebounded. In fact, the market
soon was flooded with the crop. By 1869 the nation was joined by the
railroad, which revolutionized the shipment of textiles. Cotton produced by irrigation on "pocket farms" simply couldn't compete with
that which grew from natural rainfall on vast plantations in the south
that could now be shipped inexpensively to the West. But the Washington County cotton mill managers adapted by taking on wool to mill
and acting as a wholesaler of many products; nonetheless, refunding
Brigham Young's investment never happened. The factory was often in debt and had to be helped by funds from the Caanan Livestock
Company as well as by further loans from Brigham Young.[17]

Refinancing and changing leadership was tried into the 1890s.
Finally about 1892, the factory was leased to Thomas Judd, a seasoned businessman from the well-known St. George mercantile firm
of Woolley, Lund and Judd. Under his management, the factory was
as much a store as a mill. Amazingly, Judd turned a profit for about
four years, perhaps because he paid his employees one-third in cash,
one-third in factory scrip, and one-third in store scrip. He finally announced the closure of the factory in May 1898, however.

The cotton factory made a huge contribution to Washington County. It employed scores of young women, facilitated the use of farmers'
harvests, and promoted a wide system of freighting. It was a major
link in the trade with the Silver Reef miners, and it kept the Dixie Mission well advertised throughout Mormondom. No one ever became
wealthy from the cotton factory, but it operated in the black some
years of its existence, particularly when it diversified under Thomas
Judd and became a trading center. Its demise was particularly painful
to Washington City.

Alternatives to Cotton

Since the settlers could not eat cotton, a greater urgency was given crops that could nourish them. Gardening on their town lots and farming on small acreages near the towns occupied many, if not most, of the Dixie women. Annie Atkin Tanner much later remembered her childhood growing up on such a town lot:

> I loved every foot of our lot, which was divided into two parts, the north half was our wonderland of trees and vines. We had a spreading apricot tree, which at one time, completely shaded the pig-pen and I used to amuse myself watching the pig eat the ripe apricots and cracking the pits to eat the kernels in them. We also had a chicken-coop and a name for every hen: Snow-Flake because she was black with flecks of white feathers, Limpy acquired her name from an accident which crippled one foot and then there was Speckles and others. At the back end of the lot we had an asparagus bed and still further back a cow corral. The two cows that I remember were Bess and her daughter Betty. Here was the haystack, the shed and of course, the ever present outside toilet, with its Sears and Roebuck catalogue. This I'd like to forget.18

Levi Savage of Toquerville gave a detailed description, almost day by day, of his farming activities. His record provides a picture of the year's agricultural cycle in the desert climate. Savage spent the winter months, December and January, milling wheat, digging carrots (which he sold at Silver Reef), building fences, hauling wood, and trimming grapevines. He killed about twenty sheep during that time as well as one beef cow, which he put in salt. He traveled to Virgin and Rockville to buy potatoes and then resold them at Silver Reef and Cedar City. He also sold sheep skins, collected manure and put it on his lucerne fields, watered those fields, repaired a road, plowed the garden, ordered seeds, settled several accounts including his tithing, and by late February was harrowing his fields. In March he planted potatoes and peas and cleaned ditches. By April he set out onions, planted cucumbers, more peas, radishes, carrots, and lucerne. He irrigated these vegetables and worked six days a week on ditches.

Beginning in May he was irrigating almost every day, moving from one field to another. He planted beans, parsnips, squash, and more potatoes, searched for lost animals, repaired his wagon that seemed always to break, tried to keep cows out of the fields, and repaired fences and ditches. By June he cut the first crop of lucerne, continued to irrigate, planted wax beans, watered his corn and beans, and conducted a horse drive to Kolob. In July he didn't take time to celebrate the holidays in the 110-degree heat but did horseshoeing and repaired ditches that were damaged in the cloudbursts. He planted Brimbadge corn and cut the second crop of lucerne, gathered more wood (this for making molasses), hauled hay, and watered the squash, carrots, melons.

In August Savage worked on roads again and was credited with five dollars per day toward his taxes. He planted turnips, gathered driftwood, and repaired ditches again that were damaged from heavy rains. In September he mowed lucerne, picked corn, gathered driftwood, killed three sheep, sowed onion seed, and traveled to collect debts owed him. October brought more wagon repairing, including a trip to Silver Reef to buy a king bolt. He purchased a mower for $125. The lucerne was ready for another cutting, and he hauled hay as well as manure. He attended a water meeting and slaughtered two more mutton as well as spending a full day searching for a lost cow. November was spent spreading manure and hauling cedar wood and "choring" about the farm. Then December arrived and the story began again with the winter cycle.[19]

Throughout Washington County there was one common problem: forage for farm animals. The land was so dry that grasses were often too sparse to support dense grazing. Excessive grazing had already injured the watershed and exacerbated flooding. Most villages used the town herd system — each family would send its cows with the others in the village to be herded by one or more young people during the day. This allowed the animals to be taken some distance from the village in search of forage. But it also used the range too intensively. There simply was much greater need for forage than the sparse landscape could supply.

Farmers attempted flood irrigating rangelands and discovered that grasses would come back but not stay long, especially in drought years, so it was great fortune when they discovered the suitability of alfalfa to the sandy soil. From the very earliest settlement times some alfalfa had been planted. The San Bernardino Saints who moved north in 1857 evidently brought alfalfa seed with them, increasing the limited supply. Gradually farmers learned that alfalfa was uniquely adaptable to the dry Dixie lands. Each year they planted more. And each year farmers turned more to raising livestock for a living as the alfalfa provided winter feed. Lucerne (as alfalfa was often called in Dixie) was literally a miracle for the settlers. It is doubtful that the Dixie population could have been sustained without alfalfa providing a harvestable feed crop.

Ranching, Cattle, and Indians

Many of the Dixie settlers brought cattle with them. All needed to be grazed, so it was common for the farmers to set up cooperative town herds. As the farmers discovered how limited the yields would be from their small farms, they increasingly depended upon raising cattle. This necessitated grazing the herds at greater distances from the villages, which also was often done in a cooperative system, each farmer putting some ten to twenty-five head into a larger herd. Both winter and summer ranges were sought out for these herds.

Market potential for the cattle was initially near at hand. The builders of the St. George tabernacle and temple had to be fed. Later the miners at Silver Reef were ready buyers. Once the railroad reached central Utah, area cattlemen drove large herds to Lund to be shipped north and east.

Within the first decade of Dixie settlement, the church tithing herd grew to such a size that new forage had to be found for them. Herders were sent with the animals to find new range possibilities. These early cattlemen discovered such lands along the upper Santa Clara River. Many of the explorations led cattlemen to take up ranch sites for their personal endeavors. Gunlock, Pine Valley, Hebron, Hamblin, Pinto, and the lands between (such as Mountain Meadows and Dammeron Valley) were locations where cattle raising and ranch life became more important than farming. With each decade, sheep and cattle-raising activities increased in importance. The Arizona Strip, between St. George and the Grand Canyon, was another prized area for grazing sheep and cattle, as was the Kolob Plateau above Toquerville and Virgin.

The area between Pipe Spring and Short Creek became the home of a huge undertaking — the Canaan Stock Company. In 1870 Erastus Snow organized the company with several directors including Sixtus E. Johnson, James P. Terry, Richard Ashby, Daniel D. McArthur, and

Nathaniel Ashby. Snow served as president with Joshua T. Willis as vice president. The Mormon church had purchased the Pipe Spring Ranch from the Whitmore family for $1,000. Brigham Young appointed Anson P. Winsor to operate the ranch and it became a successful venture involving several thousand head of cattle. This showed that raising livestock could be a profitable venture and attracted several enterprising people to do the same. The church divested itself of the company in the 1880s and sold to private hands. At that time, 1883, the company had some 4,200 cattle. James Andrus was superintendent of the company for several years thereafter, but it was not as profitable as before, partly because the range was over-grazed.

Most ranching in the county was not on the scale of the Canaan Ranch. A different kind of ranching started out on a modest scale. In Santa Clara, for example, there were good small farms for orchards and vegetables, but these generally could hardly sustain a family. Out from town were some fields where alfalfa was raised to feed a few cows and horses. Each farmer generally had five or six head of cattle; some had as many as fifteen to twenty-five. These animals needed to be grazed in the spring and summer, so area farmers organized a cooperative system. To the west, north, and south there was seemingly endless rangeland that could be used to supplement their farming activities. The land was very dry, so it took vast amounts of range to support the cattle. It was not a matter of a few animals per acre, rather it was a few animals per section, so herds had to range over thousands of acres.

These first settlers soon found that they had to protect their animals from the Indians, and a long and tense contest began. Indians were accustomed to living from the land, gathering seeds, and harvesting wildlife. The arrival of cattle threatened much of the grazing areas on which the Native Americans had traditionally depended. The Indians felt justified in killing cattle to provide the sustenance they had lost to the white man's incursion; it seemed fair rent to them.

The farmers and cattlemen saw things differently, especially when renegade Paiutes, cast out from tribal controls, defied agreements that had been made with their chiefs. Also troubling were Navajos who sent skilled raiding parties into Paiute territory and drove off large herds of cattle and horses maintained by the Mormons. To the livestockmen this was thievery, if not outright war. So, for the first three decades (from about 1855 to 1885), cattlemen and sheepmen were armed in defense of their flocks. Sometimes the clash between the two cultures resulted in deaths on both sides. A standard Mormon response to Indian trouble was to call people from unprotected settlements into larger communities for protection, which could last a few months; sometimes even settlers would build a fort.20 Either response was a burden because the men still had to work the land near those vacated villages and could only do so with guards standing nearby.

Charles Walker's journal gives examples of Indian raids: "Sat 10th [November 1866] News has reached us of an Indian raid on Berry Valley in which the raiders took off some 100 head of animals and shot one man in the knee....Sat 29th [December 1866] The Indians have drove [sic.] a number of our horses and mules from the vicinity of Pine and Diamond Valleys. Our men have started in pursuit. God protect them and bring them safe home again. Tuesday, Jan 1st, 1867.

"The Indians that made the raid a few days ago were surprised in the vicinity of the Pipe Spring by Capt Jas And[r]us. 6 of them were killed and all the stock recovered except 2 animals."21

The settlers of the county worked for accommodation with the Indians of the region. By Christmas 1870 one of the Navajo chiefs promised no more raids on the people of the county.22 On at least one occasion Indians were invited to speak to the people of the county in the tabernacle. Mo-ke-ak was one such Indian. He asked for peace and for help to be educated. Erastus Snow responded to this request with a promise to begin a school where the Indians could be taught to read and write.23

Either by design or by accident, county ranchers soon found themselves outside the protection of the Mormon village settlement system. Theirs was not a lifestyle encircled by community. Schools and churches were distant and neighbors were beyond sight. For some, the possession of cattle, the access to land and water, and the stunning beauty of the open range meant freedom. Some didn't mind being away from the ecclesiastical authority that prevailed in the villages. Others commuted, maintaining a domestic operation at the ranch and another in the community, to keep close ties with the church and community. During polygamy days, it was possible for some family heads to maintain one family on a ranch and another in town. Jacob Hamblin did this with one family at Santa Clara and one at Mountain Meadows. Others made similar arrangements.

The Mormon church was a major promoter of farming and to an extent was also an advocate of the cattle industry. The cattle trade got its first impetus from the management of tithing herds. Later, many church leaders were directly involved in the largest cattle project in the county, the Canaan Stock Company.

In some ranching environments like the Arizona Strip or Pinto, ranchers tried to replicate a community environment by building a school/church structure and fostering neighborly support. Gradually, as roads improved, many families moved back into the villages and men commuted to the ranches, sometimes camping there. The houses at the ranches became more like lodges, used mainly in the summer and only for a few days a week. Today, ranching in the Arizona Strip is entirely a commuter-ranch system. Pinto is largely a summer retreat, and Pine Valley has changed dramatically, becoming a second home retreat for summer vacationers. Atkinville is abandoned as are many isolated ranches. But some ranches, such as those along the Santa Clara River, are very much alive — Terry's, Holt's, George Chadburn's "New Jerusalem" below Central, the Lytle Ranch at Mountain Meadows, Blake/Gubler's southwest of Pine Mountain, and Fawcett's at Diamond Valley. The Sunset Ranch near Virgin, Maxwell and Canaan Livestock Company near Hildale, and Cane Beds Ranch near Pipe Springs are among the continuing cattle enterprises on the eastern side of the county.

One interesting example of ranching was that of Peter and Anna Anderson, emigrants from Denmark, who settled in Bellevue in 1868, where six children later were born to them. Peter and his sons wanted more land, so in 1884 they moved a few miles south to Echo Farm near the junction of the Toquerville and Cedar City road. There they took up a homestead of 160 acres, living in a dugout the first winter. The next summer the family camped at the foot of Pine Valley Mountain where they could raise a garden and make butter and cheese to ship north while they began to dig a canal to their ranch.

That waterway became the lifeblood of the ranch for two generations. It is a piece of engineering genius, delivering a steady flow of water along the top of a mountain ledge. Ravines on either side would destroy Anderson's ability to control the flow, so the ditch was constructed to prevent water from drifting either to the south or the north. It gradually descends for six miles over a stone-strewn path to the valley floor below where a pond receives its precious waters for distribution on the ranchland. This was a brilliant feat — building a farm where there was no stream. The Andersons constantly had to inspect the ditch for breaks and had to keep it clean. It was a duty akin to marching on the battlements of a castle, always keeping a diligent eye against possible enemies. All of the children were trained for life in this guard duty, shovels in hand. The ditch is still running today, and a hike to its path brings deep respect for human genius — this one mostly the design of one man and the achievement of one family. Peter's wife, Anna, wrote:

> During those early pioneer years and while homesteading Anderson's Ranch, no one can picture the hardships, misery suffering and loneliness I experienced. Always my heart yearned to run away…to run away to the ease, comfort and luxury of my home in the old country.24

Because of its location on the junction between the Toquervile highway (which later led to Zion National Park) and the highway along the Black Ridge to Cedar City, Anderson's ranch received a steady flow of visitors. At one time President Warren G. Harding stopped there, as did the Crown Prince and Princess of Sweden. Most other ranches in Dixie were much more isolated.

"Women's Work"

Agriculture was as much women's work as men's. The village system meant that the men were generally away in the fields, so the women had to manage the town lot. That meant directing the children in raising animals, gardening, and processing food. This was in addition to rug-making, spinning wool, carding cotton, sewing clothes, weaving, making soap, laundering clothes, preparing daily meals, and engaging in endless other crafts. They made lye from cottonwood ashes, baking powder from alkali, starch from potatoes, yeast from hops, and dyes from various plants. The women were also largely in charge of medicating, teaching family members, and promoting culture. They often also were the main marketers of saleable goods — all this besides giving birth to an average of nine babies per woman, nurturing them, protecting them from diseases, and transmitting their religious faith and values to each one.25

For some women, living in the county and being a polygamous wife or having their husbands on Mormon missions, life was doubly difficult. One such woman, Mary Ann Hafen, maintained her household and property through her own ingenuity, independence, and hard work. During the two years of her husband's absence she worked at picking and drying peaches, selling them to peddlers who in turn sold them in Salt Lake City. At other times of the year she picked cotton on shares. "That cotton picking was very tiresome," she wrote, "back-breaking work but it helped to clothe my children."[26] On the town lot, Mary Ann Hafen grew grapes, some of which were dried into raisins. She made jam from the California grapes and sold other varieties of grapes to peddlers who frequented the mining camps of the region.

While establishing their homes, women of the county were conscious of orderliness. Emma Hinton, wife of John Nock Hinton, along with six children lived in a 16 by 18 foot log house in Virgin. According to Lenora Atkin Meeks, Emma Hinton's home "was the epitome of cleanliness and her food preparation was immaculate." In addition to maintaining a neat and tidy house, Emma Hinton milked the family cow since her husband had never learned that skill.[27]

Alice Parker Isom was one example of many powerful women who had both domestic and business responsibilities. In 1885 when she was thirty-eight years old, her husband, George, died of bronchitis. Together they had built a successful store in Virgin and established a family of several children. The oldest, Ellen, was fifteen and the youngest, Sarah Laverna, was born two weeks after her father's death. Alice took over the store while raising her children and managing other investments. Ellen helped both at home and as a clerk in the store. Alice wrote: "After my husband's death I was appointed manager of the store and Lanthus Richards secretary. I had done most of the buying from the first and understood the business quite well. I did well with it both for myself and the stock holders." When an oil boom occurred in Virgin in 1907, Alice borrowed money and expanded her store to meet the sudden demand. She provided lumber, hay, grain, and general merchandise, which she obtained from the Mormon church-operated Zions Cooperative Mercantile Institution (ZCMI). Then the panic of 1908 struck, and her customers fled Virgin without paying her. It required a decade of effort for her to settle her accounts.[28]

Medicating Illness

Health and sickness, birth and death, medicating and attending the ill are also part of the Dixie story. A long line of health providers worked in a succession of buildings that preceded the current hospital. Prior to that, health care was left largely to families, midwives, herb doctors, prayer, and folk wisdom. One study indicates that in Washington County in the nineteenth century, babies died at about the same rate in their first year of life as elsewhere in the nation; but they died at a greater rate for the next four years. Fifteen percent of newborns died in the first year; after five years, only 71% of boys and 72.3% of girls had survived. The author postulated that the transfer from mother's milk to local water was too much for many babies: "If they had escaped the town's diseases while they were nursing, children were attacked with double force once they were weaned. Now they had to depend on polluted water and other sources of disease, and they also relied on food that occasionally ran short."29

Desperate mothers shared folk remedies, experimented with herbs, and even sought wisdom from the Indians to spare their children from deadly diseases.30 Despite the attempts, many children succumbed to common diseases. Martha Spence Heywood, a schoolteacher in Washington City; confided her anguish about her daughter to her journal.

> On Wednesday the 12th of March I first gave her the Lobelia in doses of tincture. It was several hours in her system without operating. I gave her rhubarb to work it off which she did and passed some phlegm and at this time I discovered the hard phlegm stuck to her mouth and was more convinced that the difficulty lay in her chest. She again took a turn for the better after this first administered lobelia and my spirits again revived. She seemed easier Thursday night when I went to bed and being very much exhausted I fell into a heavy slumber and woke up by her call to me and when I had come to myself I found her in very great distress with her breathing. I had some onions and I put them under her arms and oiled her well. Went after Sister Bigler that she might assist me in putting her feet in water. It was two o'clock when she came in and we bathed her feet which seemed to ease her breathing a little but until daylight she appeared to be dying but between six and seven she revived again which comforted me much....About twelve o'clock I gave her the emmetic which operated well in her system but about four o'clock she had the appearance of dying and I again gave her up. Oh, my

poor heart, how it was wrung with anguish but again she revived and
called "Mamma" which word once more heard made me crazy with
joy which continued till she was really death struck and the only
thing to desire or hope for was to have her Father come in time to see
her once again and he did arrive on Tuesday, 18th, about six o'clock
in the evening. She had been dying all day and the night before and
when he came she stretched her little arms to him and called Papa
and all that night would call to sit on Papa's lap. She died next
morning about eight o'clock, being sensible to the last breath she
could draw and [when she] ceased to breathe the bad smell ceased.
I washed her little body myself on my lap and dressed her in her own
clothes and the last sewing I did for her was to make her a pair of
shoes of white cloth.[31]

The Latter-day Saints' religious convictions were ever challenged by the lurking specter of death. Parents were often torn by the
helpless feeling of holding their tiny ones in their arms as they died.
Charles Walker and his two wives were among the grieving parents
whose faith was tested to its limit. They buried four children, one of
them a young son who drowned by slipping into a water tank. Their
last to die was an infant boy, Lowell. Charles reported, "Sat up alone
with corpse all night. All was very still save the terrified moan and
convulsive sob of his Mother. I thought that three draughts at the bitter cup would be enough for me to drink but it seems in the kindly
dealings of providence I am called to drink it the fourth time; the
Lord's will be done."[32]

These poignant accounts could be repeated a thousand times by
anguished Dixie parents who tried to relieve their sick children. Home
remedies were developed by the shared wisdom of the whole region
and sometimes moderated the suffering. Often the attendants could do
little but watch and pray. They relied much on spiritual administra-
tions to the sick. Sometimes they had access to medical practitioners,
but they could seldom do more than use similar remedies that were
available to the parents.

Frontier medicine in the last half of the nineteenth century was
greatly influenced by Thompsonian doctors whose herbal medicine
many found more acceptable than the "bleeders" who called themselves surgeons. Brigham Young was outspoken about his preference
for the herb doctors and his criticism of the physicians who bled patients to expel the illnesses.

Samuel Thompson was born in 1769 in New Hampshire. He published his remedies in a 800-page manual, *Thompson's New Guide to Health or Botanic Family Physician,* and sold it for twenty dollars, including a license to practice. His fame and methods spread widely even among some who had neither the book nor the license. Among those who used his methods was Willard Richards, friend and associate of Brigham Young. In the Washington County area, there were several practitioners in his tradition. James Whitmore, who was killed at Pipe Spring in 1866, was one of them. Priddy Meeks also practiced herbal medicine in Harrisburg and then later in Long Valley. Silas Higgins came to St. George in the 1860s; he and botanist Joseph E. Johnson maintained a pharmacy to produce medications from herbs. Israel Ivins was evidently not a Thompsonian follower, but it was said that his family was also engaged in making pharmaceuticals which he used in St. George from 1861 on. Evidently being a doctor was not necessarily a full-time job because Ivins also doubled as a surveyor.

In Toquerville the colorful John Steele advertised himself as "Dr. and surveyor"; he had associated with Priddy Meeks in Parowan from whom he learned much about cayenne pepper, lobelia, cherry stones, and steaming. Kerry William Bate described the Thompsonian philosophy: "A sick person needed to first have his body clensed [sic] with natural emetics, such as lobelia, and enemas. Second, lost heat should be restored through the use of cayenne pepper internally and hot pads and steam or vapor externally. Third, the residue of the canker should be carried away by doses of herbs."[33]

Midwives were often more available to the Latter-day Saints who were dispersed widely across the Dixie landscape. Two St. George midwives in the pioneer period were Mary Ann Hunt Nielson and Caroline Baker Rogers Hardy. Both came to Dixie with their husbands in the early pioneer period. Like many others, these two women had some form of midwife training before coming to Utah. Both lived to their nineties and delivered hundreds of babies during their years in southern Utah. They performed their services largely before the territorial government of Utah began licensing midwives in 1893.[34]

Anna Hess Milne was one of Dixie's legendary midwives. Daughter of a handcart pioneer, Anna came to Dixie with her parents in 1861. As a young girl, she married Bishop David Milne and later bore seven children. As polygamy prosecution increased, she determined to seek a means of supporting her family alone. She left her children with her mother and went to Salt Lake City to study nursing and obstetrics. She completed her studies and returned to St. George in 1893. Because she was a licensed nurse, her services were soon in great demand. She delivered babies and nursed the ill until her death in 1921. Her charge was five dollars initially and eventually became ten dollars, paid mostly in produce. When Dr. Frederick Cliff and later Dr. J. T. Affleck came to St. George, she assisted them.

Many of the Dixie midwives were called by ecclesiastical authorities to serve in the birthing process, some having trained under Dr. Ellis Shipp in Salt Lake City. Hazel Bradshaw lists Mrs. Stanton, Mrs. Tuckett, Mrs. Elmer, Mrs. Church, Mrs. Perkins, Mrs. Kleinman, Agnes Calkins Thompson, Mary A. Harradence, Ida Seegmiller, and Nancy Louisa C. Higgins, in addition to Anna Hess Milne, as midwives who served in the county.[35]

Most midwives were called to the bedside of the woman in labor shortly before the birth, and often they were a critical factor in helping both the mother and baby survive the birth. Sometimes midwives served for extended periods. Mrs. William Ellis Jones of Gunlock specialized in these kinds of deliveries. People from distant towns often engaged her to come and "live in" for a month when the mother was known to be having difficulty. Mrs. Jones left her husband and family to the care of an older daughter and pursued midwifery as a career to help support the family.

Fairs and the Gardener's Club

The Washington County Agricultural and Manufacturing Society organized the county's first fair in 1860 to promote agriculture. Some of the area communities were too recently established to have agricultural products displayed at this first fair. Other communities were well represented with exhibits of livestock, corn, cotton, garden vegetables, homemade articles from county-grown cotton and wool, braided straw hats, and moccasins made from tanned deer skin.[36]

The fairs in the 1860s were often visited by Brigham Young, who took great interest not only in the fruit displays but especially in cloth woven from local cotton. At one of those fairs, the crops of Indian chief Tut-se-gavit took first place for corn. The fairs were held at the St. George Hall after it was finished in 1865. When the St. George

Hurricane Peach Days, about 1910. (J. L. Crawford Collection)

LDS Tabernacle was constructed, the fair moved into its basement. Citizen committees took charge of the fairs, and the Gardener's Club was a major supporter. By the end of the century, the committees were expanded, including some thirty people.[37] F. L. Daggett, president of the Washington County Fair in 1908, and his committee faced some serious challenges. Although the committee at the beginning of the fair lacked funds for premiums to the winner in the various categories, the people of the county said, "Let us have a fair, not to do so will be a step backward."[38] As it turned out, the number of exhibits in some of the fair departments exceeded entries from the previous year. Such fairs continued almost annually. In addition, many local communities also promoted agriculture. These celebrations have continued to be very popular — one is Enterprise's Corn Fest Days, another is Washington City's Cotton Days.

Fruit Growing

Fairs were an important event each year in part because horticulture was highly valued. Santa Clara and Toquerville were successful garden communities, but they were not alone. In St. George, for example, Joseph E. Johnson promoted a gardener's club as early as 1865. With his energy, it continued for decades, even maintaining its own headquarters building which stands today in Ancestor Square and a wine cellar which is today part of the restored opera house in St. George. Johnson's skill in horticulture and floriculture was a real benefit to all people in the county. He cultivated trees, vines, and flowers, and operated a nursery business. He grew over 100 varieties of grapes that were well suited to the soil and climate of various parts of the county. A. K. Larson suggested that Johnson contributed more to the early fruit industry in the region than any other person.[39] Johnson also organized a pomological society in St. George with branches in other communities. Its weekly meetings were open to the public and a publication, *The Utah Pomologist*, promoted improvements in horticulture and fruit growing. These two organizations remained vital into the 1880s.

The industry of drying fruit for shipment to northern colonies was a major sustaining influence in Dixie. Enterprising peddlers were able to exchange dried fruit in Beaver, Iron, Juab, and Sanpete counties. In Salt Lake City they traded for potatoes, flour, and even equipment. Similarly they freighted foodstuffs to eastern Nevada, particularly to the miners in Pioche. They also supplied garden products to the miners in Silver Reef. This trade greatly benefited Dixie families, who had few other export products.

Another person who had beneficial influence on the agricultural development of the Southern Utah Mission was John C. Naegle, a prosperous German farmer from Lehi. He was called to go to Dixie in the 1860s because he was an expert vintner. He, his half-brother Conrad Kleinman, and Ulrich Bryner, also a German, promoted wine making in Toquerville. Naegle became a major exporter of wine and built a marvelous home with a wine cellar which is still the pride of the town and now a national historic landmark. He instructed many people in grape raising and wine making. In the north he had been a successful horse breeder. It is said that at one Time he donated 120 horses to Brigham Young. He carried on with his horse herds in southern Utah, becoming one of the few wealthy men in the area.

Peddling

The successful raising of fruit, especially in Santa Clara, led to a side profession — peddling. Initially, peddling was done by farmers themselves who took teams and wagons and their produce to the miners at Pioche and Silver Reef. Farmers would take their children, sometimes their children's friends, and a loaded wagon to Nevada towns and have them knock on the doors along each street saying "Melons, grapes, apples" or whatever was available. The peddler would honk a

The John Gubler family from Santa Clara, selling fruits and vegetables in 1905. (Lynne Clark Collection, donor — Nellie Gubler)

shrill horn to draw the attention of the whole neighborhood, who were all potential buyers.

More ambitious peddling involved freighting large amounts of dried fruit to the northern Utah communities, as far as Salt Lake City. Often peddlers also included other goods such as cattle. Once motorized trucks became available in the early twentieth century, entrepreneurs from Santa Clara and St. George began freighting fruit to California, where they would sell their goods and buy oranges and other California products to bring back and sell in Utah. They soon learned to include among their wares any product that could be profitably traded. Gradually peddling became a full-time effort — delivering fruit, vegetables, cattle, and even alfalfa wherever there was a market, and bringing goods back to sell in southern Utah. Out of this door-to-door, single-family enterprise there gradually emerged the Rocky Mountain Produce Company, with its home base in Santa Clara, as well as the Milne Trucking Line of St. George.

Those who raised and dried fruit in the Toquerville area had a wonderful nearby market at Silver Reef. The miners there were ready customers for the grapes, apples, peaches, apricots, vegetables, melons, and wine that the Mormons delivered to the mining camp. County farmers became rather dependent on that lucrative market. Toquerville producers were not the only ones who delivered food to the miners (Leeds farmers did too), but their proximity gave them an advantage in transporting the perishable fruit. When the Silver Reef mines began to close in 1890, Toquerville farmers expanded their deliveries to Pioche, which had long been advantageously served by vegetable and fruit gardeners of Santa Clara.

The trip to Pioche was a week's undertaking which was near the limit that fresh produce could tolerate. It was not unusual for many peddlers to arrive in Pioche simultaneously. Sometimes the Mormons, desperate to unload a wagonful of perishables, undercut each other in selling. This competition became the topic of discussion of church leaders who met at the home of Erastus Snow to devise a way to merchandise cooperatively. They organized the Dixie Cooperative Produce Company with David H. Cannon as president and with town representatives from Santa Clara and Washington.

It did not take long for Bishop J. T. Willis of Toquerville to respond, expressing deep resentment at the attempt to control the trade. He made it clear that the allotment of one day a week for Toquerville farmers to sell in Pioche was unacceptable. He argued that Toquerville was adapted to very little other than fruit growing; cotton did not work, and their fields were too small for grain. They were dependent on fruit and had become experts in it. They did not feel that their competition could be justifiably limited without destroying the community of fifty families. Uncharacteristically for Mormon group ventures, this protest killed the effort at cooperation. American free enterprise won out.[40]

Such peddling lasted well into the mid-twentieth century. So-called "independents" were families with small acreage and a truck. They often would haul their produce to California or Las Vegas to sell for money or trade for citrus fruit. Among others, the Spencer Reber family of Santa Clara supported themselves in this manner. Beginning in March they thinned and weeded carrots and onions. All family members labored at this and other farming activities when their time allowed. In May they harvested radishes, rinsing them in the irrigation ditch. Towards the end of June the onions, carrots, and some of the row crops were ready. They planted tomatoes by late May or early

June, at which time apricots and some early varieties of peaches were ready to pick. In early June the Reber family, like others in Santa Clara, loaded up their truck for the first of several trips to Las Vegas and California. By fall the tomatoes were ready to be picked as were some later varieties of peaches. Spencer Reber, Jr. recalls that most of the thinning, weeding, and harvesting was hard work and that some of it was unpleasant. "Even the most disagreeable aspects (such as the itching and smarting caused by peach fuzz) we were able to joke and laugh about," he adds.41

Transportation of the harvest of fruits and vegetables to Las Vegas or California was critical to the success of the independent peddlers. Boxes and crates were carefully stacked and arranged on the trucks to ensure that the heavy loads would arrive at their destination without incident. Truck loading was generally done late in the evening. Before the crack of dawn, recalls Spencer, Jr., his father would start for Las Vegas, which usually took nearly four hours of hard driving. The first test of the heavily laden trucks came with the climb over Utah Hill in the Beaver Dam Mountains. Spencer recalls one memorable incident:

> One time we were unsuccessful in selling all of our load. We had about 50 or 60 lugs of peaches left. It was one of those rare days when there were thunder storms moving across the desert. On our way home mid-afternoon, we came upon a line of stranded cars, a flash flood in California was running over the highway. As more cars joined the line forming behind us, people started walking up the road past our truck to see the flood. I climbed up in the back of the open stake bed truck and picked out a big red juicy peach and started to eat it. A guy asked me where I got it — that is all it took. Within a few minutes, we sold every peach we had and at considerably more money than we could have gotten in Vegas. When the peaches were all gone, Dad pulled the truck out of line onto the oncoming lane (which had no traffic because of the flood), drove up to the edge of the water, then to everyone's surprise, drove right across. The water just came up to the running boards, but was so muddy, the people unfamiliar with the road could't tell it was so shallow.42

Mining

The Mormons initiated some mining efforts, such as the iron mines near Cedar City. They also promoted coal mining in several locations in the state and the first copper mining at Bingham Canyon near Salt Lake as well as salt and lead enterprises. Once mining for gold and silver became the preserve of Colonel Connor and his soldiers at Fort Douglas in the Salt Lake Valley, Brigham Young strongly advised the Latter-day Saints to avoid the mines. He did not want the faithful to take up residence in mining boom towns where the lifestyle was much different from their "Kingdom of God." He also saw in mining a boom-and-bust cycle that could draw people from agriculture, ruining farms that could not easily be reclaimed when the mines came to their inevitable bust.

Silver Reef in Washington County was a case in point. According to Paul Dean Proctor and Morris Shirts, it was a Mormon, John Kemple, who originally discovered mineral riches in the Silver Reef area.[43] He arrived at Harrisburg in 1866 with prospecting equipment and lived there off and on until 1871, spending a good part of that time in Nevada. Conventional wisdom at the time said that silver could not be found in sandstone, but Kemple, a seasoned prospector, noticed coloring in the sandstone that convinced him to challenge that long-held view. He did not pursue the possibility immediately; in fact, he went back and forth to Nevada before filing his first claim at Harrisburg in 1871. He included many of the local residents of the town as well as St. George leaders E. G. Woolley, Richard I. Bentley, James Andrus, and Erastus Snow in his Union Mining District, as he called his organization; but he did not begin mining at that time. He returned to Harrisburg in 1874 and reorganized his company as the Harrisburg Mining District, filed under the new Federal mining law of 1872. Mormons claimed most of the land that later became Silver Reef, but they couldn't hold on to it.

Once silver was assayed in ore from Silver Reef, the secret could not be contained. Miners in Pioche heard the rumor and bullied their way to the site. Others filed claims, including Mormons, but they were soon jump-filed or outsmarted by outsiders. Mormons John Ferris and Elijah Thomas, for example, found ore that seemed promising but lost control of the ore in the assaying process. Once the possibility of a find was known, the rush was on.

The Walker Brothers, merchants in Salt Lake City, sent William Tecumseh Barbee to Silver Reef in June 1875. A seasoned miner in the Ophir mining area in eastern Tooele County of northwestern Utah, he was soon convinced of the significance of the unlikely find.

Barbee then publicized the discovery in the Salt Lake Tribune which set off a genuine rush. It soon became clear that Barbee intended to build a city, sell lots, establish merchandising, and become wealthy from the incoming fortune seekers. He laid out a proposed "Bonanza City," but most miners felt his lots were too expensive, so they lived in tents and huts instead. Barbee nonetheless became wealthy from his mining claims.

Much of the ore taken from Silver Reef was freighted to Pioche, Nevada, for smelting — a fact which also advertised the Silver Reef finds. By the end of 1876, a thousand people were living in the newly christened city of Silver Reef. A fair number were former residents of Pioche. The town soon developed the atmosphere of a mining boom town with saloons, dance halls, grocery stores, restaurants, Masonic and Oddfellows halls, banks, telegraph office, barber shop, Chinese laundries, boarding houses, homes, and a Catholic church and hospital.[44]

The economic impact of Silver Reef and silver mining on the county was fortuitous. Several important Mormon church construction projects in St. George were coming to an end, resulting in surplus labor even as buildings at Silver Reef were needed. Employment opportunities paying hard currency to construction workers were welcomed. Local teamsters also found work, hauling dismantled silver mills from Pioche and Bullionville, Nevada, to Silver Reef. A number of mills including the Steel Arrastra, a crushing mill, the Dupaix and Spicer, the Buckeye or Pioneer, the Leeds, the Christy, the Barbee and Walker, and the Stormont Mill were constructed at the newly organized Harrisburg Mining District. These mills and mines created a tremendous appetite for lumber. The Pine Valley mills supplied much of the lumber for the mills, mines, and community at Silver Reef. Mount Trumbull on the Arizona Strip also provided lumber for the growing community. Teamsters from Parowan and Cedar City hauled lumber from the sawmills in Iron County, infusing real money into that county as well.

During the height of activity at the mining district from 1877 to 1888, the Barbee and Walker Mine, the Leeds, Leeds Number 2, McNally, Nichols, Newton, South, and other mines produced thousands of dollars worth of silver. It is estimated that from 1875 to 1910, when the last efforts were made to extract silver from the sandstone, some $7.9 million worth of silver had been mined from the district.45

One did not have to be in the employ of the mines or in residence in the wide-open town to reap benefits. The peddling skills that the Mormons had developed to deliver foodstuffs and lumber to Pioche were most useful, and it was much easier to deliver to nearby Silver Reef. Leeds, with a population of 280, and Harrisburg, with fifty-one residents, were much smaller than Silver Reef with its population of 1,146 [1880 census], but they thrived as suppliers of foodstuffs. Nearby Toquerville, with 371 people, joined in with fervor. The proximity of these towns did not stop other enterprising peddlers from Washington, St. George, and Santa Clara from marketing their produce at the Reef for cash.

The rise of Silver Reef was a major challenge to the isolation of Dixie. In fact, there was some real concern among Mormon leaders that mining would do to Dixie what it had done to Salt Lake City — wrest exclusive political and economic control from the Latter-day Saints. When the very first rumors of a strike began to circulate, local leaders spoke out. Charles Walker reflected their attitude in his diary:

> There is at this time considerable excitement among some of the Brethren concerning silver mines and some are foolishly neglecting their legitimate business and are hunting all over the hills and mountains endeavoring to find precious metals, contrary to the counsel of those over them in the holy Priesthood.46

Relations with the gentiles at Silver Reef were cautious. One well-known exception was a friendship that developed between John Menzies Macfarlane of St. George and Reverend Lawrence Scanlan, the Catholic priest in Silver Reef. Macfarlane was a surveyor (also a musician and a judge) and was often employed in Silver Reef. He lived at the same boarding house as the Catholic priest. The two conversed at length and became respectful of each other. In one conversation they discovered a mutual problem. Father Scanlan wanted to celebrate high mass with a choir for his congregation. His church, St. John's, was unfinished and he had no choir. Macfarlane proposed that the mass be held in the St. George LDS Tabernacle where he was the choir director of a thirty-voice ensemble. Scanlan was hesitant. Macfarlane explored the idea and won over Erastus Snow and stake president John D. T. McAllister. Arrangements were agreed upon.

The choir took two weeks to learn the mass in Latin from a piece of music provided by the priest.

On 25 May 1879 the memorable event occurred. Many Catholics traveled to St. George for the service, but at least as many in the congregation were curious Mormons. Father Scanlan is reported to have started by saying, "I think you are wrong and you think I am wrong, but this should not prevent us from treating each other with due consideration and respect."[47]

The cultural distance between Silver Reef and St. George gave rise to several interesting relationships. A favorite area folktale describes how Mormons infiltrated the town. Federal agents pursuing Mormon polygamists thought Silver Reef was a safe haven in a sea of Mormons. Wilma Beal reported:

> Because Silver Reef was mainly a non-Mormon town, Federal officers worked from there in conducting raids on the Mormon polygamists. These raids were called "Polyg hunts" and proved very unsuccessful because of a fortunate arrangement between the telegraph operator at Silver Reef and the one in St. George, both Mormons.
>
> The marshals traveled mostly at night so they could not be seen. They would send word to Mr. Huston [a store operator] they would arrive at his stables at a certain hour and would like to get a fresh team quickly to take them to St. George or some other town in Dixie. A very innocent sounding message would be sent to a St. George furniture store where the telegraph office was located. The message would read "Send two chairs." This meant that officers were in Silver Reef preparing for a raid. St. George would warn neighboring towns and by the time the "Polyg hunters" reached the Mormon towns, the polygamists would be far away.[48]

Silver Reef was not the only mining location in Washington County, but it was the only significant mining town. Prospectors roamed over much of the county and adjacent territory. The discoveries of copper ore in several locations were the most productive finds. Ninety miles south of St. George in Mohave County, Arizona, copper was mined successfully at the Grand Gulch Mine beginning in 1878. Dixie men worked there, as they also did at the Apex Mine west of St. George starting in 1890. The ever active Woolley, Lund and Judd firm gained control of the Apex Mine and built a smelter in St. George on Diagonal Street.

The United Order

The coming of "outside" influences such as mining stimulated much thought in Brigham Young's mind. He had plenty of warning about the arrival of the transcontinental railroad in Utah and was concerned that it would secularize the Mormon kingdom. His reflex was to support the coming of the railroad, but he wanted to limit its secularizing influence. When the nation-wide panic of 1873 came, he and others could see the negative impact of being dependent on imports. It seemed like a good time to reinforce the concept of isolation, of being self-sufficient.

As he traveled to southern Utah for the winter Brigham Young consulted with colony leaders. Many encouraged him in his exploratory questions. He was impressed with the success of the cooperative activities of Lorenzo Snow and the Latter-day Saints in Brigham City, especially their ability to weather the 1873 panic. He harkened back to the communal economic ideas of the early Mormon church in Kirtland, Ohio. He chose St. George as the place to launch the so-called United Order.[49]

On 17 February 1874 Brigham Young, with support from Erastus Snow, John W. Young, and George A. Smith, organized the United Order of St. George. They took great care in writing the incorporating document because it was the first of many that would be based upon it. Three hundred families signed the Articles of Agreement which became a prototype for many united orders throughout the territory. The order was essentially a communitarian system: participants contributed their possessions and labor to the general order, receiving in return from its holdings what they needed to live on.

The 1874 Record of Incorporation for Washington gives a realistic picture of the situation. It lists the personal property (not land) of each participating family including wagons, animals, and farm equipment and their dollar value:

John W. Freeman	$224.51	A. R. Whitehead	$251.40
Neils Sorensen	200.00	Robert F. Goold	100.00
John E. Pace	100.00	Peter Neilsen	325.00
G. W. G. Averett	211.95	Chapman Duncan	100.25
Aaron Nelson	100.00	W. L. Jolley	100.00
John P. Chidester	100.00	John W. Smith	135.00
Henry Harriman	100.32	James Hodges	79.00[50]

From the beginning, the project was undertaken with more enthusiasm from the top than the bottom although idealism existed on all levels — there was genuine support for utopianism in Mormonism. The concept appealed to many, but even in that first meeting, the vote was not unanimous. The Saints probably most accepted the idea of stability that the order projected. Most enjoyed the idea of independence from the nation's economy; they were proud of their homespun and their agriculture, but making the plan work was hard from the very first day.

Orson Huntsman's diary from Hebron and Enterprise presents a view from the remote villages in 1874:

> This order of things caused much talk and excitement among the people, some meeting it with joy and some with sorrows, some approving of it, some disapproving of it....
>
> Sometimes I thought that I should like this order of things very well and at other times thought I should not like it very well, and in some things the United Order was better and in some it was not as good. We had been in the habit of plowing a little land here & there for wheat, corn and potatoes but this spring the best pieces of land adapted for wheat. All hands go to work, plant all the land in one field that would do for wheat was planted, and the same was done with corn and potatoes, large patches of land was planted in a day, so that our crops all had the same chance to grow and all came off at the same time...
>
> There seems to be a spirit of fault finding and of speculation growing among the people through the whole land of Zion. Those that had little authority and those that had put a little more means into the order than some others had done wanted it to stay in there, they seem to think a laboring man could live without anything, while they themselves think because they put in means to the order they could have plenty and do nothing. The Lord has said, "the laborer is worthy of his hire."
>
> There seemed to be so much fault finding, I think through jealousy, on the part of the Bishop and a few others against Bro. Terry. He worked along, stood it as long as he could, until the second day of July then resigned as supt. and drew out of the United Order entirely and had nothing more to do with it....
>
> Sept 15 As I have said, I went to the bishop to see if he could do anything for me, as I and my family were getting quite destitute for clothing. My Indian moccasins were about gone, but he said, as he

had said many times, that he could not help me, so I told him I was
about through with the United Order, also, and I had never seen a
time in my life that I could not get a little something for my family
to live on, and that I would try it again.

This month or the close of this year about ends the United Order
with most of the settlements of Zion. A very few towns or branches
of the church work in the order for several years. But for Hebron
and some others, it proved to be about ten months of experience
and disunion.[51]

The Hebron story was similar to other experiences throughout
Dixie. Exhortations and idealism for the united orders did not weather
more than a year.

Harmony or Conflict?

The isolation of the area Latter-day Saints in their remote corner
of the world meant that they were generally left to themselves to resolve conflicts as they arose. The cooperative nature of their highly
organized society promoted a general harmony, but sometimes the
very closeness and small numbers created difficulties. Since authority
was an accepted principle throughout the county, one would expect
that harmony was implemented through leadership. And it was. Considerable effort was expended to resolve disagreements and prevent
open conflict. Many institutions were devoted to that end — families,
ward congregations, town governments, canal companies.

The records of the Hebron LDS Ward give a good example of how
one Mormon village in the county maintained harmony and smoothed
out conflicts which may have occurred in business dealings, water use,
and land disagreements. At a meeting of the ward held in October
1872, J. Pulsipher reported on "some misunderstandings with Bro.
Terry and others in matters of business which was investigated til dark
when a better understanding was arrived at."[52] What does this record
tell us? First, it is clear that fellow members (ward teachers) were assigned to visit all the members regularly. Second, they reported what
they found to the bishop. In this case they found some ill feelings on
the part of Terry. His concerns dealt with secular matters rather than
religious ones, but the teachers felt compelled to urge harmony on that
topic as well. This reflects the lack of separation between the secular
and the sacred among the Latter-day Saints as well as their desire for

community harmony.

Terry, now bishop, spoke in a priesthood meeting on 2 March 1878 of his trip north and his concern. There he had heard of a member of the church "going to Law" with another member. He urged that any differences be handled without going to courts of law. A few weeks later Bishop Terry asked D. M. Tyler to report on his attendance at stake conference in St. George. Tyler detailed a sermon by local stake president John D. T. McAllister about settling difficulties and stressing that backbiting "should not be countenanced among Latter-day Saints."53

One obvious instrument of conflict resolution was municipal government. St. George City was the most highly organized of those in the county, and a perusal of the city council records shows that the community was immediately and extensively organized almost as soon as the settlers arrived. A city council was elected with Angus M. Cannon as mayor and treasurer, Orson Pratt, Jr., W. E. Dodge, and Jacob Gates as councilors, and Easton Kelsey and Benjamin F. Pendleton as aldermen. This membership changed rather often, but Mayor Cannon remained as a stable force for his full term. Other city officers included James G. Bleak, recorder; William Fawcett, water master; Hosea Stout, city attorney; John Pymm, cemetery sexton; John Oakley, auditor; Albert Tyler, pound keeper; Stephen R. Wells, streets supervisor; Israel Ivins, city surveyor; D. H. Cannon, tax collector; and Daniel D. McArthur and later Ute Perkins, town marshal. All were expected to submit quarterly reports to the council. When they failed to do so, they were summoned to the next meeting.

The city council functioned by means of a formal procedure as though its members had long been familiar with Robert's Rules of Order and established civic government. As proposals came to them, they delegated them to subcommittees made up of council members, who investigated the matters and reported back within a few days with a proposed resolution, which was usually adopted. The council devoted much of its time to allocating water and land, promoting street improvements, regulating the production and sale of liquor, trying to get people to accept appointments to labor in the service of the city, and authorizing expenditures.

Some comments in the city record capture the role the city fathers set for themselves. The 17 May 1862 entry reads: "The mayor suggested that measures be adopted to prevent the rapid riding of horses in the streets of the city; and also to prevent swearing. Referred to the committee on the care and disposition of stock." This issue proved to be a sticky one; there was not much enthusiasm for having the city government be disciplinarian instead of families. Three weeks later (7 June 1862) the record states: "Councilor Gates from the Committee on the Control and disposition of Stock stated that the Committee deemed it best to leave the matter in the hands of the Bishops. The matter was discussed, Pres. Snow and Bp. Gardner taking part in the discussion of the question. It was referred back to the committee."

Though most of the actions of the city council were devoted to building an infrastructure such as roads, ditches, cemetery, and planting shade trees, many of their activities were focused on resolving differences and disciplining infractions. For example, there was a major disagreement about controlling the water in the Santa Clara River. When St. George City was incorporated by the territorial legislature, it was given control over the Santa Clara River. Prior to that 1861 date, there were already people living in communities along the river — from Pine Valley at the source, southwestward to Gunlock and then Santa Clara farther south, and finally to Tonaquint at the junction with the Virgin River. The citizens of these communities were of the opinion that they had priority in the use of the water. This superimposition of a large population at St. George with a well-organized council government was a major threat to the earlier settlers, and much of the St. George Council time was devoted to hearings with residents along the Santa Clara. The issue was a continuing one, with Santa Clara residents feeling they were being slighted.

Another focus of the council could be said to have aimed at preventing conflict. This was the matter of "Spiritous alcohol." The council decided at its inception to control the manufacture and sale of whiskey, which became a city monopoly. The city record includes reports on manufacture and sales of liquor, with responsibility shifting among several people. For example, Hosea Stout reported that he sold fifty-six gallons of whiskey during a four-month period — about a half-gallon a day.

One visible dimension of the system of authority was Mormon church leadership. From top to bottom there were authority figures. At the top in Washington County were apostles Orson Pratt and Erastus Snow. Both refrained from direct political activity in the county, yet they coordinated the secular and the sacred. Neither of them was elected as a city or county official; however, they often attended the city council meetings and on occasion the council referred matters to them to be settled. For example, on 1 May 1865, Judge James D. McCullough asked the city council to designate a piece of land for a courthouse. The council took the request under advisement. On 20 May the council appointed Alderman Daniel D. McArthur and Councilor Jacob Gates to meet with Apostle Erastus Snow about such a site as well as one for a city jail. On 1 July a councilman reported that they were not yet ready to report, but on 19 August he announced that a site for the courthouse had been selected on the southeast corner of the block where it stands today.54 Evidently what we would call long range planning was in the hands of the ecclesiastical leader.

Life at the top was not always harmonious. It is clear that Orson Pratt and Erastus Snow occasionally disagreed. Both were strong personalities. Pratt was the senior, yet Snow seemed to take the initiative. This appeared early as the 1861 company reached the bottom of the Black Ridge. Pratt was not enthusiastic about the site Brigham Young had selected for St. George between the two lava-covered mesas. He likely knew of the sickness of the people in nearby Washington and argued for going to higher ground, up the Virgin River toward Rockville where the air and water would be healthier. Snow insisted on settling the site announced by Brigham Young. Pratt left the company and went on to Rockville where he lived for a few months.

Orson Pratt and Erastus Snow soon resolved their differences and Pratt moved to St. George. There he built one of the finest homes in the city and participated in civic and religious activities; however, he remained for only three years before accepting a mission call to Europe. Evidently he encouraged church president Young to issue that call. Some have felt that Orson Pratt was more comfortable as a missionary than as a pioneer.

The middle-level leaders were also influential and visible, particularly the bishops. Most communities had a bishop selected by Erastus Snow and sustained by the ward members. The apostle frequently invited members of the local congregation to nominate or advise in the selection process. Generally the bishops were very responsible and were clearly respected. They were lay leaders, serving mainly without remuneration and were expected to support themselves and their families while being models for their brethren. Their tasks were both spiritual and temporal, presiding over the religious meetings of their congregation (ward) as well as being deeply involved in helping the poor, arbitrating disputes, collecting tithes, enlisting volunteer labor for the many projects of pioneering, and especially being the local agent of the stake president and apostles, and even the church president who often sent heavy assignments the bishop's way. It was not uncommon for a local bishop to serve a decade or more in this demanding calling.

Problems sometimes arose when "outsiders" settled among the Latter-day Saints. Utah society was structured so that bishop's courts handled matters. One tale is told of a young man who moved to Washington City from Silver Reef. His lack of social skills was evidently considerable and parents urged young women to avoid his attention. In this case the parents' admonitions were warranted because he was able to attract a young lady's affections and soon made her pregnant. Bishop Covington called the young man in for counsel and made it clear that he would be expected to marry the young lady. The youth showed no inclination to do so or to listen to the bishop. The bishop called him before a bishop's court and had the same result. The dashing youth saw no reason to recognize the ecclesiastical court. Covington then sought counsel of Apostle Erastus Snow. The presiding leader asked the bishop to reconvene the court. The young man reappeared but still with a confident air of being beyond authority. Snow sat in the back of the room quietly listening to the proceedings until Covington called on him. He went forward, looked the young man squarely in the eye and asked him if he was sorry for his action. The youth responded no differently than he had to the bishop, giving an air that he felt in command of the situation. Snow is reported to have said without agitation, "Young man, if one of these men here doesn't kill you, I will have to do it myself." The youth reportedly left the county within the evening.[55]

There were sometimes people who had disagreements with their bishops and on rare occasions the majority clashed with their local ecclesiastical leader. In Gunlock, for example, the members were not happy with their bishop, J. S. Huntsman. Numerous criticisms were levied against him, particularly that he did not give his calling enough attention. Erastus Snow met with the Gunlock Latter-day Saints and all agreed to be more patient with each other. That lasted only a short time, however; eventually the bishop decided to leave town rather than face the continuing rejection.[56]

A contrasting tale involved a clash between the Swiss Mormons in Santa Clara and neighboring cattlemen. The Swiss were expert growers of vegetables and fruits. They became increasingly angry with the freewheeling cattlemen who could not keep their stock from invading the Swiss gardens. The conflicting lifestyles provided continuing clashes. Add to that the ethnic slurs that were often directed at the Swiss immigrants and soon Erastus Snow had a full-sized conflict on his hands. Snow called young Edward Bunker from Toquerville to be the bishop in Santa Clara. Bunker quickly came to a solution of having the community fence the Swiss lands with the ranchers help, something they could not have done alone.

For the majority in Santa Clara this settled the matter, but at least one Swiss Saint became increasingly disillusioned. Heinrich Hug, a German-speaking Swiss, had joined the church in the 1850s in his home canton, Zurich. In 1858 he immigrated to Utah and was called in the 1861 mission group to southern Utah. He was part of the eighty-five member Swiss company that settled in Santa Clara. For a decade Hug struggled, sacrificed, and held ranks with his fellow residents. His journal and especially his poetry portray his inner tensions. Hug became increasingly disenchanted with the authoritarian nature of the church leadership in Dixie. He was discouraged with the climate and the difficult challenges for making a living, but he also chafed at the discrimination the Swiss experienced. He had been a man of trust and leadership in the church in Switzerland, a real pillar. In southern Utah the Swiss seemed not to be valued; none were called to leadership positions. Hug felt that the Swiss took these insults as placid followers. The conflict over water rights between Santa Clara and St. George particularly irritated him, seeming to be the final cause of his complete break with the faith. His poetry became strident, his dreams crushed. In 1879 Hug, his wife, and children left Utah and moved to Oregon, severing their ties with Mormonism.[57] Not all conflicts were resolved amicably.

There were many frustrations about water. For example, a group of St. George farmers agreed to close several acres to irrigation in the west fields in order to divert the water to more promising fields on the east side of town. The closure was to prevent spreading the water too thin on all sides. A difficult situation arose in the Harrisburg/Leeds area. Harrisburg's water supply was always tenuous. Some seasons the creek flow was too low to meet minimal needs. Whether this was the only cause or not, the people in Harrisburg fell into arguments. Priddy Meeks felt he was under personal attack and left the town, moving to Orderville. Several other families moved north four miles to Leeds, but there the disputes resurfaced.

A similar problem arose in Hebron over the rights to Shoal Creek water. Proposals by a group of citizens to build a reservoir were criticized by other Hebron residents, including the bishop. The reservoir nevertheless was completed through the heroic devotion of a few determined crusaders. Finally, an arbitration involving the stake presidency resolved the water claims resulting from diversion of the water with the dam. A combination of drought and other discouragements eventually convinced most residents of Hebron to move to Enterprise. An earthquake in November 1902 confirmed their decision to move by ruining most of the brick homes in Hebron.

Washington County at Statehood

The isolation that kept Dixie away from the mainstream and wealth would dominate Washington County for nearly a century. The Arizona Strip and Virgin River Gorge were southern barriers to travel into the county. The Black Ridge made travel very difficult from the north. The gorge of the Colorado River and the Colorado Plateau guarded the east. The Utah Hill challenged travel to the west. The population of the county would remain isolated but fairly stable, growing slowly. The values that helped settlers achieve stability would be cherished and would enable the region to mesh gradually with the larger American society.

In 1892 historian Andrew Jenson visited southern Utah, inspecting each LDS ward. He held meetings with each congregation and collected historical documents for the Mormon church archives in Salt Lake City. The Deseret Weekly included Jenson's summary of his seven-week journey in Washington County, describing each community and giving a church census.

Jenson reported that there were 4,658 Latter-day Saints in the St. George Stake, which included all of Washington County, the Arizona Strip, and part of Lincoln County, Nevada (Panaca and Pioche). Statistics were given for each of the twenty-one wards and several branches. Non-members were not included, so the Protestant missionaries, the few remaining miners in Silver Reef, and the considerable number in Pioche did not appear in his data. Similarly with Indians; many were baptized members of the church and were included, but those who were not members were not counted.

Jenson noted that several towns including Washington had declined in population and that Silver Reef had nearly disappeared. The dam being constructed above Washington was the big hope for both Washington and St. George. The destruction of farmlands from floods was the plight of many towns, causing some people to seek opportunities elsewhere, he said. Jenson concluded that life in Dixie was still a challenge, but he shared the expectation of the local residents that they were eventually going to win the battle for a stable water supply — a vision that would soon be fulfilled by the completion of the Washington Dam, the Enterprise Reservoir, and the La Verkin and Hurricane canals, all within a dozen years of his writing.[58]

As with towns throughout the rest of the territory, Dixie communities were poised for statehood in January 1896. The Union of 11 January 1896 reported the celebration of 6 January. The people of the territory celebrated in their usual manner — meetings in the morning and dances thereafter. Speakers in the tabernacle included Ashby Snow, Daniel D. McArthur, D. H. Cannon, and Reverend G. M. Hardy of the Presbyterian church. James G. Bleak prayed with gratitude for the long-awaited statehood and John G. McQuarrie read the statehood proclamation from the president of the United States. Martha Keat gave a recitation as did Francis Higgins. A song composed for the occasion by Charles Lowell Walker, "The Star of Utah," and other music was performed by the St. George Tabernacle Choir directed by Joseph W. McAllister. The local brass, martial, and string bands performed and bells rang at the tabernacle and the Presbyterian church. In the afternoon there were dances, first for the children under ten years of age, then for those from ten to sixteen. In the evening everyone was invited to dances in two locations. All were joyous that admission to the Union had at last been accomplished.

ENDNOTES

1. *Diary of Charles Lowell Walker* I: 349.

2. Andrew Karl Larson, *I Was Called to Dixie*, 638.

3. James G. Bleak, "Annals of the Southern Utah Mission," Book A, 178.

4. The census figures were taken from the official U.S. Census records of 1860, 1870, 1880, 1900, 1910, 1920 and 1930. The census of 1890 is not available. These were made available on microfilm at the LDS Family History Center in St. George. Print copies were also consulted at the Salt Lake City Public Library, Main Branch.

5. W. Paul Reeve, "Hurricane, Utah Community Building, 1906-1920. A People's View," paper delivered at the Mormon History Association in Park City, April 1994. See also Reeve, "A Little Oasis in the Desert: Hurricane, Utah, 1860-1920." *Utah Historical Quarterly 62* (Summer 1994): 222-45.

6. Two fine books give insight into these communities. Charles Peterson analyzed the story of those who moved to the Little Colorado River settlements — St. Johns, Snowflake, Brigham City, St. Joseph, Holbrook, Woodruff, Taylor, Springville, and Sunset — in the 1880s. His book *Take Up Your Mission* (Tucson, Ariz.: University of Arizona Press, 1973) focuses on Snowflake. Jennifer Moulton Hansen has published the letters of her grandmother who grew up in St. George, married Miles Park Romney there, then followed him as his third wife to the Little Colorado and later to the Mexican colonies before returning to Dixie after his death. Her letters give a classic example of the tie to Dixie and an "inside" view of a polygamous marriage; see *Letters of Catharine Cottam Romney, Plural Wife* (Urbana: University of Illinois Press, 1992).

7. *Deseret News* 1866 vol. 16, 246. Also Reeve, "Hurricane," 8.

8. Reeve, "Hurricane," 8-9.

9. Dean L. May, Lee L. Bean, and Mark H. Skolnick, "The Stability Ratio: An Index of Community Cohesiveness in Nineteenth Century Mormon Towns," in *Generations and Change: Genealogical Perspectives in Social History*, ed. Robert M. Taylor, Jr., and Ralph J. Crandall (Macon, GA.: Mercer University Press, 1986). See also Dean May, *Three Frontiers: Family, Land and Society in the American West 1850-1900* (New York: Cambridge University Press, 1994). This study compares a Mormon village (Alpine, Utah), with an Idaho and an Oregon frontier town.

10. Larry Logue estimated a higher percentage of those practicing polygamy, 34 percent, in St. George by corroborating the census records with family group sheets in genealogical records, verifying names of deceased polygamous partners and other details. See *A Sermon in the Desert* (Urbana: Illinois University Press, 1988), 49.

11. Bleak, "Annals," 184, 92, 95.

12. Lawrence L. Linford, "Establishing and Maintaining Land Ownership in Utah Prior to 1869," *Utah Historical Quarterly 42* (Spring 1974): 126-43. See also Allan G. Bogue, "An Agricultural Empire" in *The Oxford History of the American West*,

ed. Clyde Milner II, Carol O'Connor, and Martha Sandweiss (New York: Oxford University Press, 1994), 293.

13. Linford, "Establishing and Maintaining," 137.

14. Lawrence B. Lee, "Homesteading in Zion." *Utah Historical Quarterly 28* (January 1960): 28-38.

15. Walker, *Diary*, I: 323, 325.

16. Larson, *The Red Hills of November*, 82-4.

17. Larson, *I Was Called to Dixie*, 244.

18. Annie Atkin Tanner, "My Shining Valley, St. George, Utah 1891-1972," unpublished manuscript, Dixie College Archives.

19. Levi Savage, Journal 1887-1903, Dixie College Archives.

20. Bleak, "Annals," Book A, 269. The settlements temporarily abandoned were Grafton, Gunlock, Duncan's Retreat, Dalton, Mountain Dell, Schunesburg, Northrop, Springdale, Clover Valley, and Long Valley.

21. Walker, *Diary* I: 275.

22. Ibid., I, 324. An earlier account of such negotiations appears in Bleak's "Annals," 248, describing a peace meeting of sixty-seven Indian chiefs and forty-four of their followers at St. Joseph on the Muddy River.

23. Ibid., 406.

24. Louise Leavitt Engstrom, "Island in the Stream: Anderson's Ranch 1884-1984," unpublished manuscript, Dixie College Archives.

25. Larry Logue, *Sermon In the Desert: Belief and Behavior in Early St. George* (Urbana: University of Illinois Press, 1988), 72ff. See also A. K. Hafen, *Devoted Empire Builders* (St. George: privately published, 1969).

26. Mary Ann Hafen, *Recollections of a Handcart Pioneer of 1860* (Denver: privately published, 1980), 61-2, 79-80.

27. Leonora Atkin Meeks, "John Nock Hinton: The Reconstructed Life of an English Born Mormon Convert of Virgin City, Utah." Masters thesis, Brigham Young University, 1987, 94.

28. "Memories of Alice Parker Isom and George Isom, 1838-1923," unpublished manuscript, Dixie College Archives.

29. Logue, *Sermon*, 97.

30. Wesley Larson, "Indian and Pioneer Medicine in Utah Territory: 1847-1900," unpublished manuscript, Dixie College Archives.

31. Martha Spence Heywood, *Not By Bread Alone, The Journal of Martha Spence Heywood, 1850-56*, ed. Juanita Brooks (Salt Lake City: Utah State Historical Society, 1978), 116.

32. Walker, *Diary*, I, 466.

33. Kerry William Bate, "John Steele: Medicine Man, Magician, Mormon Patriarch," *Utah Historical Quarterly 62* (Winter 1994), 74-5. See also Bart Anderson, "A Look Back — Old Time Medicine," *The Daily Spectrum*, 28 August 1983.

34. Vicky Schreiter, "Early Midwives of Southern Utah," Gregerson Collection, 1982, Dixie College Archives.

35. Hazel Bradshaw, "St. George," in *Under the Dixie Sun*, 304.

36. Larson, *I Was Called to Dixie*, 330. See also John D. Lee, "Writings of John D. Lee," Agriculture File, Dixie College Archives.

37. Larson, *I Was Called to Dixie*, 329-33.

38. *Washington County News*, 14 September 1908.

39. Larson, *I Was Called to Dixie*, 336.

40. Ibid., 264-65.

41. "Spencer J. Reber History (Part 1)1927-1977," Dixie College Archives, 21-27.

42. Ibid.

43. Paul Dean Proctor and Morris A. Shirts, *Silver, Sinners and Saints, A History of Old Silver Reef, Utah* (n.p., Paulmar, 1991), 27—29.

44. Wilma C. Beal, *My Story of Silver Reef* (1987), 7-17.

45. Paul Dean Proctor, *Geology of the Silver Reef/Harrisburg Mining District* (Bulletin 44 Utah Geological and Mineralogical Survey 1953), 70-77.

46. Walker, *Diary*, I: 330.

47. Proctor and Shirts, *Silver, Sinners and Saints*, 90.

48. Beal, *My Story*, 12-13.

49. Leonard Arrington, *Great Basin Kingdom* (Cambridge: Harvard University Press, 1958), 326-29.

50. Probate Court of Washington County, A. R. Whitehead, Clerk. 77. The typed copy is on pp. 96-98 and puts the date 1874.

51. Orson Huntsman, Diary, vol. I: 80-87.

52. Hebron [Ward] Record, I, 4; copy in possession of Heber Jones.

53. Ibid., II, 127.

54. "Record of Minutes of City Council of City of St. George," 1862-1872, Dixie College Archives.

55. Andrew Karl Larson, *Erastus Snow* (Salt Lake City: University of Utah Press, 1971), 561-62. See also Nels Anderson, *Desert Saints* (Chicago: University of Chicago Press, 1942), 339.

56. William Ellis Jones, Journal, 48, Dixie College Archives.

57. Douglas F. Tobler, "Heinrich Hug and Jacob Tobler: From Switzerland to Santa Clara, 1854-1880," *Dialogue 26* (Winter 1993): 104-28.

58. Andrew Jenson, "In Southern Utah," *Deseret Weekly* (Salt Lake City), 16 July 1892.

5

STORIES AND REFLECTIONS

The stories that people tell each other, relate to their children, record in their journals, use in their sermons, and sing in their songs are what bind a people together. Stories help define a culture. They embody the shared values that create group identity. Certainly Dixie has its rich share of stories. Some stories included here are firsthand accounts of the Dixie pioneers. Others are attributed to that early generation. Most center on daily life, families, work, and community living. In this chapter, average people tell their stories, some of which require the stage first be set for them.

Indians

The first white settlers were interested in the Indians of Washington County who, to them, were as different as the landscape. What became Washington County was the homeland of the Paiutes. Other tribes did not envy them their marginal land, and they were left to roam on foot in small bands since they did not have horses. Neighboring tribes of Utes and Navajos raided them regularly. Their brush shelters were temporary and offered no defense. For food the Paiutes roamed over vast areas to glean seeds and insects from the desert's meager yield. The land was harsh; the Paiutes were often plagued by severe hunger.

As the Mormons entered into the area, they brought a civilization that included such elements as private property, tool-driven agriculture, herds of cattle and sheep, and permanent villages. They built fixed homes, schools, and churches. They had formal law, government, and armies — all foreign to the Native Americans and not compatible with their ways of life. The history of Utah, including Washington County, is yet one more example of how the agricultural and industrial culture displaced a traditional culture.

Initially the Mormons in Washington County were optimistic that the Paiutes would accept the invitation to join their world. Their hope was that the Indians would greatly upgrade their agricultural efforts, abandon their semi-nomadic life, settle on farmsteads, build homes, and attend schools and churches. The Mormons, like other Americans on the western frontier, saw themselves as bringing civilization, especially Christianity, to their fellows.

The Mormon version of this mission was institutionalized in the call of the Southern Indian Mission. It soon came to be focused in Santa Clara under the leadership of Jacob Hamblin. Brigham Young's paternal attitude to help the Indians was nowhere better exemplified than in the life of Hamblin and his illustrious colleagues, Thales Haskell, Ira Hatch, Augustus P. Hardy, Isaac Riddle, and others.

The initial Mormon reaction to the Native Americans centered around their poverty. Brigham Young instructed the Mormons to be generous with Indians, sharing their food with them. This generosity was often tested, such as this early contact recorded by the scribe of the Southern Indian Mission, Thomas D. Brown:

> Tuesday 25 April [1854] A fine morning after leaving camp up to Corn Creek, very wet and heavy driving. About 20 Indians of Walker's band came and surrounded our wagons and finally crossed the road and stood ahead of them, after many strange gestures & much loud speaking by the eldest of them, a blanket was thrown down, we all understood this to be a demand of toll for passing over their lands, we all contributed some bread & flour & tobacco. They sat down & seemed to enjoy the bread. We passed on and soon some more came down the creek, they too had to be satisfied.[1]

The missionary accounts express attitudes about the culture clash that ensued. Brown records the Mormon's feelings at a campsite of Chief Toquer (where today's Toquerville stands) one time when the missionaries were welcomed to an evening meal and rest:

> We went over to their wickiups after our supper and found their women grinding seeds by the light of the moon, and boiling a large potful of pottage - in a conical shaped dish made from clay and sand thin and hard. This mess seemed of a darkish grey color with like chunks of bacon in it, we tasted the flour which the women were making from the seeds of grass - by rubbing them between two rocks - it tasted much like buck wheat flour or bean meal, what we fancied to be pieces of bacon, I have been told were bunches of matted ants, one of the brethren tasted this food and said these clusters tasted very oily but knew not the cause, this porridge the female stirred with a large spoon or ladle, like the water gourds of the states made from the horn of a mountain sheep, with this mess was divided on wicker baskets, flat in the shape of flat wood turned dishes, about 1 quart to each - the elder served first -this was soon cleaned out by the forefinger of the right hand inwards around the point of the thumb for a spoon…the same dish handed back and filled & passed around - they supped this up greedily, and with the head of a roasted porcupine, brains and bones, added to an entire roasted sand lark seemed added to what we gave them - to about satisfy. Then like hogs with little or no covering they huddled in the sand! Oh how Ephraim has fallen.2

The Santa Clara missionaries had great difficulty repressing their abhorrence of Indian customs. Particularly grating was the existence of a slavery system in which Utes from the north invaded their territory almost annually, taking Paiute children, mainly girls, whom they then delivered into Mexico as slaves. Hamblin records a trade of one horse and two guns for three girls:

> …the girls' father & mother cried to see them go; but they had nothing to eat and it would be better for the children than to stay & starve. I saw tears fall fast from the eyes of the oldest of the three; a girl about ten or twelve years old. I felt heart sick to see them dragged from their homes to become slaves to the Gentiles. I saw the necessity of the Elders doing all they could to ameliorate the condition of this miserable people.3

Sometimes Mormons would actually engage in this trade, buying children to prevent them from being carried off to Mexico and an uncertain existence.

Another practice that upset the Mormons was the custom of fighting for brides. Brutal fights lasting for a full day or more involved scores of Indian men who beat each other to exhaustion to determine who would win the bride. Tragically, the bride was often so hurt in the fray that she sometimes did not survive. The men were also sometimes killed, as one account illustrates:

> The name of this Indian was "Pierre," we saw him a few days before and discovered that consumption dried up his vitals, and worn him to a skeleton's form. We then pronounced his death near, he is said to have been hurt while fighting for or to obtain a wife – his second – his first still alive, which some say is customary here – the strongest and boldest being the most successful. When he lay dying his only bed was the dusty earth. I could not help reflecting "to dust we must return" — alas! poor Indians how near the soil you ever have been, at birth dropped into the dust, creeping, lying and running in it with no other table – thy work bench – thy gambling table – thy theater – pulpit – stage – bed of joy, sorrow and death; with apparent sympathy thou are surrounded by thy wives, children and friends, though at a little distance in sad and mournful silence – the head of the dying one resting on the roots of a bunch of bushoak his feet drawn up to his back, his legs and thighs wasted away except at the joints; "return to dust!" why poor dark degraded Lamanite thou never went far out of it.[4]

Similarly, the treatment of sickness and death among the Indians was hard for the Mormons to comprehend even though they faced the same dangers. Thomas Brown describes the rituals of an Indian medicine man in rich detail:

> The Indian doctor or medicine man came today, & after giving the sick woman some hot water to drink, but no herbs in it, began to sing, "nani nani nani Nani nani nani" &c., varying the sound as I have written it, first loud and then falling by degrees, then begin-fling aloud again, this he continued, til, I suppose having invoked the healing spirit long enough he would get to his knees, then roll over to his back would draw himself close up to the patient, & with closed eyes still singing lift up his hands so as to receive her, she would fall across him & he placing his arms around her & near the sore shoulder would begin to press her till she would groan, at same time his head being below apparently sucking her breast, would crawl out when breath seemed almost gone

to him, would spit out some nasty green stuff, expectorated from his own lungs or chest, would again begin a new murmuring song.[5]

After describing more such details, Brown concluded: "I know not but the general testimony is that often remarkable cures are affected."

The Indian missionaries tried consciously not to be judgmental. Hamblin respected the Indians' prayers for rain and even invited a medicine man to use his "poogi" on him when he was deathly ill. He won their respect and set a high standard for missionary dealings with the Indians. When his son once "drove a sharp bargain" in a trade with an Indian, Jacob sent the boy back to pay a better price for the blankets he had obtained. The Indian expected him back; that was Jacob Hamblin's standard — total honesty. He always acted upon the premise that Indians could be trusted, that they could communicate as well as anyone else, and that the best strategy was to confer with them. He did not talk above their heads; explaining things in a straightforward manner was the best approach, he felt. Hamblin's problem was persuading white people of these convictions. The Indians generally responded to him with respect, and he gradually became a legend among them.

Over time Hamblin developed explicit rules for his relationship with the Indians. According to Pearson Corbett, John W. Young asked Hamblin to write down these rules. They appeared in a letter to Young dated 14 April 1874, from Kanab:

1st. I never talk anything but the truth to them.

2nd. I think it useless to speak of things they cannot comprehend.

3rd. I strive by all means to never let them see me in a passion.

4th. Under no circumstances show fear; thereby showing to them that I have a sound heart and straight tongue.

5th. Never approach them in an austere manner; nor use more words than is necessary to convey my ideas; nor in a higher tone of voice, than to be distinctly heard.

6th. Always listen to them when they wish to tell their grievances and redress their wrongs however trifling they may be (if possible). If I cannot, I let them know that I have a desire to do so.

7th. I never allow them to hear me use any obscene language or take any unbecoming course with them.

8th. I never submit to any unjust demands or submit to coercion under any circumstances thereby showing that I govern and am governed by the rule of right and not by might.

9th. I have tried to observe the above rules for the past twenty years and it has given me a salutary influence where-ever I have met with them. Many times when I have visited isolated bands upon business and have been addressing them in a low tone of voice around their council fires, I have noticed that they have listened with attention and reverence. I believe if the rules that I have mentioned were observed there would be but little difficulty on our frontier with the Red Man.[6]

The early missionaries received the trust and cooperation of most Indians, but the situation changed when large numbers of Mormons were called to settle Dixie. Until 1861, families scattered in a few settlements no larger than ten or twenty homes. When the 1861 call came to go to Dixie and raise cotton, the balance changed drastically. Soon pioneer cattle and sheep numbered in the thousands, preempting the grazing lands for wildlife. The seeds Indians had gathered nearly disappeared. Indians increasingly saw the Anglos as a threat; and whites were also facing a survival test that had little room for Indians who stole cattle as their game supply dwindled. Thus began a tension that lasted three decades.

Hamblin tried to sustain an enthusiasm and compassion for the Indians, but he gradually shifted his hopes from the Paiutes to the Hopis. The Shivwits band of Paiutes near Santa Clara showed a willingness to farm and to abandon their thievery; they were fairly quick to accept baptism, but they did not sustain the intentions. The Paiutes proved to be moderately willing to coexist with the Mormons (something the Navajos were not) but Hamblin and Brigham Young came to feel that the Hopis were more likely to be receptive to their religious message. Their stone dwellings and successful agriculture seemed closer to the Anglo culture, more amenable to Christianity.

Some of the initial experiences with the Indians were not unlike those experienced by later settlers:

There were many Indians about the settlement, generally friendly in later years and often employed by the whites. The squaws especially were good to wash clothes on the washboard and to help the pioneer women with their hard tasks. In early times the Indians stole cattle. Mrs. Mary A. Hafen had related to them that Brigham Young told them a plague would come to them and they would die like rotten sheep if they did not stop. In her girlhood days a plague did come on the Indians near Santa Clara.[7]

But not all clashes over cattle were handled with warnings. For example:

> In the spring of 1867 the Indians came within four or five miles of Pine Valley and stole some horses. Most of them were Navajos with some bad Paiutes with them. Cyrus Hancock and myself were going out into the hills that day and he came along before I was ready. When I got ready there was no one to help me start a horse off that I wanted to take so I did not go that day. He was attacked by the Indians and shot through the arm with an arrow. He outran the Indians and reached home with the arrow still in his arm. I saw him as he came into town on the hind end of an ox wagon driven by William Coache, an Englishman. The oxen were on a big trot. The people gathered round and Athe Meeks pulled the arrow out. I think he took hold of it with a pair of bullet molds. They would take hold of it much like a pair of pincers. We had several head of horses in the band that was taken, among them a gray spanish mare that had a bell on. We did nothing with this mare. She just wore the bell to keep the band together. The Indians killed her, as we suppose, to get rid of the bell. An express was sent to St. George that night. James Andrus was in the vicinity of Rockville with some men. He started in hot pursuit and overtook them and killed seven Indians and got the horses.8

The Anderson ranch site was a natural trail crossing that often brought Indians by. On one occasion a large contingent of Navajos on horseback were reported. Alarmed, the children ran to hide, jumping in a dugout and hiding under sacks of grain. Their father had all he could do to divert the Indians from stealing and did not notice one poking around in the grain storage. When the Indian lifted the sack away that protected the little ones, they screamed. He looked at them a long time and then said "Boo." He then chuckled and turned away.9

Martha Cragun Cox reports a child's experience in the late 1860s on a ranch south of Pine Valley. Her parents had gone to Salt Lake City, leaving her with her brothers. One night both of her brothers were away. She was alone in their makeshift dwelling when a major storm came up. She had always feared thunder and rain. She went out to assess the clouds and saw a lone Indian on the property:

> My first thought was that he was a spy or scout for a party on a raid, but he had no gun and his limbs were naked, so I concluded he was a common Indian seeking shelter and I knew he would freeze in the

open roofless shop. I went to him and told him to come to my wickiup and warm. He said, "St. Wino, Ticaboo," meaning "Good, I'm
your friend." I gave him some supper and a seat by the fire, where we
two sat together til late in the night, while the worst storm the ranches
ever knew howled terribly outside and fairly shook the old cabin. I
felt so thankful for the company of that dirty, ragged Indian in the di-
lemma of the storm. And he was grateful for the storm. He told me
his tribe had cast him out for some very bad thing he had done and
some wanted to kill him. He would say the wind and the snow were
good because they could not find him nor track him and tomorrow he
would be away over the mountain. I asked the Indian if he had killed
someone, he said no that killing was pretty good that he had done
worse than killing. There was a little "lean to" behind the cabin into
which an inner door opened. I showed him an empty corn bin and
told him to lie down in that when he wanted to rest. When the storm
abated he went into his rest and I laid down on my cot before the fire
and went to sleep. When I awoke I found he had gone.[10]

Making a Living

Building shelter, obtaining furnishings for the dwellings, bringing water to the site, gathering and preparing food, doing the laundry,
engaging in creative crafts — these are part of the daily life of people
almost anywhere. Certainly these activities occupy the daily lives of
people today in Washington County. The following account from a
child's view gives an insight into providing the basic elements of food
and shelter during early settlement days.

Father's next interest was to provide us a better shelter. The dugout
he built was about six feet deep, twelve feet square, with a slanting
roof. Crevices between the roof poles were filled with small compact bundles of rushes held in place by a weaving of young willows.
About a six-inch layer of dirt which had been excavated from the
cellar was then put on the roof. There were no windows. The front
and only door had one small pane of glass to light up the cool cozy
room within.

Beds were made by driving corner posts into the dirt floor. Black
willow poles split were nailed close together to serve as slats on the
bed and fresh straw was used for mattresses. Comfortable pillows
were made from the fluff of the cat-tails which were gathered from
the sloughs along the creek. To save space in this little room-of-all-
purposes, an improvised table was made by laying a large plank on
top of the posts of one of the beds. Two benches made of boards,

a shelf cupboard, and a small sheet-iron stove with two holes and a tiny oven, completed the furnishings. All in all the little primitive shelter was quite comfortable; for it was pleasantly cool in the suffocating heat of the summer, and was warm in the winter months when light snow fell, rain drizzled, or ice coated the water ditches. For three years this dug-out was to serve as our home....

By this time, along each side of the wide street ran a little irrigating ditch of water. Upon the banks, to shade the sidewalks, cottonwood trees were set out. Every morning while the water was still cool and clean, each family dipped up barrels of water for household and drinking purposes. After a storm the water was roily and had to settle before it was fit to use.

Water for laundry purposes was generally softened by pouring in cottonwood ashes. Soft rainwater we generally used to wash our hair and our nicest clothes. But of course we couldn't get rainwater always. A favorite substitute for soap was the root of the "oose," or yucca sometimes called "soap root." This root looked about like a sugarbeet. Cut up and left in water it soon made a fluffy suds....

This very same year I learned how to weave. Father made me a loom. My arms were too short to reach both sides of the loom to shove my shuttle through the web, so I had to lean from side to side. I was proud of the first dress I wove. It was made in a checkered pattern one inch across of brown, blue, and white, from cotton yarn. I also made what we called jeans out of cotton warp with wool. This was used for men's suits and was very heavy cloth.

Besides making our dresses we also made our hats. We cut the ripe wheat straws, using only the long top joint. We would lay a handful of this straw in the water until it became soft. Then we braided it. I became expert at braiding from seven to thirteen straws....I guess through those years I made enough hats to fill a wagon box. I would trade them with the neighbors for things which we needed.11

Schools

Until the territory took on the responsibility of funding schools in 1890, schools were rather makeshift. Families paid a tuition for their children to attend. This meant that many children did not go to school, or, if they did, they often attended only two or three years, thus making way for a sibling to replace them. The family often either could not afford more or needed the physical labor of their offspring to help sustain the family.

The tuition system also meant that teachers frequently could not support their families on the income they made teaching. Classes were held only during the three or four winter months and tuition usually was paid not in cash but in kind. This would perhaps feed the teacher and sometimes house him or her with families of the students, but it certainly did not provide an income that would allow the teacher to build and support a home and family in the community. By the 1870s the territorial legislature began to provide limited funding for schools — initially one dollar per student per term. Parents could subtract that dollar from the tuition charge and then pay the rest of the tuition, often in kind. This meant that teachers at least received a portion of their pay in cash.

William Ellis Jones left a poignant journal describing his itinerant teaching career in Santa Clara, Gunlock, Hebron, Hamblin, and their environs. Because school was only held sporadically, he spent most months of each year making adobes or bricks. This would require him to build a brick oven in each town where the buildings were to be constructed. Many of the homes still standing in Pine Valley are the result of his brickmaking, and his reputation was as a brickmaker, not a teacher. Other times he labored in his small orchard — he never ac-cumulated more than three acres — to feed his family; schoolteaching was almost a sideline.

Jones's wife, Dinah Vaughan, was a sought-after midwife who of-ten lived in with an expectant mother for a few weeks, even in distant towns. This supplementary income was necessary because William taught school for only three or four months each year and only in those years when the local trustees hired him. He suffered from a system that left his fate in the hands of local trustees who often did not de-cide whether to employ him until shortly before, or even after, school started. He never knew if he could depend on employment, and he went some years without a class to teach. Other years he had to travel some distance from his home to find a classroom.

Martha Cragun Cox tells a more typical story. After marrying into a polygamous family, Cox found herself in constant need of a supplemental income. In 1881 she was informed that the non-Mor-mons who had taken up residence in the Muddy Valley after the Mor-mons left were in need of a teacher. They were not favorably inclined toward Mormons, but families there with children had notified her

St. George First Ward School House and Students. The building was completed in 1864. (Lynne Clark Collection, donor — Nellie Gubler and the Washington County Daughters of the Utah Pioneers)

that the trustees would be hiring a teacher. They informed her that a qualifying examination would be held on 6 August. Her baby died and was buried just two days before the examination, so she could not arrive on time. Her family's need for money was great, however; this prospect could bring fifty dollars a month for three months. She was determined to go anyway, even though she would arrive after the appointed date.

> I knew that the very name of "Mormon" was hated in Nevada that no Mormon woman had ever taught there — that only one Mormon man had ever been allowed to hold a certificate in that state. That Samuel O. Crosby and Zera Terry both good young men that I had known were not even allowed to be present at school teachers' examination. I knew that the officers of the state had virtually driven the Mormons out of the Muddy Valley. I had occasion many times afterwards to ask myself the question, "Why did you make the venture?"[12]

Cox had quite an adventure with the examiners who, at first, did not want to give her the exam. They eventually agreed and brought her a test on chemistry, Latin grammar, and U.S. history, obviously intended for high-school teachers. She forcefully explained that the people of the area asked her to come and teach second grade to their children, implying that the examiners were being devious in attempting to exclude her. One examiner asked her which college she attended. The other quickly changed the question, asking her if there was a high school in St. George and whether she attended it. She replied, "Yes they do have a high school but the learning that has served me best in work as teacher was gotten outside of high school. I burned the midnight oil for it, as others have said who learned by the same method." She won the examiners over and began a series of years teaching in Nevada while her sister wives helped raise her children.

From today's vantage point, it appears that schools were not a high priority in pioneer Dixie because of the poor facilities and short terms. The actual case was quite the contrary, however; schools were among the citizens' highest concerns. Most towns set up a school before they built their own homes. The school building was the central community structure and was usually the site for church meetings, frequent dances, plays, and other socials.

In St. George the schools were quite small because there were four of them, one in each ward. They were not used for church meetings generally, so they could be smaller; but once the larger St. George Social Hall was constructed, it also hosted school classes. Josephine J. Miles has left a record of her childhood experiences in the St. George schools. She includes the names of many of the early teachers: Orpha Everett, James G. Bleak, Orson Pratt, Jr., Judge McCullough, a Mr. Kessler, a Brother Burgon, George Spencer, Samuel Miles, Eleanor Woodbury (Jarvis), Mariette Calkins, Sarah Clark (Crosby), Cornelia Lytle (Snow), and G. G. R. Sangiovanni were among the very earliest. Later teachers included John Macfarlane, Joseph Orton, a Sister Liston, Barbara Mathis, Annie McQuarrie, Mary Mansfield (Bentley), Richard Horne, Caddie Ivins McKean, Susa Young Gates, Seth A. Pymm, David LeBaron, Zina Clinton, a Mr. Schultz, a Mr. Peck, Martha Cox, a Mrs. Purse, Retta Cox, Ruth Fawcett, Emily Spencer, and Annie W. Romney. Miles wrote:

> Sister Orpha Everett was my first teacher in about 1872 or 1873. The school was held in the west room of her home. There were no conveniences of any kind — a four legged, long stool furnished seats. There were no desks, blackboards, charts or maps. We had few books, but were just past the stage of having an old Book of Mormon, or other Church book for a reader.

When our supply of slate pencils became exhausted, a hike to the foothills north followed, where by expert selection, the soft pieces of slate rock, suitable, were secured. We had good times together and chewed each other's gum in perfect friendliness, with never a thought of the dreadful disease germs later to be discovered.

Methods and equipment improved gradually, and about 1888, there was an appropriation from the State of 50 cents per student per term of twelve weeks. This gave a little cash to go along with our pickles, brooms, wood, molasses, etc., for we still had to collect our own pay from the parents, furnish our own wood, clock, brooms, etc., and hire our own janitors.

In 1890, the free school system was established, and the state paid the teachers. The schools were graded. This was more than a step forward — it was a bound. Prior to this, all grades were in one room, under one teacher, in each ward. This new system enabled the teachers to do better work with less exhaustion. Just imagine eighty-five pupils, of all grades, in the upper room of the Fourth Ward School House; three in a seat, when seated at all; many little ones sitting patiently around the edge of the platform. There was one small blackboard, no maps, charts, nor other apparatus. This was my experience one winter.

All of the schools were crowded. Strange as it may seem, some bright pupils advanced rapidly, and were good Third Readers at the end of their first year, and also could write nicely and do simple problems in arithmetic. They were graded by reading and we promoted them when we saw fit. We may not sympathize very deeply with the "overworked" teacher of today, although we know the requirements are greater. If the requirements then had been greater, we would not be here to tell the tale.

In 1894-5, I taught the Central School — the 5th and 6th grades and a class of left-overs. There were 119 enrolled. I had no assistant. There was no playground, nothing attractive nor convenient, but many inconveniences. The higher grades were taught by John T. Woodbury in the basement of the Stake Tabernacle.13

Administration of the schools was left to each community where school trustees were selected. It was their job to engage a teacher and provide a room for the teaching. There was no countywide school system that hired a cadre of teachers until much later. Each town was on its own. Since very few people had professional training to be teachers, trustees generally had to settle for someone who had the basic skills of reading and writing. Later a county superintendent of schools was appointed and began certifying teachers by administering a test to the prospective teachers. Although this was not uniformly done, it became the norm. Several of these tests have survived. One from 1887, for example, included the following questions:

> Conjugate the verb to write in the 3rd person, the singular and plural number, of all the tenses of the indicative mood. What are the leading industries in the U.S. and in what localities do we find their chief seats? A speculator bought 25 acres of land for $10,625, and after dividing it into 125 village lots, sold each lot for $250. How much did he gain on the whole? On each acre? On each lot?
>
> Physiology and Hygiene: What changes do the blood and the air undergo in the lungs? What forces propel the blood through the body? How does alcohol affect the blood and the heart? Why does not a fall hurt a child as much as a grown person?
>
> Geography: What produces the change of day and night, and the change of the seasons? Give some proofs of the rotundity of the earth. Name the great divisions of land and water and also give the races of people. Define the different kinds of government existing among men and state under what form of government we live.
>
> Orthography: How many sounds are in the English language and how are they represented? Give a few leading rules governing the use of capital letters. What does a difference of accent sometimes serve to do? Give an example.
>
> Education: Write an essay expressing your philosophy of Education.[14]

One of the candidate's examinations is found in the Dixie College Archives. It reads: "Care should be taken that the heart, as well as the brain, should be educated; if the latter is cared for to the neglect of the former, we will see the intellectual knave, destitute of the true object of education." It is interesting that the author (in 1887) saw Dixieites as a favored people.[15]

A report for Gunlock in 1882 gives the following picture: twentythree students were enrolled although only eighteen were attending. Another five of that age group were not enrolled. The value of the school included twenty-five dollars for the land, fifteen dollars for the furniture and $600 for the building. The report was signed by trustees Jeremiah Leavitt, Joseph S. Huntsman, James W. Hunt, and William E. Jones.

A budget report for the Pine Valley School District in the year 1884 shows an income of $341.65, with about half coming from tuition and half from territorial school apportionment. The male [full-time?] teacher was paid $200 and the female [part-time?] teacher $90. At the same time the town of Washington reported 102 students enrolled. Again, about half of its budget of $608 came from tuition and half from territorial taxes, with $385 being paid to one male teacher.16

By the 1880s a county superintendent took over the testing responsibility and even the job of visiting schools to make reports to the state, but the local trustees still did the hiring and were responsible for buildings and teachers' salaries.17

An alternative to this Mormon and state system came in the form of schools sponsored by Protestant churches. Nationally, several Protestant churches — particularly Presbyterian, Congregational, and Episcopalian — undertook to "Christianize" the Mormons. In their minds the practice of polygamy by Mormons was tantamount to their being infidels. While their representatives in Washington were pursuing legal means to eradicate the practice through Federal legislation, some churches undertook to proselytize Mormons back into mainline churches. Their strategy was to locate schools in Utah. They anticipated that parents would recognize the superiority of the Protestant schools and would want the best for their children. Once children came to the schools, perhaps the parents' confidence would be won over, and families could be brought back to Protestantism. Professionally-trained teachers were sent on missions to Utah. Congregations in the east collected funds to build schools and pay salaries. Many such schools were opened throughout the state.

Washington County was the scene of some such developments. Reverend A. B. Cort from Chicago came as a missionary to St. George in the 1880s. His welcome was not warm but he persisted, especially in establishing schools. Reverend Duncan McMillan had established Presbyterian schools elsewhere in Utah and soon accepted Cort's invitation to do so in Washington County. Young women were sent as missionaries to start schools: Virginia Dickey was the teacher in Washington, Fannie Burke taught in Toquerville, and a Miss Stevenson taught in St. George.

As statehood neared, Reverend Galen Hardy came to St. George where he and his wife enrolled seventy students from 1893 to 1898 when his mission ended. Reverend Clayton Rice took up the mission in 1908 and was well liked in St. George, but the congregation and school dwindled. He left in 1911 feeling that not much could be done in St. George, despite the friendships he had made.

Religion

Religion was a dominant element in the daily life of Washington County's people. It was the driving force, the purpose for creating this portion of Zion in the desert; it was the common bond that united the people not only in their villages but beyond them to the whole territory. The fusion of religion with all other elements of daily life was almost total. Often the commercial and political leadership overlapped with the religious hierarchy.

Education, entertainment, daily labor, family life, health and sickness, clubs, theater, celebrations, recreation, schools — all were pervaded by the religious convictions and values of the people. It was not institutional structures alone that produced this fusion; individual commitments to the shared religion were also important. With that common bond, the people regarded canal building, road construction, erecting dams, and creating civic structures — as part of building up Zion. Planning and enlisting work groups were often the subjects of religious meetings.

Life in a village Mormon ward was fairly communal. Though each family worked its own land, built its own shelter, and assumed responsibility for its own actions, there was much shared life. Perusing the minute books of the Hebron LDS Ward from 1872 to 1879, for example, one comes across the following entries:

> 27 Oct 1872 Z. Parker reported that his visits indicated that his half of the town was in good condition. J. Pulsipher said that his half was also but that he and Bro. Terry worked on a misunderstanding until well into the night and felt better.

> 26 Jan 1873 Teaching meeting. Encourage our women and girls to read good books and not waste much time with novels. Fast meeting well attended.

> 2 Aug 1874 Reported that Jacob Hamblin has built a fort on the Colorado River to keep Navajos from coming up to steal horses. 12 Feb 1875 Bishop Jones of Panaca, Director of the Washington [cotton] Factory visited, urging members to subscribe to the factory. $300 was raised.

2 March 1878 Bishop T. S. Terry admonished the members against taking a difference before a court of the land instead of a bishop's court. He decried such an instance in Salt Lake.

5 May 1878 Problem of wild horses eating up the range was discussed in Priesthood meeting.

9 June 1878 Priesthood meeting voted to have irrigation water four hours per lot this season.

29 August 1878 The bishop discussed some ill feelings between some of the brethren. This was talked over and everything was made right. "Good counsel was given by Bishop Terry and others, exhorting the brethren to try to live together in peace as a band of brethren and God would bless us."

16 November 1878 Bishop expressed gratitude for the superior harvest — 1700 bushels of grain "with which God has blessed us." He further presented the water ditch accounts, showing the tax per lot this season to be $3.50.18

If these entries seem to lack spiritual content, it is because they are minutes of the priesthood meeting rather than the sacrament services. Religion to these people included more than worship. It permeated relationships with each other, work, town policies, reading material, allocating labor, planning the harvest — virtually everything in the daily life of the people.

The word "counsel" surfaces often in the record. This refers to a dimension of the authoritarian lifestyle that characterized the Dixie community. It was common for members to "seek counsel" of those whom they sustained as their inspired leaders. They sought such counsel in decisions about staying in the area or moving elsewhere, about remaining as missionaries or asking for a release, about taking another wife or changing jobs. People were not required to seek counsel, but it was common. The "double edged" dimension of seeking counsel was that once one sought counsel, it was expected that one would follow it. The counsel was usually sensible, even gentle, but it was given in the context of the greater good for the whole group.

The people of Dixie were often anxious to ask for such advice from Erastus Snow. Even more valued was counsel from Brigham Young who was always willing to deal with personal requests. Elizabeth Wood Kane, non-Mormon wife of Colonel Thomas Kane, who helped negotiate the peace of the Utah War, accompanied Brigham Young on a

tour through the southern colonies. She described one of these regular
sessions where the Latter-day Saints came to seek counsel:

> I noticed that he never seemed uninterested, but gave an unforced
> attention to the person addressing him, which suggested a mind free
> from care. I used to fancy that he wasted a great deal of power in
> this way; but I soon saw that he was accumulating it. Power, I mean,
> at least as the driving wheel of his people's industry.[19]

Daily Religious Life

Lenora Cannon Gardner of Pine Valley provides a Mormon woman's view of life inside a Washington County LDS ward:

> Jan 5 fast day I went to fast meeting and to testimony meeting. I was
> appointed to hunt up something to go to the World's Fair. Jan 7 Went
> to Primary. Geo. started school [teaching]. Jan 12 Abraham Burgess
> came for me to go and help make his baby's clothes that was dead.
>
> Jan 14 I got up very poorly but I went to Primary and after supper Pa
> and I went to Celestias and to Jeters and spent the evening. Lizzie
> brought Halley home to stay allnight.
>
> Jan 15 Pa and I was invited to Sister Lloyds to selabrate Sister Slades
> birthday. went to meeting in afternoon and evening meeting.
>
> Jan 16 Comenced to sno. I cut Pa's blue flanel shirt it snowed 5 or
> 6 inches.
>
> Jan 21 Finished Angus shirt. Lizzie went to Alice's set her calico
> quilt together. I went to primary
>
> Jan 22 I went to meeting. Amanda Hale, Royal S. and John Chad
> was here for supper
>
> Jan 28 pleasent but cold boys took wagon and went to G.V [Grass
> Valley]. I was poorly did not go to Primary
>
> Jan 29 I was sick and did not go to meeting went in the evening.[20]

Seven days in thirty-one were devoted to attending religious meetings, the majority of them as an officer in the children's activities on
Saturdays. She dressed the body of one dead child for burial and con-
soled a girl whose mother died. She did washing for another twice,
made a fire at a neighbor's house, and "hunted up" a quilt to send to
the world's fair. She and her family made five visits to friends' homes
for social occasions and had overnight visitors in their home twice. It
was a full month in a communal setting. Weekday religious activities — a children's program called Primary — were held largely in

homes. Even Sunday School meetings were in homes. Monthly fast-and-testimony meetings held in the church on the first Thursday of the month were important to her as a time when members spoke of their own spiritual feelings. Her days and those of her female peers were punctuated by a regular routine of religious meetings.

There was another equally important side to Pine Valley religion: weddings, births, missionary farewells, deaths, reading clubs, spinning and sewing bees, caring and fasting for the sick, quilt-making sessions with sister neighbors, and above all, visiting. These activities often required considerable preparation and time away from home, dressing a body for a burial, helping as a midwife, gathering rags for rug-making, preparing food for a wedding. Relatives and friends often came for visits that lasted several days. All this was centered around religious sisterhood. In many ways it was a rich life; certainly it was a communal one. The residents took great pride in their Pine Valley community. The church building was a masterpiece and families were central to the religion.

Religious life in St. George was more institutionalized than it was in the villages. For one thing, the St. George preaching meetings were held in the tabernacle and often provided the occasion for hearing celebrated leaders such as Erastus Snow or many of the other apostles who traveled through. Visits from Brigham Young brought memorable sermons:

> Sunday 29 March 1874 Br Brigham spoke in the afternoon, quite lengthy for him, on a variety of subgects, [sic] showing that what we were entering into now was only the first step toward learning the order of Heaven, and the Lord wanted us to learn it that we might learn more and more, that after a while we might take another step, then another, and so on by faith until we should become aquainted with the order of heaven, and know how to conduct ourselves when we got there but at present pulling against each other as we wer[e] now doing, we would never enter into the Kingdom of our Father, and this step was the commencement of "Thy will be done on earth as it is in heaven." ....And again, as he has done time and time again, [he] counseled the saints to be selfsustaining and strive to make within themselves that which they needed, and urged them to entirely forego the fashions of the world and practice industry, economy, prudence and frugality, in all their ways of life, in diet, Clothing, labor etc. Said that the Prophet Joseph told him that Peo-

ple were very apt to take cold when sitting over closets [outhouses] when cold damp noisome air came up when attending to the wants of nature and more especially females. Made some sound and sensible remarks on eating and what to eat to promote health and longevity, also on sleep and sentitation [sanitation]. Remarked that he would like the people to study chemistry, astronomy, and kindred sciences that we might know and comprehend what we used and had to do with every day and learn the comp[o]nent parts of the elements that surrounded us and be able to make them subservient to the building up of the Zion of God in the last day. Said that the Earth on which we dwell was a mere speck among the vast creations of God, and the inhabitants of other worlds would fail to see it even with the most powerfull telescope we were in possession of. Showed the benefits that would arise from wearing clogs or wo[o]den bottomed shoes on this cold damp mineral ground, and gave many very useful hints on home and domestic economy.[21]

Charles Lowell Walker was a devoted Mormon. For a time he served as second counselor in a St. George bishopric, but most of the time his callings focused his efforts on visiting members in their homes, blessing them during illnesses, and teaching Sunday School. He was particularly active in bands, theatricals, lectures, and community celebrations for which he composed poems and songs. The picture we get from his wonderful journal is of a developing urban atmosphere — there were many cultural and religious events in St. George. He participated almost weekly in Erastus Snow's prayer circle, composed of the apostle's close associates. He attended several church functions each week and responded to them candidly in his journal. He read the Deseret News regularly, keeping up on international as well as national and territorial news. This is also reflected in his musings. As a result, he held passionate feelings against the so-called "enemies of the church" in Washington, D.C., who were escalating the legislative attack on polygamy. But most of his entries reported on meetings he attended, such as his following candid reactions to a conference:

Br Covington represented Washington Branch. Bore his testimony to the truth. Robt Gardener spoke of the Rise of St. George, on tithing, etc. The General Authorities of the Church were presented (in a bungling manner by Bishop McArthur) and unanimously sustained by the People. A good spirit and feeling prevails. The Church teams that Started from here last May for the Frontier to gather the Poor have just arrived looking pretty well. P.M. F B

Wolley gave some items concerning the death, murder of Dr King Robinson. He was the noted claim jumper, and no one seems to mourn his loss. Bishop Bunker spoke well of the Clara settlement. Br. Snow exhorted the saints in the outer Settlements to be watchful and guard against the attack of the redmen. Showed the course the government officials had pursued among this People. Exhorted the Saints to faithfulness, to read the scriptures and Serve God. The conference adjourned until the first Friday in May 1867. We had a good time and I believe the saints felt blest from the good teaching they received during the conference.22

Every few months a St. George Stake conference was held in the local tabernacle. Since Dixie was so isolated, very few people were able to travel to Salt Lake City to the semi-annual conferences of the Mormon church. The stake conferences thus served as the major religious gathering for people in Washington County. The meetings were held for three days — Saturday, Sunday, and Monday — which meant that members from distant communities had to stay overnight in St. George. This included people from the communities "up river" (Toquerville to Shunesburg) as well as those from Nevada and Arizona.

These occasions required formidable arrangements. People in St. George opened their homes and often hosted as many as twenty friends and relatives. Housewives cleaned their homes and cooked plenty of food ahead. One person recorded: "All cooking was done on a large scale and included dried corn (soaked and simmered to tenderness), baked beans, bottled fruit, rice pudding, etc. On Friday at least twenty-five pies and three or four kinds of cakes must be baked and stored in the screen-doored pastery cupboard on the south side of the pantry. The deep shelves held pies three deep."23 People camped out in yards and even on the town square. Church leaders from Salt Lake City as well as from the stake spoke in two meetings each day. The three days served as a time for many other dealings — commercial, cultural, and ecclesiastical. They were an important time for family visiting, even for courtships.

So the Dixie folks undertook their pioneering through a union of religion and society which reflected an inner expression. To many county residents if not most, religion was the most basic expression of their lives. They loved to dance, they flocked to the theater, they read books, they attended lectures, but all of that was supportive of and integrated into their religion.

Recreation

When the people of Dixie woke up each morning, they did not have to ponder long about what was ahead of them. Work was clearly the first priority and it dominated their lives. Survival was guaranteed for no one; however, people also needed some relief from work. Mary Bertha Wood Hall recorded her girlhood memories of fun times in Grafton:

> When I was a girl, even a little bit of a girl, we'd have to piece quilt blocks. We'd all get together after school almost every day. We'd have to piece two or three quilt blocks before we could play. When we'd get that done, we'd get up and play ball, run races, ride horses or just anything.

> When we were teenagers we had a lot of fun. We danced what you call old-time dances: Virginia Reel, Quadrille, Minuet, Three Step, Schottische, Danish Slide-off, Round dances and many others. When anyone would get married, we'd have a dance. It sure was fun. The dances were really started by us young kids, but the older people came just because they like to dance.

> The cowboys like to come to the dances, too. They worked out there at Canaan at the big cattle ranch, and Cane Beds. Oh, they loved Grafton. They would sing and dance. Oh, it was really a pleasure to have those guys come.

> Grafton had more music than any place I have ever seen. Nearly every night or every few nights, everybody in town with music would get out there in front of the school/church building and start playing. There would be accordions. They'd get on those steps and start playing, then everybody would come. Everybody would sing and everybody would dance. There was really a lot of pleasure that we got out of the hours we spent there.[24]

J. H. Jennings spent his boyhood in pioneer Rockville where he came as a lad in 1862 with his parents who he said "volunteered" to come. He dictated his childhood memories at an advanced age, focusing especially on the entertainments in the town:

> Our amusements were going to church once a week and dancing. Sam Kenner was the fiddler, he also liked to play the banjo and sing for us. We had very good times dancing barefoot on the dirt floor. The first winter, church was held in the Stock's dugout because it was the largest place available.

The next spring we built a bowery of cottonwood branches just west of Jacob Terry's log house. Here we held church and celebrations on the 4th and 24th of July, and whatever other amusements we had. We made swings on the cottonwood trees and went swimming in the river. There were few horses that first winter so we did very little horseback riding. Later when horses became more plentiful we spent what time we could horse racing and taking our best girl for a ride.

Sometimes we had an evening when we had a play or maybe it would be dialogues and songs and recitations. Charles N. Smith often read to entertain the crowd. After the program was over the benches would be pushed back and then we danced or had a spelling school. In spelling school we chose two leaders. They would stand facing each other and would take turns calling someone from the crowd to come up and stand by them until there would be two long rows facing each other. One person gave out the words, first to the leaders, then back and forth down the line. If you missed the word you had to sit down. The side that had someone standing last, won out.25

In St. George dancing was highly appreciated, though it was undertaken with greater resources. Charles Walker records: "Thurs 20 [January 18701 At work as usual. At night went to a united Musical Ball consisting of the St. George and Santa Clara Brass bands, the St. George choir, and the St. Geo. Martial Band. Spent the night in dancing, playing and singing. Got home about 2 o clock a.m."26

Another way of relieving the pressures of living in the heat and austerity was to make fun of it. Charles Walker also was a boon to Dixie for his sense of humor and poetic pen. He wrote songs and eulogies and verses for many occasions. The following is one of his most famous. St. George's mayor during the 1996 statehood centennial, Daniel D. McArthur, sings it from the podium whenever he gets a chance, so the present generation is learning it all over again:

ST. GEORGE AND THE DRAGON

Oh, what a desert place was this
When first the Mormons found it;
They said no white men here could live
And Indians prowled around it.
They said the land it was no good,
And the water was no gooder,

And the bare idea of living here,
Was enough to make men shudder.

Chorus
Mesquite, soap root, prickly-pears and briars,
St. George ere long will be a place
That every one admires.

Now green lucerne in verdant spots
Bedecks our thriving city,
Whilst vines and fruit trees grace our lots,
With flowers sweet and pretty.
Where once the grass in single blades
Grew a mile apart in distance,
And it kept the crickets on the go,
To pick up their subsistence.

Chorus

The sun it is so scorching hot,
It makes the water siz, Sir.
The reason why it is so hot,
Is just because it is, Sir.
The wind like fury here does blow,
That when we plant or sow, Sir,
We place one foot upon the seed,
And hold it till it grows, Sir.

Chorus[27]

Leone Russell McMullin records another pleasant diversion from the tedium of pioneer labor:

One fall Mother, Father, Uncle Lorenzo Russell, and myself, went out on Goose Berry Mountain to gather pine nuts. We came to an Indian camp, they were gathering nuts too, so they insisted on us roasting ours along with theirs. After they were roasted, they had us keep all we could get out of the cones, whether they were from our cones or not. Their methods of roasting them was to dig a shallow hole several feet across, pile the cones in the hole, covered with brush then cover with dirt and at several places around the mound the brush was set on fire, the dirt kept it from burning too fast and it heated the pile of cones enough to roast the nuts. After a long time, it was uncovered and the mound was surrounded by Indians with a shallow basket. A large rock [was used] to crack the cone open on a smaller rock for a hammer, the nuts were put in the shallow basket and tossed to winnow out trash and empty nut shells.[28]

The 24th of July (Pioneer Day) was a time to celebrate. Arthur K. Hafen records:

> I remember, as a boy in Santa Clara, sleeping on an outdoor deck and being awakened at daybreak by the roar of salutes fired in St. George, and hearing the reverberations and echoes along the hills. Old Glory was hoisted and music by string or brass band was brought to the home of every family by serenaders. In St. George it has been chiefly the martial band (fife and drum corps), but a brass band also played an important part in activities. This band was a community band, until later years the school sponsored a band. Other communities also had their martial band, which survived through the years.
>
> The patriotic meeting was spiced with wit and music, and was enthusiastically attended by everyone. Sports on the public square were attended just as enthusiastically, and old and young alike participated. Novelty races, such as sack races, egg races, potato races, nail driving by women, sewing buttons by men, and a great variety of sports made fun for all. Of course, refreshments were not forgotten, prominent among which was the large barrel of lemonade from which each in turn might quaff. Children danced to the tune of a fiddle with organ accompaniment in the afternoon, and in the evening the same musicians set the adults afire. They danced with zest, and really enjoyed it. All ladies present shared, in varying degrees, in the dance, for each fellow felt duty-bound to dance at least once with every girl present.[29]

Dixie Wine

Mormons of the twentieth century are widely known for their abstentious lifestyle, so the subject of wine making in Dixie is to some Mormons something of an embarrassment. Stories abound about Dixie wine, almost in the tone of revealing a forbidden secret. It certainly was not such to the early Dixie settlers. For example, John S. Stucki recorded in his autobiography:

> The main object of President Brigham Young in sending our people to Dixie was to raise cotton for the people to make clothing from. (There was no money to be obtained for very many years.) We also were to raise wine to be used for the Sacrament of this people, although water was used until this people could have wine of their own making which was to be the pure juice of the vine. I had the chance to furnish the first wine for the Holy Sacrament in Santa Clara, which was a great pleasure for me to have the right to do.[30]

The warm sandy soil of Dixie invites the vintner. Grapes thrive on the hillsides and bask in the summer sun. As a result, several villages specialized in raising grapes, especially Toquerville and Santa Clara, but people in Leeds and St. George and Washington were also proud of their grapes and active in wine making. The Dixie vintners learned quickly that wine making produced a saleable product that had many shipping advantages over bulky cotton bales. Wine not only was compressed into small packages but had a ready market. An obvious advantage of wine making was the proximity of mining camps where the product sold briskly. Pioche, Nevada, first provided a market and later Silver Reef became a boom town and a natural source for sales. John Conrad Naegle and his half-brother, Conrad Kleinman, learned the art of growing grapes and making wine in their youth in Europe. Naegle brought a wine press and distillery from California, and they became wine producers in Toquerville.

Cotton in its raw condition was not useful to anyone until it was milled, made into cloth, and then into clothes. Wine, of course, created its own problem; the lofty ideal of preparing sacramental wine was quickly diverted to social uses and then, unfortunately, frequently to overuse and drunkenness. And consumption was not confined to gentiles. The abuse of the sacrament was a constant source of tale telling. Some elderly gentlemen were reported to have sometimes taken three or four long sips of the wine as the sacramental cup was passed along the rows. Eventually problems with abuse caused church authorities so much frustration that they decided to end the use of wine for the sacrament and discourage any production of wine.

Wine and wine making have been a natural almost irresistible, source for folktales. Olive Burt, for example, combines the themes of polygamy, gentiles and wine making in this tale that conveniently makes its heroes and villains fit the local scene:

> Mother liked to tell about what happened to one ripening barrel in Toquerville. It was in the 1880's when U.S. government agents – deps - for deputies – were hunting men living in polygamy-cohabs. One of the most active deps was a fellow named McGeary. One night he came with an assistant named Armstrong to Toquerville to catch a cohab....McGeary told his aide to go around to the back to watch while he stayed in front: they'd sure catch the miscreant that way.

The second dep went around to the back of the small house.

There he saw a barrel with a canvas cover held tight with a hoop. He thought he'd step up onto this canvas to get a look in at the tiny window. But his weight dislodged the canvas, and down he went, kerplunk into the barrel. For only the briefest moment did he imagine he had fallen into the rain barrel. The fragrance of the ripening wine soon informed him. He climbed out, licked his chops, and then, using his cupped hands as a dipper, he went to work.

Some time later McGeary became curious about the stillness at the rear of the cottage. He tiptoed around, saw his companion stretched out on the ground fast asleep, took in the situation — and using his cupped hands as a dipper, went to work. The cohab and his plural spouse had an undisturbed night — and in the morning two red-faced deputies hurriedly left town.31

William B. Ashworth, speaking of drinking wine in St. George, said: "At the Sunday meetings the Bishop would inquire if there was anyone present who had over indulged during the week and wished to confess before partaking of the sacrament, they would have the privilege of doing so. Usually some of the elder brethren's consciences would smite them, and they would arise and confess to indulging a little too strongly. They were passed on each time and forgiven."32

Bob Naegle tells a story that took place when he was in the sixth grade in about 1907 or 1908. There were five fifty gallon barrels of wine in the tithing celler. In an effort to obtain some of the wine, a few of the youths in town broke out a window. Naegle continued:

A friend and I were the smallest kids in town and we could crawl through the window by getting our shoulders kittywhompas and the older boys lowered us to the floor. They told us to go over and pull out a hose down the barrel and blow on it a little bit until the bubbles came and then draw on it and put the end of the hose in a gallon jug. Dewey tried two or three times and couldn't do it. So I gave a big suck on it and got a mouthful of two or three swallows. We filled 4 or 5 jugs that way.33

All of this is folklore, which means that the tales may tell us as much of the teller as of the events. Certainly Dixie is a place where tale telling is a favorite pastime, and Dixie wine is a rich source of tales.

Polygamy

If wine making and wine consumption have generated many folk-tales, certainly polygamy has done the same. That form of marriage was not unique to Dixie, of course; it was a trademark of the early Mormon church. One practitioner of Dixie polygamy was Catharine Cottam Romney. As one of the "prettiest girls in St. George' according to her older brother George, Catharine attracted suitors and by her eighteenth birthday had a proposal for marriage. But she preferred Miles Romney, eleven years her senior, who was already married. He was an actor, master carpenter, orator, and budding community leader. Being Romney's plural wife was preferable to Catharine to having a husband her own age all to herself. Not a few young women believed that their eternal status depended a good deal on the spiritual level of their spouse; and an established leader seemed more attractive to many of them. Catharine is an example of those polygamous wives who preferred polygamy to monogamy. There were certainly polygamous wives who would have preferred a monogamous relationship and many who found plural marriage most taxing. But a reading of Catharine Cottam Romney's letters, recently published, makes it clear that she defended the practice not only loyally but insistently.

Stories told about polygamy are legion. One that captures the sympathy of some for plural marriage involves the cotton factory at Washington. A fondness has always been attached by many to the cotton mill and continues to this day. Many stories circulate about its social value. For example, C. L. Christensen from Sanpete County is supposed to have made a freighting visit to the mill. Upon his departure, his wife reportedly told him not to return without bringing back a second spouse! When Christensen arrived at the factory, he had plural marriage on his mind. There he discovered a golden opportunity: the score or more young women who worked in the factory usually took their lunches out to the nearby hill where they enjoyed their sandwiches and each other's company. When Christensen noticed this practice, he confidently strode toward the group, climbed up on a rock, and called for their attention. "I am C. L. Christensen from Sanpete. I will be here today and tomorrow and I am looking for a second wife. Take a good look. What you see is all I am. I am young and hard working and will accept inquiries the rest of the day here." Reportedly, he was able to communicate effectively because he rode away the next day with his new wife.[34]

Tales of eluding Federal marshals are told and retold today as humor. They portray the enigma of a generally law-abiding people who were opposed to the nation's polygamy laws. A favorite tale is told of Dudley Leavitt, a well-known husband of five wives, who was surprised while bringing in a load of cotton to the cotton mill. One of the young girls at the front desk saw Federal marshals McGeary and Armstrong drive up; she yelled to Leavitt to run and hide. Leavitt figured that to hide would not work. Grabbing a cap and oil can from a machinist, he donned a worker's hat and began actively oiling the machinery. He climbed a ladder and crawled along a top scaffold and worked diligently, clearly in sight. The officers shifted the cotton about, kicked boxes, looked in barrels, and looked for trap doors, but they found no polygamists.

The families who practiced polygamy in Washington County chose one of several options for their domestic arrangements. Sometimes families lived together in one house. Certainly the census records show several cases where two families were in one home. Another choice was for the families to live in separate houses in the same neighborhood or town — a preferable choice where wives did not get along well. Catherine Cottam Romney's account of her family described both systems at differing times. She first enjoyed living with one of the senior wives; later on, when another wife was brought into the family, the relationship did not develop closely and she lived separately. At one time, during their residence in Arizona, Romney's wives lived in three houses, all on the same block. Yet another arrangement was for families to be housed in different towns. Jacob Hamblin located one wife and her children at his Mountain Meadows ranch while two other wives lived in Santa Clara in the same home.

When the Manifesto was announced in 1890 by Mormon church president Wilford Woodruff, withdrawing permission for further polygamous marriages, many families in Dixie welcomed it; they were exhausted by the long Federal prosecution of polygamists.

Others felt a loyalty to "the Principle" and were not pleased with the decision to suspend the system. Polygamy did not end immediately; it required several years for families to adapt.

ENDNOTES

1. Thomas D. Brown, *Journal of the Southern Indian Mission*. Ed. Juanita Brooks (Logan, Utah: Utah State University Press, 1972), 10.

2. Ibid., 44-45.

3. Juanita Brooks, "Indian Sketches from the Journals of T. D. Brown and Jacob Hamblin," *Utah Historical Quarterly 29* (October 1961): 356.

4. Brown, Journal, 43.

5. Ibid., 23.

6. Pearson Corbett, *Jacob Hamblin, The Peacemaker* (Salt Lake City: Deseret News Press, 1952), 270.

7. "Biographical Sketch of Elethra Calista Bunker, 1859-1901" (St. George: WPA, 1938), 7.

8. "Biographical Notes from the Life of Joseph I. Earl, 1852" (St. George: WPA, n.d.), 42.

9. Louise Leavitt Engstrom, "Island in the Stream: Anderson's Ranch, 1884-1984," 11, 15, unpublished manuscript, Dixie College Archives.

10. "Biographical Record of Martha Cragun Cox," Dixie College Archives, 48.

11. Mary Ann Hafen, *Recollections of a Handcart Pioneer*, (Denver: Privately published, 1938), 36-37, 39, 40-41, 47.

12. Cox, "Biographical Record," 74.

13. Josephine J. Miles, "History of Education in St. George," paper read at Daughters of Utah Pioneers, St. George Chapter, 28 January 1923. Miles lists others who taught in early St. George: Louise Worthen, Elida Crosby, Elizabeth Snow, Martha Cox, Josephine Snow, Mary E. Cook, Laura Gardner, Mame Ashby, Alice Worthen, Mr. J. A. Whitelock. After 1885 the teachers she remembers in St. George included Eliza Lund, Andrew Winsor, M. M. Harmon, Mary Redd, Isabell McArthur, Annie Cottam (Miller), Mary Nixon, Martha Snow, Zaidee Walker, Mary Judd, Mr. Romney, Eva Cannon, Mary DeFriez, Edith Ivins, Julia Sullivan, Mary Judd, Ella Jarvis, Charles A. Workman, Louisa Cox, Rachel Cottam, Kate Kemp, Mary Thompson, Jennie Lund, Josephine Jarvis, Rosina Jarvis, John T. Woodbuiy, Sr., Nephi M. Savage, and Lena Nelson.

14. "Tests to Teachers, and Some Scores," in Schools and Education folder, Dixie College Archives.

15. Ibid.

16. "School Trustees Annual Financial Report, 30 June 1884," in Schools and Education folder, Dixie College Archives.

17. Superintendents in Washington County prior to 1915 included George A. Burgon, 1868-72; Joseph E. Johnson, 1872-77; Miles P. Romney, 1877-81; Adolphus R. Whitehead, 1881; Moroni Snow 1881-83; Joseph Orton, 1883-85; John T. Woodbury, 1886-91; Levi N. Harmon, 1891-1900; Charles A. Workman, 1901-07; Edward H. Snow, 1907-08; W. O. Nisson, 1909-12; and Charles B.

Petty, 1913-15.

18. "Hebron [ward] Record," II, 134-40.

19. Elizabeth Wood Kane, *Twelve Mormon Homes* (Salt Lake City: Tanner Trust Fund, 1974), 101.

20. "Journal of Lenora Cannon Gardner," Dixie College Archives.

21. Walker, *Diary*, I, 385.

22. Ibid., 271-72.

23. See L.D.S. Conferences in Utah's Dixie, in "Histories and Stories," typescript, Dixie College Archives, 30.

24. Mary Bertha Wood Hall, "Excerpts from the Life of Mary Bertha Wood Hall," *Honoring our Ancestors* (Hurricane, UT: Homestead Publishers, 1988), 54-55.

25. "Life Story of J. H. Jennings," as told to Anna Jennings Wood in 1940. Dixie College Archives.

26. Walker, *Diary*, I: 305.

27. Ibid., 369.

28. James T. Jones, "Old Grafton," unpublished manuscript, Dixie College Archives.

29. Arthur K. Hafen, *Dixie Folklore and Pioneer Memoirs* (n.p.: published privately, 1961), 16-18.

30. *Family History Journal of John S. Stucki, Handcart Pioneer of 1860* (Salt Lake City: Pyramid Press, 1932), 52.

31. Olive W. Burt, "Wine-making in Utah's Dixie," *Lore of Faith and Folly*, ed. Thomas E. Cheney (Salt Lake City: University of Utah Press, 1971), 145-52.

32. Dennis R. Lancaster, "Dixie Wine," *Sunstone 3* (Summer 1976): 81.

33. Dennis R. Lancaster, "Dixie Wine," Master's thesis, Brigham Young University, 1972, 96-105.

34. "A Hint to Young Men in Search of Wives," *Utah Historical Society, 29* (July 1961): 299-300.

6

Cultural Life

Theater

The isolation of Washington County meant that the residents were dependent mainly on themselves for any form of "high culture" — music, theater, literature. Fine arts would have to be generated largely in Dixie. If there were to be drama, it could not come from outside. No railroad would bring a troupe; roads were so bad that few bards would wander by. Either Dixie would be a cultural desert or the people would have to create a life of enlightenment themselves.

In St. George, theater productions quickly became an expression of cultural life. A core of devotees grew into the St. George Dramatic Association, including Miles Park Romney, Charles Lowell Walker, Joseph Orton, Sarah Clark, Mary Romney, R. C. Lund, E. G. Woolley, G. A. Burgon, and many others. Regular productions began in the Bowery and moved to the St. George Hall as soon as it was completed in late 1863. The players preferred the basement of the Tabernacle after it became available. Then they shifted to the winery and its 1875 addition, the Social Hall.

Theater was not a church calling, however. It was a self-initiated community effort of those who had the inner desire to act. Such folks

St. George Opera House/Social Hall, constructed in 1875 and 1880, was a major culture center for the Dixie community. (Lynne Clark Collection, donor — Orpha Morris)

found each other, then organized an amateur acting company. Individuals such as Joseph Orton initially and A. W. Ivins and C. E. Johnson later stood out as crucial in the tasks of organizing, obtaining scripts, and even directing. Joseph Orton was most important for the first decade or two of theater in St. George. He kept a distinguished group together from 1862 to 1877, and some of those people continued on after that with a new generation. Actors included Artemisia Snow Seegmiller, Jacob Gates, Susa Young Gates, Dan Seegmiller, Horatio Pickett, and E. G. DeFriez. This was a dynamic group that became very popular, staging productions regularly and drawing large audiences.

The core group of thespians was amazing in its staying power and excitement for its members' avocation. Later, as each group of players began to tire, a new one seemed to appear. The second group of players was as impressive as the first. They undertook to add a large wing on the already enlarged winery. By 1880 that addition was completed, seating as many as 400 people (it seats only 200 today). The building came to be called the "Opera House," and productions featured another new group of thespians: Frank Snow, Joseph Bentley, John T. Woodbury, Ashby Snow, Brigham Jarvis, and Martha Snow Keate.

Most actors stayed with their avocation for several seasons, some for more than a decade. They developed a popular following, becoming local celebrities. Among them were Sarah Clark, Mary Romney, Joseph Orton, Miles P. Romney, and Tony Ivins. The casts of the varied plays also included many well-known citizens such as Judge McCullough, Artemisia Snow (Seegmiller), George Brooks, A. R. Whitehead, J. F. Gates, C. E. Johnson, James G. Bleak, Charles Lowell Walker, Erastus Snow, Orson Pratt, Jr., Frank Woolley, R. C. Lund, G. A. Burgon, and at least a hundred more. Some of their children, such as Zaidee Walker and several Bleaks, also appeared in later years.

In 1895 yet another cadre came on the scene in a series of short-lived local companies: The Clark Theatrical Company, Higgins Brothers Theatrical Company, John S. Lindsay Company, Lyceum Dramatic Company, and St. George Dramatic Company. The latter included Charles Whipple, W. A. Nelson, John T. Woodbury, Arthur Miles, Brigham Jarvis, Jr., Martha Snow Keate, and Walter Keate. Their vitality kept the theatricals in production until 1910 when they gave way to the new Dixie College, which staged performances, especially musicals, in the Opera House until about 1927. Thereafter, the college productions moved to the Dixie College building, and in 1930 the Opera House was sold to Utah-Idaho Sugar Company to serve as part of a sugar-beet-seed factory. That building was restored in 1995 and is being used once again as a cultural facility in the center of town.

For almost fifty years, various home-grown dramatic organizations presented theater pieces at least monthly, often as much as every other week. There was probably more theater produced in St. George then than there is now, even with all the high school and college productions of the present day. One does not have to search far for a reason to explain the decline — the advent of motion pictures. After 1910 the Opera House was used for a while to show moving pictures as well as for staging college musicals.

The theater had an impact in the lives of both the actors and the audiences. It was an important feature of pioneer Dixie society. Audiences were large, actors were well-known adult citizens, and the corps of performers succeeded through three generations. It was common

Cast of one of the early productions performed in the Social Hall. (Lynne Clark Collection, donor – Edna Cloward)

for them to perform in Silver Reef where there were large, boisterous audiences who appreciated the performances. St. George drama groups also performed at Washington, Leeds, and elsewhere. Mainly, however, people saw them perform in their St. George theater.

Initially the performances featured farces and vaudeville type melodramas including *The Drunkard's Wife*, *The Farmer's Daughter*, *All That Glitters Is Not Gold*, *The Yankee in Cuba*, and *Rough Diamonds*. These were the products of the St. George Dramatic Association which was founded in 1864 with Franklin B. G. Woolley as manager; James G. Bleak, director; William A. Branch, prompter; and Thomas Crane, doorkeeper. A perennial favorite was *The Golden Farmer*.

Occasionally an outside influence affected Dixie theater. Charles J. Thomas came from Salt Lake City to give instruction to the thespians. He remained in town for several weeks and was warmly received. In 1879 the Harris Comedy Company included St. George, as well as Silver Reef on its tour, but mainly theatrical performances were done by local players. The theater provided mostly light entertainment, focusing on comedy, farce, and melodrama.

One of the area's popular young actors, Anthony W. Ivins, later became a successful rancher, mayor of St. George, LDS apostle and a member of that church's First Presidency. In a talk to students, he reflected on his days on the stage:

> Among other things we had dramatics in those days [early days of St. George]. I chanced to be one of the performers, and my wife here another. We were playing "East Lynne." If the College hasn't played it, I will bring my family up to see it if you will put it on in Logan. We were so successful with it in St. George that we took it up to Silver Reef. A great number of Cornishmen had been brought to work in the mines there. The house was crowded with people. I was playing the part of Sir Archibald, and my wife's sister was playing Lady Isabel. When it came to the part where Lady Isabel on her knees pleads for forgiveness (of course I had to be the stern husband who reprimanded her for the mistake she had made), there walked down the aisle a big Cornishman with his sleeves rolled up to his elbows, who shook his fist at me and said: "Damn you, forgive her!"

> Later, in another play, were in a complication on the stage which indicated that I had been the individual who had gone off with some money which did not belong to me. (Of course it was apparent to the audience that I was entirely innocent.) It looked bad for me, however, until a boy jumped on one of the seats and shouted: "Tony didn't take it! That man over there took it!"[1]

The achievement of the players was amazing — maintaining a full season each year for five decades, stimulating the community to construct a building, and drawing full audiences while maintaining their own employment, family, and church responsibilities. The community needed this entertainment as a diversion from the toil of Dixie living, and the leaders knew it. Perhaps that is a major reason the theater enjoyed regular support. The cadre of theater players reads like a Dixie Who's Who. The theater, for both thespians and audiences, declared that Dixie was a focal point. It may have been isolated, but it was not insignificant. The nation may not have known about Dixie, but its people were creating civilization there. St. George was a city in the making. Communities in Arizona, Nevada, and southern Utah recognized it as a city, for the accoutrements of civilization were thriving — the temple, the tabernacle, and the theater.

Music

If theater was a spontaneous outgrowth of the people of the county, music was both an effort initiated by the common people and a program planned by Mormon church leaders. Brigham Young and George A. Smith knew that life was going to be hard in Dixie. They planned right from the start for diversions to make life more bearable. One was music. For that reason Charles John Thomas was called to St. George in November 1865. He stayed until May 1868 and organized a choir, a brass band, and a children's choir. He also gave private lessons.

A self-initiated choir under the direction of James Keate existed before Thomas arrived, starting within weeks of the pioneer company's arrival in late 1861. A brass band appeared in St. George too. It was short-lived but was just the first of many that followed.

Santa Clara was the home of a famous brass band. In 1864 John R. Itten inherited several band instruments which he gave to the community of Santa Clara. This enabled George Staheli, a talented coronet player from Switzerland, to organize a first-rate band which at times included John G. Hafen, Charles Hildebrandt, Gottlieb Bliggensdorfer, Henry Kuhn, Sr., Bastian Strausser, Herman Bosshard, John Keller, Jacob Bosshard, George Staheli, Jr., and John Staheli. For a long time George Staheli had to copy music from various sources to provide scores for the players. The Staheli band became known widely, especially because it often played at Fourth of July celebrations and welcoming ceremonies for dignitaries as they entered St. George. Staheli also organized a Swiss choir that became well-known, often performing for stake conferences in the tabernacle. The choir usually sang in the German language. Brigham Young and other leaders could not understand the words, but they applauded the choir. Both the choir and band quickly brought acclaim to Dixie.

Bands were also a trademark of Washington City. It took a community effort to obtain instruments. Around 1910 the band won a first-place rating at the Washington County Fair. At that time, its members included Frank Staheli, Emmeline Sproul, Angus Sproul, Mazel Sproul, Edward Nisson, Willard O. Nisson, Della Nisson, Israel Neilson, Ina Neilson, James Cooper, LaMar Pearce, LaFayette Jolley, Byron Barron, and Clinton Averett. This and other bands did a lot for the community spirit at holiday celebrations and dances.

In St. George, John Eardley organized a band in 1868. William H. Thompson became its leader in 1877. He also organized a juvenile band which continued until 1902 when Woodward School came into existence and took on the tradition.

The Thompson Band, an early musical group.
(Lynne Clark Collection, donor — Archie Wallis)

John M. Macfarlane was brought to St. George from Cedar City by Erastus Snow, specifically to continue the work of Professor Charles Thomas after he moved to Beaver in 1868. Macfarlane trained a choir which continued until 1885 for the St. George Tabernacle. That choir became a central part of the community, singing at the tabernacle and temple dedications, stake conferences, annual holidays, funerals, and once at Brigham Young's birthday celebration. The choir was not large, usually between fifteen and twenty singers, but it was well trained. Initially the membership included Mary Ann Sullivan, Emma and Eleanor Adams, Artemisia and Elizabeth Snow, William McAllister, Joseph Orton, William Kemp, Horatio Pickett, William O. Miles, Maggie and Eleanor Jarvis, Louis Worthen, Annie McQuarrie, Barbara Mathis, Mary Worthen, and others.[2]

Two rather famous events occurred during John M. Macfarlane's tenure as choirmaster that are often retold in the folklore of Dixie. The first was when his tabernacle choir cooperated with Reverend Lawrence Scanlan of Silver Reef by learning a Catholic mass in Latin and performing it in the St. George Tabernacle.[3] The second signal event in the Macfarlane years of music was the composition of a simple hymn for Christmas. Wanting to do something special for a Christmas choir concert, Macfarlane asked Charles Lowell Walker to prepare verses he could set to music, which was a natural thing to do because Walker composed poetry for almost all civic celebrations. Walker brought

Macfarlane some words but the composer did not sense a melody to match them. Macfarlane tossed and turned one night in bed and then suddenly an idea came to him. He woke his wife and dictated both words and music to her until the song was completed. That Christmas the choir proudly performed an original hymn, "Far, Far Away on Judea's Plains." The song did not gain immediate recognition but has gradually been included in many Christmas collections in the English-speaking world. It is included in LDS hymnals and is now a standard part of Mormondom worldwide.

John M. Macfarlane left St. George in about 1885 after serving as a local judge for several years. He was followed in his music assignments by Horatio Pickett and later by Joseph Warrington McAllister. Both offered classes in reading and singing music for the general public. His son, Joseph William McAllister, took over the stake choir, became a music teacher at the St. George Stake Academy when it opened, and directed musicals in the Opera House. The opening of the Woodward School in 1901 provided an opportunity for music training for all young people up to the eighth grade. Instructors included Mary Lund Judd, A. L. Larsen, Henry Otti, and Joseph W. McAllister.

When the St. George Opera House was completed in 1880, theater productions took most of its space, but musicals occasionally were produced. These included *H.M.S. Pinafore* in 1886 and 1889, and *Rob Roy McGregor*, *Under the Palms*, *Queen Esther*, and *Children of Israel Wandering About in Egypt* in 1891. Woodward School musicals were also presented there, *The Merry Milkmaids*, *Priscilla*, and *Olivette* between 1906 and 1908, for example. These productions gradually gave way to a prolific series of musical productions presented by the St. George Stake Academy (later Dixie College) after its founding in 1911.

The years of the academy/college in downtown St. George from 1911 to 1963 brought forth a major musical tradition. The names of William Staheli (band), Joseph W. McAllister (choir), and Earl J. Bleak (band-orchestra) are linked to the importance of music in Dixie. Professor McAllister produced many operas while Professor Bleak supported that effort as well as organized dance bands, marching bands, and an orchestra. Stella Christian Bleak served as the piano accompanist for many of the musical productions. Thus, by the time Washington County had passed the turn of the century, much of the county's musical life moved into the schools where it still thrives. Today the high schools in the county feature bands, choirs, and musical productions that draw large audiences. The college expands upon that tradition with theater, musicals, choirs, bands, symphony, and a community concert series.

Newspapers

One of the most amazing appearances in the dry desert of Dixie was an early manuscript newspaper. Given to serious reflection, humor, history, and news, this handwritten circular, *The Vepricula*, appeared on 1 May 1864 and continued bi-weekly for a year. It was the product of a group of men whose minds were compelled to expression even though their lives were quite occupied with survival needs. They met before each edition appeared to critique each other's efforts and prepare the final copy. Evidently the newspaper circulated, because on one occasion the writers urged their readers to pay a modest fee in kind. We have no way of knowing how widely the copies circulated.

The authors wrote with classical pseudonyms, a device quite common in literary circles in America at that time. Orson Pratt, Jr. wrote as "Veritas," George A. Burgon was "Signor," Joseph Orton signed himself "Cerus," G. G. R. Sangiovanni was "Ego," and Charles Lowell Walker "Mark Whiz." All five of these people were also active in the theater. Several of their articles were philosophical examinations of timeless themes: Hope, Evil, Association, the Will, Reason and Faith, Reading, Writing. Their reflections are as pertinent today as then. For example, consider this lofty paragraph:

> The anxious student should sedulously cultivate the art of composition, for by its assistance he learns to collect and arrange those items of useful information which are the real foundation of erudition. A man cannot become a good politician, a statesman, an author, nor a philosopher, until he has formed his opinions, and established them as criteria whereby to direct his future actions; and this disideratum is best obtained by carefully analyzing general principles, and giving on paper an originality to the result.[4]

Some editorials were much less high-minded: "Washington County is rough and uninviting in many respects. Yet if we will adapt ourselves to the surrounding circumstances we need not want for the common comforts of life....I hear individuals complain of hard living, who fail to provide themselves with dried fruits, beans, peas, and corn, and make no effort to have turnips, carrots, and parsnips, for winter's use."5

There were articles on principles of government and free speech. In October 1864 the paper announced the beginning of the season's lyceum series which featured debating clubs. On 15 May 1865, Cerus reported on his visit to outlying schools and a proposal for joint text-book purchasing. Veritas produced an essay, "Musings," which was a rationale for optimism. He argued that people have within them the power of response to the world about them. Some have a tendency to shirk from the unknown and to see death lurking at the end of each tun-nel. He felt that early training was fundamental so people did not live placidly, allowing life to come upon them. Mental effort can transform life and is as important as physical effort, according to the author.

In the early period, a most unusual publication appeared, *The Min-eral Cactus*. Edited by G. G. R. Sangiovanni, one of the original five writers in *The Vepricula*, its title was soon shortened to *The Cactus*. It was printed at the shop of the newspaper *Our Dixie Times*. The editor devoted the publication mainly to humor although its editorials were usually straightforward.

One of the more interesting men in early Dixie was Joseph Ellis Johnson. Known as an expert nurseryman and one who encouraged fruit growing, Johnson was also the promoter of several newspapers (as well as other endeavors including being a notary and a producer of medications). *Our Dixie Times* began in January 1868 under his sponsorship and was renamed the *Rio Virgin Times* in May of that year. By 1870 Johnson shifted his efforts to the *Utah Pomologist and Gardener*, which united his nursery and journalistic interests. That paper in turn added the title *Silver Reef Echo* to its masthead. As min-ing began to boom, the *Echo* became independent and appeared six days a week.

Joseph Carpenter seems to have taken up the publishing task fol-lowing J. E. Johnson. He experimented with a couple of efforts as a teenager and then in 1878 produced the *Union*. It was renamed the *Union and Village Echo* in 1882. In 1879 Carpenter undertook a daily called the *Evening Telegram* which lasted only briefly.

John R. Wallis produced a weekly, the *Washington County News*, from 1898 to 1900. He resurrected it in 1908 and continued to publish it until 1933. In the interim period, D. U. Cochrane of Oregon bought the *Washington County News* and published the *Dixie Falcon* for a year before leaving the area. The *Dixie Falcon* was largely a political paper with news from the national scene as well as from local correspondents in the county towns. Its discussion of water reclamation in the West could be timely today: "The West contributes to eastern improvements. Why should not the converse hold good?" The editor opined that eastern states were not losers through western reclamation — a fairly timely view but only popular in the West. According to the writer: "The benefit of a comprehensive system of government irrigation works to the arid west can hardly be underestimated, and it is high time the West was waking up to the situation, and doing its share towards getting Congress to take action."[6]

The railroad was a major topic. In addition to listing the special rates for conference round-trips to Salt Lake City (from Lund $7.50, from Modena $9.25, and from Urvada $10.00), the paper continued:

> Some seem to think that it is a foregone conclusion that the railroad is coming through here. Nothing could be more foolish than this thought and nothing more fatal to the chance of that event happening. Along other possible routes people are bestirring themselves in putting forward the advantages which their route affords and in no uncertain tones either. They want the railroad. So do we. The good things do not come without an effort. Something should be done in regard to this at once.[7]

The *Washington County News* entered the journalism scene in 1908 and continued to publish until 1988 under several different owners. It is a prized possession for Washington County, a source for much of the county's twentieth century history.

There were other short-lived papers, the *Southern Star* in 1895, the *Dixie Falcon* in 1901, the *Dixie Advocate* also in 1901 which was renamed the *Virgin Valley Enterprise* about 1907.

The *Tri-State Advertiser*, a weekly, began in 1963. In 1972 it became the *Southern Utah Free Press and Southern Utah News-Advertiser*. In 1972 it was sold to Gail Stahle and renamed the *Color Country Spectrum*, becoming a daily in 1976. Stahle in turn sold it to Thomson Newspapers of Toronto, Canada. It continues as the daily newspaper of Washington and surrounding counties and is now named the *Daily Spectrum*. In 1992 Tom Backman published a few issues of the *Red Desert Digest* as a competitor to the Spectrum, but that paper did not survive.[8]

One factor that made the existence of newspapers difficult in pioneer times was obtaining newsprint. Without railroads in the county to bring in newsprint, it was not easy to remain in production. Costs were high. Advertising was hard to obtain. People had little money, so it was difficult to get subscribers. There was no shortage of writers and venturers who wanted to produce newspapers, but sustaining one was difficult. This helps explain why, with a dozen efforts between 1864 and 1908, only one newspaper sustained production for the next eighty years.

Books and Discussions

As early as 1864 there was an attempt to establish a library in St. George. The territorial legislature authorized the establishment of such a book repository. Key citizens were named to a library board; they included Orson Pratt, Sr., Erastus Snow, Franklin B. Woolley, Angus M. Cannon, Jacob Gates, Orson Pratt, Jr., and James G. Bleak.[9] This library board maintained a small collection of books in the St. George Hall and even sponsored lectures. The books were obtained from private subscription funds.

The modest library appears to have been moved to the Lyceum building nearby on Main Street when the LDS Mutual Improvement Association agreed to take over care of the books about 1875. The Lyceum had housed a bakery that was built during the construction of the tabernacle and temple. When construction finished, the bakery building became available and was deeded to the Mormon church's Relief Society and the Mutual Improvement Association. It was remodeled and rededicated in 1884, with a reading room included. The books were to be read in that room rather than circulated.

A more ambitious library had to wait until 1910. The state legislature had authorized cities of the third class to levy a one-mill tax for the use of libraries. Mayor George F. Whitehead proceeded to establish a library in conjunction with the St. George Stake Academy which was then under construction. A room in the college building was devoted to a library and the books were moved from the Lyceum to the Academy. The next mayor, Thomas Judd, applied to the Carnegie Foundation for $8,000 to build a separate library building located west of the tabernacle. The city added $4,000 to the budget and by 1916, the next mayor, James McArthur, also serving as library board president, saw the project finished. In 1919 Mayor Albert B. Miller facilitated the transfer of the library to the supervision of the Washington County Commission, and it became a county facility.[10]

Throughout the pioneer period, there were occasional public lectures. The Seventies Quorum of the LDS church sponsored some, and a short-lived "School of the Prophets" was instituted in 1868 to include members from Washington, Santa Clara, and St. George. These two endeavors were closely tied to ecclesiastical leadership. The next generation ventured more on its own, establishing the St. George Literary Society in January 1894. Andrew Karl Larson described the society's activities as focusing mainly on literature and politics.[11] Society members read Welch's English Literature together and discussed parts of it at each meeting. The minutes book includes the members' names: Fred Woolley, Kate Kemp, Edith Ivins, Elias Kemp, Walt Adams, Alex Andrus, Tom Andrus, Louie Woolley, Lizzie Lund, George Lund, Mary Morris, Louie Miles, Morgan Thurston, Harry Thurston, W. G. Miles, By Ashby and Maud Snow. Alma Nelson, E. G. Whitehead, and Alonzo Clark apparently joined later. The Literary Society evolved into the Utah Club which became more of a debating society, focusing on a study of the U.S. Constitution.

Journal Writing

Since survival was the chief concern during the 1852 to 1877 period, people of Washington County Dixie turned most of their efforts to hard physical labor: work to bring water to the land, work to make the land produce both food and cotton, work to build civic structures, homes, and roads. It was a time of toil. The years that followed to 1930 demanded continued physical labor because the yield from the land was so sparse, the roads so desperately hard to improve, the freighting so challenging in the heat and sand, the range so vast for animals to graze, the water so minimal to store for the driest seasons, the food so scarce to feed the many mouths in large families. Work seemed to dominate life.

Work, however, was not the whole story. In fact, the traces those generations left behind are balanced between work and words. Words emerged in the form of celebrations, choirs, bands, poetry, newspapers, sermons, letters, journals, drama, and songs (to say nothing of meeting minutes, legal documents, surveying notes, and other civil records). Humane letters poured forth right from the start, especially in journals.

James G. Bleak was perhaps the first case in point. When Brigham Young organized the Southern Utah Mission in Salt Lake City in 1860, he selected a diverse group with many trades that would create a balanced community. Bleak was called to be clerk of the mission. He was assigned to keep a journal of the venture. That was but the start of his writing of words.[12] Bleak was a man of official written words. His words survived — in city council minutes, church council records, court records, business records, and especially in his journal of the Southern Utah Mission which he compiled from those records. The settlement of Dixie is documented as richly as was the Philadelphia Convention, as solidly as was Puritan New England.

Today we have a score or more of magnificent journals where words speak to us — words from those who labored by day and wrote by night. John D. Lee, for example, was a man of action, an entrepreneur par excellence. He bought and sold, built and farmed, freighted and repaired, but somehow he also was impelled to write. He was a great booster of Dixie in the earliest days. He presided over a large family and had many sons engaged in his far-flung enterprises. He dealt with Indians as well as Salt Lake authorities. He was a judge and a legislator. All of this stands quite apart from the single event, the Mountain Meadows Massacre, for which history judges him.[13]

One powerful journal such as John D. Lee's is special for any community, but there are more. Charles Lowell Walker provides a counterbalance to Lee. Walker was a follower, not a leader; an aesthete, not a merchant; a reflective creator, not a commander. Walker was a town dweller, Lee a man on the move. Introspective and spiritual, Walker was also one of the strugglers who never accumulated a surplus, while Lee quickly became affluent from his wide-ranging industry. Both, however, were men of words. Lee's boomed from every pulpit he saw and every marching field he commanded. Walker wrote from the back pews and in the late nights. His poetry gradually won the hearts of the whole colony and his songs became their vehicle for ritual and celebration. Here were men of words, worthy of the American Revolution or the Civil War, who just happened to be isolated. Their words are largely unknown in America, but their quality is worthy of the dreams they express.

There are also many more: Thomas D. Brown, who recorded the Southern Indian Mission and also protested John D. Lee's authoritarian leadership at Fort Harmony; Jacob Hamblin, whose prose belied his limited education but whose adventures with the Indians are more powerful than legends; Orson Huntsman, whose six volumes make record of a life he claimed was insignificant as he wandered from town to town, but who eventually transformed Shoal Creek by building the Enterprise Reservoir; Martha Cragun Cox, who was a perceptive school teacher and polygamous wife; William Ellis Jones, another struggler who never acquired enough to bountifully support his family, who taught school, made bricks, raised fruit, and served in the Gunlock bishopric, and who at times anguished but loyally followed the faith; Joseph Fish, whose extensive record of Enterprise was but one of his achievements in pioneering; Lenora Cannon Gardner, who brings a full description of women's lives in Pine Valley including midwifery, weaving, visiting, religious instructing, and building community cohesion; Mary Ann Hafen, who recorded her girlhood in Santa Clara; Levi Savage, who farmed and traded with Silver Reef, was involved in continuing disputes in Toquerville, dodged Federal marshals, and went to prison for polygamy.

These were people of words — in journals, songs, lectures, newspapers, and drama. They were writing to us. Their sense of destiny was clear. Seldom did ambivalence challenge the meaning of life for them. They arose in the morning committed to the tasks that faced them. They saw their chores as well beyond routine. They measured their days by their achievement, both for their kin and their kingdom. They tried to be at harmony with their neighbors in their very communal lifestyle. It was not always easy. They spoke to those who would inherit Dixie; they expected that life would always be sparse (how shocked they would be to see today's luxury), but they expected those who came after to perpetuate the purpose and not become lost in the material. So they used words in many venues. They preached, they testified; but they also described and enlivened. The result is that their lives are very much with us, if we will but read their words.

ENDNOTES

1. Albert O. Mitchell, "Dramatics in Southern Utah, From 1850 to the Coming of the Moving Picture." Masters thesis, University of Utah, 1935.

2. Reed Paul Thompson, "Eighty Years of Music in St. George, Utah, 1861-1941." Masters thesis, Brigham Young University, 1952, 29.

3. Bernice Maher Mooney, *Salt of the Earth*, 274.

4. *The Vepricula*, 15 May 1864, Dixie College Archives.

5. Ibid., 1 Sept 1864.

6. *Dixie Falcon*, 22 September 1900, Dixie College Archives.

7. Ibid.

8. The following list of Washington County newspapers was compiled by Loren Webb.

    • *The Vepricula* (The Little Bramble), May 1864 to 15 June 1865, semi-monthly written by Orson Pratt Jr., George A. Burgon, Charles L. Walker, Joseph Orton and Guglielmo Gustavo Rosetti Sangiovanni.

    • *Our Dixie Times*, 22 January 1868, renamed *Rio Virgin Times*, 13 May 1868. Edited by Joseph E. Johnson.

    • *Utah Pomologist*, 1 April 1870 edited by Joseph E. Johnson. Name changed to *The Utah Pomologist and Gardener*, then to *The Utah Pomologist and Silver Reef Echo*, then to *The Silver Reef Echo*. Sold to G. W. Crouch and James N. Louder and renamed *The Silver Reef Miner*.

    • *The Mineral Cactus*, 25 February 1868. Name changed to "The Cactus" 19 September 1868. Edited by G. G. R. Sangiovanni.

    • *The St. George Juvenile*, semi-monthly 1868; Joseph Carpenter renamed it *The St. George Enterprise*, November 1871.

    • *The Union*, 14 June 1878. J. W. Carpenter renamed it *The Union and Village Echo*, June 1882, Bloomington.

    • *The Southern Star*, 20 July 1895, weekly, James T. Jakeman.

    • *The Evening Telegram*, 8 April 1879, Joseph Carpenter, daily except Sunday.

    • *Washington County News*, 18 June 1898 to 28 July 1900, John R. Wallis.

    • *The Dixie Falcon*, September 1901, D. U. Cochrane.

    • *The Dixie Advocate*, 6 September 1901, Charles S. and Joseph F. Wilkinson renamed it *The Virgin Valley Enterprise*, 1907.

    • *The Washington County News* (renewed), weekly, 30 January 1908 with John R. Wallis as editor and publisher to 1933, then owned by Edgar and Hazel Simpson until late 1930s. Owned by Clyde and Nora Lyman until 1958, then by Frank Mountford until 1973, then by Jim and Asa Mountford until 20 March 1986. Owned by John Rogers, publisher, and Jeannette Rusk, editor, until 8 March 1988.

    • *Tri-State News Advertiser*, weekly, 1963, Kanab, Hurricane, by Errol Brown and Ben Brown. Became *Southern Utah Free Press and Southern Utah News-Advertiser*, 1972. Sold to Gail Stahle and became *Color Country Spec-*

trum. Became a daily on 24 March 1976, renamed *The Daily Spectrum*, 1982. Sold to Thomson Newspapers, January 1984. Became "The Spectrum" in 1994. Notable editors LaVarr Webb, Jr., Carrick Leavitt, Paul Challis, Brent Goodey, Chris Miller, Janet Fontenau.

- *The Southern Utah Sun*, 7 January 1986 to 13 June 1987, LaVarr Webb, Sr. as publisher and Gaylen W. Webb as editor.

- *Red Desert Digest*, Tom Backman, editor, 1992.

- *Senior Sampler*, November 1989, Michael and Donna Stanley, sold 1994 to Van and Maureen Willson.

9. Bleak, "Annals," Book A, 200.

10. See *Under the Dixie Sun*, 334.

11. Andrew Karl Larson, *I Was Called to Dixie*, 511.

12. Caroline S. Addy, "James Godson Bleak: Pioneer Historian of Southern Utah." Masters thesis, Brigham Young University, 1953.

13. John D. Lee, *A Mormon Chronicle. The Diaries of John D. Lee 1848-1876*, 6 vols., ed. Robert Class and Juanita Brooks. (San Marino, CA: Huntington Library, 1955.) These handsome volumes provide one of America's truly great journals. They are candid, and they also capture the fervor of the Latter-day Saints' kingdom building.

7

WATER

Water is the key resource in a desert. Land seems boundless, but water is scarce. Not only is rainfall limited in Dixie (eight inches average annually) but its flow across the landscape is also sporadic. Sometimes small rivers and streams are placid and easily used, other times they dry up. They occasionally become roaring floods and turn destructive when cloudbursts come. The speed of the accumulation, little hindered by vegetation, creates a force that uproots trees and rocks, hurling them as if they were toothpicks. In minutes the force cuts into soft riverbanks and washes away the soil the river has deposited for decades. Thus farmlands are decimated and sent downstream as mud and debris, eventually reaching the Colorado River. Over time, grazing by cattle and sheep denuded some of the range in Washington County, causing water to run off hillsides even more quickly.

Canals and Dams

Diverting water to thirsty crops and maintaining diversion dams and irrigation ditches was a constant cooperative challenge for the settlers in the county during the first four decades of settlement. The Virgin and Santa Clara rivers were not easily tamed. Scores of men, working cooperatively, spent each winter building or repairing yet another dam or ditch to divert the waters of the Virgin. The construction and maintenance of the Old Virgin Ditch, the Jarvis Ditch, the Price Canal, and finally the Washington Fields Canal made the "desert blossom as the rose" — at least in spots.

Once those few plots were blossoming, a second generation was on the scene. They were anxious for land. Fathers were not ready to give their land to their sons, sometimes because they were still young themselves, sometimes because they had younger plural families to support. The need for land and water increased with subsequent generations.

Settlers faced numerous engineering and technical problems in their efforts to coax the water onto the land. Washington City farmers came together to dig several tunnels (named Schlappi, Beard, Pickett, and Sproul) through the Shinob-kiab, only to have them fill with silt, reducing the flow of water through the tunnels and causing flooding up the canal from the tunnels.[1] The Old Virgin Ditch had to be constantly guarded and maintained against breaks, and the farmers using it spent many days annually removing silt from the canal; however, by 1880 the ditch had become too expensive to maintain and was abandoned.

Brigham Jarvis of St. George invented a system of sand gates, providing a means of clearing the Jarvis Ditch of silt. Through the Jarvis method for removing silt-laden water, a series of sluices made it possible for a canal to be self-flushing, removing silt with less manpower and expense. In 1870 a group of promoters, including William Carter, William Fawcett, George Jarvis, William P. McIntire, Mathew Mansfield, Henry Gubler, Joseph Birch, Addison Everett, and John Larson, began building a new dam and ditch.[2]

Floods were not respectful of the Jarvis Ditch nor of the next dam project higher up the river. After a huge effort to build a permanent dam from 1886 to 1889, developers including Marcus Funk, John R. Chidester, Anthony Ivins, and Andrew H. Larson, expected a yield. No sooner was that major achievement completed than the largest known flood to date came and literally defied all their efforts, twisting their dam's well-engineered pilings and gates with its massive force.

This "dam versus flood" cycle was a life-and-death matter. Were the floods to win over the Mormons' attempts to conquer the Virgin, the area's best agricultural land (the Washington Fields) would have to be abandoned. Time after time, people found the inner resources to try again to beat the floods on the Virgin. Financial costs had to be overcome — volunteer labor was requisitioned again and again by canal companies. Many people concluded the endeavor was self-defeating and chose to move, some going to Garfield or Emery counties, others to Arizona, where new Mormon colonizing efforts were underway. The population of the city of Washington dropped from 600 to 312 in 1892.3

Those citizens who stayed organized yet another expensive effort, this time to build a permanent rock dam farther upriver that would double the acreage that could be watered.

This great effort required outside help. A. W. Ivins went to Salt Lake City and convinced Mormon church leaders to participate even though they had their own major financial crisis with the Federal government.

Many Latter-day Saints gave their tithing as labor and volunteered their energy to the project. This was a "do or die" undertaking. It came at a time when previous economic supports had dried up — the cotton industry, the mining boom, the church building projects. Agriculture had become the only base for the economy. Again it meant strenuous labor in frigid water with no guarantee that their venture would not meet the fate of at least ten previous attempts. Leaders from earlier efforts, George F. Whitehead, Alonzo Clark, William Mathis, Henry Schlappi, Jack Beard, Horatio Pickett, and Andrew Sproul, Sr., were central in the effort. This dam, completed in 1891, allowed the canals to be finished by 1893 in time to meet the deadline for land-filing claims. It proved to be a real victory. It held and served as the basic structure to open up the Washington Fields to permanent productivity. By 1896 the "Report of the State Board of Equalization for Utah" noted that there were 11,122 acres in the county used for agriculture and assessed them at $14.00 per acre, second in value only to Salt Lake County at $14.80.4

Cottonwood Project

St. George City has its own water story to tell. Two springs coming from the Red Hills inside the city limits had a lot to do with locating the city where it is today, snuggled close by those springs. Together they produce just over two cubic feet of water per second, and they have been consistent for 135 years. A few smaller springs also feed into the flow. Some 400 acres and perhaps that many homes were sustained by channeling water through an elaborate ditching system requiring constant care.

Old-timers love to tell of city regulations that sent them out to the ditch each morning about 5 a.m. (in the summer) and 7 a.m. (in the winter) to fill the family barrel with water. They would then wrap the barrels with wet burlap to keep the water cool. This had to be done early because by 6 a.m. (8 a.m. in the winter) cows were allowed out in the street where they were gathered from individual corrals and herded to a common grazing spot. The first thing the cows wanted to do was drink from the ditches, fouling the water for the rest of the day. For the next twenty-three hours the water was sent down various ditches to provide watering turns for gardens and farms.

Before long, St. George residents realized that the city would continue to grow and that they would need a more ample water supply than the Red Hills springs provided. By the mid-1860s, they had explored widely and knew of a wonderful large spring on the southern face of Pine Valley Mountain, some eighteen miles away. Lyman Hafen tells the story of bringing culinary water to St. George in several phases over the next decades.[5] As he suggests, the project had its most effective organizer when Anthony W. Ivins was elected mayor in 1890. His efforts helped divert the Cottonwood Spring water from its natural flow into the path of the Washington cotton mill, then by canal to St. George.

The next strategy, just six years later, was more ambitious. Following a plan offered by Brigham Jarvis, the St. George City Council authorized building a canal to bring water directly from the Cottonwood Springs to St. George, bypassing the Cotton Mission mill creek. Jarvis's plan was controversial; many people felt he was trying to make water run uphill. He had established his route with homemade surveying equipment, a simple spirit level and tripod. The city council listened to Jarvis's proposal and had Isaac Macfarlane recheck his figures. They then committed $2,000 and authorized Jarvis to issue labor certificates. It was an enormous undertaking. Hafen recorded:

> Yet with nothing but teams, wagons and crude horse-drawn excavation equipment, a crew of townsmen went to work with high aspirations. They built a ditch that wound more than 15 miles down the

rocky knolls, and sprawled down the lava flats — mile after mile — to the city. Meager wages, paid in the form of water "scrip" (to be redeemed later), were promised to the men who dripped sweat and shed blood along every inch of the canal. But their pay came mostly in the satisfaction of building a lifeline from the mountain to the town. And instead of two years, the project took more than seven.6

Arrival of the Cottonwood Springs water in 1898 assured St. George of a water supply for the next several decades. Official completion took until 1903 when the headgates and storage system were finished. The water flowed from the mountain in an open canal, however, which meant that nearly half of the water sank into the ground or evaporated on the way. The other problem was that the range cattle and sheep quickly discovered the canal and fouled the water while they drank.

The availability of plentiful water encouraged citizens to pass a bond election in 1907 which financed installation of pipes from the headgates to individual homes, ending the old practice of dipping from road ditches. Still the water coming out of those taps was often filled with red sand if there had been rainstorms; certainly other impurities came out too because the canal was not enclosed. In 1920 another bond election was held, this time to raise $72,000 to enclose the city's water in a distribution system of wooden pipes. Later cement pipes replaced the wood. (More recently, iron and plastic pipes have replaced the cement ones.)

Completion of this project was not accomplished until well into the 1930s with the aid of Federal Reconstruction Finance Corporation funds amounting to $150,000. These dollars were devoted to enclosing the canal from the Cottonwood Spring all the way to the city headgates. Finally in 1937, people could celebrate; they turned on their taps and received clean, cool water, a feat that would have brought tears to the eyes of their grandparents. (This New Deal largesse may have been one reason why county residents moved in large numbers to the Democratic column in the 1930s.)

Enterprise Reservoir

The saga of water development in Washington County — from the first diversion of streams to the later engineering undertakings — was not confined to the large communities of Dixie. For example, some people who lived in Hebron realized that there was not enough watered land to guarantee the future of their community in the northwest corner of the county. Since ranching rather than farming was the main concern of Hebron citizens, it seemed initially that Hebron could survive without irrigating much land. That was all right for a few cattle operators, but the small, self-sustaining families needed farmland and substantial gardens, so they diverted Shoal Creek water onto the land around Hebron. Many people left Hebron to search for more land, some going to Wayne County; others tried various locations in Washington County and elsewhere.

Orson Huntsman was one of those who settled in Hebron but later moved because he could not get enough water to support his farm; however, other places had similar problems, so he eventually returned. His active mind kept him searching for a solution to the water shortage; he began talking with his neighbors about a major project — building a large reservoir at the head of Shoal Creek and bringing water in a steady, all-year delivery canal to the desert lands below Hebron. This was revolutionary in a way; it meant skirting Hebron and creating a new community.

For Huntsman the idea was not just talk. He gradually took on the responsibility of molding public opinion. In this he was initiating a typical American frontier effort, something quite different from the church-planned land distribution of the first villages that earlier had shaped Dixie. His was a venture of individual initiative without the convenience of prestige or authority on his side. Huntsman soon found that convincing people might be harder than building the dam. The older citizens of Hebron did not want to impair their holdings by diverting water to the proposed new community, Enterprise, even though it had a much larger potential as envisioned by Huntsman. His own father-in-law, Hebron bishop Thomas Terry, was not enthusiastic. He urged Huntsman to move to Beaver Dam, where the bishop kept a hiding spot for polygamists being pursued by Federal marshals. There was sufficient water there for one more family. That plan did not appeal to Huntsman, however; it did not solve the situation at Hebron. The reservoir idea had a potential for supporting dozens of families, not just one; he foresaw a community several times the size of Hebron. In 1891 he hired Isaac C. Macfarlane of St. George to survey a townsite of 130 lots about ten miles below the reservoir site. He then filed on those 320 acres which he named Enterprise under the Federal desert land entry system. He reported:

> The people of Hebron, or most of them, did not want any stock in Enterprise, so I had to work on the people outside of Hebron to get a company organized. I preached reservoir for about three years in all of the surrounding towns. I went as far north as Parowan and as far south as the settlements in the Muddy Valley; also to Clover Valley and Panaca in the west. I visited all these places two or three times a year and found a few people in most of the towns who would like to take stock if a company were organized.7

Such single-mindedness made Huntsman almost an outcast in Hebron. At best he was considered an irritant. One of the turning points in Huntsman's search for support was in St. George. He asked the LDS stake presidency to organize a meeting during the September 1892 stake conference where he could propose the reservoir and attract investors. Because of the press of time in the regular meetings they did not oblige him, but Thomas Judd and Huntsman stood at the doorways of the tabernacle and informed the exiting congregation of a meeting early the next morning. Huntsman was skeptical that the stake presidency did not support him, but the next morning a large crowd was at the tabernacle early, including the presidency. He received a lot of verbal support, perhaps because Isaac Macfarlane gave a positive report of his survey.

Stake President Daniel D. McArthur, A. W. Ivins, and Thomas Judd all spoke in support of the reservoir. They formed a committee, including Huntsman, to write a prospectus and have it printed. That writing took several months. Huntsman wrote the first draft based on Isaac Macfarlane's information. He took it to Ivins who corrected it, then Huntsman paid a printer eight dollars for a thousand copies. It read in part:

> It is the design of the company to construct a reservoir on the head of Shoal Creek at a point known as Little Pine Valley in Washington County, Utah with a capacity sufficient to irrigate an area of 5,415 acres of land. The estimates are based upon a calculation by which the capacity of the reservoir shown to be 2,758,145,277 gallons which will give a depth of 16 inches of water over the entire surface of 5,415 acres of land.
>
> The reservoir will be one mile long by half a mile wide and the average depth of water will be about 45 feet. The ground covered by

this area of water has an underlying strata of granite under its entire surface and there will consequently be very little loss, seepage or evaporation.

The land to be irrigated lies at the mouth of Shoal Creek where a very desirable townsite has been selected and surveyed on the county road between Hebron and Hamblin and is a fine sandy loam, very rich and admirable, adapted by climate and otherwise to the production of small grain, alfalfa and corn.

This land is subject to entry under the Desert Act and it is the design of the company that all benefits to be derived through the cheap acquisition of titles shall be shared by all who assist in carrying the enterprise to a successful termination.[8]

The dam was described to be eighty feet high, twenty feet wide at the bottom and eight feet at the top. The cost of the reservoir was estimated to be $18,947.00 and the canal at $12,923,00 for a total cost of $31,870.00. The sponsoring committee consisted of Thomas Judd, Isaac C. Macfarlane, Orson W. Huntsman, Anthony W. Ivins, Zora P. Terry (Hebron), George M. Burgess (Pine Valley), and Alfred Syphus (Panaca, Nevada). On 12 September 1893 a formal company was organized with Bishop James Andrus as president and George A. Holt as secretary; work then commenced on the reservoir. No one knew it would take sixteen years to complete.

A year later a glitch arose when George A. Holt was appointed bishop of Hebron. He switched gears and started a move to resurrect Hebron. He led an effort to build new ditches, dams, and roads to Hebron and keep the Shoal Creek water there instead of allowing it to flow to Enterprise.

Huntsman and a few friends kept working on the reservoir during the winters. An itinerant mason, Chris Ammon, actually laid most of the stone, working at the task steadily. Then in November 1902 a severe earthquake hit the entire area; Hebron, especially, was damaged. The quake's center seems to have been in Pine Valley; it was felt in Salt Lake City. Chimneys were toppled throughout Santa Clara and Pine Valley. Many of the rock homes in Hebron were damaged beyond repair. By that time, some families had already moved to Enterprise or elsewhere; the earthquake prodded the rest to move and sell the water they controlled to the Enterprise Reservoir Company.[9]

The Enterprise Dam. (Photo by J. J. Booth, Heber Jones Collection)

Negotiations began immediately with the town of Hebron which was asking $19,000 for the water rights while the company was offering $14,000. Unable to agree, they decided to place their case before the stake presidency and bind themselves to accept its decision. On 23 January 1904 the presidency — consisting of Edward H. Snow, Thomas P. Cottam, and George F. Whitehead — heard both sides and determined that the company should pay $17,500 in capital stock, and the people of Hebron would turn over the water of Shoal Creek. The way was open to complete the project, but the work dragged on slowly. Then in the spring of 1911, A. W. Ivins, now an LDS apostle, subscribed for 1,000 shares of stock in the Enterprise Reservoir Company to get the project moving. This amounted to about $7,500 and was a final factor in bringing the reservoir to completion.

Huntsman was not an aggressive capitalist. Rather than seek profit from investment, he hoped to benefit a whole community and only be one of those who gained access to water and land. The initiative and persistence of Orson Huntsman, the sustained and skillful labor of Chris Ammon, the support of stake leaders, the investment of scores of local people in the Hebron/Enterprise area, and the foresight and resources of Anthony Ivins and many others brought about a marvel, the Enterprise Reservoir. To this day the reservoir is the key element for sustaining agriculture in the area. Groundwater pumping has been added as a source of water and makes large-scale agriculture possible, but between 1920 and 1950 the reservoir was the lifeline for people in the northwest corner of Washington County.

La Verkin Canal

The La Verkin and Hurricane benches were obvious places where productive agriculture could be developed. The earliest settlers inspected both sites in the 1860s, but both required that water be brought to them from the Virgin River. Because the riverbed was depressed in a deep gorge between the two benches, water could only be delivered to the promising lands if it were captured before it entered the gorge. Proposals to do this were considered in the 1860s but the costs involved seemed prohibitive; nonetheless, the idea always challenged enterprising men.

In 1888 the widely involved entrepreneurs Thomas Cottam and Thomas Judd decided to venture. They hired Isaac Macfarlane to make a survey, and together they estimated that a canal could be built for $25,000. They formed the La Verkin Fruit and Nursery Company which included themselves, Eva Hardy as secretary, and Robert G. McQuarrie and Isaac C. Macfarlane as directors. Their idea was to establish orchards and vineyards on the La Verkin Bench and promote major agriculture. This would be a large-scale enterprise, not a village farming system.

Several people invested in the company, including Charles H. Rowe and Charles Brown of Salt Lake City and St. Georgers Andrew W. and Frank Winsor, Hector McQuarrie, and Samuel Judd. Men were hired to build a dam on the river and work on the canal. They were paid in Washington cotton factory scrip (Thomas Judd was leasing the factory at that time) and in company stock. The work was strenuous, hacking out a ditch in stone, even building a tunnel some 900 feet long:

> They went to work on the ledges, shooting them down so that they could obtain a bed for the ditch. They made the grade six or seven feet wide, with a fall of about one inch in ten rods except near the upper end where the grade was somewhat steeper. The powder holes for blasting the ditch out of the grade thus provided were placed about six feet apart, filled with black powder, and exploded. Without tearing, the exploding powder lifted the rock, a great mass, so that about a rod of ditch could be made for every two shots (two were always placed together). The work moved along at a satisfactory pace, and in due time the stockholders had it completed.[10]

Everything appeared in readiness. In anticipation, the company had planted many acres of almond trees and grapes. They then turned the water into the ditch. The grade was adequate but little water came out to the land. The builders quickly discovered that the water was sinking into gypsum sections of the canal. That discovery was the start of numerous efforts to salvage the canal. They tried plugging the areas with cotton from the Washington factory. Mud was applied, making some improvement; but not until nearly 1900 did builders turn to cement, which had just become available and which finally solved the problem. In the interim, the company found it necessary to give much of the land to individual stockholders. They raised some capital thereby and finally cemented the canal all the way from the tunnel entrance to the dam.

The long-range result was quite different from what the originators envisioned. They had hoped for large-scale agriculture and an important company; but La Verkin actually became a community of individual farmers. The canal still remained the lifeline, and La Verkin did become a very productive area, especially for fruits and nuts. It also became a safety valve for families who could not find land elsewhere.[11]

Hurricane Canal

Heroic tales abound in Dixie history, but none are more moving than those of the Hurricane Canal. Today we may prefer stories like those of Jacob Hamblin and the Indians where there seems to be more adventure, or perhaps we revel in the tales of outlaws on the Arizona Strip. But for sustained heroism and lasting impact, the tale of conquering the Hurricane Cliffs by building a canal is of real importance.

The story begins with the same fundamental problem: where could the second generation find land and water to establish homes? By 1890 the idea of founding villages had passed. It was being replaced with the need to expand irrigation facilities and add farms for new families. The problem with the "up river" communities — Virgin, Rockville, Grafton, Springdale, and Shunesburg — was that their farming land was shrinking, not expanding. Floods had washed away much of the original farming area. Many families had moved away in discouragement. The grown sons of those who stayed faced the crucial question: would they have to leave Dixie to support their families?

The idea of harnessing the Virgin River as it cascaded down the Hurricane Fault and diverting it onto the vast Hurricane Bench came very early. Erastus Snow and John M. Macfarlane examined the site as early as 1867 but despaired of getting the engineering equipment to build such a canal. The possibility languished for many years, just as other big projects like the Cottonwood Canal and the Enterprise Reservoir had to wait until sufficient capital and engineering expertise made them possible.

James Jepson of Virgin was the vital figure in the initiative. He discovered that John Steele of Toquerville was also thinking of the same idea. They selected a site in the Virgin Gorge where the walls were solid limestone. They proposed building a dam at that point, then digging a canal along the side of the gorge to bring the water from the dam to the Hurricane Mesa. The canal would be a seven-and-half mile channel through rock cliffs, requiring dynamite to carve out a bed for the water. In several places wooden flumes would have to be constructed to carry the water over breaks in the stone course. The canal would have the advantage of diverting the flow above the Pah Tempe sulphur springs, thus capturing the water while it was still good for crops.

Jepson agreed to solicit the support of people in Virgin and the upper towns while Steele recruited in Toquerville and elsewhere. In June 1893 they formed an enabling committee which wrote by-laws, then organized a canal committee. J. M. Ballard of Grafton, David Hirschi of Rockville, Martin Slack, Sr. and W. A. Bringhurst of Toquerville, and Jepson drew up a constitution. Jepson was elected president of the company with J. C. Willis, vice-president, L. N. Harmon, secretary, and James M. Ballard, J. F. Langston, John W. Isom, and L. J. Slack as directors.[12]

Work on the canal began in the winter of 1893 with J. C. Willis as construction superintendent. Nearly 100 men subscribed to the stock option and initially large crews arrived to begin the daring task of chipping out a canal from the side of the canyon's cliffs. The digging was most difficult. Picks and shovels were the main tools; the men had to lower their tools and supplies as well as their food down into the gorge. Horses could not make it through the rock ledges, nor could workers get wagons near, so the they had to sleep under wagon covers.

Some unemployed miners drifting about the country came to the area seeking jobs. Since local men were working for shares, the miners were not offered pay. In their desperation, they were willing to work for board. They brought skills of digging in rocks and using explosives that were sorely needed. This addition of non-Mormon skill and technology was a crucial benefit. The newcomers also added color, humor, and evening music to the band of workers who numbered as many as 300.

After two winters, the canal company ran out of capital and discouragement set in. Tunneling and pick-and-shovel work had been backbreaking, but now even harder stone blasting lay ahead. Enthusiasm for the task dwindled. Twice the dam broke, raising the question of whether the canal would ever receive water, but a third dam held. Only a few workers stayed with the dream. Some winters as few as three men kept at it. Those discouraging years dragged on. Wooden flumes were built where the canal could not be chipped out of the rock, but the builders had to have more capital to undertake the heavy blasting.

Officers of the canal company met and decided to approach church leaders in Salt Lake City, aware that a civic undertaking could hardly justify using church funds; nonetheless, James Jepson was asked to plead their case with the church leaders. Boarding a train at Lund for the capital, Jepson first met with Mormon church president Joseph F. Smith. The following morning Jepson presented a report to the Council of Twelve and Smith. The church was itself in financial difficulties and as a matter of policy had generally refused further financial obli-

Hurricane Canal Crew at La Verkin Hot Springs. From left to right: Sam Crawford, Bishop Hunter, Jess Lemmon, Joe Fames, Alfred Jones, John Hirschi. (W. L. Crawford Collection)

gations. At the meeting, several apostles and President Smith asked Jepson about the project and how much money was being requested from the church. Jepson explained that they were not asking for a donation from the church but rather for the church to purchase $5,000 worth of stock. It was discovered that the dollar amount Jepson was requesting for the project was about the same amount church members from the five wards involved had paid in tithing the previous year. Following a few additional minutes of consideration, the leaders agreed to purchase $5,000 worth of stock in the Hurricane Canal Company. Jepson later wrote, "When that motion carried, it seemed the happiest moment of my life."[13]

This external infusion of capital was crucial, leading to the final success of the project. Arrival of the water meant families could start building homes on the bench. Within two years, about a dozen families had arrived. Soon more came; there was no difficulty finding takers for the land because about seventy-five members of the canal company had filed on the land during the canal construction to secure it for the company. Within a few years, 2,000 acres were under cultivation, watered by the Hurricane Canal. Today that acreage has been expanded to 4,000, including other water sources. The water came through a canal suspended in a rock-lined delivery channel elevated above the town on the edge of the Hurricane Fault.

One of the tasks the newcomers to Hurricane inherited was "ditch riding." The canal had to be inspected constantly to prevent breaks and leaks. It was a tedious but absolutely crucial job. Frank Lee was one of those riders who will long be remembered because he died in an accident while riding the ditch. In this he joined at least one other, an Indian boy whose name has not survived. Lee lost his life in the construction to make the Hurricane Canal the lifeline for a whole new community. That canal delivered water to Hurricane for eighty years until 1985 when the water was placed in a pipeline, avoiding the old ditch route.

In retrospect, the building of the Hurricane Canal characterizes Dixie — the terrible challenges of weather and landscape, the urgent shortage of land and water, the pulling together to conquer these difficulties, the need of outside capital, and the endurance to carry out large projects that required years to complete. Some years later, James Jepson took George H. Brimhall, president of Brigham Young University, the length of the canal. Brimhall marveled that such a group of men would tackle a problem so difficult without capital. Jepson answered by asking the question, "Do you remember how Brigham Young called a group of people to Dixie and only about half of them responded?" "Yes," President Brimhall had heard something like that. "Do you remember that of the half who came, only half remained?" "Yes." "Well," said Jepson, "the men and women who built this canal are the children of those who stayed!"14

Mead/Adams Study

Just as the Hurricane Canal was being completed, the U.S. Department of Agriculture was also finishing an ambitious study of irrigation in the United States. It was headed by Elwood Mead, who was later honored for his work by having Lake Mead (created by the Hoover Dam near Las Vegas) named for him. One volume was devoted to Utah. A chapter by Frank Adams examined "Agriculture Under Irrigation in the Basin of Virgin River." This important study gives a detailed picture of the water situation at the turn of the century in Washington County.

Adams spent a year in Washington County examining each of the canal companies and water projects. He garnered an understanding of the area's history and came to appreciate the ethic of Dixie. His observations are insightful:

> The type of institution in the Virgin Valley is essentially coopera-tive, as it is elsewhere among the Mormons. If the rights of one settlement to water are encroached upon by the farmers elsewhere, the natural method is to stand firm as a local unit until the wrong is righted. If new lands must be brought under ditch to keep the young men at home on the farms, the usual procedure is a joining of forces until the result is accomplished. If water for irrigation is to be dis-tributed, the only way the settlers know is to work together until each man has his rightful share. Thus it is that a forbidding country has been made fruitful where individual effort would have failed.... The farmer of the Virgin River is the farmer of small means and modest wants. Yet his 5 acres of alfalfa is his fortune.[15]

Stressing cooperation in the "forbidding country" and the search for land for second-generation sons, Adams went on to describe the Mormon village system:

> The farms on Virgin River, as elsewhere in Utah, are in community groups surrounding or not far from the settlements from which they are worked. Only in rare instances does a farmer live on his farm, but instead, in the village made up of his neighbor farmers. This compact village type considerably alters agricultural methods and makes the farms less diversified than is common in intensely cul-tivated farm homes. There is no place in the field for the fruit and vegetables that ordinarily supply so much of the farmer's living. Those products are grown in the village dooryards, where they can have the requisite care and attention. His field is essentially a one-crop field, generally alfalfa, or it may have also wheat or oats. He hauls his product 1, 2, or 4 miles to town, where he stacks it for the winter's feeding.[16]

Adams lists 6,504 acres in Washington County as well as 7,200 more in Kanab and the Muddy River Basin, bringing the total to 13,700 acres. He suggests that this amount could be increased to 61,700 acres if more water sources could be developed, but that would only bring the percentage up to 1.4 percent of the land surface.[17] One example of such an increase was occurring before his very eyes as the Hurricane Canal was being completed. He was deeply impressed with this development and described it at length. In one excerpt he said: "This undertaking has been carried on, not as an investment, but solely to create homes for the sons and daughters of the early settlers in the upper Virgin River towns."18

Adams concluded that the silting problem made it impractical to store reclamation water in the channel of the Virgin River. In this he was an indirect prophet of the later Quail Creek project that devised a way to divert Virgin River water away from the channel for storage.

Adams discovered that the farmers of Washington County had not filed their water claims with the county recorder. Water, under the laws passed by the territorial legislature, was distributed by the county selectmen (county commissioners of today). These men served as the "guardians of the streams" and were charged to distribute the water with equality and fairness based on the demonstrated need of the farmer. The county selectmen, acting on behalf of the common good of society, appointed watermasters to assist them to see that water was distributed fairly and used properly. The county selectmen issued water certificates to individual water users; through the common practice of usage, these became the basis for claiming rights to water. Until recently, little litigation over water rights has occurred in the county. Frank Adams and Elwood Mead noted at the turn of the century, "the irrigators from Virgin River are endowed with a propensity to peace, and are fairly well agreed as to their own and neighbor's rights."19

Despite this picture of harmony and isolation, Adams noted that there was some conflict over water, particularly on the Santa Clara River.20 St. George City Council was given control of the flow of the Santa Clara River by the territorial legislature in the city's original charter of January 1862. The St. George-Santa Clara Canal Company was formed to give Santa Clara its established rights prior to 1862 as well as to give St. George its rights according to the charter. Nonetheless, the administration of water between Santa Clara and St. George for garden purposes was a continuing challenge for the Washington County Commission. An 1865 court settlement set out the parameters. The St. George-Santa Clara Canal Company was set up to deliver water to the lands in Green Valley, so there would be a basic plan; nonetheless, numerous compromises were necessary to implement the court order, and even then there were occasional harsh feelings.

Pine Valley was also given irrigation rights by the St. George City Council in the early 1860s, but that arrangement did not settle all future arguments. Serious disagreements about water on the upper creek were still unresolved, leading to a lawsuit taken to Federal court. In State of Utah v. Royal Hunt, the United States Court in Salt Lake City on 20 May 1901 held that Hunt could appropriate the use of water from springs on his property and that the watermaster could not claim that water, as he had done, for users downstream.

It is important to understand that the distribution of water in Utah followed a different pattern than it did in some other western states, notably California. The tradition of riparian rights, inherited from English law, was that land ownership included water ownership. The mindset of the Mormon leaders as they entered the Great Basin was different even though many of them had lived in New England and England. Their concern was for the thousands of Latter-day Saints who were yet to come west. They did not want those who came first to have preemptory rights over those who would come later. Also, they were concerned that water would be in short supply in the Intermountain West. They chose to settle there because no one else wanted the land, and shortage of water had a lot to do with that undesirability. It was clear that water would have to be dealt with differently than in the riparian tradition.

Brigham Young believed that people should have the right to use water, not to own it. Even before the Territory of Utah was organized, Young implemented that policy in the legislature of the Mormons' proposed State of Deseret. When the Federal government organized the Territory of Utah, the legislature stated on 4 February 1852: "The County Court has the control of all timber, water privileges, or any water course, or creek to grant mill sites, and exercise such power as in their judgment shall best preserve the timber and subserve the interest of settlements in their distribution of water for irrigation or other purposes." University of Utah economics professor George Thomas wrote of the Utah system: "The water of the streams and the lakes of the territory [of Utah] belong to the public and are subject to appropriation by individuals or to grants by the legislature or subordinate bodies created by it; [this] shows a far keener appreciation of the needs of the arid regions."21

Litigation was not often necessary. The Washington County Court and the St. George City Council, which were granted control of the water, were successful arbitrators and administrators, and their appointed watermasters enjoyed respect from the farmers. When Adams arrived soon after 1900, he found that the farmers did not feel it was necessary to file for water, nor were there court cases challenging allotments of water.22

The Newcastle Venture

In Washington County, some major engineering efforts were undertaken that failed to meet dreams to deliver water. In 1911 the St. George City Council undertook a project to store the Cottonwood Canal water delivered by the prized pipeline. The city council commissioned the building of a reservoir above the town near Black Knolls on the Red Hill. An earthen dam was built with lava boulders, taking twenty years to complete. It came to be called "Hernia Dam" because the huge boulders were so hard to move. Unfortunately, the soils underneath the reservoir were so porous that the structure would never hold water. Almost unknown by today's residents, it stands as a silent monument to the toil of its builders.

A much more ambitious idea was the Newcastle Reclamation Project. A private, for-profit undertaking, the effort involved the idea of delivering water from the Colorado drainage basin up into lands of the Great Basin. Proponents argued that there were few large tracts of flat land in the Virgin River Basin but that there were great flat areas just north, near the successful Enterprise area. If water from the upper Santa Clara River could be brought there, large farms could be sustained.

In 1902 Congress passed the Federal Reclamation Act. This made Federal funds available for irrigation efforts in arid lands, and it attracted several northern Utah entrepreneurs who saw the Escalante Desert as a likely site for water reclamation. They were convinced they could apply for Federal funds to underwrite the water project and then use the funds to develop city lots and farms in the proposed development at Newcastle. Willard Jones was instrumental in stimulating interest in the endeavor among Salt Lake City investors. Jones grew up in Cedar City and obtained an engineering degree from the University of Utah. His enthusiasm guided the formation of the Newcastle Reclamation Company in 1908. The idea was to build a canal from the headwaters of Santa Clara Creek in Pine Valley to Grass Valley, bringing that water to a spot where they would build a reservoir. At the back of the impounded lake, they would dig a canal to a tunnel through the mountain into Pinto Canyon where it then could flow down the canyon into Newcastle.

It was a daring plan, but one fraught with difficulties. First, there was the problem of getting the cooperation of Pine Valley residents so developers could take water normally belonging to the Santa Clara users and divert it into the Great Basin. There were also the challenges of constructing a canal with the correct fall as well as a reservoir to store the water and raise its level so that the water could be taken from the back end of the resulting lake. Then the tunnel had to be constructed. Finally came the challenge of attracting sufficient capital and Federal funding to underwrite these endeavors and turn the whole prospect into a profit-making venture.

The amazing thing is that so much was achieved. The canal was built using Japanese labor and by 1914 water was delivered to the reservoir. The tunnel was completed. The dam was finished by 1919 and the ditch was dug to the tunnel opening. A tremendous sales-promotion scheme was undertaken, including laying out the town of Newcastle and building a hotel where prospective buyers were courted, even to the detail of having limousines with chauffeurs available to wine and dine potential investors.

This undertaking had all the elements of capitalism: formation of a company, attraction of investors, a sales campaign, construction of major infrastructure, and an incentive for profit. But the dream ran into tough realities, situations that the distant investors had not sufficiently considered. The major difficulty was that the reservoir leaked, just like "Hernia Dam." Soils were too porous to create a lake large enough to back the water to the canal which entered the tunnel. The inventive developers did not let that stop them. They changed their plan, extending the canal out of Pine Valley directly to the tunnel. But then they ran into objections of Pine Valley and Central residents, including the water companies downstream from Pine Valley.

Steven A. Bunker, a Grass Valley rancher, was sufficiently aggrieved to sue. The company had filed on Pine Valley water, so that was no contest; but feelings in Pine Valley were very strong against the Newcastle people. Bunker had a much stronger case because the project builders had constructed a ditch right through his ranch. The ditch had the effect of draining a meadow and ruining its grazing value. Bunker's life became a tragedy over the problem; he sought redress unsuccessfully for fifteen years and finally had a mental breakdown.

Although some water continues to flow through the tunnel, the Newcastle project never materialized. The hotel burned down a few years after its construction. Wells that were drilled in the town failed to produce sufficient water to make up for the flow that never materialized from the dam in Grass Valley. Attempts to divert some Shoal Creek water to Newcastle set Enterprise and Newcastle into conflict. Litigation was costly and feelings in the area were polarized. One can hike to the site today and see the tunnel, the ditch, and the reservoir, but the thousands of irrigable acres in Newcastle are still desert.23

Recent Water Development

Since construction of the dramatic projects — Cottonwood Canal, Hurricane Canal, Enterprise Reservoir — area water development has been a steady process. St. George leaders soon discovered that the Cottonwood Creek water, as clear and wonderful as it was, would not be enough to sustain a growing community. When the city was nearing 3,000 people in the late 1930s, leaders began looking for supplementary water sources. Under the leadership of Bill Baker in the 1940s and 1950s, the city bought water rights from ranchers along Pine Mountain and from farmers along Mill Creek near Washington.

City crews, led by Baker, worked consistently on water projects to increase the inflow to the Cottonwood pipeline by capturing spring water in East Fork, Cottonwood, Sullivan, and West Fork canyons. They constructed collection boxes on the Blake and Gubler side at Big Pine, Quaking Aspen, Slide Canyon, and Carter Springs. Often they had to carry cement in on pack animals and camp out at the construction sites because they were not accessible by road.24

The management of the whole water system for St. George was getting to be extensive, and the city fathers realized that expansion of the system would be an ongoing necessity. In December 1943, the city council assigned water-system supervision to a three-person commission that had been set up a year previously to administer municipal power and light facilities. That commission, made up of Mathew M. Bentley, LeRoy H. Cox, and Harold S. Snow, hired councilman Clair

Terry to be its secretary, requiring him to resign from the city council. He was succeeded in 1949 by Rudger McArthur, who became the director and continued in that position until 1952 when Lynne Empey took over for nine years. Rudger McArthur returned to the position until 1985 when Wayne McArthur was appointed director.

Since it is the St. George Water and Power Board's responsibility to develop new sources of water, the board has continued as a major institution in the county. Later members of the council included Brown Hail, Shirl H. Pitchforth, and H. Bruce Stucki. Board membership recently has been expanded to include Randy Wilkinson, Ross Hurst, and Craig Booth.

Gunlock Reservoir

The Gunlock Reservoir was one of the water and power board's early successes. Initially the board hoped that the Federal government could be induced to fund this smaller project as well as a comprehensive "Dixie Project" for the whole area. That did not happen; the city itself took leadership in promoting the dam on Santa Clara Creek. The St. George-Santa Clara Canal Company, the Santa Clara Canal Company, the Bloomington Irrigation Company, and the Seep Ditch Company banded together to seek funds from the state power and water board. Wayne Wilson of La Verkin served on that state board, representing five counties of southern Utah, and helped gain funding.

Jay Bingham, an engineer from Salt Lake City, was instrumental in the design and construction of the Gunlock Reservoir. Governor George Dewey Clyde was an advocate of the project and a supporter of Jay Bingham. Bingham recounted that Clyde had been involved in water investigations in Dixie in the mid-1920s when Federal economists concluded that the county could not sustain an arable economy because of inadequate water supplies.[25] The reservoir was begun and completed in 1970 at a cost of about $1 million; however, the amount of water it stored was less than it would have been if the Federal government had built the Dixie Project, as was originally hoped. The water is used for irrigation purposes. An additional benefit has been in keeping the six wells charged that St. George City has developed just below the dam. Those wells produce culinary water that fills the 1.7-million-gallon storage tank located on the north end of the Black Hill in the city. They produce seven million gallons of water daily.

Another major success was an undertaking to find water in Snow Canyon. City employees Rudger McArthur, Glen Gubler, and Shirl Pitchforth searched through the upper canyon area in the late 1970s. Dr. Harry Goode and Robert Cordova were employed by the city and were instrumental in analyzing the geology. Pitchforth recalls:

> Dr. Harry Goode from the University of Utah stood with Rudger McArthur and me on the lava flats south of T Bone Mesa giving us advice on water aquifers as relating to the fault line on which we were standing. After advising us that we would be likely to find water on either side of the fault line but with dubious quality, he suggested we explore Snow Canyon. Our immediate answer was "Where is the fault line?" The next morning we met Dr. Goode at the mouth of Snow Canyon and he proceeded to instruct us on the possibility of finding water on the west side of the canyon near the fault line.26

Water witching was also used to select the site for drilling in Snow Canyon. Both approaches led the searchers to a place where drilling hit clear water at depths of from 700 to 1,000 feet. The spot was located inside the state park, which required careful negotiations. Santa Clara and Ivins joined in the effort and some water was shared with the park. Six wells are now pumping in the area, producing three million gallons of water a day.

Kolob Reservoir and the Baker Dam

Private property owners on Kolob Mesa were concerned about flood control in the late 1940s and 1950s. The St. George and Washington Canal Company and the Hurricane Canal Company began negotiations with the intention of building a reservoir on the mesa. Ray Schmutz, Evan Woodbury, LeRoy H. Cox, and Woodrow Staheli represented the former, and Wayne Wilson, Winford Spendlove, and Raymond DeMille the latter. Wilson won a concession from promoters of the Washington Fields on grounds that the Hurricane water was less dependable. Hurricane received 60 percent and the St. George Irrigation Company 40 percent of the water. The Hurricane Canal Company then made application to the Utah Water Resource Board for an interest-free loan of twenty years, which was granted. They assessed stockholders in order to buy property and construct the reservoir. That loan was paid off in the mid-1980s and the water added to the Virgin River, improving its flow for both irrigation companies.

A similar plan was followed for the Baker Dam below Central. The Santa Clara Irrigation Company and the town of Ivins joined together to gain a twenty-year interest-free loan from the Utah Water Resources Board. Once the project was approved by the state board, some people of Ivins and Santa Clara and St. George had second thoughts. They were concerned that the dam would endanger the proposed Dixie Project. Leaders from Central (Grant Keyes), Veyo (Jimmie Bunker), and Gunlock (Lee Leavitt) felt that the Dixie Project was a long time away from completion. They decided to go ahead with the Baker Dam. George Moses-Patrick Dougal became the contractor. The new company was led by Lee Leavitt, president, Max Cannon, first vice-president, Melbourne Cottam, second vice-president, with Lewis Bowler, Ether Leavitt, and M. Truman Bowler as directors. Truman Bowler was secretary-treasurer and remained a major leader in water development in the county. The dam was dedicated 9 June 1954. Twenty years later, in 1976, it was paid for through water-user fees and has been a boon to farmers throughout the area.

The Dixie Project

The county's biggest water dream came on the heels of Hoover Dam near Las Vegas. There, massive investment by the Federal government created Lake Mead in 1935 and provided the water and electric power that made modern Las Vegas possible. Local leaders in Washington County caught the spirit of Roosevelt's New Deal. The idea of a big dam on the Virgin River seemed to them as justified as was Hoover Dam. Such a reclamation project could realize a long-held dream to capture the potential provided by large runoffs during the early spring and from summer cloudbursts. Washington, D.C. officials seemed to favor water development in the West.

Much of the initiative for the so-called "Dixie Project" came from Hurricane residents, including former mayor Wayne Hinton, former state senator David Hirschi, Claude Hirschi, J. Monroe Ballard, John W. Spendlove, Emil J. Graff, D. W. Gibson, Henry Gubler, Eugene Wadsworth, George Stevens, Chauncey Sandberg, Alvin Larson, Flint Wright, Rulon Langston, and J. Morris Wilson of La Verkin. Judge LeRoy Cox was an early backer. Others involved in lobbying for the project included William Barlocker, George Snow, Philip Foremaster, Ray Schmutz, Claude Frei, Winfred Spendlove, Wayne Wilson, Evan Lee,

Austin Excell, Orval Hafen, Dixie Leavitt, Lorin D. Squire, Malm Cox, and Governor George D. Clyde. This provided a broad base of leaders from throughout the county and beyond. Senator Frank E. Moss became lead man for the request in Washington. Representative Laurence J. Burton was helpful in the U.S. House of Representatives.

A proposal was submitted to Congress in October 1961. The request was for $42 million, anticipating a large dam just below Virgin City and another (which eventually became the Gunlock Reservoir) on the Santa Clara. The Gunlock, Veyo, and Santa Clara farmers and ranchers were often impacted by drought and were anxious to have a steady agricultural water source.

With backing from various local, state, and Federal interests, Congress authorized the Dixie Project. The huge reclamation project, authorized at $42.7 million, was to be repaid in part from selling electricity from hydroelectric power generated at the dam. Further engineering and geological studies of the proposed Virgin City dam site revealed that the gypsum and limestone floor of the canyon would not hold water. The geological problem could only be solved by a costly process of pumping cement under high pressure into dozens of drill holes. It was further discovered that the dam site was located over a fault line and severe crack lines in the earth's crust. The fault line forced the relocation of the dam site twenty-five miles downstream, and the relocation of the proposed dam resulted in the loss of its capacity to produce electricity. This loss, the additional loss of productive farmland, and increased costs for the new dam site would have increased the overall price of the project to $58 million. Clearly the costs for the project had risen well beyond the means of Washington County to repay the Federal government.[27]

The Dixie Project therefore was not funded. Wayne Wilson remembers making the announcement that the local Water Users Association was recommending rejection of the project.[28] It was a major decision, but farmers felt the financial obligation was too big due to the fact that the project would not produce income from power generation. Many people at the time felt that the decision not to undertake the Dixie Project was tragic.

Quail Creek Reservoir

An outgrowth of the Dixie Project was the establishment of the Washington County Conservancy District, an entity that was required if the project was to be funded. Even though the project was not funded by the Federal government, the conservancy district became a key planning agency. The district board anticipated tremendous population growth in the county. The discovery of the Dixie area by retirees made it clear that the once-isolated desert communities had become a destination for increasing numbers of people. The possibility of doubling the population each decade on a sustained basis was alarming, however. The development of residential projects like Bloomington and Green Valley convinced the board that such growth would continue.

An alternative to the Dixie Project was on the minds of members of the district board. Under the chairmanship of Ron Thompson, the conservancy district board sought alternative funding mechanisms. It considered a proposal from Ellis Armstrong at the Bureau of Reclamation for a site near Purgatory, and it looked at a proposal from the SM Corporation for a 10,000-acre foot reservoir, but the board finally decided on a project proposed by Creamer and Noble Engineers in St. George. It used as its precedent the Gunlock Reservoir, turning to the Utah State Water Board for loans to fund a new reservoir. This one was to be located at Quail Creek.

The dam provided a solution to Frank Adams's warning in 1904 that a reservoir directly on the Virgin River would be destroyed by silting. The Quail Creek plan diverted water from the Virgin River through a canal system to avoid silting. The district presented a bond election to county residents (instead of canal companies) for $20 million, and it passed. Bonding enabled the creative idea to be implemented; construction began in 1982 and the reservoir of 40,000 acre feet was half full and in use by 1987.

Power generation in connection with Quail Creek was a controversial matter. Water falling from the diversion canal above the reservoir allowed for some generation of electricity. The question was whether to grant that privilege to Utah Power and Light Company or to the Dixie Rural Electric Association (REA) which supplied power to several parts of the county. The conservancy district board was split on the matter, with strong feelings on each side. It was a question of receiving a firm commitment of funds from a commercial company, Utah Power, at a set amount or to gamble on the possibility of a growing amount over time from a locally owned cooperative. Wayne Wilson was the chair and broke the tie vote in favor of Dixie REA, thus keeping power production in local hands. This proved to be a great revenue producer. The Dixie REA is not a Federal agency; it is an electric-power-generating cooperative which includes several communities in Washington County and southern Nevada.

This undertaking was built without direct involvement by the St. George Water and Power Board, which would become its largest customer. Some delicate negotiations were required resulting in the city building a water treatment plant just below the reservoir. The city contracted to lease 10,000-acre feet of water, more than doubling the entire supply then available to St. George. The plant was constructed and ready for use as the reservoir filled with water.

Then crisis struck. Like many other attempts to store water in Washington County, the Quail Creek dike began to leak. Soils under the lake were porous, and water seeped under the dike. Many attempts were taken to fill the leaks with cement, but the leaks continued. Members of the board began considering options. They looked at two similar dams which suggested some alternatives. Then, on New Year's Eve 1989, at 11:45 p.m., the dike broke. A massive flow of water burst out, scarring the land and rushing onto the floodplain of the Virgin River. Warning signals sounded, but many people thought they were midnight celebrations for the new year. Quickly word spread, and all emergency personnel were called into action. Water rushed into the Washington Fields, swept away livestock, and destroyed fields and barns. The Quail Creek dike was destroyed, a loss of $12 million. The bridge to the Washington Fields was destroyed as was the iron bridge in Bloomington Hills. The highway to Bloomington Hills was washed away, nearly isolating that suburb. Fears for the 1-15 bridge and the Bloomington bridge mounted as the waters approached, but the two bridges held. Several homes were flooded in Bloomington as the water reached the 100-year floodplain level. Miraculously, no lives were lost, but the property damage was high.

The dam had held; the dike was the structure that broke. The Washington County Conservancy District and its executive, Ron Thompson, were targets of criticism because they had built an earthen dike instead of a cement one. District officials met through the night and determined to rebuild immediately on the basis of the other dams they had inspected. They talked to Governor Norman Bangerter by telephone; he came to the site the next morning and met with the district leaders. He joined them in a quick decision to rebuild, setting a tone of rallying to meet an emergency. A plan was announced to rebuild the dike — this time not as an earthen structure resting on top of the porous soil but as a cement intrusion into the soil and side hills that would surely hold the water back. The governor pledged state support. Wayne Wilson had talked to members of the Utah Water Resources Board and gained a commitment from them to support another loan. He reminded them that all previous projects from Washington County had been paid back on time and assured them the same would occur with Quail Creek. There were a few tense hours, but unity was maintained both at the county and state levels. Within the year the replacement dike was underway, and was completed in two years. Fortunately the raging waters escaping from the dike had flowed below the St. George water treatment plant, sparing it from damage, so when the new dike created a renewed Quail Lake, the facility was ready to produce high-quality culinary water.

One might think that the final success of the Quail Creek project would solve Dixie's culinary water needs. For the 1990s, communities involved in it can serve their growing populations, but the spiraling population increases will soon consume that capacity. Future growth of the county will require major expansions of water storage, as has been the case since the first springs and streams were diverted in the 1850s and 1860s.

Water remains the most critical challenge for Washington County. Both ground-water and surface-water possibilities are promising. Geologic studies have identified new sources of ground water, and state and water conservancy district planning has pinpointed sites for additional dams and dikes.[29] There are, however, increasing numbers of environmental and political constraints that limit these water development options. Ultimately, water availability will be the prime limiting factor to further development of Utah's Dixie.

ENDNOTES

1. Andrew Karl Larson, *The Red Hills of November*, 110-2.

2. Andrew Karl Larson, *I Was Called to Dixie*, 361; see also Bleak, "Annals" Book B, 43.

3. Larson, *I Was Called to Dixie*, 368.

4. Report of the State Board of Equalization, 1896.

5. Lyman Hafen, *Making the Desert Bloom* (St. George: Publishers Place, 1991), 11-4.

6. Ibid., 12-3.

7. "Diary of Orson Huntsman," vol. II, 30ff.

8. Ibid., 37-42.

9. J. Stewart Williams, and Mary L. Tapper, "Earthquake History of Utah, 1850-1949," *Bulletin of the Seismological Society of America 43* (July 1953): 203. See also Andrew Karl Larson, "Irrigation and Agriculture in Washington County," in *Under The Dixie Sun*, 54-5.

10. Larson, *I Was Called to Dixie*, 376-8.

11. Ruby Webb, *A Brief History of the La Verkin Hot Springs and the La Verkin Canal*, (n.p.: Daughters of Utah Pioneers, 1986), 32-40.

12. James Jepson, Jr., *Memories and Experiences of James Jepson, Jr.*, ed. Etta Holdaway Spendlove (n.p.: Lucy Barnum and Zina Barnum, 1944), 20-1.

13. Jepson, *Memories*, 26.

14. Alice Gubler Stratton, "The Story of the Hurricane Canal," *St. George Magazine*, Vacation Issue 1991, 11-29.

15. Elwood Mead, *Report of Irrigation Investigations in Utah* (Washington, D.C.: U.S. Government Printing Office, 1904), doc. 720, 58th Congress, 2d Session, 213.

16. Ibid.

17. Ibid., 262.

18. Ibid., 220-2.

19. Ibid., 227-31.

20. Ibid., 235-44.

21. George Thomas, *The Development of Institutions Under Irrigation* (New York: Macmillan, 1920), 44-5.

22. Mead, *Report*, 227.

23. York Jones and Evelyn Jones, *Lehi Willard Jones* (Cedar City: n.p., 1972), 145-61; see also Walter Jones, "Newcastle Reclamation Project" (1985), Dixie College Archives, Gregerson Collection, 26.

24. Lyman Hafen, *Making the Desert Bloom*, 40.

25. "An Unexpected Visit with Governor George Dewey Clyde," letter from Jay Bingham to Douglas D. Alder, 8 August 1995, Dixie College Archives, Water File.

26. Letter, Shirl H. Pitchforth to Douglas D. Alder and Karl Brooks, 10 September 1994, Dixie College Archives, Water File.

27. David Lloyd, "The Politics and History of the Dixie Project, Utah," paper submitted to Dr. Frank H. Jonas, Western Politics Seminar, University of Utah, 1968, pp. 8, 11, Dixie College Archives, Water File. See also *Dixie Project, Utah*, House Doc. 86, 88th Congress, 1st Session, 21 March 1963, and United States Department of the Interior, Bureau of Reclamation, Region 3, "Definite Plan Report on Dixie Project, Utah," June 1967.

28. *Washington County News*, 22 March 1973, 1. See also Wayne Wilson, interview 19 November 1994, Dixie College Archives.

29. *Utah State Water Plan: Kanab Creek/Virgin River Basin* (Salt Lake City: Utah Board of Water Resources, 1993), 2-4.

8

END OF ISOLATION,
1930-1960

From the arrival of the Mormons in the 1850s and 1860s onward to 1930, the people in Washington County were relatively isolated. The railroad did not penetrate the county despite several schemes to entice investors to bring it into Dixie. Between 1903 and 1911 several proposals seemed near finalization. The Iron County Record of Cedar City announced on 17 July 1903: "Milford and Dixie are to be connected by an electric railroad, according to the plans of George F. Lane, the Milford mining operator, who says he has secured ample capital for the enterprise and the work will be commenced within ninety days. The line will be 130 miles long and will go by way of Beaver and Parowan, running four miles west of Cedar and on to St. George." Work never commenced.

The commercial clubs of Washington County and Iron County joined to lobby railroad officials in Salt Lake City to choose the Cedar City to St. George route down the Black Ridge for a proposed railroad to the Grand Canyon. Throughout the year 1910, boosters from Cedar City wrote letters and articles in the Iron County Record expressing confidence that the railroad would come to Dixie. The boosterism and

Wagons loading freight at Lund, Utah, the closest railhead to St. George until 1923. (Wm. L. Crawford Collection)

optimism were assertive, but the capitalists in Salt Lake City were not moved. The rail line was laid farther west, skirting Washington County; thus the commerce and outside capital that usually accompanied the "iron horse" went elsewhere.

The alternative to the railroad was wagon roads into Washington County; however, they were a major deterrent — difficult to traverse, particularly down the Black Ridge between Harmony and Toquerville. To the south, navigation on the Colorado River never did materialize as a significant route even though Brigham Young had considered that possibility. Dixie was not connected to national traffic and was hardly connected to Utah travel; it remained isolated.

That did not mean total isolation, however. Obviously the settlers themselves had reached this land of sand and sunshine. They engaged in a lively freighting trade with their northern compatriots. Miners also flocked to Silver Reef in the late 1870s, but most had left by the early 1890s. Mail came regularly. Cattlemen drove herds to market, mainly to the railheads at Modena and Lund in western Iron County. California immigrants followed the Spanish Trail through the western edge of the county. Mormon church leaders visited regularly, as did Federal marshals seeking polygamists. Folks came up the "Honeymoon Trail" from the Little Colorado River settlements to be married in the St. George LDS Temple. Some Dixieites traveled two days to the railhead and rode the train to Salt Lake City for the Mormon church's semiannual general conference, family visits, or trade; nonetheless, Dixie remained quite isolated, a fact which brought both advantages and disadvantages.

Zion National Park

Gradually outside influences began to interrupt the peaceful isolation, the monolithic culture, the agrarian austerity that pervaded Dixie. One of the first elements of change began quietly. Off in a remote corner of the county where the tiny Mormon villages of Springdale and Rockville were devoted to subsistence farming along the banks of the Virgin River, an event occurred that would transform the region. In 1909 the U.S. government designated a canyon of the Virgin River as Mukuntuweap National Monument after an Indian name for the area. This came as a surprise to most county residents, but it was the beginning of a process that would eventually give Dixie its international reputation for scenic beauty and its largest industry — tourism.

The designation of Mukuntuweap National Monument by presidential proclamation signed by President William Howard Taft was the result of an extended process of discovery of the area by "outsiders." Two of John Wesley Powell's associates in the explorations of the Grand Canyon, Clarence Dutton and Frederick Dellenbaugh, helped bring Zion Canyon to national attention. Dutton explored the canyon in 1880 and included florid descriptive language in his 1882 U.S. Geological Survey report:

> Nothing can exceed the beauty of Little Zion Valley....In its proportions it is about equal to Yosemite, but in the nobility and beauty of the sculptures there is no comparison. No wonder the fierce Mormon Zealot, who named it, was reminded of the Great Zion, on which his fervid mind was bent — "of a house not built with hands, eternal in the heavens."[1]

Much later, in 1903, Frederick Dellenbaugh visited Zion Canyon and took photographs which he published in the January 1904 issue of Scribner's Magazine. That same year several of his oil paintings were exhibited at the St. Louis World's Fair. This exposure brought

Aerial view of Zion Lodge area in 1923-4.
(National Park Service Photograph, J. L. Crawford Collection)

notoriety but did not open up the area to travel because existing roads were merely wagon trails.

Leo A. Snow, U.S. deputy surveyor and resident of St. George, following months of survey work in southern Utah which included Zion Canyon, wrote in June 1909:

> A view can be had of this canyon surpassed only by a similar view of the Grand Canyon of the Colorado. At intervals along the west side of the canyon streams of various sizes rush over the edge of the chasm forming water falls from 800 to 2000 feet high. The stream in the bottom of the canyon appears as a silver ribbon winding its way among the undergrowth and occasionally disappearing from view. In my opinion this canyon should be set apart by the government as a national park.[2]

A little over a month after receiving Snow's report, the Acting Secretary of the Interior made a recommendation to President Taft for the creation of Mukuntuweap National Monument. President Taft signed the proclamation the same day — 31 July 1909.[3]

With the stroke of Taft's pen, southern Utah was changed forever. The national monument designation was amazingly uncomplicated. It preceded the creation of the U.S. National Park Service but came at a time when several people in Washington, D.C., particularly Stephen T. Mather and Horace Albright, were anxious to designate scenic lands for national preservation. These two men became the founding director and assistant director of the United States National Park Service. The national monument label came without a long lobby from local folks; in fact, it came almost effortlessly because naming the monument did not require an appropriation or congressional approval.

In 1917 Horace Albright visited Mukuntuweap National Monument. Albright, like other early visitors to the area, was taken with Mukuntuweap's scenic beauty and grandeur, and he moved quickly to expand the acreage of the monument and to change its name. He later recalled in a report to Stephen T. Mather, director of the National Park Service, that "Mukuntuweap National Monument was too small and the name was too hard to pronounce, and the people there called the place 'Little Zion'...." Albright returned to Washington to begin work to enlarge the monument and to change its name. Former governor William Spry and church leader Heber J. Grant were strongly supportive of the name change and the campaign to include the monument in the national park system. Senator Reed Smoot from Utah agreed to sponsor the bill expanding the size of the monument and changing its name to Zion National Park.[4]

Over time, several people were appointed as park superintendents but the one consistent person to carry on the work of developing the park was Springdale resident Walter Ruesch, who began as custodian of the park in 1917 and remained at his post under various titles, constructing many trails and buildings until his retirement in 1948.

Friends of Zion National Park enjoy early park stories such as those of Nephi Johnson and the Indians who were hesitant to enter the canyon with him because they felt the canyon was the dwelling place of the spirits; Isaac Behunin's farming in isolation near the present-day lodge; David Flanigan's famous cable to bring lumber from the upper mesa down into the canyon for milling; and especially the building of the Zion Tunnel in 1930. This latter development was a major factor in opening the canyon to automobile traffic, thereby encouraging that new phenomenon — the tourist.

C.Y. Rozencrans and William L. Crawford standing on a platform of the upper cable frame which was built by David Flanigan between 1888 and 1901. (Photographed by Putnam and Valentine, Los Angeles, California, J.L. Crawford Collection)

Utah Parks Company

The designation of the monument as a national park and resultant nationwide publicity of Zion and the other scenic and geological wonders of southern Utah and northern Arizona increased the number of visitors to the park following World War I. The National Park Service quickly found itself unable to provide adequate accommodations for the growing number of visitors to the park. The Union Pacific Railroad and its newly-established subsidiary, Utah Parks Company, agreed to provide high-quality accommodations at Zion National Park and the other national parks in the region. Tourists traveling by rail were brought to Zion by a railroad spur from Lund to Cedar City where a fleet of orange buses owned and operated by Utah Parks Company transported visitors to Zion, Bryce, and Grand Canyon national parks.

By 1923 the Union Pacific Railroad had absorbed the LA & SL Railroad, established the Utah Parks Company, and taken over William W. Wylie's and Parry Brothers' Zion operations. A new lodge with separate guest cabins was opened for business in 1925, retiring the Wylie tents as guest housing, though they were kept as employee housing until about the beginning of World War II. The new cabins were built without bathroom facilities, making a chamber pot a necessity in each room. Showers and other modern appurtenances were provided at the lodge center. By 1929 there were nearly 150 "standard" rooms and twenty "deluxe" — the deluxe including "comfort stations."

The Great Depression of the 1930s spurred the addition of a different type of facility near the south entrance to the park. A cafeteria and less-expensive cabins operated from 1935 to 1973, at which time the cafeteria was closed and the cabins were removed.

To accommodate increased tourism and to meet the needs of the Utah Parks Company, the National Park Service built a bridge across the Virgin River at Rockville. The relationship between the National Park Service and the Union Pacific Railroad was not always an amicable one. One early conflict was over roads and 200 acres owned inside the proposed Bryce Canyon National Park. The railroad agreed to sell the land to the Park Service, which in turn agreed to build the Zion-Mt. Carmel highway and tunnel to accommodate Utah Parks Company buses.[5] The cooperation between the Utah Parks Company and the National Park Service did encourage more tourists to visit

Opening Day at Zion Lodge, 20 May 1925.
(Photograph by Harold Russell, J. L. Crawford Collection)

Zion Park and the other wonders of the region. In 1924 there were 8,400 visitors to Zion Park, double the number of the previous year. The figure continued to multiply until the hard times of the Great Depression when the number of visitors leveled off at about 55,000. In 1995 there were nearly three million visitors to Zion Park, adding greatly to the economy of Washington County.

The tunnel shortened the distance to Bryce Canyon by seventy miles and to Grand Canyon by twenty. A significant concession had been made previously when, in 1924, the Park Service went outside its boundary to install a bridge across the Virgin River at Rockville, bypassing Hurricane and shortening the distance to Zion National Park by thirty-three miles, a crucial benefit to the Utah Parks Company and its buses which took tourists to all three national parks. National Park Service Director Stephen Mather donated $5,000 of his own money to that project.

Utah Parks Company officials underestimated the impact of the private automobile. They believed that the remoteness of the national parks in the southwestern United States would convince most people to take the train and be guided through the parks on buses. The company invested in rustic lodges, cabins, and dining facilities and provided memorable entertainment. In actuality automobiles came regularly from early days, and by the outbreak of World War II, the majority of visitors were coming to the parks by automobile. From 1943 to 1945, the parks company closed its facilities because of the war. When they re-opened, the automobile was king. Soon both train service to Cedar City and connecting bus service to the parks were abandoned.

All of this changed Washington County. People from throughout the nation and some from beyond its borders were coming to the land of red sand and considering it not as primarily desolate and dry but as profoundly beautiful. After years of exporting a modest volume of agricultural goods and struggling with a life of scarcity, Dixie residents had a new product: beauty. It took some time for local businessmen to realize the significance of this shift. Here was something that did not need to be shipped away; the consumers came to the source and, when they left, the beauty remained. The visitors also served as word-of-mouth advertisers. There were new outside allies to help in this trade — the Union Pacific Railroad, the state of Utah, and the National Park Service. Here was the outside capital that had long eluded county developers. Southern Utahns could develop a new source of employment for their sons and daughters and there were new opportunities for entrepreneurs.

Zion Natural History Association

Zion National Park benefited greatly from public-spirited citizens, including Juanita Brooks, Herbert E. Gregory, and Arthur Bruhn, who responded to requests for volunteer service to promote it. This was facilitated through the Zion Natural History Association (ZNHA) that was organized in 1929 as the Zion-Bryce Natural History Association but split in 1961 to become independent. ZNHA is a non-profit organization chartered by the National Park Service and incorporated under Utah law for the purpose of supplementing interpretive activities of the park through the publication of books, maps, guides, pictures, and documents. ZNHA operates the bookstores in the park where publications and other items are sold. This arrangement ensures that the Federal government ia not in competition with local businesses.

By the 1970s, the volume of tourists to the park was enormous and the sale of tourist materials substantial. Because of the weight of association duties, the National Park Service required boards of directors to assume management of all business, freeing the chief naturalist for official government business. Victor Jackson remained as coordinator between the park and the board of directors. Under the direction of the board chairman, St. George community leader Robert N. Sears, the board assumed a much more independent role, increased the size of the board of directors, opened membership to the public, and hired a professional executive director, Jamie Gentry. Sears also organized "The Friends of Kolob" as a fund-raising effort which was successful in encouraging people to donate $100 or more to become life members. The "Friends" group was later absorbed into ZNHA. A million-dollar addition to the visitor center was built in the 1980s. An additional visitor center was constructed at the 1-15 entrance to the Kolob section of the park.

One of the most memorable projects of the association was to sell the forty-seven tourist cabins that were being replaced by permanent and updated facilities. Sears and J. R. Madsen spent hundreds of hours supervising their removal and sale, and the men were able to raise $48,000 for the park with this project. In recent years ZNHA has formed the Zion Canyon Field Institute and the Zion National Park Foundation.

ZNHA is one of the most successful services of its kind throughout the national parks system. It is a member of the Association of Partners for Public Lands (APPL) which holds annual conventions and whose 1996 national convention was held in St. George.

Automobiles

The Washington County News in the 1930s was replete with advertisements enticing county residents to purchase Chevrolets and Fords at prices ranging from $475 to $675. Half-ton, 1-1/2 ton, and large chassis 1-1/2 ton trucks were also popular. Those vehicles soon made peddling and freighting a big business in Dixie, overcoming some of the drawbacks of the lack of a railhead in the county. Though oiled roads were rare, auto buyers were soon found in the county, and travelers from outside came in ever-increasing numbers in private automobiles. Service stations appeared, as did restaurants. Local merchants became seriously involved in the trucking business. By 1 April 1928 there were 490 cars and trucks licensed in the county. This was the beginning of something more profound for Dixie than the railroad was for neighboring Iron County because it was a mode of transportation that would only grow.

Early automobile travelers in Washington County faced many difficulties.
(Lynne Clark Collection, donor — Orpha Morris)

National and local automobile clubs took to the road promoting tourism by automobile, endorsing hotels, and lobbying for good, all-weather roads. Nationally, the Lincoln Automobile Club, with a growing membership of automobile owners, and the Arrowhead Trail Automobile Association lobbied Congress for the construction of a national highway linking the east coast with the west coast. In Utah, the Arrowhead Trail Automobile Association was active in promoting the Salt Lake City to Los Angeles route, passing through Washington County. In the 1920s and 1930s, the Arrowhead Trail from Los Angeles to Salt Lake City was a project that brought national attention to Washington County. It was part of the national promotional campaigns developed by the automobile industry to increase the average American's desire to own automobiles. The famous race driver, Charles Bigelow, was particularly effective as an automobile lobbyist and developed close ties in St. George.[6] He was close to Warren Cox who built the Arrowhead Hotel in St. George. Cox's hotel became a haven for travelers on the Arrowhead Trail, as did Snow's and the Liberty Hotel.

Partly because of Bigelow's effectiveness, there was a growing interest in automobile tourism to the national parks in southern Utah and northern Arizona. The Salt Lake City Commercial Club organized an automobile expedition of five cars and seventeen people in September 1914 to demonstrate the viability of auto tourism to southern Utah. The automobile expedition invited Warren Cox of St. George to join the group as its travel guide from Salt Lake City to St. George.[7] Meetings were held along the route to encourage local townspeople to sustain this new economic venture and support improved roads in the state.

The expedition was not without incidents, however. At many locations in Washington County members of the expedition were forced to "camp out," there being no adequate facilities. Breakdowns occurred frequently, and the lack of gasoline facilities required the expedition to place tanks of gasoline along the route in advance.

Roads in the county and south to the north rim of the Grand Canyon were difficult for the automobiles. The drive up the Hurricane Cliffs to Kanab was much more difficult than anticipated, resulting in the temporary abandonment of two of the five cars.

The expedition brought further attention to the scenic wonders in the county and southern Utah while also demonstrating that tourism by automobile was possible. On the heels of this first and successful tourist expedition, ambitious businessmen in the county built sleeping and eating establishments for weary tourists and service stations for their automobiles.

Roads

Any significant automobile travel in Washington County depended on there being oiled roads. Crusading automobile club members braved gravel roads, but normal high-volume auto traffic depended on hard-surfaced roads. The Zion Tunnel road provided a case in point. It opened Zion National Park to a whole array of visitors and created a major tourist business. The development of other such roads was necessary to transform Utah's Dixie.

Roads had been a challenge from the earliest arrival of white settlers. The first roads began as rude wagon trails in the same general routes that the main routes follow today: down the Black Ridge from Harmony to Toquerville, then on to Washington through challenging sand deposits and finally to St. George. This road would later become Highway 91 and eventually Interstate 15.

Very early a trail was hacked into the Hurricane Cliffs above To-querville so that settlers could settle the upper Virgin River valley at Grafton, Virgin, Rockville, Springdale, and Shunesburg. A road later would be built up the hill outside Grafton to Kanab. That in turn was replaced by the Rockville mountain road. Another series of roads led toward Pine Valley, Mountain Meadows, and Hamblin (with connections to Gunlock), and later extended from Central to Enterprise. A road from Washington, called the Warner Valley Gap Road, went out through Fort Pearce, up the Hurricane Cliffs, and on to Pipe Spring, Moccasin Springs, Kanab, and Long Valley. Wagons that went to the Muddy River settlements lumbered from St. George to Beaver Dam and then over difficult terrain, either crossing the Virgin River many times or taking a dangerous alternate route over the desert sands.

County road development and maintenance was the responsibility of the three elected county selectmen (county commissioners) and the probate judge — collectively known as the county court. The court hired superintendents of roads (or several superintendents for different roads) to supervise their development and maintenance in the county. The county court levied taxes and labor assessments for the maintenance of county roads. It was not unusual for Mormon ward congregations to obligate themselves to road building. It was also possible to pay church tithing or delinquent taxes by working on the roads.[8]

John R. Young was appointed superintendent for the St. George and Pine Valley Road in the 1860s. Young reported to the court in June 1867 that he collected, through donation of labor on the road, $907.85 of the $978.50 that was needed for its improvement.[9]

From the outset, Dixie Latter-day Saints in Washington County were able to persuade the territorial legislature to appropriate modest sums toward road building. This made it possible to pay workers a dollar or two a day for hard labor on roads, but the allotments were always merely a portion of the cost. For example, in 1878 the legislature appropriated $3,000 "for widening of the dugways, removing rock from the road, and graveling or otherwise covering what is known as the Grapevine Sand, and generally repairing and straightening the Territorial Road from the head of the Black Ridge Dugway through Bellevue and Leeds, to St. George,...."[10]

After the turn of the century, it was a common practice for inmates from the state prison in Salt Lake City to work on major road-building

This 1915 camp at Anderson's Ranch accommodated prisoners constructing a state highway. (Mildred Larch Collection, in the possession of Harriet Leavitt)

projects. Zion National Park benefited from such labor. J. T. Woodbury reported in the Deseret News of 18 October 1913 that convicts would be working on a road to the county line toward Cedar City. State appropriations grew over time so that by 1936 the state made $60,000 available for another project, the Snow Canyon road.

Improved construction machinery, technology, and engineering, as well as stronger bridge materials, greatly improved county roads and bridges at the turn of the century. In 1924 the county constructed a steel bridge over the Virgin River near Rockville which greatly improved access to Zion National Park by Utah Parks Company buses. This sturdy bridge is still being used by travelers today. Equally important to the transportation needs of the county was the erection in 1925 of a steel bridge a few miles south of the Iron-Washington county line on the newly-established road called the Arrowhead Trail. Other bridges were also built by the state to serve the transportation needs in the county. In 1934 a bridge was erected between St. George and Hurricane, considerably shortening the route between the two communities. In 1937 a steel bridge was erected over the gulch near Pah Tempe, improving the road between La Verkin and Hurricane.[11]

The link of St. George with Las Vegas had historic roots back to the days before the Utah War when Las Vegas was a Mormon outpost. Because Washington County, Utah, and Clark County, Nevada, share comparable elevation and other physical similarities, travel and trade between the two areas developed easily. The connection between St. George, Cedar City, and beyond to Salt Lake City was politically and culturally essential to Washington County residents, so St. George was a vital point along the proposed Arrowhead Trail to Los Angeles. Completing an oil surface road all the way so automobiles could travel easily was of prime importance.[12] The St. George Chamber of Commerce undertook an aggressive advertising campaign, especially in the California press, presenting St. George as a tourist mecca and also as a good site for conventions. In the late 1920s, segments of the Arrowhead Trail (later designated U.S. Highway 91) were oiled. The last segment to receive oil was completed in early January 1931. The Washington County News reported: "With the completion of this seven mile stretch (Harrisburg to Anderson's Ranch) the last unimproved link on the Arrowhead Trail in this County will be finished."[13]

State funds were used to make improvements to Main Street in St. George because it was part of the Salt Lake to Los Angeles highway. This oiling greatly reduced the dust kicked up by increased automobile traffic and was a blessing for residents living nearby. It also benefited downtown businessmen.

Tourism

Completion of national and state highways brought a transformation almost unimagined to Washington County. A new zest infected businessmen; motor courts, restaurants, and gas stations were built. The challenge at first was to attract people to stay a night instead of driving through. That was the initial vision; later, ideas would surface to attempt to entice visitors to stay longer than just one night.

The eastern half of the county became involved in the tourist trade as soon as Zion Canyon became an attraction. J. L. Crawford, one of the advisors for this history, contributed the following synopsis of early tourism connected with Zion National Park:

> When Zion National Park came into being in 1917 there were three hotels in Hurricane (Isom, Reeve and Bradshaw). At least two hotels were doing business in St. George (the Arrowhead and Snow's)

William Wylie operated this tourist camp in Zion National Park from 1917 until 1923. (Photo by Putnam and Valentine, Los Angeles, J. L. Crawford Collection)

and certainly drew part of their clientele from the Arrowhead Trail (later U.S. Highway 91), some of which could be classified as "tourists." Those three establishments in Hurricane can attribute their beginnings to the sheep industry; and specifically to the Gould's Shearing Corral which began operation in 1910. That huge sheep-shearing establishment naturally drew buyers and salesmen to the area and the need for accommodations was apparent. The exact year the hotels came into being isn't known and each was most probably a home turned into a boarding house, but each acquired the name "hotel" and stayed in business for many years.[14]

Director Stephen T. Mather of the National Park Service, seeing the chaos that existed in the tourist industry around Yellowstone, took steps to eliminate business competition in the parks, turning concessions into virtual monopolies. That year the Parry brothers — Gronway, Whitney, and Chauncey — who owned the Cedars Hotel in Cedar City, made application to operate transportation and hotel services in Zion National Park and at the North Rim of the Grand Canyon. About the same time, Douglas White, passenger agent for the Los Angeles and Salt Lake Railroad, made a similar application for his company. An agreement was reached whereby the railroad company would operate the hotel services while the Parrys ran the stages from Cedar City to Zion and Grand Canyon's North Rim.

W. W. Wylie, although aging, was hired by the railroad company to build camps at both Zion and Grand Canyon national parks, patterned after the Yellowstone operation for which he had become famous. The camps provided tents stretched over wooden frames and floors, a modest accommodation that was better than camping but not as expensive as park hotels. The camps were open for business by the spring of 1917. Wylie's son-in-law, Robert McKee, managed the Grand Canyon camp. Wylie and his wife remained in Zion. The Wylies gained a reputation as excellent hosts, serving appealing meals and providing clean sleeping quarters — no small accomplishment since they had to contend with box-elder bugs, caterpillars, skunks, and sand. Most of their foodstuffs were purchased locally, thereby helping to establish a fine rapport with the local residents, several of whom were hired to help run the camp. These accommodations were somewhat primitive by today's standards, although water was piped to the kitchen and a centrally located shower bath. One or two outside taps and privies took care of other needs.

In 1972 the Utah Parks Company was disbanded and the Union Pacific railroad company donated its property, less rolling stock, to the National Park Service which planned to close all overnight facilities inside the park except campgrounds. Because of objections from the public, however, it found a new concessioner, TW Services. Although bathrooms had been added to the standard cabins following World War II, by 1984 they had been replaced by modern motel-type, multi-room structures.

The Utah Parks Company had a franchise that constituted a monopoly within the park boundary. There also was little competition from outside for many years. The small operations that began in nearby communities had little or no effect on business inside the park. The Utah Parks Company ultimately failed because of the demise of railroad passenger business as the American traveling public turned to automobiles.

Whether Wylie set the pattern for future tourist camps or not, the many that sprang up in the vicinity — and all over the country — provided similar accommodations, except they were wooden structures instead of tents. A typical camp, or "tourist court' consisted of single,

The Bradshaw Hotel in Hurricane, c. 1910.
(Photograph by William L. Crawford, J. L. Crawford Collection)

plain, frame cabins with bare essentials such as bedstead with mattress, a chair or two, a table with a washbasin and pitcher. An outside tap provided water. Toilets and bathrooms were located centrally. There were four such courts in Springdale and two in Rockville, beginning about 1927. The two in Rockville didn't survive, but one is still in use in Springdale. It began as the Olsen Tourist Camp but has changed hands several times, being upgraded in the process. Another court, the most successful, was built by John A. Allred, who also operated a restaurant. Although his rooms were the old single-cabin type, both rooms and restaurant were considered to be rather high class. None of the establishments took on the name "motel" until after World War II. By 1970 Allred had sold out, and the modern Pioneer Lodge and Restaurant now (1996) occupies that location.

Tourism in the Eastern Part of the County

The up-river communities of the county remained rather quiet into the 1950s, at which time new tourist businesses began to appear. Even then most activity seemed to be in Springdale, except for a cafe and a few cabins in Virgin that have long since disappeared. As of 1994 there were nine thriving motels and three restaurants in Springdale, with the prospect of more being added. A convention center was added in 1996. In recent years, bed-and-breakfast establishments have become popular in all towns. Springdale, Rockville, and Virgin all have a few. This appears to be about the only kind of business the people of Rockville allow in their town.

Until quite recently, both Hurricane and La Verkin remained quiet towns, with only the Swan Motel offering up-to-date tourist accommodations. La Verkin may still be classified as a bedroom community; however, within the last decade one motel and various other businesses have blossomed along state Route 9. Hurricane is rapidly expanding southward into what used to be farmland, and westward across the Virgin River to Interstate 15. There are four motels in Hurricane. Hildale, on the Utah-Arizona line, has one motel and a restaurant. The tourist industry continues to expand in the county.

Campgrounds have always been part of the national park scene, but only since World War II have they become common while taking on a new look with the advent of the recreational vehicle. Those campgrounds provided by the National Park Service remain old-fashioned to the extent that they don't furnish electrical, water, and sewer hook-ups. They do, however, have conveniently located dumping stations. Commercial campgrounds are now found in nearly every town, taking advantage of the popularity of the travel trailer and motor home (RVs). At this writing, Springdale had only one commercial campground, La Verkin had one, and four were in Hurricane. As most RVs are self-contained, a one-night stay in a campground without hook-ups is acceptable, so the Zion campgrounds are full nearly every night during summer months.

Tourists and St. George

The motel, gas station, and restaurant business in St. George has been one of continuing expansion. The arrival of U.S. Highway 91 in 1930 enabled the city to become a vital tourism center. Located midway between Salt Lake City and Los Angeles, the city quickly developed a hotel business at the Tabernacle and Main Street junction where the Snow and Arrowhead hotels were located. Then "Jockey"

Hail and others in the local Democratic party convinced the state government to move Highway 91 one block north to what later would be called "the Boulevard." In the 1930s it was simply "100 North"; today its formal name is "St. George Boulevard" and it has become the motel/restaurant lane. Hail built the Liberty Hotel on the 100 East block, soon to be followed by some twenty other accommodations between 800 East and 500 West. These included Fred Schulze's cabins (at Dick's Cafe); Motel 91 and Cafe operated by Bill and Lida Prince; the Colonial, west of the Sugar Loaf Cafe run by Bert Milne (it later moved to 400 East and was called the Milne Motel); the Red Mesa owned by Bert Covington; the Holt Brothers' Sands; the Twin Oaks at 300 West; the Desert Edge Motel next to the Sands; the Thompson Motel; Blaine Andrus's Bennett Motel; the Shady Acre, where Julio Paolasso and Melvin Larson were in charge; Clarence Force's Big D Motel; the Travel Inn owned by the Wittwers, across from the Sugar Loaf Cafe; Lynne Empey's LynMor Motel; the Lamplighter Trailer Park on the west end; Hail Motel at 200 East operated by Brown Hail and Richard Jenson; and Andy Pace's motel at 100 West. When all of these were operating in the 1950s, there were about 500 beds available. In contrast, there were 2,500 in 1995 (plus 500 more in the rest of the county).

When the freeway arrived in 1973, a whole new arrangement developed as motels were built near the two St. George exits — South Side, Four Seasons, Thunderbird, Motel Six, Travel Lodge, Comfort Inn, Regency, and Chalet were built on the north very recently. Ramada and Hampton Inn opened on the east side of the freeway at exit 8. At exit 6 on the south end of town, motels including Heritage Inn, Budget 8, Super 8, Ancestor, Claridge, and Comfort Suites have been built in the 1990s.

Despite these developments, other motels were built in the center of town: Anthony Atkin's Travel Lodge at 100 West, Sid Atkin's Rodeway Inn in the 200 East block (recently renamed Singletree), Wittwer's Coral Hills across from Dick's Cafe, Weston's Lamplighter in the 400 East block, and the Coronada in the 500 East block.

Certainly one of the biggest developments was the coming of the Hilton Inn on the south end of town (exit 6). When it was built, it seemed far away from town and very ambitious. A golf course was developed in conjunction with the inn. John and Daisy Morgan were the proprietors, and they invested heavily in television advertisements in the Wasatch Front market. The image of those ads — sunshine, golf, recreation — reinforced the southwest image that the chamber of commerce had initiated in the 1940s with its theme: "Where the Summer Sun Spends the Winter." Northern Utahns increasingly came to see St. George as a destination recreation spot. The Hilton became a major attraction, which was then matched by the Holiday Inn on Bluff some twenty years later. These two facilities have been active in attracting conventions to St. George.

The restaurants that captured the tourist market from the 1930s to 1960s included dining facilities in the Arrowhead and Liberty hotels; George Pace's Big Hand Cafe at the junction of Main Street and St. George Boulevard (where Ancestor Square is today); Dick's Cafe, which became famous when movie industry crews were on location in St. George; the Sugar Loaf Cafe at 300 East and Boulevard, operated initially by Don McDonald and later by the Atkin family; the Whiteway malt shop owned by the Whitehead family, across from the Big Hand Cafe; the Desert Kitchen at 800 East; the Wishbone, run by Walter Fuller, which later became a Chinese restaurant called John John's (where Zion's Bank is today on the Boulevard) and the Trafalga Restaurant run by Fenton Terry. These restaurants have all disappeared except Dick's, which is slated for removal. They have been replaced by some sixty other dining establishments, which testify to the brisk trade supported by tourists and residents alike.

The development of a sleek highway and many passing automobiles caused someone at the newspaper to consider the future. On 16 April 1931, a brief article appeared near the bottom of the second page, not making any waves, but it certainly was an early prophecy.

A Golf Course is the first step toward making St. George a winter resort. People from the North who generally spend their winters in California say that our greatest asset and opportunity lies in this direction. Our climate is unexcelled and there are many places in the valley which could be made into a first-class golf course. Governor Dern is one of our biggest boosters and at the banquet in his honor two weeks ago, and in letters to local people, [he] urged that we develop along these lines and take advantage of our natural resources.

As it is now we have nothing to hold the vacationist. He stops for a few minutes or stays over night, goes to a picture show, gets a glimpse of the surrounding scenery and is gone the next morning. A large majority of these people if we had a golf course, and other like amusements, would remain a few days and in some instances, as the town became better known, would establish winter homes here.[15]

Aviation

Another sign that Dixie was overcoming its isolation was the arrival of airplanes. An early airport, southeast of Washington City, was started in 1924. By 1948 it had become an emergency Civil Aeronautics Authority (CAA) facility, but it was abandoned in 1955. Another small strip was established as an air-mail field west of Little Valley on the road to the Arizona Strip. In the 1920s, Maurice Graham, a Western Air Express mail pilot, landed on a race strip atop the Black Hill during bad weather. Graham's landing may have led local officials to settle on that location for the official St. George airport. In the early 1930s, city officials established an airport on the hill in St. George, and in 1940, they blacktopped the main runway and built a small hangar and terminal building.

Dixie College joined in the operation. In 1938 the college, under the leadership of President B. Glen Smith, gained authorization to offer an aeronautics program. The class was first given in the fall of 1940 after a hangar was built, an airplane obtained, and an instructor, E. L. Anderson, appointed. By January 1941 seven students had passed their CAA flight tests: Van Blaine Cutler, Kanab; Lester Cottam, Merlin Milne, and Keith Hafen of St. George; Ray Sorenson, Orderville; Bill Frei, Santa Clara; and Lowell Terry, Rockville.

The story from that beginning is one of gradual improvement of the gravel airfield, hangars and terminal. The road up the hill was widened and graded in 1940. The city appointed Lee Owens as the local manager and the facility was dedicated with much ceremony in May 1941. These efforts were rewarded in 1946 when Western Airlines gained approval to stop in St. George. In October of that year, Challenger Airline began a daily flight to Salt Lake City. Neither of these services lasted long, however.

During that decade Owens had his hands full searching for funds to enclose the facility with a fence, improve the runway, and eventually finish a hard surface and install lights. After the hard surface was added with a grant of $84,000, the airport was dedicated once again in 1958. All those improvements were a prerequisite to the establish-

Washington County Soldiers at Camp Lewis, Washington, November 1917. (Lynne Clark Collection, donor — Archie Wallis)

ment of regular air service by Bonanza Airlines beginning in January 1958. That commercial effort lasted only two years. In November regular airmail service began but the airport remained largely a facility for Dixie College, commercial flight training, and private planes.16

World War I and the Depression

As was the case throughout the nation, Washington County citizens served in the military in World War I. Some 321 men and women entered the service from among 1,250 who were registered with the Selective Service. Of those, eleven died: Daniel Lester Keate, Sterling Russell, David L. McNeil, and George C. Felter of St. George; Wallace Gray and Glen J. Reber of Santa Clara; Charles E. Scannel of Orderville; Moroni Kleinman of Toquerville; Isaac H. Langston of Springdale; and Alton Hiatt and Ray C. Coleman of Enterprise.

The members of the Selective Service board in Washington County served voluntarily, without pay, and completed three rounds — 5 June 1917 (543), June and August 1918 (74), and September 1918 (633) — totaling 1,250 registrants. Following the war, the county and the city presented 321 medals to those who served as soldiers, sailors, marines, and Red Cross nurses.17

The United States entry into the war created an enormous market for agricultural goods, and farmers in Dixie thrived as never before. Trucking of agricultural produce boomed, overcoming the lack of a railroad. For a short time, Dixie residents thought they were going to be an agricultural power, but the war ended as abruptly as it had started for Americans. Markets for foodstuffs dropped dramatically; the county slid quickly into economic difficulties and felt the Great Depression a decade early.

Mining for copper at the Apex Mine southwest of St. George also fell off. The trucking of ore to the smelter located on Diagonal Street in St. George had employed many men as had the mining and providing of charcoal. The demand for copper declined precipitously with the end of the war. Activity at Apex slumbered until World War II revived the price of copper.

When the Great Depression of the 1930s hit the nation, people in Dixie were not initially alarmed. Black Friday did not even merit an article in the 31 October 1929 issue of the Washington County News. Few people were involved with the stock market, and everyone was already accustomed to scarcity. City fathers soon noted difficulties as valuation of property declined, however. The income from taxation for municipal government and county spending also waned. Total valuation for the state of Utah was $728 million in 1930 and $618 million in 1931, a drop of $110 million. Taxable valuation of St. George City in 1930 was $859,400 and $840,000 in 1931, a drop of $19,400. A dramatic example of the Depression was seen in the 10 December issue of the News — some thirteen pages (seven columns per page) of tax delinquent notices. In comparison the delinquent notices published on 5 December 1918 occupied a page and a half. The editor complained that his staff could not write news or meet the printing deadline because everyone at the paper was setting type for the delinquent tax list.

Just as alarming was the fall in farm prices. Between 1929 and 1931, wheat prices dropped from $1.03 to 46 cents per bushel in Utah, oats from 60 cents to 35 cents, potatoes from $1.10 per bushel to 45 cents, eggs from 32 cents to 22 cents, butter from 47 cents to 31 cents, and sheep from $8.70 per 100 lbs to $3.10. At the same time, tax burdens actually rose slightly.

Many banks in Utah closed during the early 1930s. Six failures were announced on 21 January 1932. Washington County was fortunate that two of its banks, the Bank of St. George and the State Bank of Hurricane, were able to avoid closure. David Hirschi was instrumental in working with northern banks and preserving the Hurricane institution. The Dixie Stockgrowers Bank in St. George closed in 1932.

Many people in Dixie suffered greatly during the Depression. Erinn Bowler, described the plight of her grandfather Marion in Gunlock:

They faced problems in farming during the depression, the biggest of which was the constant struggle to keep from having to sell their farmland because of crop and livestock failures. For example, in 1928 his father spent a great deal of money on a herd of goats, which at the time seemed like a good investment. Unfortunately when the economy faltered the next year, the goats became worthless and the entire investment was lost.

"As if the depression was not enough, during the same time we had the worst drought in our history." His father gladly accepted the job of running the Drought Relief Program. "No one turned down any job that paid money," he emphasized. This meant that, during the summers of 1932 and 1933, he seldom saw his father who, "practically worked around the clock, running the farm and working at any other job that came along." At one point, Bowler said, "father was put in charge of well drilling to get water for crops which were burning up." Then he got a job inspecting livestock, "which the government was paying $10 a head to have them killed, because the drought was so bad there was no feed on the range for them."[18]

Another Bowler family memory of the Depression was captured in Erinn's account:

I will never forget the day the bank went broke. It was just before Christmas. Dad had been able to raise about $70. He had sent it by mail to the Dixie Stockgrowers Bank to be deposited to his checking account. The next morning we received word the bank had gone broke. Mother was in tears and Dad was very upset. He knew if this money had reached the bank it was gone, and that was the only money they had to buy Christmas with. Dad finally contacted some friend in St. George who worked in the bank. He found out the money had not as yet reached the bank. This friend got the money out of the Post Office and dad was able to get it back. What happy excitement ran through our house when we received this word. Mother and Dad told us without this money there could be no Christmas presents. Imagine $70 for thirteen people. And to think that meant each of us would get an orange, a pair of high top shoes, a twenty-five cent pocket knife, or a piece of candy for Christmas.[19]

The Depression had a huge human impact. People lost jobs; even worse, some lost their farms to foreclosure. Some had to wait to attend high school, and when they did graduate, there were few jobs. Bowler returned to Gunlock to work on the farm but had no prospect of attending college, even though there was one nearby. As with many people, the Depression made a deep personal impact on Bowler, the future mayor of St. George, who said: "I own everything. If I can't pay cash, I wait. I never borrow."[20] This mindset became widespread in Dixie, complementing the long-held experience of "doing without."

Schools quickly ran out of funds to pay teachers' salaries. Despite many attempts to avoid it, including agreements by teachers to teach three weeks without pay, Washington County schools closed early — on 28 April 1933. Another measure of the intensity of the Depression was that 3,835 people applied to the Red Cross for wheat and flour in April 1932. The wheat was used largely for animals, including 1,946 cattle, 497 horses, 304 hogs, and 8,222 chickens.[21]

The New Deal

The election of Franklin Delano Roosevelt was welcomed by the majority of Washington County citizens; 1,678 voted for him and 1,328 for the Republicans. Soon various programs sponsored by President Roosevelt's New Deal legislation began to impact Dixie. In general, they were not seen as outside intrusions. The majority wanted a solution to the Depression and soon sought to participate in the various relief programs offered by Congress.

One of the most innovative efforts was intended to provide employment for housewives. The initiative was taken by Juanita Brooks who at the time was serving as St. George Stake Relief Society president. Working with Nels Anderson, a former resident of the county and a writer for the Federal government in Washington, D.C., Brooks devised a plan to employ Mormon women in Dixie to type copies of the original diaries of Washington County pioneers and later residents. As part of the Works Progress Administration (WPA), dozens of diaries and journals were borrowed and transcribed by women in the county, with the original diaries being returned to the families. Today these transcribed diaries and journals are found at Brigham Young University, Dixie College, the Huntington Library in California, and elsewhere. This kind of work provided supplemental income for dozens of families living in Washington County and, equally important, it helped preserve important historical records.

A successful New Deal program was the preservation of food. Several canning centers established in the county by 1934 had canned 15,500 cans of peaches, 1,400 cans of tomatoes, 650 cans of meat, and 100 bottles of meat. These canning centers provided full-time work for sixty women and fifteen men on county relief. The men and women were paid a salary, the cans and sugar were furnished by the Federal government, and the fruit, vegetables, and other food items were purchased from local farmers. The canned goods were then provided to needy families through a county-operated storehouse.[22]

The distribution of food for needy families and feed for animals was a thorny task, fraught with jealousies and criticism. The newspaper editorialized that "no man has a right to take the wheat unless he needs it, no more than he has a right to take money out of the United States treasury. No individual is entitled to more wheat than his animals can eat in a sixty-day period." At that time, 1,400 fifty-pound bags of flour and $7,620 worth of wheat had been distributed to needy Washington County residents, with $9,000 more expected. Unfortunately there was bickering about how much each county and each state received. The News responded to this: "It is assumed by too many that the flour and wheat are gifts in which all have an equal right, rather than an effort on the part of relief agencies of the nation to help those really in NEED."[23]

With assistance from the Federal Emergency Recovery Administration (FERA), Henry Pickett and county officials directed a campaign to improve local sanitation. Materials were provided to construct privies for homes not having such accommodations. Neither the city nor the county had yet developed a sewer system or septic tanks.[24] This was yet another program that provided work for individuals while solving serious community problems. By 1934 it was reported that 24 percent of the people of Utah were on government relief rolls, and that to October of that year $372,841 had been spent by the Federal government in Washington County for relief.[25]

The most welcome of all WPA projects was funding to complete the piping of water from the Cottonwood Canal. Cold and clear water from the source springs was transported to the residents of the city through eighteen miles of open canal. There was a significant loss of water from seepage and evaporation. Flowing under bright sun, the water, by the time it reached the residents of St. George, was warm and had become polluted from grazing animals. The WPA project provided for steel and concrete pipes buried underground to transport culinary water for thirsty St. George residents. The total cost for the project was about $140,000, with the WPA contributing nearly a third of the cost. About fifty local workmen were employed for the better part of a year to complete the project.[26]

The building of a junior high school in Hurricane and one in St. George were assisted by WPA funds which provided 46 percent of the cost of construction. Numerous other projects were completed with Federal help, including a new post office in St. George which opened on 30 September 1937. WPA funds of $13,000 were helpful in completing the Mechanic Arts Building at Dixie College. Another appreciated Federal program was the government's insuring of bank accounts to the amount of $5,000 in 1934.

The social security system was established during the Depression. Of the 12,000 Utahns eligible for assistance, some Washington County residents were among the 15 percent who participated. Another Federal agency, the Home Loan Program, aided some home buyers. Even as these Federal programs were aiding county residents, the local newspaper complained that Federal taxes were too high.[27] The Washington County News editorialized against the mounting national debt, decrying wild spending by the Federal government. Almost in the same breath, however, the News complimented the Federal government for its various projects in the county.[28]

The most remembered New Deal effort was the Civilian Conservation Corps (CCC). This program initially employed 300,000 (eventually 2.5 million) young men nationally, in 1,500 camps. They were placed in military-style quarters, generally in remote areas, to work on national park lands as well as forest projects, park buildings, road improvements, land conservation, and dam construction efforts. This brought many young men from outside Utah into the county to reside and work under army-like supervision. Some Utah youths were also included in the corps. This provided a real infusion of new blood into the isolated communities of Washington County.

The CCC leaders knew there would be opportunities for clashes with the local residents, so they kept the young men under tight control. On the more positive side, they undertook a public-relations campaign which included weekly news articles in the local newspaper.

Bridge Mountain Civilian Conservation Corps Company 962, Zion National Park, 1935. (National Park Service Photograph, J. L. Crawford Collection)

One article noted that $180,000 was brought into the county as a result of the CCC.[29] Open house invitations to the public as well as various recreational activities were standard modes for public relations. CCC teams played in local leagues so that people would have regular but controlled contact with the young men. Towns sponsored open-air dances in which CCC officials brought the youths to the pavilion then transported them back to camp right after the event. Baseball games, dances, and other socials resulted in several romances and marriages. Some of the young CCC men, including Frank Holland, Bill Strickland, Joe Prims, Don Horn, Skylar Maggart, Jimmie Sammons, Bill Ewell, Max Huff, and Rowland Platt, settled in Washington County. Ray Squiers came with a training program at the airport and remained. Other young men returned home with their new Dixie brides.

Local resident Don Horn of Washington City recalled life in the CCC camp.

> [It was] run like an Army camp. We got up to a bugle in the morning, and there were an Army captain and a lieutenant in charge of the camp, but I believe everyone else was a civilian. Everyone in the work force was a civilian. We did a lot of road building, grading and graveling. Most of our entertainment took place in Hurricane. The CCC would send a truck to bring all the boys who wanted to go, down to Hurricane on a Saturday night.[30]

Fundamentally the CCC efforts were intended to benefit the local communities, so it was expected that residents would be sympathetic. Certainly that was generally the case in Dixie. One company, the 961st, originally worked near Panguitch but was transferred to St. George for the winter, during which time the men worked on flood control for the Santa Clara Creek. A long dam was built about a half mile above the Shivwits Indian Reservation. It included both dirt-fill and masonry walls. The St. George Chamber of Commerce also requested CCC to help build a road to Dammeron Valley.

Camps were established at Leeds (recently restored by local residents), Veyo, Gunlock, Pinto, and Enterprise. The Veyo camp crews constructed a dam and recreational facilities at Pine Valley. In Washington City the CCC was particularly active grading and improving city roads and streets. Corpsmen built a dam and canal on both the south and north sides of town. Two camps were located in Zion National Park where their crews completed dozens of projects, including landscaping, building construction, basket dams to prevent the Virgin River from cutting away acres of meadowlands, comfort stations, campgrounds, fireplaces, trails, road grading, boundary fencing, and an outdoor lecture circle.[31]

Through the many New Deal projects, Washington County was drawn somewhat more into the American fabric. Closer ties were established with Washington, D.C. The local economy was made more dependent on outside help, and non-resident officials and inspectors came into the county — all at the invitation of the local people.

Dixie College Becomes a State Institution

Dixie College in St. George nearly became a fatality of the Great Depression. The LDS church, its patron, faced tremendous financial challenges and church leaders chose to withdraw from the higher-education arena as one solution for coping with the Depression. This had long been under consideration, but the Depression certainly influenced the decision to close Dixie College.[32]

Attending Dixie College was one way for Washington County youth to cope with the county's isolation. From the very beginning of the southern settlements, county residents had built schools and theaters, bands and choirs, lyceum series, and literary clubs. Eventually they persuaded the LDS church to support a stake academy. It began in

Dixie College under construction, c. 1910. (Courtesy — Mildred Larch)

fits and starts, initially in 1895; firm commitments finally brought forth a college building in 1911. The LDS church pledged $20,000 toward its construction if the community would raise $35,000 in labor and materials and support the school in other ways. This meant that the citizens must yet again donate to a community project, this one of major proportions. They responded. For example, one campaign (of several) raised funds just for the maple floor of the auditorium in the building after the major structure was nearly done. One hundred and forty-nine people donated amounts from fifty cents to twenty-five dollars. Many of the donors were prospective students, and most donations were between one and five dollars. The donation list, found among the papers of Joseph K. Nicholes at Dixie College, reads like a Who's Who of 1911 Dixie. Begun in 1909, the handsome sandstone building was ready for its initial class in 1911. This enabled young people to pursue higher education opportunities without leaving the county.[33]

Beginning as a high school-level academy, Dixie gradually moved to become an accredited junior college. Local leaders adopted a plan that was gaining popularity around the United States to combine the last two years of high school with the first two years of college; thus they had a four-year institution for students from ages 16 to 20. This meant that the college worked closely with the Washington County School District, which paid for the first two years of the students' training. The plan allowed for joint use of buildings and faculty.

Located in the heart of downtown St. George, adjacent to the tabernacle and the city/county library, the college quickly became a center of community activities, especially cultural events such as theater, music, and lectures. Dixie College athletic teams also became a focus for community boosters. The college leaders in turn solicited support from the community to provide housing for students who came from nearby Nevada and Arizona towns such as Panaca and Bunkerville. Local citizens supported the college by providing equipment, employing students, and attending college events.

Without a doubt the college and the Dixie community became one. Enabling students from the area to obtain a college education was pivotal in human terms. Even though there was another college fifty miles away, few could have afforded the costs of traveling that distance and paying for board and room. Having a college in the county seat also gave stature to St. George that it could not have attained otherwise. The LDS temple was certainly a great source of pride and importance, but the college enabled hundreds of young people to enter professions, establish businesses, and become national leaders. It was these young people who, in the long run, brought significance to Dixie out of proportion to its population.

By 1921, however, the LDS church began to close academies, citing the problem of competing with tax-supported education in areas where LDS members paid both taxes and tithing to underwrite colleges. Church leaders had concluded that, as with public elementary education, the church did not need to maintain a separate parochial system in order to sustain the faith. The first church academies to close were St. Johns Academy in Arizona and Cassia Academy in Oakley, Idaho. Eventually, nine church-supported academies throughout the Intermountain West were turned over to the states to operate or were closed.[34]

The immediate result of the initial closures was the strengthening of the remaining academies. Two-year teacher training courses were initiated in seven of the academies — including Dixie College. But as the financial crisis of the Depression more deeply affected the church, its leaders in Salt Lake City decided to close more campuses, retaining BYU in Provo as the lead institution with only one or two others. Initially on the list for closure, Ricks, in Idaho, and Juarez, in Mexico, were spared, and the others were closed.

On 31 January 1931, Elder Joseph F. Merrill, LDS church commissioner of education, notified President Joseph K. Nicholes of Dixie College that financial support for the college would terminate at the conclusion of the 1930-31 school year. He stated that the church would provide $5,000 a year for two years to help transform the college into an excellent high school. He urged President Nicholes (who also served as St. George Stake President) not to seek assistance from the state legislature to continue the college. His reason for such a request was clear. He pointed out that the legislature had just agreed to accept Snow College and Weber College for state support. Merrill feared that a request from Dixie would endanger plans for the continuance of the other two and that all three would die. Not stated, but easy to infer, was the fact that there was already a state-supported college in southern Utah in Cedar City.35

Evidently President Nicholes kept that letter confidential because a movement began immediately to seek state support for the continuance of the college. Nicholes, along with W. O. Bentley and members of the St. George Chamber of Commerce, held discussions with many community leaders. Once that movement gained strength and the attention of the legislature, church leaders in Salt Lake City supported the local delegation. They repeated their pledge to provide $5,000 for the next two years, this time as a transition to state support of the institution.

The campaign to win legislative and gubernatorial endorsement was an uphill battle. Governor Henry Blood was determined not to expand state expenditures during the hard times of the Depression. Legislators had to be convinced that there was good reason to have two colleges in southern Utah. There was no one to convince state leaders other than the local residents themselves. The state board of education was not campaigning for Dixie College (though it eventually received the assignment to supervise the two-year college). Mormon church leaders were not taking the initiative, but they offered the campus, valued at $200,000, to the state. Dixie had one inside person at church headquarters in Anthony W. Ivins of the LDS First Presidency, a consistent supporter of the college who had grown up in Dixie. He was an avid reader, a prolific writer, and a promoter of education, and used his influence in the church on behalf of his home county during this debate. At his funeral in late September 1934, he was described as a fighter for the continuation of Dixie College, a huge task.[36]

Arthur F. Miles was the local representative in the legislature who carried the bill in the 1933 session. Former legislator David Hirschi of Hurricane also helped. Others in the community who worked with legislators included Joseph S. Snow from the St. George civic clubs, state representative Othello C. Bowman of Kanab, and David H. Morris. Orval Hafen represented the chamber of commerce as its president.

Prior to the 1933 session, Miles and others convinced the legislature to make a trip to St. George to inspect Dixie College. In a session held in the St George Tabernacle but sponsored by the chamber of commerce (with Orval Hafen presiding), President Nicholes reported that 546 students currently were enrolled — 221 of them in the junior-high programs, 153 in the senior-high curriculum, and 172 in college. He said: "Dixie College is more than a school. It is a community enterprise. It is a cultural center. It has been developed through the efforts and self-sacrifice of the people of our section."[37]

The local committee felt it had a 50-50 chance of success. W. O. Bentley, Nicholes, David Hirschi, and Joseph S. Snow stayed in Salt Lake City for most of the legislative session, supported with funding raised by the local chamber of commerce. They were able to gain the cooperation of leaders at Weber College and Snow College, whose support was absolutely critical. They also enjoyed tacit support from LDS church leaders. One crucial person opposed the idea, however — state senator Wilford Day of Parowan. He argued from the beginning that having two colleges in adjoining counties in rural southern Utah was not necessary. With a good road now available in all seasons, students could travel to Cedar City, he maintained. His arguments were loud on the floor of the Senate, but the alliances built behind the scenes overruled him handily.

In the House of Representatives, there was a clear majority for the bill, but the question of an appropriation was the next hurdle. Governor Blood was adamant about not increasing the state budget. A compromise finally was reached in which Dixie College was made part of the state system, but no appropriation would be made to the school until the next legislative session in two years. Since the LDS church agreed to provide $5,000 toward faculty salaries and the community was determined to keep the college, legislators argued that the college could survive on tuition, Washington County School District support, and donations until an appropriation could be made in two years. That was acceptable to the governor.

The issue of Dixie College did not occur in a vacuum. The "hot potato" before the legislature in 1933 was the matter of repealing the Eighteenth Amendment — Prohibition. Thirty-five states had passed its repeal; if Utah were to vote for repeal, national prohibition of alcoholic beverages would be ended. Delegates from some sections of the state were very anxious for repeal, particularly those from Price. Reportedly, horsetrading occurred in which the Carbon County vote supported Dixie College and the Washington County vote went for repeal of the Eighteenth Amendment and to support Carbon County later in its bid for a junior college.

Though these were austere terms, they brought celebrations in Dixie. The local newspaper spoke with pride:

> The action is conceded by Dixie residents to be one of the most vital movements to the development of this territory since the settlement of the Dixie mission in 1861. Education has always been one of the foremost objectives of the pioneers of the region, and the continuation of the local school is unquestionably an item of the greatest interest to every home in which there are boys and girls who are anticipating advantages of a college education.[38]

Continuing, the paper set an optimistic tone: "At the end of that time [two years] it is expected that the condition of the state's finances will be such that an appropriation can be made at least comparable with that for B.A.C., Weber and Snow colleges."[39]

That time came quickly. Arthur Miles, who guided the legislation through, was replaced by Francis Joseph Bowler. He inherited the task of getting an appropriation two years later, an amount comparable to that received by Snow and Weber colleges, so Dixie could become a credible junior college. Bowler's son Truman recalled being with his father for two weeks during the next legislative session. They stayed in the Newhouse Hotel where accommodations were less expensive and walked the eight-block distance between the capitol building and the hotel. "One night about at the Federal Building Dad stopped and said, 'You know we might as well not go home if we don't get the appropriation.' I think it was $38,000."[40] They were fortunate in the support they received from Weber College and Snow College and from legislative colleagues.

Without question, that was an important moment for Washington County. Success was brought about specifically by well-organized local leadership who applied pressure directly at the legislature. State and church leaders must have received many protests from every community where academies were closed. That the Dixie leaders surmounted such grim economic circumstances is a credit to them. Once the victory at the legislature was achieved, its supporters came home and organized the Dixie Education Association to raise the financial support to get the college through the tight years ahead. Their experience in lobbying convinced them that they simply could not drop the problem in the lap of the state.

In 1953 Governor J. Bracken Lee convened a special session of the legislature and succeeded in passing a bill to transfer Dixie College, Snow College, and Weber College to the LDS church, the original owner. There was a good deal of support for the idea in St. George, but the people of Ogden were very critical of it. They succeeded in placing an initiative on the ballot in 1954 which passed statewide although people in Washington County opposed it. By a majority of 2,649 to 482 the Washington County voters preferred returning the college to the LDS church.[41] The success of the referendum statewide prohibited the transfer, so almost by default Dixie continued as a state college.

An example of community support for the college occurred in 1954. College President Glen Snow became aware that nearby ecclesiastical leaders were hesitant to send their young women to Dixie because there were no official dormitory facilities for girls. He determined to remedy the situation. He had a building designed then arranged for trailers to be removed from some land near the college in order that the building could be placed there.

There were no state funds available for the project. Snow turned to the college's Building Trades Department headed by Wayne McConkie, and together they enlisted faculty and students to construct the dormitory. The carpentry class laid out the site. With picks and shovels, students dug the foundation and heat trenches, hauling the dirt away in wheelbarrows. Faculty members such as Arthur Bruhn joined in during afternoons and evenings. The new president Ellvert Himes was often on site with a shovel. Civic clubs and other citizens helped in the evenings. Some like Bill Barlocker donated money, others labor. Women's clubs held fund-raisers. McConkie led the night shift and Clair Stirling of Leeds headed the day shift. In a two-year period, without state funding and mostly without pay, these volunteers built the Dixiana Dormitory. The facility was a symbol of community support, faculty dedication, and student vitality. It helped the college maintain a spirit of progress.

The Dixie Education Association quietly continued as a patron of the college thereafter, slowly collecting a sizeable fund. When the right time came, they had the money and the political connections to help the college move to a new campus on the edge of town where space was sufficient to allow for an expanded institution. President Ellvert Himes met with the association in the 1954-55 academic year and presented the problem: there was no more space downtown to expand the campus. The legislature was about to appropriate funds for a new building, but no site could be found. The leaders finally decided to consider the idea of a completely new campus. Once that plan took hold, land was found quickly. Orval Hafen was then in the Utah Senate. He and others proposed the concept to the legislature. The Dixie Education Association would buy six city blocks and give them to the state in return for locating the new building (the gymnasium) there and beginning plans to gradually move the entire campus to the new location. The plan was approved, and the gym was completed in 1957.

Results of this citizen commitment continue, and its impact since 1935 has been immensely positive. Clearly the college came about through community effort, was saved from extinction by the same kind of effort, and was propelled toward expansion by citizen funding and direction. No wonder people in the county feel strongly that they own the college. It is not the preserve of professional educators; it is the possession of the citizens of Dixie.

Electric Power

One more accommodation resulting from the Great Depression was the change from private to public ownership of electrical power in St. George. Citizens complained that prices had dropped for many things with the market decline in the 1930s but power rates had not.

Many customers were unable to pay their power bills. The St. George City Council drew up a resolution on 18 March 1933 demanding a 25 percent rate decrease. All of this caused people to think about municipally-owned power again.

The first power company in St. George was a private business formed in 1909. It brought electricity to the city rather belatedly, nearly thirty years after Salt Lake City had electrical service. In less than a year of its operation, city fathers became critical of the company, and with the support of a city vote, they passed a bond to purchase the system which the city operated until 1916 when it needed to upgrade the plant. Also, the city council soon wearied over the management role and began looking for an opportunity to sell the facility.

Another community election was held, and by a similarly large margin, citizens approved the city council's recommendation to sell the system. The highest bid came from A. L. Woodhouse of Richfield, who was granted a twenty-five-year franchise to supply the city with electrical power and gave birth to what became the Southern Utah Power Company. Over the next two decades, the company expanded to include Cedar City and the Washington County communities of Enterprise, Hurricane, and Springdale. Additional power plants were built at Gunlock, Veyo, and La Verkin.

As that twenty-five-year franchise renewal date neared, the mood in the St. George area was to go back to municipally-owned electricity. In 1940 Albert E. Miller, who had been mayor and a state legislator, proposed changing to municipal power. He argued that since the private system was profitable, the municipal one could be profitable too.[42] His argument was countered by Reid Gardner, manager of Southern Utah Power, headquartered in Cedar City, who claimed that a municipal system would not be profitable because expensive generating equipment would have to be installed. That set the tone for an intensive public debate, creating a fervor seldom seen in Dixie.

An election committee (consisting of E. Eric Snow, chair, Byron Taylor, George P. Lytle, Albert Fawcett, Andrew McArthur, Arthur Cottam, Newell Frei, Wilford Schmutz, Paul Seegmiller, and James Andrus) opened a formal campaign on 27 March 1941 for approval of a municipal power system, with an election date set for 6 May 1941. They sponsored pamphlets, neighborhood meetings, advertising, and letter writing in the newspaper. Mathew Bentley argued the case for a public utility, fending off criticisms by the Southern Utah Power Company. His letter to the newspaper reflects his precise accounting manner as he dealt with bond rates, equipment costs, and the very interesting possibility of cheap Federal power in the future from Hoover Dam. In the same edition, Orval Hafen wrote in opposition of the move to public ownership. His equally long four-column article was a reflection of his legal demeanor, challenging the logic and validity of the proposers' arguments. He called for exact research instead of enthusiastic promotion, pointing out that the city had no good data on the water flow essential to operate a new plant.[43]

The controversy heated up from there. Helen Reichmann entered a housewife's doubts, suggesting that locating the new plant in the city park would interfere with radio reception in that neighborhood, that the Cottonwood Canal water used to generate the plant's power would have to be chlorinated after it passed through the plant, and that the plant would not generate enough electricity to supply the town's needs at peak times like Christmas.[44] Proponents answered her in a large advertisement a week later.

M. J. Miles wrote a measured letter with nine reasons for adopting the system, pointing out that employees of the power company naturally argued for its retention, and although that was their right, it did not necessarily make their logic sound. He claimed that if it were sound for the city to own its own water system, which no one doubted, it was equally sound to own the power system. The Southern Utah Power Company also placed large advertisements but was not able to stem the tide.

Considerable argument centered around Provo's recent move to municipal power. People discussed how well that project was going. Joseph K. Nicholes, respected past St. George Stake president and past president of Dixie College who now lived in Provo, sent data and encouragement for the public system. This letter and other information were advertised by the proposing committee, mayor, and city council in the last newspaper before the 6 May election day. The bond election for $300,000 passed 952 to 287 in the largest election turnout in the city's history to that date.

Quick action was required to make the transition to public power. The city had already engaged a Mr. Bletzaker to build the plant and Mayor D. C. Watson hired Ken Parkinson of Murray to manage the facility, which he did for the next thirty-two years. The building of the power plant took longer than expected, and the city encountered serious difficulties with Southern Utah Power Company which announced it would turn the city's power off on the day their contract ended. It took a court order to prevent that. Belatedly, the switch was turned on in April 1942, and St. George had its own power system, which it still maintains. The possibility of acquiring inexpensive electrical power from Hoover Dam and later from Glen Canyon Dam became a reality in succeeding years, a great advantage to the community that subsequently grew beyond anyone's expectations.

Dixie-Escalante REA

The development of electrical services to the rural areas of the county was closely connected with the Dixie Rural Electric Association, the Escalante Valley Rural Electric Association, and the Littlefield Rural Electric Association. The Escalante association was started by Parley Moyle, who was attempting to farm in the Newcastle area. By using an old truck engine to drive a pump, Moyle succeeded in bringing enough well water to the surface to supply a small irrigation system and grow successful crops. That venture was very limited, so he and several neighbors applied for Federal funds to organize a rural electric cooperative, which was granted in 1946. A lot of effort was required to get Federal government support and even more to find equipment to build a functional system, but Moyle remained with the project. The Escalante Valley REA group hired Leon Bowler as manager because of his previous experience with the Southern Utah Power Company. With that electricity, several farmers successfully pumped well water and maintained farms in the Newcastle area west of Cedar City.

Rumell Reber, Louis Reber, Afton Reber, and Clifford Peterson organized the Littlefield Rural Electric, also in 1946, to facilitate the delivery of electricity from Hoover Dam. The power arrived in 1952 after rather complicated negotiations with Arizona. The Dixie Rural Electric Association was organized in 1946 under the leadership of Evan Woodbury. He and several neighbors (Walter Cannon, Wallace Iverson, Charles R. Sullivan, Clare Sturzenegger, Daniel H. Heaton, and George H. Seegmiller) appealed to the Southern Utah Power Company to supply their farms with electric power, but the company declined. By 1948 lines had been built to thirty customers by Dixie

REA which contracted with Ken Parkinson of the St. George Utilities Department to maintain the system. The Dixie REA served everyone south of 700 South in St. George, west to Santa Clara, and east to the Washington Fields and Berry Springs.[45]

In 1974 the Dixie REA merged with the Littlefleld REA and four years later joined with the Escalante Valley REA. Leon Bowler became the manager of the combined associations and continues in that position today (1996). Membership has grown to 4,500 and includes those in Newcastle, Beryl, Modena, Pine Valley, Bloomington, Bloomington Hills, Washington Fields, and Littlefield, Arizona.

Telephones

The installation of telephones was not nearly as controversial as was that of electrical power. It was also more of a force for opening communication beyond Dixie, even though long-distance service outside the county required relaying the call through each central — for example, to Cedar City, then Beaver, Fillmore, Nephi, and Provo to Salt Lake City. A backup at any central office could cause a delay.

Telephones were actually an adaptation from the telegraph, using the same wires and poles, merely replacing telegraph keys with telephone receivers. In 1904 telephone equipment was installed by the Southern Utah Telephone Company, an enterprise organized by Edward H. Snow and a group of local businessmen. They linked St. George with Toquerville and Cedar City, where messages could be relayed north through the state. Initially there was one phone in each town, requiring all customers to come to that instrument. When a call came for a person in town, runners would be sent to find the person and bring him or her to the receiver. Children were often given a dime for being runners. Soon thereafter residential phones began to be installed, but the rates were expensive, one dollar per month.

As the number of phones increased in St. George, there were two operators, one for local calls and one for long distance. Alma Nelson was the first operator, assisted by his sister, Jennie Nelson Hall. The people in Gunlock worked together to set up their own company called the People's Progressive Telephone and Telegraph Company. It served Moapa, Bunkerville, Mesquite, Santa Clara, Enterprise, Newcastle, Pine Valley, Central, Veyo, Gunlock, and some ranches.[46]

The year 1930 was a turning point for telephones in Washington County, the same year that U.S. Highway 91 was completed. The Mountain States Telephone and Telegraph Company purchased Southern Utah Telephone Company on 1 April 1930. At the time of acquisition, there were 336 telephones in St. George and twenty-seven in Hurricane. The acquisition of Southern Utah Telephone expanded long-distance telephone service for the residents of the county.[47]

Most of the phones were on party lines with four receivers each. The people of the area came to know the telephone operators by name as the communication network bound them together. By the 1930s, it required five operators at a time to meet the county's needs. Several of these operators still live in Washington County and have vivid memories. Alice Holland recalled her saddest day at the switchboard: "I was at the switchboard alone and the oil well explosion occurred south of town, killing about a dozen people. The board lit up like a Christmas tree as people called about their family members and wanted to know what had happened."[48] The explosion occurred on 6 March 1935. Nine died instantly, one the following day, and four others were injured.

Telephone operators were important to the functioning of the town. Local operators served as alarm clocks, provided wake-up calls to their customers and calls for nighttime water turns, gave the time of day, answered emergencies for doctors and police, and rang the noon siren. Helen Bennett, one of the early telephone operators, reviewed the procedure for an emergency: "When there was a call for the police, we put a red light on at the Tabernacle and they would see it from wherever they were patrolling and call us for information. The volunteer firemen also called in for addresses of the fire."[49]

Oil Exploration

The story is told that Bishop Joshua T. Willis discovered some rocks with unusual coloring twelve miles east of Toquerville; he felt they were manganese ores that could be mined to bring new fortunes to the poor pioneers. He quietly preserved them to show Brigham Young on his next visit; however, Young is said to have told Willis to bury the ore because the time had not come for the Latter-day Saints to be involved in mining. Other tales are told that Erastus Snow thanked the Lord for the mines at Silver Reef in a prayer at the St. George

Oil derrick at Virgin. (Wm. L. Crawford)

Tabernacle, but it is quite clear that he intended the Mormons to profit from the mines indirectly. They could supply the miners with lumber and food in exchange for coin, but he and other leaders urged their followers not to move to the mining camps and be directly employed in the mines. The values of the mining camps were not those the Latter-day Saints should condone.[50] These stories reinforce the general idea that the Mormons wished to maintain their isolation and develop agriculture as the base for their economy. However, this situation was changing by the turn of the century.

When oil drilling began in 1907 near the entrance to Zion National Park, it was generally welcomed. The prospect of a new income source seemed to outweigh worries about outside capital taking over the economy. About fifteen wells were drilled two miles northeast of

Virgin, most of which produced little. Some flowed enough to sustain a flame, and three captured about thirty-six barrels of oil a day. That was enough to raise big hopes, so drilling continued. Up to 140 wells were drilled to a depth of 1,000 feet.[51]

One of the avid promoters of oil exploration in the Grafton/Virgin area was Henry Doolittle, superintendent of the Dixie Apex Mine, a good forty miles southwest of Virgin. He was an entrepreneur extraordinaire, investing in copper mining near Shem — the Apex Mine — as well as doggedly supporting oil explorations. Doolittle wandered into Washington County from Riverside, California, in 1904 and soon progressed from working in the mines to buying property and searching for other mining opportunities.[52]

Beginning about 1920 regional drilling for oil picked up and Washington County was an active location. In addition to the areas near Virgin and Grafton, there was a lot of activity from Bloomington to the Arizona Strip as far as Littlefield. The Arrowhead Petroleum Corporation was busy working what it called the Escalante Wells and the Punch Bowl Well. In contrast to the "outsider-insider" relationship that existed in the silver mining days of Pioche and Silver Reef, the oil-drilling effort directly involved local people as employees and shareholders. The St. George Chamber of Commerce promoted local investment in the companies, held meetings to court outside investors and organized field trips to the drilling sites.

Oil exploration in the county was a risk. Investors had to be constantly encouraged to reinvest and Washington County News articles provided that reinforcement.[53] An inspector from the oil company working in the Virgin oil field provided hopeful indications to would-be investors: "I will stake my reputation that this will become one of the most important fields in the United States." He added that a "gusher production may be expected" at a depth between 2,300 and 2,500 feet.[54]

Perhaps in response to such reports, local businessmen organized a holding company to attract capital to drill for oil. The News reported that the following were involved in the company: Joseph Prince, Albert E. Miller, F. A. Reber, Kumen D. Williams, Dr. Clare Woodbury, George Hale, and A. B. Andrus.[55] This was just one side of the financial picture. There were buy outs and mergers of national companies that impacted the drilling as well as other ups and downs. With each new disappointment there was a call for new equipment and a drive to lower depths, but the printed news continued on the upbeat side year after year. For example:

> Oil indications on the Punch Bowl dome, being drilled by the Arrowhead Petroleum Corporation are increasing daily. The bit is now at a depth of between 1300 and 1400 feet and is nearing the end of the Kaibab lime formation, ready to break into the Coconino sands.
>
> Oil showings are increasing as depth is made, and for the past few days from a quart to a gallon of live oil is brought up with every bailing. It is of a light high-grade nature, and evaporates within a few minutes after being brought to the surface.[56]

Certainly the people of Washington County were changing their attitudes about outsiders, isolation, and a lifestyle of agrarian austerity. They were ready for more affluence.

Many of these hopes were dashed in one second, though. Arrowhead company officials had decided to lower a large explosive charge of nitroglycerin into its Escalante Well #2 with the expectation that they were very near a breakthrough, and the explosion would bring in a gusher. A crowd of a hundred people went to the site to see the anticipated flow of oil on 6 March 1935. As the explosive was about to be lowered into the well, it blew up from unknown causes. The blast damaged several automobiles used to carry visitors to the wellhead. The explosion wrecked the 120-foot steel derrick and started fires in adjoining lumber and oil-rigging buildings.[57] And, most tragically, the explosion killed ten people, including Charles Alsop — president and general manager of Arrowhead Petroleum Company — and his wife. A well driller, C. M. Flickenger, Joseph Empey Jr., an electrician, his son-in-law, Cail Nicholson, and Billy Maloney, a worker, also died. Onlookers killed included Olive Bleak Snow, Ray Nelson, and Joseph Kitterman. Leah Cottam died in the hospital a few hours later.

Drilling continued at some sites for a few more years, but the disaster took the wind out of the drillers' sails; the momentum, nursed so hopefully, stalled. Washington County would not experience significant oil production.

ENDNOTES

1. Clarence Dutton, "The Tertiary History of the Grand Canyon District," (Washington, D.C.: USGS, 1882).

2. Quoted in Angus M. Woodbury, *A History of Southern Utah and Its National Parks* (n.p., 1950), 187. The original typescript of Leo Snow's full report is in the Dixie College Archives through the generosity of his sons and daughters.

3. Ibid., 188.

4. Horace Albright, interview, by J. L. Crawford, 10 April 1979, Dixie College Archives.

5. J. L. Crawford, interview, Washington County Centennial History Committee, Dixie College Archives.

6. See Charles Bigelow scrapbook, Dixie College Archives. Bigelow became so fond of St. George and so closely identified with its tourism that he chose to be buried in the St. George cemetery. The Arrowhead Hotel, built in 1926, and Snow's Hotel, built in 1921, were the main facilities to cater to the automobile drivers. A third hotel, the Liberty, was added in 1929 by George W. "Jockey" Hail to serve the growing number of tourists coming to the county.

7. Helen Gibbons, "The 3 mph Adventure—Horseless, Helpless Carriages," *Deseret News*, 8 May 1980, C-i.

8. Bret Whittaker, "Road Travel and Development in the St. George Area," 1980, Gregerson File, Dixie College Archives.

9. Washington County Court, Roads, Bridges, Highways, 5 June 1867, 5 March 1867, Record A, 6 March 1876, Record B, William R. Palmer, archivist. Copy in Dixie College Archives, in "Roads" file.

10. Journals of the Legislative Assembly of the Territory of Utah, Twenty-Third Session, for the year 1878.

11. J. L. Crawford, "A Tale of Two Bridges," *Washington County News*, 13 September 1984.

12. Ezra C. Knowlton, *History of Highway Development in Utah* (Salt Lake City: Utah State Road Commission, n.d.), 178.

13. *Washington County News*, 8 January 1931, 1.

14. This statement was written by J.L. Crawford at the request of the author.

15. *Washington County News*, 16 April 1931, 2.

16. Kathy Cottam, "The St. George Airport: Past, Present, and Future," Gregerson Collection, Dixie College Archives. See also Sid Atkin, "History of Aviation in St. George," in *Legacy, Art and History in Utah's Dixie* (St. George: St. George Art Museum, 1996).

17. *Washington County News*, 26 April 1934, 6.

18. Erinn Bowler, "The Reality of Human Suffering as a Result of the Great Depression," ms., 1988; in possession of Marion Bowler.

19. Ibid.

20. Ibid.

21. *Washington County News*, 21 April 1932, 1.

22. *Washington County News*, 16 August 1934, 1.

23. *Washington County News*, 26 May 1932, 2.

24. *Washington County News*, 21 March 1935, 1.

25. *Washington County News*, 7 March 1935, 1.

26. *Washington County News*, 26 June 1936, 1.

27. *Washington County News*, 22 March 1934, 6, 8.

28. *Washington County News*, 16 June 1932. *The Washington County News*, 1 March 1934, 4, noted that the national debt had risen to $314 per person.

30. *Washington County News*, 12 January 1988, 7.

31. *Washington County News*, 6 June 1935, 6.

32. Other academies included Murdock Academy in Beaver, Utah; Snow College, Ephriam, Utah; Weber College, Ogden, Utah; Ricks College, Rexburg, Idaho; St. Johns Academy and Gila Stake Academy in Arizona; Millard Academy, Hinckley, Utah; Brigham Young College, Logan, Utah; Brigham Young College, Provo, Utah; Latter-day Saints University, Salt Lake City; Uintah Academy, Vernal, Utah; Cassia Academy, Oakley, Idaho; Fielding Academy, Paris, Idaho; Oneida Academy, Preston, Idaho; Emery Academy, Castle Dale, Utah; San Luis Academy, Manassa, Colorado; Big Horn Academy, Cowley, Wyoming; Snowflake Academy, Snowflake, Arizona; and Juarez Stake Academy, Colonia Juarez, Mexico.

33. Edna J. Gregerson, Dixie College, *Monument to the Industry of a Dedicated People* (Salt Lake City: Franklin Quest, 1993).

34. Thomas Alexander, *Mormonism in Transition* (Urbana: University of Illinois Press, 1986), 164-5. The first to close were St. Johns Academy in Arizona and Cassia Academy at Oakley, Idaho. Then the Gila, Arizona; Uintah, Utah; and Snowflake, Arizona academies ceased to function. In 1923 the Fielding Academy in Paris, Idaho, Murdock Academy in Beaver, Utah, Emery Academy in Castle Dale, Utah, and Oneida Academy in Preston, Idaho, were notified of their closure. San Luis Academy in Colorado and Big Horn Academy in Wyoming were turned over to their respective states.

35. Joseph K. Nicholes, Correspondence File, 1932. Dixie College Archives.

36. *Washington County News*, 27 September 1934, 1, 5.

37. *Washington County News*, 9 February 1933, 1.

38. *Washington County News*, 23 March 1933, 1.

39. *Washington County News*, 23 February 1933, 1; 2 March 1933, 1; 9 March 1933, 1; 11 May 1933, 1.

40. M. Truman Bowler, Interview, by Douglas Alder, August 1993, Dixie College Archives.

41. *Washington County News*, 4 November 1954, 4.

42. *Washington County News*, 8 February 1940, 1.

43. *Washington County News*, 10 April 1941, 6.

44. *Washington County News*, 24 April 1941, 9.

45. Loren Webb, "Brief History of Dixie-Escalante Rural Electric Association," ms. in Gregerson Collection, Dixie College Archives.

46. Roark Smith, "The Growth and Development of the Southern Utah Telephone System," Gregerson Collection, Dixie College Archives, 6.

47. Ibid., 9.

48. Elaine R. Alder, "The Heartbeat of St. George," *St. George Magazine,* July-August 1993, 67.

49. Ibid.

50. Andrew Karl Larson, *I Was Called to Dixie*, 315.

51. Osmond L. Harline, "Utah's Black Gold, the Petroleum Industry," *Utah Historical Quarterly 31*, (Summer 1963), 294. See also ElRoy Nelson, *Utah's Economic Patterns* (Salt Lake City: University of Utah Press, 1956).

52. Brest van Kempen, "Harry Doolittle—An Honest-to-Goodness Splendid Citizen," 19, typescript, Dixie College Archives.

53. *Washington County News*, 17 December 1931, 2.

54. *Washington County News*, 12 August 1926.

55. *Washington County News*, 9 September 1926, 1.

56. *Washington County News*, 3 September 1931.

57. Orval Hafen, Diary, 1, 26; ms. in possession of Bruce Hafen.

9

AMERICANIZATION
ESCALATES

Culture: Motion Pictures and Authors

After 1930 Dixie's absorption into the American fabric accelerated with each decade. For example, like other Americans, people
in Washington County fell in love with moving pictures. With the
demise of vaudeville theater in St. George came the rise of the movie
house. Two main theaters became gathering places: the Wadsworth
and the Gaiety Electric Theater. The production of films in Hollywood
was such that these theaters could show four to six different movies
a week. In the week of 16 November 1939, for example, the Wadsworth offered "Drums Along the Mohawk" with Claudette Colbert
and Henry Fonda on Friday, Saturday, Sunday, and Monday. Tuesday and Wednesday there was a double feature, "Law of the Pampas"
with William Boyd and "Television Spy" with William Hendry and
Judith Barnett. Over at the Gaiety Theater "When Tomorrow Comes"
was showing Thursday, Friday, and Saturday with Irene Dunne and
Charles Boyer. Sunday and Monday brought "Fifth Avenue Girl" with
Ginger Rogers, Walter Connoley, and Veree Teasdale. Tuesday and
Wednesday there was a double bill: George O'Brien in "The Fighting
Gringo" and Jack Holt in "Hidden Power."[1]

The Electric Theater, St. George.
(Lynne Clark Collection, donor — Nellie Gubler)

Movie stars probably figured more prominently in the lives of area people than had the actors at the old opera house. Certainly films were a major factor in absorbing people of southern Utah into the larger nation as a whole. Along with the whole country, county residents fell in love with Clark Gable, Gary Grant, Claudette Colbert, and Irene Dunne. Dixie began to abandon even more its byway ethic. This was happening over the entire landscape of small town America but it would become especially strong in Dixie. By the time southern Utahns became ardent fans of Hollywood stars, they found themselves in a movie location where they saw Henry Fonda, John Wayne, and others in the flesh.

Many residents' principal forms of entertainment were the movies and Friday and Saturday night dances. The period between 1930 and 1950 was often termed the "Big Band Era." Radio sets brought the big bands right into homes. That generation was entertained by Benny Goodman, Duke Ellington, Tommy Dorsey, Glenn Miller, and many others. Local bands, of course, were not as big nor as famous, but the quality was good. The best-known local group was Earl J. Bleak's orchestra which not only played for dances in St. George but also in other towns, especially New Harmony and Santa Clara.

Dixie Academy Band, directed by Earl J. Bleak, far left.
(Lynne Clark Collection, donor — Ferrol Tait)

Dancing also was big at Zion National Park. The Utah Parks Company always had excellent dance orchestras at the lodges. A prerequisite for a young person to get a summer job at one of the lodges — Bryce, Zion and Grand Canyon — was a talent for some form of entertainment. Vocal and instrumental talent was in demand. A few Dixie people such as Howard Cannon, Gene Morris, Vella Ruth Morris (Hafen), and Carl Workman were mainstays in the Grand Canyon programs for several years.

Nearly every town, no matter how small, had an orchestra, sometimes made up of members of one family. In most towns there was a dance on Friday nights. The piano was the core instrument of most dance groups; the saxophone, a twentieth-century instrument, replaced the violin (or fiddle) as the lead. Following the sax was the trumpet. For many years the tenor banjo appeared in bands and provided rhythm along with (or without) tap drums. A trombone often was next to be added. Many saxophonists doubled on the clarinet. Larger orchestras may have had a bass instrument.

Open-air dance halls with floors made of wood or concrete were popular. Partygoers traveled far to attend dances at places with such exotic names as "Purple Haze", "Shady Dell," or "Airdome" and dance to the music of such orchestras as "The Footwarmers." At New Harmony there was the "Bluebird," the "Santa Rosa" was in Santa Clara, and the "Starlite" was at Anderson's Ranch. Others which did not have romantic names were the American Legion floor in Hurricane and Dixie College's outdoor dance floor. Springdale had a wooden dance floor built by J. A. Allred in the mid-1920s, which was removed after a short time to make room for a tourist court. Rockville had a dance floor for a few years, and Virgin built one after World War II.

Another sign that Dixie was no longer so remote as it had once been was the appearance of two Dixie authors on the national scene. Here the story was the reverse. Instead of becoming fans of distant celebrities, the local citizens saw people they knew very well become known beyond the Rocky Mountains. The first to break into renown was Maurine Whipple, whose novel *The Giant Joshua* was something of a sensation. The book is a fictionalized version of the pioneer settlement of St. George, using folktales of the region and playing upon the national fascination with polygamy. Its villain is a domineering, patriarchal polygamist husband while the heroine is his much younger plural wife. The harshness of desert life, the beauty of the red hills, and the leadership of Erastus Snow are all portrayed in refreshing style.

Whipple came to the attention of Boston's Houghton-Mifflin publishing company in a writing contest, after which she was encouraged in the writing of her book. Once the publishers accepted it, the company initiated a marketing campaign and the book reached the best-seller list. Whipple received national attention and went on a national speaking tour in 1941, the book's publication year. The *Washington County News* followed her awards and tours and greeted her upon her arrival home, mentioning that 25,000 copies of the book had already been sold.[2]

The reception of *The Giant Joshua* in Dixie was mixed, however. Three hundred people attended a favorable book-review lecture of four books about Utah by President Glenn E. Snow: *For This is My Glory*, by Paul Bailey, *History of Utah* by Andrew Neff, *Children of God* by Vardis Fisher, and *The Giant Joshua*. A month later, in February 1941, Mrs. H. C. Thomas lauded the book in a review at the public library.

Nonetheless, some people took offense at Whipple's view, which they felt was an attack on polygamy. There are still mixed feelings about the book in Dixie, but in the wider circle of literary critics, *The Giant Joshua* is considered by many as the best Mormon novel to date.[3]

Whipple received another boost when *Look* magazine commissioned her to do a photo essay titled "Meet the Mormons." They sent their photographers to travel the state with Whipple, and the article appeared in the 10 March 1942 issue, featuring twenty-five photographs with Whipple's text. The issue was certainly a best-seller in the county. Newsstands could not get enough copies to meet the demand. Whipple was also invited to write a popular introduction to Utah by national book publisher A. A. Knopf. That highly illustrated book appeared as *This Is The Place: Utah* in 1945.

On a different level, Juanita Brooks brought acclaim to Dixie with her history of the Mountain Meadows Massacre.[4] The result of years of research and record collecting, this book itself was controversial, detailing the most tragic event in southern Utah history. Its historical characters are the progenitors of families in Washington and Iron counties today. Many members of the families involved have strong feelings about the event. Brooks was treading on delicate ground in tackling the subject. It was widely known that Brooks was working on the study, and some Dixie families and LDS church officials had genuine anxieties about its appearance. Reviewers hailed the book and academic libraries included it in their collections. The *Mountain Meadows Massacre* has been reprinted several times, but like most academic books has not enjoyed the wide circulation of Whipple's novel.

Juanita Brooks's later biography of John D. Lee was equally controversial for the same reasons as the book on the massacre.[5] These undertakings called attention to her many other articles and books. Before either of these works appeared, Brooks had written widely, especially about Dixie history. Brooks's first dream was to be a fiction writer, and she submitted several manuscripts in that vein. Her work had more appeal when she used folk tales and local lore. Her story "The Water's In" was of this genre and was printed in *Harpers* May 1941 issue and later reprinted in the *Reader's Digest*, a major coup.[6]

Brooks also traveled and lectured, more in the Intermountain region than nationwide. She proved to be a most engaging speaker, spinning her folktales and becoming a folk figure herself. The picture she painted of herself was of a mother of many children who taught in college by day and wrote by night. She claimed she worried about her neighbors' opinions of a mother neglecting her children to write books, so she kept her typewriter on her nearby desk and placed ironing over the machine when visitors dropped in, as they often did.

There are other tales that are told in Dixie about Juanita Brooks. For example, her son Karl enjoys telling that one night she wrote until two or three in the morning. She had put baby Karl in his buggy out in the backyard to sleep in the cool air while she typed. She got so tired that she went to bed, forgetting that the baby was outside. She jumped out of bed when the sun hit her face, dashed to the yard, and found Karl still asleep. There are stories of her searching out documents, guiding women in preserving them, presiding over Relief Society activities, disciplining young women as the dean of women at Dixie College, and engaging the city government in good causes — all fortifying her status as a legendary figure in the region.

The reception of her work in Dixie was also mixed. Some people wished she had left the old controversies to die, and some saw her as contentious. Others, like Orval Hafen, eulogized her. Many of her advocates were her students. In general, the appearance of her two controversial books brought her more respect outside Dixie than within, but she had an adroit way of rolling with the local feelings and remaining very much involved in community affairs. Brooks is the subject of a prize-winning biography by Levi Peterson.[7] Whipple, on the other hand, had a heightened sensitivity. Over the years she became reclusive and never did complete her long-heralded sequel to *The Giant Joshua*.

Today portraits of both Whipple and Brooks hang in the Dixie College Library, alongside one of Andrew Karl Larson. The latter was another productive writer and contemporary of Brooks and Whipple. All three directly influenced each other. Larson's books enjoy increasing respect and are currently available in new editions. H. L. Reid, a professor at Dixie College, and Angus Woodbury of the National Park Service in Zion Park were also writing local history at the time, and their works are still being read. Dixie was fortunate to have several authors influencing each other in the same town at the same time. Since Dixie College had fewer than 300 students, and the town had a population of approximately 5,000 people, such productivity was stunning and has not been matched since. These authors' works made Dixie an adopted home for many readers.

Civic Clubs and Celebrations

In the decade prior to World War II, civic clubs emerged, particularly in St. George, Hurricane, and Washington. These were comprised of local groups of men who banded together for social and civic purposes (women were included in later decades). They affiliated with national organizations — chambers of commerce, Lions, Rotary, Junior Chamber, Elks, American Legion, Veterans of Foreign Wars, Kiwanis, and Exchange clubs. Many civic clubs were interested in creating parks, fostering patriotism, and conducting celebrations. These groups signaled a shift from a rural to an increasingly urban community, from a religious to a secular society, and from a localized to an Americanized identity. That these people chose to use their personal time for civic purposes suggests that they not only had the time but also had a lively sense of community.

The St. George Chamber of Commerce was established in the 1920s. One of its most beneficial activities was organizing the campaign to save Dixie College in 1933. Chamber president Orval Hafen used his office effectively to demonstrate to the governor and legislature that the community was solidly determined to keep the college going. By the 1940s a dynamic group devoted their energy to the community through the chamber; they included Frank Holland, Jack Ricketts, Neal Lundberg, Arlo Prisbrey, Andrew Pace, Anthony Atkin, Clark Empey, James Andrus, and Wendell Snow among others. Their goal was to improve facilities for the growing number of tourists. The chamber took an active part in raising funds for the airport and road improvements, as well as generally promoting Dixie.

Dr. Howard Reichmann, nephew of Dr. Wilford Reichmann, was active in promoting Rotary International in Utah around 1940. The local newspaper published an article by him about the national standards of Rotary.[8] On 28 August the paper reported that the Rotary Club awarded graduating pilots their certificates. The increasing importance of the airport and several pilot training programs offered there were points of pride in the city. The Elks were active locally at the same time. They were instrumental in building a baseball diamond adjacent to the Sun Bowl (rodeo and football stadium) in St. George.

An article in the Washington County News detailed an elaborate flag ceremony to which the Lions Club invited the community on 19 June 1941. The ceremony reflected the increasing feelings of national loyalty as World War II began in Europe.

The Lions Club has had a unique role in Dixie, partly because of its vigor and partly because it linked rural and urban settings. Though the Lions undertook projects like other clubs (they improved the road up to the Sugar Loaf and built picnic tables there), their major project has been the Dixie Roundup Rodeo. Gunlock, Enterprise, Veyo, and Hurricane also held rodeos, but the Dixie Roundup has attracted larger crowds, more contestants, and financial prizes. Two hours of calf roping, team tying, kid calf riding, wild-cow milking, and bronco riding under the direction of Robert Hurley drew a crowd of 1,200 to the first Dixie Roundup on Veteran's Day, 11 November, 1935.[9] Dixie Roundup has since become an annual community celebration with added features including parades and a queen contest.

Facilities for the Dixie Roundup were temporary, located where the Elks baseball field (Lundberg Park) now is situated. Each year volunteers took weeks to set up the stands and take them down. Enthusiasm often dwindled for the removal part. The idea for a permanent facility came during one of those long assignments to dismantle the stands. Neal Lundberg and Reed Leigh came up with an idea in 1941. They took their idea to the Lions Club, which assigned them to find a suitable location. They surveyed the area and proposed land located near St. George Boulevard and 700 East. The Lions went to the city council and received a forty-nine year lease on the land in return for building a permanent rodeo facility.

The outbreak of World War II interrupted the project. By the time the war was over, the thinking about the site had changed. Mayor Eric Snow suggested moving the location to some land adjacent to the city park. He felt that the city would not have funds to develop that land for many years, and it was an eyesore, even a safety problem. The club agreed to give the original lease back to the city in return for a lease on the present site. Funding for the rodeo grounds was a major problem; Lions Club members were encouraged to each donate a minimum of $100 to the project. The club then turned to the community at large, asking for a similar amount per person. A total of 1,300 people contributed to the rodeo grounds.

During the planning, Lundberg convinced the club to expand the size of the facility, enabling high schools and the college to use it for football. By 1947 construction of the facility was far enough along that the Roundup was held there. Since then much money and labor have been spent on the facility. The Lions are rightly proud of this benefit to the whole community, and the Roundup continues to be one of the area's major events each year.

For decades before the Roundup took over the honors, the 24th of July was the biggest celebration annually in Dixie. An early tradition began of going to Pine Valley for the festivities. In pioneer times, the trip was an all-day effort. When automobiles arrived, roads were so precarious that some cars had to be abandoned part way along the route. In 1926 the News warned celebrants that the road was not good enough for cars to make the steep grade, so the paper's advice was to camp at Diamond Valley.[10] Bad roads did not limit the attendance. In 1934, for example, a major celebration was undertaken featuring local leader Anthony W. Ivins and LDS president Heber J. Grant as speakers. Certainly their presence showed that the Pine Valley version of July 24th (Pioneer Day) was important. Often the celebrations were centered on the public square, behind the Dixie College building. Activities almost always included contests, banquets, songs, and even fireworks — an all-day affirmation of the Utah settlement story.

World War II

Most of small-town America, including Washington County, was transformed by the entry of the United States into World War II. Many of the nation's youth were sent to military service either inside the nation or into the war theaters in the Pacific, North Africa, or Europe. Their lives were changed in many ways. About sixty area soldiers did not return, becoming casualties of the war.[11]

For others the war was a chance to leave Dixie as employment beckoned, especially in Las Vegas and California or in northern Utah's war plants. Many kept ties with their home communities and some sent their children back for college or later returned for retirement.

Fighting the war from the Dixie homefront was not unlike what citizens did in towns all over the nation. At first in 1939 there was a division of sentiments. Local newspapers queried "Can We Stay Out?" or "Shall We Send Our Youth to War."[12] People returning from

Europe were asked about their experiences. In Dixie returning LDS missionaries had views to share. Rulon Orton returned from serving in Czechoslovakia and published an article on the situation there following the Nazi takeover. He described the widespread depression among the Czech people. Donworth Gubler was critical of the German leadership while Woodrow Dennett was completely supportive of Hitler, arguing that the dynamic new Germany simply needed the land of its neighbors on which to expand.[13]

The Selective Service registered 900 area young men. Initially volunteers met the draft quota (October 1940) but by January 1941 conscription began. Defense stamps and bonds were sold by the American Legion auxiliary to schoolchildren and in local stores; the local unit of the National Guard — Company C, 115th Engineers — was activated in March 1941; the St. George Airport was guarded and later citizens were instructed not to go near the area; the FBI began meeting every few months with local officials to plan actions for countering any possible subversion; rationing began with rubber tires, then gasoline, and later some foods; production of nonessential items such as slot machines and juke boxes was cut back; sheepskins (shearlings) were sought to make flying suits; a civil air patrol was organized; Washington City was designated as a site to receive evacuee children should the Pacific Coast be bombed — all were examples of the war's impact in Dixie.

Paul Crosby recalls that the activation of the St. George National Guard unit well before the U.S. entry into the war was a major event in Dixie. After waiting for the camp to be prepared, the unit went to San Louis Obispo in March 1941 for training. The group was not kept completely intact — others joined the unit and the officers were transferred elsewhere. The soldiers built pontoon bridges in Yosemite National Park for practice and defended the Los Angeles Harbor and defense industries against possible Japanese subversion. Thereafter, many of the soldiers were shipped to Europe where some participated in the Italian and French campaigns; others served in the Pacific. One result of their activation was that enrollment dropped at Dixie College.

One soldier's experience could serve as an example of the combat encountered by many. Elmer Pickett was a sergeant in the local national guard company in October 1940, when the unit first anticipated activation. The married members of the company were allowed to get out of the activation; fifteen did, and new recruits had to be quickly enlisted to get the company to full strength — eighty men — before shipping out. Because the barracks were not ready in California, the company unexpectedly spent nearly six months waiting in St. George. The "Rec Hall" on the Dixie College campus was used as their armory, and their parade ground was the playing field next to the Woodward School.

Captain Howard Cannon was commander of the unit, with Clarence Moss as first lieutenant and Calvin Andrus as second lieutenant. (Cannon later became a U.S. Senator from Nevada.) Finally in March 1941, the 115th departed for San Luis Obispo to receive training in bridge building and road construction. Immediately upon arrival, the officers were transferred to other units because the army policy was to have National Guard officers not remain with troops from their home.

Pickett recalls that unforgettable Sunday morning on 7 December 1941 when Pearl Harbor was bombed. Within hours the 115th company was sent to the coast to lay barbed-wire obstacles in the ocean to serve as a deterrent against potential Japanese amphibious landings.

During their months in California, several members of the St. George unit qualified to attend officer's candidate school, among them Elmer and Evan Pickett, Spence Truman, Glade Wittwer, and Paul Crosby. After training, the group was split up. Some, including Scott Prisbrey, went to the Pacific; Doyle Sampson, Barnard Hafen, Phil Squire, Elmer Pickett, and others went to Europe. They landed in Morocco after the main fighting of the invasion had occurred but helped in the "mopping up." Then they shipped over to Tunisia and joined General George S. Patton in another follow-up operation.

The invasion of Sicily was the unit's test of mettle. The Germans fought fiercely and thousands of Americans were killed. Americans fought their way straight across the island. Elmer Pickett was injured just as the troops reached the ocean on the north side; he was sent to a hospital for six months. He returned to his unit which by then had fought its way up the Italian peninsula beyond Naples and was bogged down at Messina. Pickett and his fellows, specialists in amphibious landings, were sent around Messina to undertake the famous landing at Anzio Beach. Pickett remembers that this was not a glorious performance as supplies and back-up failed, and the landing was nearly thwarted. Famous journalists Ernie Pyle and Bill Maulden covered this story and knew members of Pickett's company.

After Rome was taken, Pickett and his men were sent on yet another landing, this time in southern France. They fought up the Rhone River, finally reaching the Rhine River, where the company built pontoon bridges while a battle was raging about them. Then it was on to Ulm and Nuremberg and finally Munich. Pickett's company was among those who first reached the Dachau concentration camp. He reported that the horror of the camp so incensed some American soldiers that they broke discipline and simply shot German guards in summary executions. Americans took on the awful task of burying hundreds of bodies that were stacked up in the camp, evidence that the Germans were trying to cremate the victims prior to the Americans' arrival.[14] J. L. Crawford was among the soldiers who witnessed the liberation at Dachau. He told of the horror and described the railroad freight cars that arrived at Dachau with only a few people alive. Maurice Tietjen of St. George recalled being at Dachau a few weeks after the liberation. Many prisoners were still there being nursed back to health before they could be released.

In comparison to the terror of combat and danger of death faced by many soldiers, those at home had a much lighter load. Of course, they spent their days and nights in anxiety for their loved ones at the battle front. These concerns outweighed the irritations of daily life at home, nonetheless, there were memorable dimensions of wartime in Washington County. Rationing is one thing residents remember about the war. Fern Crawford tells about the process from the merchants' side:

> During WWII it became necessary to ration sugar, shoes, meat, certain groceries and especially tires and gas. Tires and gas were in three categories A, B, and C. Doctors had priority. Farmers and other individuals were served in proper category. Counties received only a few tires periodically. Farmers were allotted off road gas in limited amounts. All car owners were allotted small amounts of gas. All families received ration stamps for commodities on the ration list. These stamps came in various colors marked accordingly. Nylon hose, while not rationed, were in short supply. To eliminate complaints, merchants sometimes had a drawing for the few pairs of hose they received.
>
> Office of Price Administration, organized for rationing purposes, sent an OPA official to contact each business, explain the procedure and return later to check on compliance. Lists of all items the business was selling were typed in three columns. Heading of the

three columns were COST PRICE, SELLING PRICE, AND REGU-
LATED OPA PRICE. Should owners be found not complying and
be reported, a $10,000 fine was charged. OPA Court would be held
to determine the charge. An example — one merchant was fined for
selling a can of mushrooms for 49¢ but in checking his chart found
he could have been selling the mushrooms for 59¢. Had it been otherwise he would have been responsible for the fine.15

Gas rationing had a clear impact on the county as tourism declined. Zion National Park was actually closed for a time to reduce
gas consumption.

One way to measure the impact of the war in Washington County
is to look at the statistics. Between 1 October 1940 and 30 June 1946,
1,095 residents were either inducted or enlisted in the armed forces.16
At the time, the county population ranged from 9,269 in 1940 to 9,836
in 1950, so one out of every nine was serving in the military.

Upon returning, many soldiers flocked to college courses. The Federal GI Bill made college attendance much easier. Enrollment swelled
at Dixie College as well as elsewhere in the state. Some of the return-
ees also joined the ranks of the American Legion and the Veterans of
Foreign Wars; they then undertook more ambitious civic projects.

The biggest change occurred in the lives of the people who had
been away. Those who returned often brought a new perspective with
them. They had been in big cities and seen a consumer society where
average people earned wages that were still rare in Dixie. It was a
materialistic America, a nation with seemingly endless opportunities.
They found places where they could live beyond their home town.
Some felt an urge to get beyond the Rocky Mountains and Great Basin,
but others felt the homing loyalties to live in the land of their fathers in
the raw beauty of the desert. Many returned with a determination to
launch some kind of a career that would bring about a change in Dixie
that would make their homeland more part of the America they had
discovered. Farming might be a fond sideline but not a likely career.
Increased prosperity, they felt, was both possible and desirable.

Trucking

The advent of the automobile brought people into Dixie, especially
as tourists, but development of the companion vehicle, the truck, was
perhaps an even greater influence to end Dixie's isolation. Although

freighting began in the first decade of white settlement with horse-drawn wagons, the motorized trucks developed in the 1920s and there-after made a huge difference. Trucks gradually came to surpass the impact of the railroad in other parts of the state.

In 1917 Joseph J. Milne obtained a Garford truck with hard rub-ber tires and began freighting foodstuffs to Modena and Lund. Arvel Milne tells of traveling with his father in that old truck with a grub box, a single spring, and a bedroll attached to the side of the truck. It was hooked up so the spring would swing down perpendicular to the ground and be held onto the truck siding at right angles. They would drive to Anderson Ranch the first night and sleep on the spring. Then they would drive on to Cedar City and west to Lund the second day, get their load and return to St. George and Santa Clara the third and fourth days. Most of their work became what was called "Less than Truckload Freight" (LTF), bringing hardware and other goods to Dixie from the railhead. Arvel recalls some of his impressions of trucking as a boy:

> We had some turnouts. My father had a big whistle that ran off the exhaust and some bailing wire that came up through the floor board with a ring on it. You would pull the ring and that would blow the whistle and I was the whistle boy. I thought that was a pretty im-portant job to pull on the ring and blow the whistle and let the cars down below know we were coming so they would pull into one of these turnouts.[17]

By the 1930s the Milnes had obtained trucks with inflated rubber tires that could make the trip to Salt Lake City in one day, bypass-ing the railroad. Sometimes they trucked fresh produce to Salt Lake City, but soon their staple product was oil and gas which they picked up at the railroad in Cedar City for Continental Oil Company. At one time they had the contract for a major construction project near Jacob Lake and supplied the oil and gas for all the heavy equipment. When the Public Service Commission required trucking firms to obtain a certificate, Milne filed, paid the tax, and received certificate number two. They soon had six or seven trucks and much of the Salt Lake City market. In 1933 they bought the Southern Utah Truck line with certificates for Millard and Juab counties, but they kept their main of-fice in St. George. Gradually they expanded their operation through several western states.

In the 1930s a group of Santa Clara businessmen (Norman, Emil, Ensign, and Clement Gubler) formed the Southern Utah Produce Company. At the same time, Harvey and Rulon Stucki and Lester and Reed Wittwer were working together freighting largely to Las Vegas and California. The two groups joined in 1941 to form the Rocky Mountain Produce Company. They built a warehouse in Santa Clara and in 1945 took on new partners from among the employees in the company — Don C. Frei, Stan Ray, and Arlo Prisbrey.

Both the Milne and Rocky Mountain companies expanded their respective freight operations during and after the war. Milne hauled freight throughout Utah and to Idaho and Wyoming while the Rocky Mountain Produce Company developed freight service to Las Vegas and California. In 1955 the two companies merged their freight operations. The Rocky Mountain Company (RMC) continued to handle food-and-produce hauling, remaining separate from the general freight operation. Arvel Milne served as president of the merged company, with members from both companies serving on a five-member board. Milne Truck Lines eventually employed 1,200 people throughout the western United States. In 1979 Milne Trucking sold out to Sun Oil Company, one of the nation's largest oil firms. Thereafter it experienced the fate of other mergers, eventually disappearing as new executives emphasized differing priorities.

The Rocky Mountain Company continues to maintain its identity as a food distributor with its headquarters in St. George. Today it is a dynamic business, operating in the intermountain states from its St. George hub. It distributes food, manages Sam's Clubs, and invests in real estate. The company receives its supplies from the Pacific Coast states, Texas, and Mexico. It is a full-service food distributing company. St. George, by virtue of the excellent freeway, 1-15, is located in a prime position. H. Bruce Stucki, RMC president, notes that the St. George location enables his company to operate in the state of Utah where regulations do not stifle his firm and where the work ethic of the people makes his company productive. Yet St. George is close enough to California, Nevada, and Texas that he can ship goods to the hub relatively cheaply and rapidly. The company now employs 250 people in St. George with a payroll of $2.5 million.

Dairying for Las Vegas

One of the first avenues for bringing a higher living standard to Dixie was to link its economy to the boomtown of Las Vegas. During World War II one such link had already been forged — dairying. The establishment of Nellis Air Force Base in Las Vegas in 1941 created a large market. Kenny Searles was associated with the huge Anderson Dairy in Las Vegas and was usually searching for more milk producers. Even before the war, some Dixie farmers had been sending milk "on the mail" to places outside the county. Elmer Harmon sent cans to Beaver and Julius Wittwer transported milk to Mesquite. St. George dairyman Harry S. Gentry met with Kenny Searles, who agreed to be his agent if he would get more cows, build a milkhouse, and have a delivery ready two times a day.

These local farmers and soon many others, including Art Rogers and Don and Duane Adams, moved quickly to qualify for a Grade-A rating — which meant installing coolers and a separate milking barn. They acquired an insulated truck and greatly enlarged their operations. Their dairy association eventually included fifty-five producers in Washington County, involving farmers in the St. George-Washington-Hurricane area and along the road to Central and even to Pine Valley. Murray Webb and Boots Cox had dairy herds near St. George. The Gentry family had all six of their grown sons involved in the operation. By 1956 the association had switched to a tanker that shipped 6,000 gallons a day. Some operations were so efficient that one man could milk eighty cows an hour. Certainly this Las Vegas connection had a major economic advantage for Washington County.

Ranching

The Taylor Grazing Act of 1934 put an end to open grazing on Federal land (though the Forest Service had been regulating some forest lands before that time). Ranchers recognized that the range had been overgrazed and needed protection, but they were apprehensive about the role they would play in the councils that would make allotment decisions. Development of big trucks had ended the necessity of long cattle drives to the railhead at Modena or Lund. As a result, the cattle industry experienced a great boom; World War II also gave it a bigger market. The ranchers were concerned because ranching was clearly well adapted to the Dixie region.

Branding cattle at John R. Crawford's corral in present-day Zion National Park. (J. L. Crawford Collection)

Despite the new regulations, there were several ranchers who developed large operations on the Arizona Strip, including Rudger Atkin, Anthony W. Atkin, the Esplin family, the Bundy family, Andrew Sorenson, John Pymm, the Foremaster family, and James W. Nixon. These ranches on the Arizona Strip were either survivors from or successors to the holdings of Preston Nutter, a cattleman from Texas who had brought in capital and became the powerhouse on "the Strip" in the period before the Depression. Some had worked for Nutter in the area west of the Hurricane Fault or for B. E. Saunders south of Pipe Spring where he had run the LDS church herd and then purchased it.

A different kind of ranching was the cooperative herding practiced by neighboring farmers. On the west side of the county, farmers from Pine Valley, Central, Gunlock, and Santa Clara on the northwest and some from Littlefield, Arizona; Barclay, Nevada; and Beaver Dam ranged their cattle together. Most farmers had five or six head of cows; some as many as twenty-five. These needed to be grazed in the spring and summer so farmers organized a cooperative herd system. Grant Hafen recalled the excitement of the roundup:

> They gathered everyone's cattle, started way down around Bunker-ville and Mesquite. Bunkerville and Mesquite cattle and all were gathered and when they got up to Littlefield of course they took their cattle out and took them up on the Littlefield mountain and the others came up the Beaver Dam Wash. They drove them up as far as Little Bull Valley and came into the Beaver Dam Wash. The Clover Valley cattle were cut out and taken up that canyon to Clover and the others went up Jackson Wash toward Gunlock.
>
> I remember when I was a kid being up there below Gunlock at what we called the old sand trail and helping turn the cattle into the cor-rals when there were at least 1,200 head of cows walking up that creek and going into that corral.
>
> When those cattle came in it was a great event. Sometimes there were six or eight wagons up there at the sand trail from Santa Clara with hay and things for their horses. It was just a regular outing for the kids to go up there and see the cattle and ride the horses.[18]

The next part of the job was to get the cattle to the railhead for ship-ment to market. The farmers along the Beaver Dam Wash and the Santa Clara Creek did not have far to go to get to the railroad; but the ranchers from the Kolob-Virgin-Hurricane area had a much longer drive. Lu-wayne Wood recalls his boyhood in 1923 when he went along. That was before Federal regulations and before most fences, so cattlemen in the Canaan Gap and Arizona Strip ran their cattle in common on the land and could drive them to the railroad across the land.

> At the completion of the roundup, which took several days, we drove the herd to Virgin, Utah, a distance of about 30 to 40 miles. There we separated the cattle according to brands with each owner arranging to take his own cattle except for the ones to be trailed to the railroad. Joseph Haslam and my father were running some cattle jointly, and we took about 200 head over Kolob Mountain, through Oak Valley, and to the Haslam Ranch at Crystal Springs.
>
> When we returned to Virgin, some of the men had started with the herd that we were driving to the railroad at Lund, Utah. We caught up with them near Toquerville. The thing I especially remember was the dust! When about 700 head of cattle are on the move, there is a big cloud of dust. We filtered it the best we could by breathing through our bandannas. In driving that many cattle, we split them

into three bunches, with two riders behind each bunch. It took about four to five days to make the drive from Virgin to Lund. Since we had no corrals, it was necessary to night herd. Two riders, one on each side of the herd, would ride around the cattle all night long. With a large herd of cattle, they sometimes stampede, and riding around them at night helps keep them quiet.

We travelled the main road (gravel and dirt) by way of Anderson's Ranch (where the highway which now goes to Zion National Park, Hurricane, etc. leaves Interstate 15), Pintura (then named Bellevue), the Black Ridge, Kanarraville and Hamilton's Fort, we went north toward Iron Springs which is about 6 or 7 miles west of Cedar City. From Iron Springs we travelled northwest about 25 miles across the Lund Desert to the Union Pacific railroad at Lund.[19]

The ranching that still remains is mainly extended family enterprises that have proven viable. The old drives are gone, replaced by truck shipping. Some cattlemen range their cattle (area sheep are gone) on private lands, but most graze the cattle where permits allow them to use Federal lands. Thus they are subject to government regulations that limit the number of animals allowed to graze. There is only a fraction of animals on the range compared to the number in 1900 when Frank Adams reported that there were 7,000 head of cattle and 15,000 sheep in Washington County and 3,000 cattle and 40,000 sheep in Kane County. After the Taylor Grazing Act, the sheep industry declined and eventually disappeared from the region. Political and environmental proposals to limit the use of land have created a major conflict between ranchers and Federal agencies.

Small operations seem to be dying out as the older generations disappear. Knowing that small ranches could not sustain a family by themselves, many members of the younger generation have gone to college and taken up a vocation. Some keep a few cattle out of nostalgia. Ed Bowler of St. George tells how his father, Truman, made it very clear to him that his love for the cowboy life must not divert him from a profession. Ed, now a successful executive of a title brokerage firm, has raised a son, Kip, who is a superb roper, but Ed has instructed him similarly. The Bowler cattle operation served as a good part-time job while Kip went to college, but now he is moving on. Truman moved back to Gunlock to tend the cattle as a retirement project until his death in 1995. None of the Bowlers ranch full-time, but all of them have the cowboy lifestyle in their blood.

Dry Farming

Dry farming methods were put into practice in at least three locations: New Harmony, Smith's Mesa, and the Big Plain. A fourth area,
somewhat smaller, was that comprising Cave and Lee valleys in the
Kolob region. The higher elevation — between 4,000 and 5,000 feet
— meant a few degrees cooler temperatures and perhaps a little more
rain or at least a better chance of retaining moisture.

The Big Plain, a few miles south of Rockville and just east of present Apple Valley, was opened to homesteading in 1912 and was taken
up mostly by residents of Rockville and Springdale. A photograph
taken in 1915 refers to this area as a "Demonstration Farm." Smith's
Mesa and Kolob were owned and farmed by residents of Virgin, Toquerville, and Hurricane. At one time there may have been as many as
10,000 acres of wheat growing on Smith's Mesa.

The dry farmers produced a crop only every other year, plowing
the idle ground and allowing it to lie fallow on alternate years, but
keeping it weed free to preserve water. About fifteen inches of rain per
year for two years were required to produce a crop, usually the turkey-
red variety of wheat which was planted in the fall early enough to
sprout before snowfall and harvested fairly early the following summer. Twenty bushels to the acre was considered an average yield.

One team of horses could pull a binder, a machine which bundled
and tied the grain, dropping the bundles on the ground to be picked
up and stacked in wait for the thresher. The header was pulled by two
teams, and a wagon with a large box was driven alongside to receive
the grain which was delivered by conveyor belt. The load was then
taken directly to the thresher or stacked. The first combines to come
into the area required six teams (twelve horses) to operate, but they
cut, threshed, and sacked the grain in one operation. One man drove
while another sewed the sacks shut. Gasoline-powered tractors soon
replaced horses, but eventually engines were put into combines, making them self-contained.

Dry-land wheat farming reached its peak in Washington County following World War II. Emil J. Graff had purchased most of the Big Plain,
some of Smith's Mesa, and a lot of land near New Harmony. He also
farmed at Garrison, Utah, and in Nevada. For many years, he employed
as many as fifty men in his farming operations. Dry farming still goes

on, but now a crop is watermelons. As with grain, a drier than normal year may mean crop failure. Such was the case in 1994; however, the previous year Merl Tobler shipped in excess of 100 tons of melons from Coal Pits Bench near Virgin. He and a brother-in-law, Clinton Isom, are now experimenting with growing pistachio nuts in the same area with promising prospects, the main threat to success being squirrels.

The Downwinders

In the 1950s, the United States government's nuclear testing in the Nevada desert periodically sent clouds of radiation fallout over Washington County. From that day to this, some county citizens have been vocal critics of the nuclear testing which invaded the county. Their story, mentioned here, is part of a larger picture. The conflict between the Federal government and the downwinders is complex. These residents of Washington County have come to believe they are victims of one of the deadliest cover-ups in the nation's history. The Federal government, on the other hand, feels it had sufficient safeguards in place to assure safety to the residents during nuclear tests at the Nevada test site that included aboveground and underground tests.

During World War II Nazi Germany was working on an atomic bomb; the prospect of seeing them first to make such an awesome weapon pushed the United States into the Manhattan Project in 1941. By 1945 a test atomic bomb was fired at Alamogordo, New Mexico, followed quickly by the two used in Japan at Hiroshima and Nagasaki. Politically they worked, as Japan soon surrendered. The Federal government continued to test atomic weapons because of the developing Cold War pressure for the U.S. to remain the most powerful nation in the world. Much of the testing took place in Nevada, with some of the nuclear fallout drifting over Utah.

The residents of Washington County lived a rural lifestyle, spending a lot of time outdoors, eating produce from their own gardens and drinking fresh milk; however, they seemed to suffer more leukemia and other cancer deaths than normal. This, in a state where cancer incidence generally was lower than in the rest of the United States, makes the problem more dramatic.

Before the military uses of atomic power were explored, the main concern about radiation was in connection with medical functions of x-rays. Radiation safety in the health professions was recognized before weapons testing began but was minimal because those at risk were limited to doctors and x-ray technicians. To state unequivocally that one person or another died or was afflicted by cancer caused by radioactive fallout from the Nevada Test Site is not possible. There is little doubt that radiation can cause cancer; however, the link between a given radioactive exposure and a tumor can only be drawn statistically. For medical researchers as well as for lawyers who argued their cases in a Federal court, this was a difficult statistical problem to resolve. In the end, however, many people felt betrayed by their government.

The historical record is full of family tragedy blamed on the fallout. Throughout the area, many families were hit particularly hard. In this traumatic situation, people began to raise questions. These feelings gave birth to several groups whose collective purpose was to bring relief to families who had suffered, to bring facilities and treatment closer to them, to bring an acknowledgment of guilt and admission of wrongdoing by the Federal government, to bring compensation to those who had paid for pain and treatment, and to bring an end to all nuclear testing. Erma Thomas, Elizabeth Bruhn Wright, Janet Gordon, Preston Truman and others took up the fight and organized groups in the 1960s and 1970s to support individuals in seeking redress from the government. Citizen Call, Downwinders, and Hospice of Southwestern Utah were groups that became active in these causes.

Governor Scott M. Matheson, who later died of cancer, objected to testing, as he stated in a letter to the United States Department of Energy: "I object to the disregard for the rights of Utahns to know when there is even the possibility of risk for increased radioactivity in our state as a result of nuclear testing in Nevada."[20] Protest groups began to challenge the need for testing to continue. They began to draw a cause-and-effect case in attempting to show that radiation was the source of much of the cancer. The U.S. Center for Disease Control authorized a detailed study on that issue in 1977.

Although protests continued, nothing suggested any urgency; however, congressional hearings in January and February 1978 decisively changed all that. Publicity had prompted thousands of calls and letters to the Center for Disease Control. During 1978 and 1979, congressional hearing rooms echoed with tough questions and repeated challenges to Energy Department claims. Only after 1978 did Congress for the first time seem to grasp that aboveground tests had over-exposed to radiation many hundreds of people, including those who lived downwind of the tests in Washington County. Technically, as official spokesmen sought time and again to explain, that simply meant exposures were slightly in excess of then-current guidelines, which in any event included what were widely believed to be large safety margins. Overexposure in itself, however undesirable, showed this was not necessarily harmful. Valid as such niceties might be in principle, however, they seemed almost irrelevant to the cancer-stricken residents of Washington County.

After many legal tests by a number of plaintiffs in the courts, most of which were denied, downwinders finally benefited financially. On 15 October 1990, President George Bush signed into law the Radiation Exposure Compensation Act. It authorized a $100 million trust fund from which those who lived downwind during the years of aboveground testing could be awarded $50,000 if they had contracted certain radiation-related diseases. The act was later amended to remove the $100 million ceiling and to allow uranium miners and test-site workers also to participate in the compensation. As of September 1994, 1,003 claims had been approved for a total of $50,120,000 payment; 829 claims had been denied, and 125 were pending. The act included an apology from the Federal government and has been followed up by a formal statement of apology by President Bill Clinton. It appears that the controversy that began in the late 1970s is nearly resolved at last. That such a resolution should be political, rather than scientific or legal, underscored the fundamental nature of the controversy.[21]

The New Polygamy

Just as people in Washington County were becoming increasingly Americanized, ever more like the rest of the nation, one group in a remote corner of the county was heading in the opposite direction. Theirs was a quest for renewed isolation. The fundamentalists of Hildale, Utah, are a private people; until recently they lived almost undercover. They weave into the history of Utah and Washington County in inextricable ways. To some their lifestyle seems unAmerican, to others they appear to be a group of hard-working, industrious, and, for the most part, law-abiding citizens. Their ideology dates back to before the beginnings of the county, and their story crosses back and forth along the Utah and Arizona border. Their original stronghold at Short Creek has disappeared from maps but thrives now as the twin towns of Hildale, Utah, and Colorado City, Arizona.

The doctrine of plural marriage in the LDS church dates back at least to 12 July 1843 when Joseph Smith, Jr. received and recorded what became the 132nd section of the Church's Doctrine and Covenants and provided the scriptural foundation for Mormon plural marriage. The practice was lived quietly for about a decade before it was made public by Orson Pratt under the direction of Brigham Young on 29 August 1852. What Pratt said became the policy on plurality of wives. Nothing substantive was ever added beyond this initial justification of the doctrine. He described "celestial marriage" as a sacred and binding contract for time and all eternity whereby the faithful could ensure a large and righteous posterity. The purpose of the principle, according to Pratt, was procreation. This was about the closest the church would come to providing a guideline for living and practicing plural marriage. Mormons, as free agents, were left to find out for themselves how to conduct their affairs. Regardless of Mormon efforts to legitimize polygamy or practice it under claims of freedom of religion, national public sentiment stood violently opposed to its practice, classing it with slavery as a "relic of barbarism."

In 1857 a Federal army was dispatched from the east to put down a supposed rebellion in Utah, and for the next thirty plus years the United States government was active in attempting to stamp out the practice of polygamy through various pieces of legislation. These laws made lawbreakers out of Mormons who practiced polygamy. Polygamous Mormons fled the state, went into hiding, or moved to Mexico.

The acceptance of polygamy among the Mormons began to end when President Wilford Woodruff presented the "Manifesto" to the October conference of the church in 1890 for a sustaining vote. He had issued it a month earlier, stating in part:

Inasmuch as laws have been enacted by Congress forbidding plural marriages, which laws have been pronounced constitutional by the Court of last resort, I hereby declare my intention to submit to those laws and to use my influence with the members of the Church over which I preside to have them do likewise. I now publicly declare that my advice is to refrain from contracting any marriage forbidden by the law of the land.[22]

While the intention of the Manifesto was clear, however, there is little doubt that plural marriage ceremonies continued to be performed with the tacit approval of church leaders. Polygamy was becoming as hard to stop as it was to start.

Strife that had come from without now came from within the ranks of the church as painful questions remained in the minds of many of the faithful. In 1904 President Joseph F. Smith issued what has come to be called the "Second Manifesto" which closed the door to approved new plural marriages; however, there remained a significant minority who opposed the practice's demise out of religious beliefs. As conflict arose with this group of polygamists, they sought their own leaders and their own locations to congregate together.

Short Creek, Arizona, on the Utah border, became a settling place for the polygamists community as early as the 1930s. The remote site had long been known by the Mormons; in 1858 Jacob Hamblin discovered Pipe Spring, about twenty miles east of Short Creek, and recognized the area as great grazing ground for cattle. Ranchers took cattle there as early as 1866, but that year five white people were killed by Indians — James Whitmore, Robert McIntyre, and three members of the Robert Berry family — Robert, his wife Isabella, and his brother Joseph. These events brought fear to the Mormons; permanent settlement in the area seemed impossible. The area remained unpopulated until 1912 when Jacob Lauritzen brought his family there. They diverted water from the canyon, imported machinery, lived in a tent and struggled for survival. By 1920 other families had joined them and a school was started with Charles Hafen of Santa Clara as the first teacher. A wooden schoolhouse, a few permanent homes, a store, and post office followed. By 1926 there were about 100 people in the area, and in 1931 twenty-four children were enrolled in the school.

The tie to so-called fundamentalism for Short Creek came when Isaac Carling went to Salt Lake City to work in the Baldwin Radio plant. Nathaniel Baldwin was an important Utah inventor and industrialist who became the financial patron of the fundamentalist movement. Many of his corporate officers and other employees were active in the movement in Utah; among them were Lorin C. Woolley, John Y. Barlow, Israel Barlow, Leslie Broadbent, and Lyman Jessop.

Increased pressure from the LDS church served to polarize fundamentalists, and many looked to Short Creek as the future home of the movement. The Utah Legislature elevated "unlawful cohabitation" from a misdemeanor to a felony in 1935, which made the border town look more attractive as a place where practitioners of plural marriage could step across the Utah line quickly to avoid arrest. With the conviction of Price Johnson and I. Carling Spencer in December 1935 in an Arizona court, the state line between Utah and Arizona became even more important, as polygamists could avoid law enforcement officers from either direction.

In October 1936, the Declaration of United Trust was filed and recorded in Kingman, Arizona, legally creating a trust and taking a giant step toward a united order lifestyle for area polygamists. In November 1942, a new United Effort Plan (UEP) trust was recorded in Kingman, Arizona, strengthening and making more clear the legality of the trust.

The decades of the 1940s and 1950s saw considerable conflict between the fundamentalists and government officials, as well as some internal conflict. In 1953 a raid by the Arizona state government to break up the community by taking children away from parents was a dismal failure. Though 263 children were seized, within three years all had been returned to their families in what had become an expensive and unpopular public embarrassment.[23] The raid was traumatic for all and today has gained legendary status. This would also represent the last legal prosecution of fundamentalists affiliated with the Short Creek community for practicing plural marriage.

In 1961 an oiled road was finished from Hurricane, Utah, to Fredonia, Arizona. This opened access to Short Creek and in a symbolic way exposed the fundamentalists to the world. The name of the location was officially changed the following year to Colorado City for the Arizona side and Hildale for the Utah side. Hildale was incorporated as a Utah town in 1962. The area has grown, and the combined communities numbered more than 4,000 residents in 1995.

Education is important to the fundamentalists with about 1,500 students enrolled in elementary and secondary schools in the two communities. College also is considered important and the United Effort Plan often financially assists students to attend college and apply their skills for the common good. Some students enroll at Dixie College or at Southern Utah University, but most attend the branch of Mojave Community College in Colorado City. Recently the John Y. Barlow

Horse drawn hearse at Leroy Johnson's funeral. Meetinghouse and the Canaan Mountains are in the background. (Nancy Rhodes)

University was opened by the fundamentalists of Colorado City. As yet unaccredited, it aspires to become a much larger center of learning for its members.

Under the leadership of mayors Dan Barlow of Colorado City and David Zitting of Hildale, the area has enjoyed economic growth and positive interaction with the outside world. A new airport, a manufacturing plant, a convenience store, and a restaurant all suggest economic vitality.

After the death of Leroy Johnson in 1986, an internal conflict among fundamentalists spilled over into a bitter Federal-court battle. A minority group of plaintiffs has contended that the United Effort Plan trust was a business venture from which they could withdraw, taking their contributions as well as title to real property which they had occupied but which had been deeded to the trust. The much larger majority defendant group contends that the UEP was a voluntary charitable organization advancing the religious community, which means the past contributions were gifts and need not be refunded. This has divided the community and families and led to creation of a splinter group which calls itself the "Second Ward." The dispute has more to do with legitimate religious authority than it does with polygamy. A final decision was hailed by both sides as a victory; it allowed the trust to evict the splinter group but not without compensating those who were put out.24

Hildale/Colorado City has grown in numbers, prospered financially, and gained confidence as a religious community. Members of the two towns are usually easily identified by their modest dress, conservative hair styles, and lack of makeup. Due to their common large family structure, many can get a real bargain when they purchase a family pass to some events being held in the area. The median family income is low, partly because family incomes have to be divided among so many.

The Hildale/Colorado City area has opened up considerably, looking to improve its relationship with the outside world while retaining its unique religious culture. Economic expansion in Colorado City and in other group holdings has accelerated with the development of cabinet making, commercial landscaping, chicken and egg farming, candy making, and other businesses. Innovative public school financing and aggressive expansion of public services continues under both church and civic sponsorship. Internal conflict in the UEP remains, but the Short Creek community seems clearly here to stay.

Shivwits Indians

Another group of people who have remained somewhat isolated are the Shivwits Band of the Paiute Indians in the opposite corner of the county. The land west of Ivins has traditionally been the home of the Shivwits. For decades the Indians have resided there after moving from the west side of Santa Clara where they had coexisted with the white Mormon missionaries.

In recent times the band has organized as one of five among Southern Utah Paiutes. The others include the Richfield Band, the Kanosh Band, the Cedar City Band, and the Indian Peaks Band. The Shivwits Band lost its tribal status in the 1960s when U.S. government policy shifted toward assimilation instead of dealing with Indians as separate tribes. After lengthy negotiations, the Shivwits regained tribal status in 1982.

Between 1978 and 1980 the band moved to Sand Hill which is on the North Ivins Bench above the meadows where they previously lived. The Federal government built some homes and a community center there, a major improvement over the previous housing which was some distance from culinary water. The families "rent to own" those facilities. There are about 100 Shivwits Indians in the community. Present members of the tribe, including Angus Snow, Wallea Baker Graman, Dollie Big Soldier, and Donnitta Snow, report that the Shivwits have felt isolation and discrimination. Though the Indians have long been valued employees of area farmers and ranchers, many have felt a lack of acceptance in the Anglo culture. Some of them became members of the Mormon church in pioneer times, and today many grow up as Mormons; nonetheless, they report feeling looked down upon in schools and commercial life.[25]

Another difficulty the Shivwits Indians face is that their relationship with the Navajo Indians has always been uncomfortable. In recent decades, many Navajos from southeastern Utah and northeastern Arizona have moved into Washington County to seek employment or to attend Dixie College. The Native American Program at the college has been attractive mainly to Navajos, so the Shivwits have not readily adopted it. The latest development among the Shivwits is a proposal to build a golf course and hotel on the reservation. This holds promise as an employment opportunity for the tribe and seems feasible because they have both the land and water to sustain the operation.

Religious Diversity

The preponderance of Mormons in Dixie does not mean that other Christian denominations do not exist in Washington County. Roman Catholicism, as noted previously, was important in the life of people in Silver Reef when Reverend Lawrence Scanlan built a chapel, hospital, and school there in 1878. Within a decade, however, Silver Reef was a ghost town and Catholicism had to wait eighty years until Bishop Joseph Lennox Federal dedicated a church in St. George on 8 June 1958. Catholic priests served both the Cedar City and St. George parishioners in the 1950s. About fifteen families made up the Dixie core group, but the church services also welcomed tourists. In 1980 the first full-time priest, Reverend James M. Greenwell, was appointed for St. George, leading some eighty families and 250 members.

The priests and members of the congregation have actively served the community, including the "snowbirds" who come to spend the winter in Dixie. They have taken on a mission to care for the homeless, destitute, and the ill; and the parish also maintains a thrift shop.

Growth of population in the county in the last thirty years has brought Roman Catholics into Dixie, making it necessary to plan for a major expansion of church facilities. With great effort and community support, a fine new church was built on the same site and dedicated in April 1991 by Bishop William K. Wiegand. A spacious social hail was added in 1995. The parish in 1995 counted some 480 families; in addition, there are many visitors who attend the weekly masses. Priests serving the parish have included Father Everett Harman from 1955 to 1965, Father James Coyne from 1958 to 1968, Father George Davich from 1967 to 1970, and Father Francis Kunz, C. M., from 1970 to 1980. Father James Greenwell became the first full-time priest in St. George in 1980. Reverend Paul Kuzy has been the parish priest since 1984.[26]

The Presbyterian mission to Utah focused on both religious and educational efforts. In 1880 Reverend A. B. Cort from Chicago came to St. George with the intention of building a church and conducting a school. He was not received warmly by the local people who were defending their belief in polygamy against the Federal government and many Protestants who urged the government on in its anti-polygamy efforts. Reverend Cort helped several Protestant women begin schools, including Anna Stevenson in St. George, Virginia Dickey in Washington City, and Fannie Burke in Toquerville. In 1883 Mrs. A. E. Blackburn and her daughter Nellie came to St. George as teachers. In 1891 Catherine Watt came to the area as did a Miss Rever. In 1893 Reverend Galen Hardy and his wife arrived in St. George. They had considerable success with their weekday and Sunday schools. Reverend Hardy died in St. George in 1898.

These were professionally trained teachers and their schools offered a quality of education not available in many LDS ward schools. The Presbyterians hoped that the Mormons would send their children to the schools and would then gradually move back into mainline Christianity. It was a creative strategy; however, although some Mormons sent their children to the schools and took advantage of the fine opportunity, hardly any changed their religion.

In 1901 the first Presbyterian church building was dedicated. It served the community until it was sold to the Roman Catholic

Presbyterian school kindergarten, Sarah Conklin teacher.
(Lynne Clark Collection, donor — Helen Barber)

church in 1950. The assignment was difficult for the ministers as they received little support from the Mormon community. Reverend Clayton Rice came to the area in 1908 and used friendliness and community activity as tools to break into Dixie. He loved the desert and enjoyed the people on a social level. He directed plays, coached baseball, taught violin, and trained debaters. He was well received, but only a handful attended his sermons. Other ministers also found little success.

Sarah Louisa Conklin came to St. George in 1913 as a Presbyterian school teacher and became a legend. In addition to teaching large classes, she joined the Mormon community by working with Mormon Relief Society sisters to help the sick and sorrowing. After retiring from missionary service in 1933, she remained in St. George doing what she had always done in the community. She died in 1949, and her funeral was held in a Mormon chapel because the Presbyterian church was too small for the number attending the funeral. With her death, Presbyterian activity in the area virtually ceased for two decades.

In 1980 Roger and Katy Hansen moved to St. George. They had been Presbyterian missionaries at Wasatch Academy in Sanpete County. Seeing the influx of people to Washington County, they sensed the time was right to reorganize the Presbyterian congregation. Reverend John Mahon was called in 1987 by the Presbytery of Utah to organize a Presbyterian Church in St. George. Within a year the congregation, meeting in the Senior Citizen Center, numbered 100 families. On 10 June 1990 the group broke ground for a new church building, dedicated 20 January 1991; a picture of Sarah Louisa Conklin hangs in the narthex. In 1993 there were 260 members. The church members are active in the community, and the congregation serves as a welcoming group for a continuing flow of newcomers.[27]

The 1960s saw the development of several other Protestant congregations in Washington County. Among them were members of the Southern Baptist Church. Initially Baptists held services in the home of Mrs. Nell Bass under the leadership of Reverend Kenneth Medford Hutson from Cedar City. Later they met in the Elks Lodge hall and then at the Veterans of Foreign Wars (VFW) building. Then they moved to the museum of the Daughters of Utah Pioneers and later to the Washington County Library in St. George. Reverend Sam Moses was called to the St. George Baptist Mission in June 1964. Shortly after, the Sunday School superintendent Dave Stewart found property for sale at 300 South and 600 East in St. George. A loan from the Home Mission Board of the Southern Baptist Convention allowed a church to be built there. It was begun on 14 July 1965, with forty-five members attending, and completed in October of that year. The building has been expanded as the congregation has grown. Several other Baptist churches have been built, one across the street from Dixie College on 100 South, where Reverend Alex Wilkie served for many years and built a strong congregation. He retired in 1992 and was replaced by Reverend Ellis Keck.

An examination of the Washington County telephone book shows the present diversity of religions compared to the near uniformity of religion just four decades ago. Those denominations listed include: Assembly of God, five Baptist churches (including ones in Mesquite, Washington, Hurricane, and St. George), Southland Bible church, Roman Catholic church, Oasis Community church, Christian Science church, Episcopalian church, Jehovah's Witness, Lutheran, New

Covenant Christian Center, Presbyterian church, Religious Science church, and Seventh-Day Adventist church.

ENDNOTES

1. See *Washington County News* advertisements for a running record of movies playing each week.

2. *Washington County News*, 24 April 1941, 1.

3. Maryruth Bracy and Linda Lambert, "Maurine Whipple's Story of *The Giant Joshua*," Dialogue VI, no. 3-4, 55-62. See also Eugene England, "The Dawning of a Brighter Day: Mormon Literature after 150 Years." *Brigham Young University Studies 22* (Spring 1982): 49. Veda Hale of St. George is writing a biography of Whipple.

4. Juanita Brooks, *The Mountain Meadows Massacre* (Stanford: Stanford University Press, 1950, re-issued by University of Oklahoma Press, 1962).

5. Juanita Brooks, *John Doyle Lee, Zealot-Pioneer Builder-Scapegoat* (Glendale, CA: Arthur H. Clark Company, 1962).

6. *Washington County News*, 8 January 1942, 1.

7. Levi Peterson, *Juanita Brooks, Mormon, Woman, Historian* (Salt Lake City: University of Utah Press, 1988). Brooks wrote twenty-one books, including works she edited, and some fifty articles.

8. *Washington County News*, 22 February 1940, 1.

9. *Washington County News*, 14 November 1935, 1.

10. *Washington County News*, 3 June 1926.

11. *Under The Dixie Sun*, 439-40, printed the photographs of fifty-six men who died in the service. Paul Crosby examined the list and identified four men who should be added from *The American Guidebook*, in his possession and in the Dixie College Archives.

12. *Washington County News*, 4 February 1937, 4 and 20 July 1939, 2.

13. *Washington County News*, 7 September 1939, and 19 October 1939.

14. Elmer Pickett, Interview by Douglas D. Alder, 17 November 1994, Dixie College Archives.

15. Fern Crawford, "Office of Price Administration (OPA) and Rationing," manuscript in Dixie College Archives.

16. Allan Kent Powell, *Utah Remembers World War II* (Logan: Utah State University Press, 1991).

17. Arvel Milne, Interview, Washington County Centennial History Committee, 19 December 1994, Dixie College Archives.

18. Grant Hafen, Interview, Washington County Centennial History Committee, 22 August 1994. Dixie College Archives.

19. Luwayne Wood, "Cattle Roundup and Trailing to the Railroad at Lund, Utah, Late May and June, 1923," unpublished manuscript, Dixie College Archives.

20. *Salt Lake Tribune*, 9 October 1980.

21. The literature on nuclear fallout and the downwinders is extensive. The following is a selected list:

- Irene Allen, et al., *Plaintiffs vs. United States of America Defendant*. Civil No. C 79-05 15-J.
- Howard Ball, *Justice Downwind; America's Atomic Testing Program in the 1950's* (New York: Oxford University Press, 1986).
- Rosalie Bertell, *No Immediate Danger* (n.p.: The Women's Press, 1985).
- Philip L. Franklin, *Fallout — An American Nuclear Tragedy* (Tucson: University of Arizona Press, 1989).
- H. N. Friesen, *Fireballs at Dawn* (Las Vegas: U.S. Department of Energy, Nevada Operations Office, 1993).
- John G. Fuller, *The Day We Bombed Utah* (New York: New American Library, 1984).
- Carole Gallegher, *American Ground Zero* (Boston: MIT Press, 1993).
- Samuel Gladstone and Phillip J. Dolan, *The Effects of Nuclear Weapons*, 3d edition (Washington, D.C.: Department of Defense and Department of Energy, 1977).
- Barton C. Hacker, *The Dragon's Tail. Radiation Safety in the Manhattan Project, 1942—1946* (Berkeley: University of California Press, 1987).
- Barton C. Hacker, *Elements of Controversy: The Atomic Energy Commission and Radiation Safety in Nuclear Weapons Testing, 1947-1974* (Berkeley: University of California Press).
- Richard L. Miller, *Under the Cloud: The Decades of Nuclear Testing* (New York: The Free Press, 1986).
- Thomas Saffer and Orville E. Kelly, *Countdown Zero* (New York: G.P. Putnam's Sons, 1982).

22. Conference Report, October LDS Semi-annual Conference, 1890. See also "Official Declaration," *Doctrine and Covenants*, (Salt Lake City: Church of Jesus Christ of Latter-day Saints).

23. Much has been written about that event, including Martha Sonntag Bradley, *Kidnapped from That Land* (Salt Lake City: University of Utah Press, 1993), and B. Carman Hardy, *Solemn Covenant: the Mormon Polygamous Passage* (Urbana: University of Illinois Press, 1992).

24. Damon Cline, "Judge: Without compensation, there'll be no eviction," *The Spectrum*, 24 January 1996, 1.

25. Interview of Shivwits Tribal Members Mart Snow, Angus Snow, Wallea Baker, Merrill Wall, and Dollie Big Soldier, by Washington County Centennial History Committee, 24 May 1993, Dixie College Archives.

26. Bernice Mooney, *Salt of the Earth* (Salt Lake City: Catholic Diocese of Salt Lake City, 1987), 274—5; see also Mary Winfield, "A Historical Sketch of Catholicism in Utah's Dixie," Gregerson File, Dixie College Archives.

27. John R. Mahon, "Strangers in Zion," St. George, Utah: Good Shepherd Presbyterian Church, Dixie College Archives.

10

THE NEW PIONEERS

A new Dixie was struggling for birth after World War II, but the delivery took twenty years. From the return of soldiers in 1945 until the opening of the first golf course in Dixie, twenty years passed. They were the same years that saw Palm Springs, California; Scottsdale, Mesa and Phoenix, Arizona; and Las Vegas, Nevada create a Southwest mecca, a magnet to the "sunshine lifestyle." Those twenty years were the time in Dixie for creating a new vision, one that would produce much more than a golf course, one that would create Dixie as a destination point for retirees and sun worshippers.

Southern California had been the American glamour spot in the 1930s and 1940s. Many southern Utahns moved there to seek their fortunes, especially in the war industries. It continued to be a place of ranch-style homes, automobiles, ocean breezes, sunshine, and flourishing industry. After the war, the dry southwestern desert became highly attractive because air conditioning, entrepreneurs, and real-estate speculators came to extend the California-style developments. The Phoenix-Mesa area became a haven for retirees who moved there from the Midwest and Pacific Northwest. (Florida was becoming a similar attraction, mostly for Northeasterners.) During the birth of Sun

City near Phoenix and the amazing development of Palm Springs and Las Vegas, southern Utah slumbered, even though it had the similar mild winters and enticing scenery.

The World-War-II generation returned to southern Utah with new attitudes. They had been in Europe or the Pacific or at least in major American centers. Some of those who came back home felt in their bones that Dixie's isolation and agricultural ways were going to change. Some were anxious to promote that change; at least they wanted to make room for their generation. They intended to modify the austere farming lifestyle that had been the tradition of Dixie. One said:

> I decided in the army I was coming back to St. George and help the community become something new. There was an amazing change here just during the war. There was a spirit about Dixie. One does not find that in the big time. That spirit motivated us in 1946. I could see something could happen. I believed in it.[1]

This indigenous entrepreneurial attitude helped create a turning point in Dixie as it did in much of the United States. In Washington County the deep traditions did not facilitate quick change. The county was poor compared to much of the rest of the state; there were no heavy industries and large businesses. Dixie had missed the period of major outside investment that occurred in northern Utah between 1880 and 1930. Capital that came with the railroad and big mining did not come to Washington County. Capital accumulation was difficult, so the new generation had a real challenge. National programs were a help, especially the GI Bill that helped send a high percentage of the returning soldiers to college and small Federal loans that helped some of them start their own businesses. There was some investment by oil seekers and in the Apex Mine, but the county was not a place where absentee investors poured their funds. New Deal programs helped, but the tremendous investments in defense installations during World War II in northern Utah also missed Washington County.

The twenty years following World War II were a time of transition for Dixie; they marked the birth of the area as a destination — a place where travelers would come in large numbers, where they would stay several days, maybe even months or permanently. It was a winter retreat, a recreation spot, a culture base, a business center, a retirement community — a world-level destination worthy of the Grand Canyon and Zion National Park. That was the vision, not unlike that which characterized Palm Springs, Scottsdale or even Las Vegas.

Certainly no one person was its author. Anthony W. Ivins and Heber J. Grant urged part of the idea on people in the 1930s saying "build a golf course." As early as 1931 the Washington County News suggested a golf course as a way to lure tourists who came along Highway 91. Orval Hafen outlined the whole picture and took steps to give it a jump start by building new homes and setting up a dude ranch, but the golf course had to wait for Neal Lundberg and Sid Atkin's promotionalism in the mid-1960s.

The major elements were already in place — incomparable scenery, warm weather, a national highway, motels, restaurants — but attracting the capital for large projects was difficult. The state had moved beyond the colonial capital stage where outside investors controlled its fate, and into the period of home-owned development. Anything big would likely require Utah venturers with capital connections. What was needed were local entrepreneurs, people who took initiatives and risks. These were the new pioneers. By 1965 the gestation was over, and the new Dixie was about to be delivered — one the first pioneers could have hardly imagined — from movie making to industrial parks, airports to condominium communities, shopping malls to reservoirs, freeways to convention centers.

Orval Hafen's St. George — Transition to Change

One of the developers confided his aspirations to his journal. Beginning in 1932 and continuing to 1962, Orval Haven captured the hopes and the frustrations of the period. The theme of his journal is "discontent" with Dixie. He was convinced that people did not have to continue to live under the marginal conditions that had long constrained the region. The time had come, he felt, where the good virtues of the solid folks in Dixie ought to produce a modest measure of plenty, if they could just catch the vision of economic possibilities.

He questioned whether he should stay in Dixie and help change the region or whether he should move to a larger playing field where better career opportunities awaited. His years studying law in Washington, D.C., and Berkeley, California, convinced him that he was capable of succeeding in the faster race. He had to decide what his life was for. The power of his journal is that this central question

never subsided. In some ways his story represents a whole generation. Orval and his father, John Hafen, were symbolic of the changes
coming to Dixie. John was widely respected for his virtues of honesty and hard work. Steady in his farming, he gradually accumulated
large herds of cattle which he ranged in Bull Valley west of Enterprise in the summer and near Beaver Dam in the winter. Despite his
prosperity, he remained frugal to the end. Orval includes this anec-
dote as illustration:

> One Sunday Ruth and I drove over to Santa Clara to visit father.
> He told us he had bought a new suit, but in looking him over, Ruth
> noticed the coat and pants didn't match. She called it to father's at-
> tention and asked, "Why is it you have on the coat from the new suit
> but the pants from another suit?" Dad said, "Well, I just didn't want
> to come out in the new suit all at once."[2]

In comparison, Orval and Ruth represented the lifestyle of the
new generation, taking their children on trips, trading in an old car for
a new one regularly, and building a fine home on the hill overlooking
the city. They were not extravagant, but they were clearly from a different generation. John Hafen was hesitant to install a refrigerator or
telephone, even though his means exceeded those of his son. Orval is
said to have commented that he wanted a new car, he could afford a
new car, and he deserved a new car, but it would be hard to justify to
an all-Swiss jury.

The vision we get of St. George through the eyes of Orval Hafen is
of a community caught in scarcity. He opened his law office in 1930,
seventy years following the settlement of St. George. In his eyes the
community was still restrained by the limits of marginal agriculture.
Arable land was scarce; farmers were constrained to work on small
acreage. Surplus for obtaining material comforts was rare.

Of even greater concern to Hafen was the fact that seventy years
had taught the people of Dixie to accept those limitations. He knew
why: many folks in Dixie valued other things above possessions —
children, faith, character. The question was whether an improved economy would derail the people from their higher goals. Hafen occupied
his time largely in promoting that economic development, but he often
paused to assess whether the pioneer values were still intact.

As early as 1935 Hafen had a rather clear vision of the new Dixie.
Here is his first expression of it:

If we are to believe the present signs of the times, it won't be long
until much of the Intermountain West will be a vast playground for
the nation. Dixie seems destined to undergo quite a change. Instead
of the isolated little farms and cattle ranches, we may be in the midst
of a recreational center, which will entirely change our attitudes,
our outlook, our associations, our opportunities. Boulder Dam is
finished; the five-day week and the thirty-hour week are here; we
are the gateway to the parks and playgrounds of Utah; in a few years
yachts and pleasure boats will be plying the waters of Boulder Lake
[Lake Mead]; thousands of people go to see the dam every month
now; more will continue to come. Pine Valley Mountain, Zion Park,
Bryce, Grand Canyon, and more parks to be created around us, will
draw millions of people in the next few years. Our stockmen have
been fighting this past winter with their backs to the wall; they are
faced with the possibility of having their livestock industry driven
out to make way for the sportsmen, hunters, and lovers of recreation.
It is hard for them to see the handwriting on the wall.3

With the exception of not foreseeing the construction of Glen
Canyon Dam and the resulting Lake Powell, Hafen hit the bullseye
four decades before Dixie was ready to create golf courses, condominiums, retirement communities and other amenities to lure people
to the area lifestyle. He watched Las Vegas become a dynamic center
in a much less scenic place than Dixie, wielding influence with the
Federal government to get an air force base, atomic testing grounds,
and a magnesium plant. He confided his amazement about the Las
Vegas development to his journal. But visits to the glitzy casinos only
increased his resolve to focus his life on raising his children in quiet
St. George: "[I] feel a bit sorry for the folks who crowd the divorce
courts, and dedicate their time and their energies to getting something
for nothing. I guess we're just provincial, small-town folks."4

Despite these reflections, his discontent would not evaporate.
One telling sentence suggested, "St. George doesn't figure much in the
world's progress."5 His Swiss father, John, knew that his son had to
be independent, but finally decided his patriarchal musings deserved
expression. On 22 May 1936 this man of few words penned his heart
to his son, almost in biblical tones:

You are living in a goodly land, blessed in every way that you could
desire, a beautiful home that should be the pride of your hearts, and
friends on every hand and blessings, with more than you can do, living in the land of your birth. [,] The home of your kin[,] and yet you

seek a land of strangers wherein to dwell. Why should this be so? Is it for wealth or fame that you are thus lured to seek a better place? The good master gave his life among his own and thus obtained a fame divine and why should you seek to leave home, country, kin and friends? Is it because their worth to you is less than strangers yet unknown? No, it must not be so. Your father, mother, brother, sister, all bid you stay to share their joys and woes. Will your happiness be greater to be separated from your kin and friends forever? Consider well this matter. Our people in this part of the country have need of you more so than anywhere else, and the grave of your infant son will have to be cared for by others. These sentiments and many more I want to call to your attention.

Father.[6]

Orval stayed, and he became a leader in state politics. His election to the Utah State Senate was a watershed for him; the senate was his venue. His ability with words, his financial acumen, his legal mind, and his vision, all combined to thrust him quickly into leadership. He became not only an effective advocate for the county but a cogent thinker for the state as a whole. He was one of the designers of a new governance system for higher education in the state. He was the chief author of a bill creating a state parks system, one of which would later be Snow Canyon State Park.

From his office at the state capitol, Hafen thought as much about Dixie as when he was at home. The distance gave his thoughts perspective, convincing him that his original vision was correct:

While in Salt Lake I promoted the idea whenever, wherever and however I could, that Dixie's contribution to this intermountam country was her unique combination of warm winter sunshine and lavish color. I have dreamed for many years of capitalizing on this in the way of a winter resort, golf course, etc.[7]

This was eight years before the first golf course was built in St. George, twelve years before the birth of Bloomington's homes and condominiums. On New Year's Day 1958, Hafen wrote a lengthy appraisal of his efforts. He realized that the public expected leadership from him in Dixie, and he outlined what should be done: "I want to do something about getting a golf course established so that we can begin to attract people in the winter-time. If my building plans 'catch on' I would like to go on with my project and help the town grow in a planned way."[8]

Nine months later he continued that kind of commentary: "I can't get away from the feeling that the destiny of Dixie lies in her climate and her scenery and that perhaps my mission is to help bring this about." Today Hafen's vision seems obvious — it is the Dixie everyone knows, but it hadn't come about in 1958. Zion Canyon, yes, Union Pacific's promotion of the parks had done that, but St. George was not yet a southwest haven. There were many obstacles:

> Yes, Dixie has many problems; it has been terribly isolated in the past; its people are limited in their contacts with the outside world; they are provincial in many ways; Dixie needs public and private finances; it needs industries and payrolls and more homes and more people.

> The old pioneers did their part in establishing a foothold in this forbidding, awesome land. That was their mission, and they accomplished it in spite of seemingly insurmountable obstacles. A new day and new problems are now moving on the stage. Someone must start out where they left off. There is SO MUCH to do to catch up with other sections of the state and with other states. This country is crying for leadership and bristling with opportunities.9

Ever the realist, Hafen did not get carried away with his dreams. Realities had to be faced. The cattle industry in Dixie was being severely constrained by government regulations about numbers of animals on the range; the sheep industry was gone. Mining was languishing; oil prospects were illusory. Some residents could not pay their telephone bills. People could not afford the homes Hafen was building in St. George. He was deeply hurt when good friends took his old option and moved away, some to Las Vegas, others to Salt Lake City or elsewhere. But there were occasional high points that sustained him. He was impressed with Juanita Brooks's biography of John D. Lee which dealt with the Mountain Meadows Massacre, the great tragedy in the life of Lee and the whole region. Another upbeat moment was attending the first Shakespeare Festival in Cedar City in July 1962; he commented that the use of local talent did not hamper the quality of the performance. Listening to an autobiographical talk by the successful Hurricane businessman and rancher Emil Graff also moved Orval: "He made one arresting comment in his talk. He said 'We find ourselves here and we have to do what we can with what is here. It just happens that our lot is cast in this area, rather than somewhere else, and so we must try to see what opportunities are here and to develop them.'10

One project which Hafen had no idea would be his last was the dream of a major tourist attraction. He purchased some land adjacent to what had just become Snow Canyon State Park and dreamed of creating a tourist theme park. His ideas were bold — a tram to take people up over the red cliffs, buffalo steak meals, Indian goods for sale, a lodge, cabins, horse trails, and a golf course, perhaps one without grass. There would be pomegranates and dates, figs and pecans, maybe even camel rides.[11] This man of practical matters actually set about building such a gamble. He succeeded in producing a well that brought water to the surface. He spend hours digging ditches and was felled by a heart attack while doing so.

The St. George we see today would not surprise Orval Hafen — the golf courses, the motels and restaurants, the condominiums and real estate developments, the airport, the conventions, the retirement communities and even the impressive tourist facility Tuacahn, on the very site of his Snow Canyon land, Padre Canyon. To some, these developments that began one year after his death (1964) may have seemed almost foreign to Dixie; but there was a generation that saw the potential and acted to create the new attitude and entrepreneurial possibilities. Orval Hafen was only one of these entrepreneurs, but he helps us understand the times because he wrote down his aspirations in three volumes.

Snow Canyon State Park

With Senator Orval Hafen well placed in the legislature, it was an easier step to the next action. The state was actively involved in establishing a state park system. Hafen, county commissioner Rudger Atkin, and Jim Lundberg encouraged Harold Fabian of the state parks commission to visit Dixie. They wanted to show him a proposed state park in Snow Canyon — the amazing concentration of sandstone cliffs and lava flows between Pine Valley and St. George. The canyon was named for the Snow family who ranched there, including Erastus and William Snow and their descendants. It was a tourist's delight and had the great advantage of being conveniently located near St. George.

During that visit, the team negotiated the state's purchase for $20,000 of Joseph Blake's 898-acre ranch in Diamond Valley. It was transferred to the state parks commission in 1959. Washington County had already donated 296 acres in the area to the state parks. Additional private tracts totalling 640 acres were purchased by the state in 1960. In 1964 the U.S. Bureau of Land Management transferred title for 3,854 acres of Federal land to the state of Utah, bringing the total park acreage to 5,688.

The county and the state began improvements immediately, constructing a water line to the area that is now the Shivwits campground and improving Highway 18 through the park. That work was completed in 1977, and hot showers were added to the campground in 1984. The park quickly became a popular site for tourists, in part because it was made famous by many western movies filmed in the park.

Movie Making

At age twenty-nine, Dick Hammer came to Dixie in 1933 after working in California. At first he was employed at the Beaver Dam Lodge on Highway 91, later at the Liberty Hotel in St. George. He was a restless fellow who tended to be a promoter. He opened a hamburger stand on the highway in downtown St. George when there was only one thin lane of hardtop with plenty of dust on either side. From his profits and savings, he expanded the site into the present Dick's Cafe. The atmosphere there was attractive not only to tourists and motel guests but also to locals. It has become a unique institution, partly because of the movie, *The Electric Horseman* with Robert Redford, which featured the cafe's interior. It is also popular because movie stars congregated there, as well as a regular morning coffee bunch that spun yarns and talked politics.

The fact that Hammer had a respectable portion of the tourist trade wasn't enough for him though. He looked for other opportunities which led him to Kanab. There the Parry brothers were attracting movie makers, with their actors and production crews staying at Parry's Lodge. Hammer wanted to be in on that kind of business. Before settling down in St. George, he had gone to Hollywood to try a movie career. He was trained as a stunt man and performed in several films, but that seemed like a dead end to him, so he drifted north. As a restaurateur, he thought of combining his two interests.

Motel-owner Brown Hail became Hammer's partner in the movie-making idea; they didn't hesitate to ask the Parrys for their secret and the Parrys didn't mind sharing it. They told Hammer and Hail that the key was developing personal friendships with Hollywood producers and directors. The Parrys even told them who to contact. Hammer and Hail engaged a photographer to shoot footage of Snow Canyon and other possible sites in Washington County. They took their film to Hollywood and met with cameramen at the major studios. They met a cool reception at first because the cameramen were not too impressed with the footage. Hammer's engaging personality and the Parry contacts gave them a chance to meet some producers, however. The cameramen advised their bosses to send them to the sites so they could shoot their own film. That was the turning point.

In 1953 *When a Man's a Man* starring George O'Brien and Veronica Lake came to St. George to be filmed. Hammer and Hail moved into high gear. George Pace joined them, providing his motel to house the film crews. Their strategy was to impress the Hollywood crews. Clean accommodations and good meals became the formula: serve plenty of food hot and fast. Delivering a field kitchen with meals to the shooting site on time was crucial. They had to feed up to 500 people three times a day, sometimes catering from wagons, sometimes at the cafe. Each movie star had to be provided with a trailer and a waiter to serve meals, clean up, and provide personal attention. Most films needed cattle and horses. Hail and Andy Pace contracted for the livestock.

The enterprise involved the whole town. Hollywood companies hired scores of people in St. George — carpenters, painters, cattle and horse providers, and others to take bit parts or to be in crowd scenes. Hammer hired helpers for the big catering jobs. He spent much of his time glad-handing, and it paid off. He became a friend to stars and producers. He also took bit parts, often as a stunt man. Brown Hail was a key force in the chamber of commerce and the Lions Club where Andy Pace was also active. They were locals who could win over the participation of the community.

The business turned into a bonanza. Film companies didn't mind paying good prices for food and lodging; they wanted service more than cheap rates. Workers who came in with the film companies were good customers in local stores. Building sets also brought plenty of business to town. Dick Hammer, Brown Hail, Karl Hutchings, Joe Hutchings, and Andy Lytle focused on moviemakers. Between 1953 and 1983, they provided food and lodging for dozens of films — movies which helped publicize Dixie. The red hills of Snow Canyon, Grafton, and Zion Canyon became standard fare in the nation's movie

Snow Canyon movie location for *The Conqueror*. John Wayne is on horseback and director Dick Powell, in white, is seated above. (Cuba Lyle Collection)

houses. The movie industry ended Dixie's isolation as people all over the world began to make the region a prime tourist destination.

If Hollywood could come to Dixie, so could the whole world. At Dick's Cafe they could see the memorabilia of the films and meet Dick Hammer, who would tell his stories, especially of his continuing friendship with stars like John Wayne. Other stars who frequented Dick's Cafe included Jane Russell, Gabby Hayes, and Slim Pickens,

Tom Mix in 1924 in Zion Canyon for the filming of *The Deadwood Coach*, one of the first full-length movies. (Wm. L. Crawford)

but of them all, John Wayne built the strongest bond. He and Hammer became good friends and visited each other's homes. One time Wayne sent Hammer a gift, a pickup truck, because he thought the truck looked like it belonged in St. George with Hammer.

Zion National Park was also a major attraction to movie makers. Pathe News had come there as early as 1913. J. L. Crawford reports that the first full-length movie made there was *The Deadwood Coach* by the Fox Company, starring Tom Mix in 1924. Shortly after that, between 1925 and 1929, two more films were made, *Forlorn River* and *The Vanishing Pioneer*.[12]

Industrial Parks

In 1961 the Hawthorne Company, a manufacturer of camping gear, was seeking a location in the West to build a manufacturing plant to produce tents, sleeping bags, and backpacks. State officials suggested that St. George fit Hawthorne's criteria for size and location and notified the St. George Chamber of Commerce. Chamber leaders Bruce Stucki, Jim Lundberg, and Neal Lundberg went to St. Louis to inspect the home plant and invited the Hawthorne executives to visit St. George two weeks later.

When the trio returned to Dixie, they spent a feverish fortnight preparing a proposal for Hawthorne. Within those few days, they organized the Dixie Development Corporation, a publicly-owned corporation. Doyle Sampson sold stock to 120 people. They obtained an option on a piece of land and had it cleared for construction by the time of the visit. The visitors were impressed and soon negotiated a fifteen-year contract to lease a proposed building and begin manufacturing operations. With this contract in hand and $300,000 in stock sales, the corporation negotiated an $800,000 bank loan. They had a large warehouse-style building completed for the 1962 move-in date. Hy Thomas, executive director of the chamber, Leon Jennings, and Dexter Snow were other officers of the corporation which existed solely to attract business to the area. None of the officers received a salary, and no stock has been put up for sale.

Through later mergers, Hawthorne became known as the Kellwood Corporation; their products bore the Kelty label as well as labels of some chain stores such as Sears. This employer brought a stable business to the community and has maintained a workforce of about 150 people since that time. Harold Hess has been its manager as well as a leader in the chamber of commerce.

Over the years, the Dixie Development Corporation paid off its loan and added new portions to the building. Later it added other buildings in the industrial park area on the east end of town. Several private ventures such as the Rocky Mountain Company also moved to that location, creating a robust industrial area. Bruce Stucki remains as president of the Dixie Development Corporation, with Mansfield Jennings, Doyle Sampson, and John Palmer as officers.

In 1992 the Dixie Development Corporation negotiated a ten-year lease for a $1.8-million building they had constructed with similar financing. Quality Park Products moved in and produces envelopes there. The building is located in a second industrial park developed in 1980 by St. George City under Mayor Grey Larkin. Other companies such as Ramco, producer of solenoids, are located in the new Mill-creek Industrial Park near Pine View High School.

Another industrial park is emerging near the freeway exit to Hurricane. Winding River Corporation was involved with Hurricane City and the Utah Division of Community and Economic Development in attracting Wal-Mart Corporation to locate a distribution center there. They competed with Cedar City and Richfield for a site. It was necessary for Hurricane City to annex the land and provide water and power to the complex. Road improvements also had to be made. In an amazingly short time, a massive warehouse was constructed and readied for occupancy in 1992. The Winding River Corporation is now selling land nearby for commercial use. The Sant Corporation is constructing a housing development that will occupy both sides of the highway and thus include both Washington City and Hurricane jurisdictions.

The Red Hills Golf Course

"What do you mean, build a golf course? No one around here has any time to golf." That was the reaction of many frugal farmers in Dixie. Though pundits had been talking of golf since the 1930s, no one seemed able to overcome the majority opinion that life was for working, not playing. Even Dixie promoter Mormon church president (and golf player) Heber J. Grant had suggested that Dixie businessmen invest in a golf course. In those early days the Washington County News editorialized on the golf course idea but it was a fleeting suggestion which did not catch on.[13] Gradually the post-war generation began to talk of it more seriously. More than once civic committees met over lunch to ponder such a proposal. Out-of-town visitors kept the issue alive, often asking why St. George didn't have a course. The assumption was always that it would have to be a private venture. Several sites were considered — one in Washington, the present Southgate site, another on property east of town, and a fourth southwest of St. George. The discussions never quite started the capital accumulation rolling though.

In 1960 Jim Colbert, a professional golfer, was in town and contacted Sid Atkin, who was serving as president of the chamber of commerce. Colbert asked what he could do to help St. George get a golf course. That lit a fire in Atkin who had participated in several of the earlier conversations. He went to previous mayor Joe Atkin and sought advice about how to get the project going. Joe advised Sid that he needed a "workhorse" and a committee — the former to get the work done, the latter for input. Sid and Joe Atkin thought Neal Lundberg would be a prime workhorse. Lundberg agreed to join Sid Atkin on the project. Their next step was to commission Bruce Stucki, recently home from the University of Utah with a business degree, to do a formal feasibility study. He agreed and included an examination of two recently completed golf courses, one in Provo and the other in Price. He determined that they would need to sell forty rounds a day at $1.25 per round in order to generate $17,000 annually. Expenses would be $16,000, leaving a slight surplus.

Atkin and Lundberg approached a big name in golf, Ernie Schneiter, Sr., for advice. He provided a new approach by asking, "Does the city own any property?" The three conferred with Lynne Empey and Andy Price at the city office. They examined the huge map on the wall which recorded all city property and identified possibilities, including the Watercress Spring area of eighty acres which was then serving as a city dump. Schneiter said that area would be fine for nine holes but not eighteen. Atkin and Lundberg realized that the demand for eighteen holes had been one of the sticking points for previous promoters. Atkin argued that the first nine holes was the real challenge; if they could get nine in, someone else would build the next nine. They drove to the site, and Schneiter said he could make a nice nine-hole course there.

The next problem was water. The water adjacent to the land was owned by a canal company and thus not available. The men decided to undertake the design while searching for water. They did not have to wait long. Jay Ence, who would later become the community's leading home developer, was drilling for water on land to the west. Ence was willing to provide water for the course if his drilling succeeded, which it did shortly. Thus the city negotiated with Ence.

City leaders had always been fiscally conservative, and the idea of government financing a golf course was fraught with problems. Admittedly, most citizens of the city would never use the golf course, and if that were so, how could the city council justify using tax money to underwrite what was essentially a business promotion idea? Yes, the golf course would promote community recreation, but privately owned tourism would benefit most. Should tax money be used to promote economic development? That was a rather new concept. The proposers were clear in their minds that a bond election would not pass to raise the funds. William "Bill" Lassiter, a new investor in the St. George Bank from Louisiana, suggested that the city issue revenue bonds. If the city council agreed to issue $60,000 worth of revenue bonds, the St. George Bank would purchase them, saving the city a tax increase.

Lundberg, Atkin, and their committee began making the rounds to civic clubs with their idea, Bruce Stucki's feasibility study, and the plan for a revenue bond. With that base of support and input they went to the city council made up of William Barlocker, mayor, with Mathew Bentley, Grant Johnson, Clayton Atkin, ElMyrrh Cox, and Neal Lundberg as members.

In the discussion, Mayor Barlocker urged postponement, arguing that he could close a private deal to put a course on the Southgate site within several months. Atkin and Lundberg argued that the momentum was underway as it had never been before. It must not be squandered or it might not rise again. Many private efforts had floundered in the past. Atkin quoted Abraham Lincoln as saying that government does for people what they can't do for themselves. The council respected the proposers, who had most of the city leadership lined up in support, and on 3 August 1964, they voted four to one to authorize a $60,000 bond and the use of the city property. Barlocker, as mayor, did not vote; Mathew Bentley was the dissenter.

The council appointed Neal Lundberg to take the lead from the city side in executing the construction. From that point on, Lundberg became an even greater driving force. He enlisted the Elks and Lions clubs to donate labor. The Elks pledged to build a clubhouse which the city employees constructed. Lundberg also recruited other volunteers. Marion Bowler was elected mayor during the construction, replacing Bill Barlocker, and presided over the opening of the course. Gene Schneiter, Ernie Schneiter's son, was appointed golf pro and people began playing on seven holes before the course was even completed.

Though the Red Hills Golf Course was soon surpassed by many other ventures and other courses, its creation served as a turning point for St. George. Here, finally, the dreams of many had been realized. Washington County was reaching out to tourists. Community leaders had found a way to design and finance a major project. The idea of making St. George a recreation destination had taken its first big step, soon to be joined by several others. Here was evidence that sunshine, scenery, and tourism could make things happen in southern Utah.

The 1-15 Freeway

If the 1930 connection to the Arrowhead Trail (U.S. Highway 91) opened the era of tourism for Dixie, the completion of the 1-15 freeway truly linked the region to the world. For a century and a quarter isolation had been the condition that had both blessed and cursed Dixie. The fact that the railroad could not be enticed into the county was a major deterrent to trade and commerce. That alone helped keep incomes lower in Dixie than elsewhere, but that was not the only factor; there was a lack of large agricultural lands.

Much changed with the arrival of the interstate in 1973, again an influence from outside. Dixie residents did not cause the freeway to be built; like the naming of Zion National Park, outside forces were absorbing Dixie into the national fabric.

Local leaders were not silent on the matter though. County commissioners, St. George mayor Clinton Snow, and county business leaders were keenly aware that the location of the freeway would have a huge impact on the county's future. They knew of towns such as Levan near Nephi that had been nearly eliminated from the map because the freeway shifted the highway route away from the previous road that had benefited them. Determining the site of the route was a political decision of the highest import. County commissioners and Mayor Snow met several times with Utah Department of Transportation planners to stress the need for off-ramps leading to Hurricane, Washington City, and both the north and south entrances to St. George. Snow lobbied for an off-ramp that would lead traffic directly onto St. George Boulevard.

Farmers were opposed to having the interstate go through the Washington Fields and St. George businessmen were anxious that the route be west of the mesa. There was rather quick agreement on the route of the road, which meant that the interstate would actually bisect the city of St. George. Portions of the freeway would have to be elevated on earthen hills, very much affecting the flow of traffic inside the city. City leaders felt that problem was a fair trade-off for bringing the traffic into the city. Locating the interstate east of the mesa would have avoided that problem, but it was never a serious option because it was not as direct and because local leaders lobbied for the route through St. George.

Clearly the eastern part of the county would be bypassed. The proposed freeway route would leave Toquerville, La Verkin, and Hurricane off the route, as Highway 91 had already done. Washington would have the Highway 91 traffic taken off Telegraph Street, but an exit would be just a block away. Santa Clara would be left out entirely.

An important decision for the highway designers was to avoid going over Utah Hill (the route of old U.S. 91), often plagued with snowstorms and the site of many fatal accidents. They determined to undertake the enormous expense of cutting through the Virgin River Gorge. That decision would later be a major benefit to developers at Bloomington, but it meant the death knell for the fruit-stand business in Santa Clara.

Leaders in St. George, including city and county officials, worked extensively with the Utah Department of Transportation in the planning. Businessmen, especially restaurant, service station, and motel owners, had real anxiety that the freeway would divert people from stopping in St. George. Up to that point, tourists had to drive through town which made stopping for food, gas, or rooms easy for them. With the freeway, drivers could keep going at high speed. They would have to intend to stop if they were to patronize Dixie businesses.

Truman Bowler recalled the first day, a Sunday, after the formal opening of I-15. Motel owners, restaurant workers, and gas station help stood around waiting for people to stop, but few did. Many felt their anxieties justified. Within a few days, business picked up, however, ending the worst fears, but within a few years the location of the off-ramps wrought a major change in St. George, though less so in Washington or Hurricane. Most St. George motels, hotels, restaurants, and gas stations were located in the middle of town while the off-ramps were several blocks away making the property near the exits extremely attractive; most of the new construction of such facilities has gradually moved from the center of town to locations near the off-ramps.

Another element in the 1-15 story is that of the Virgin River Gorge route through the Arizona Strip which linked Utah and Nevada, a vital commercial connection, but it merely passed through Arizona without benefiting that state's economy. The state of Arizona had little motivation to spend its Federal highway funds on an expensive project which would not create anything they could tax. The twenty-nine-mile section of 1-15 from St. George to Littlefield was carved through the Virgin River Gorge, exposing millions of years of geologic layering in 500-foot cliffs created by the cuts (and the 2,000 feet of mountains above the cliffs). The cost was approximately $61 million, and the project took more than a decade to complete. A good deal of persuasion was needed to get Arizona to undertake the freeway project. Governors Calvin Rampton of Utah and Jack Williams of Arizona had a good relationship and were able to work through the issue. One problem was that the freeway through the gorge would be one of the most expensive stretches in the whole nation. In the end, Utah had to agree to spend some of its Federal highway funds on the Arizona section, matching Arizona's appropriations. With the recent completion of the joint Arizona-Utah port of entry, substantial truck fees are being collected, and Arizona is recovering some of its investment.

Bloomington

One of the most dramatic changes to come to Dixie was the development of a planned luxury community, Bloomington. A group of northern Utah investors were responsible for this venture. Two young men, Ellis Ivory and Roger Boyer, both of Salt Lake City, had begun a real-estate development company that had undertaken projects in Idaho and Colorado. Clark Ivory, Ellis's father, and a lifelong land investor, already had an interest in ranch property at Bloomington. Paying $250 to $500 per acre in 1965 and 1966, Clark Ivory purchased farms from Romain Sturzenegger and George Larson on the south side of the Virgin River and from Dan Heaton on the north side, near where the pioneer town of Bloomington once stood. He assembled about 1,200 acres in these dealings. It was not unusual for people to approach Clark Ivory about obtaining an acre from him, so they could build a retirement cottage.

Clark Ivory's passion in life was raising horses and he considered using the land for that purpose. He also gave serious thought to raising carrots on a large commercial basis for the California market, but that idea never materialized. The two developers began to eye Ivory's land. In the meantime, they arranged a liaison with three other Utah entrepreneurs, brothers Clifton, Franklin, and Glendon Johnson. The latter had close contacts with companies which became their source of investment funding.

The Johnson brothers joined their Johnson Land Company with the Ivory and Boyer Company to form Terracor. They made quite a splash in Salt Lake City by purchasing a grand old mansion on South Temple Street and restoring it for their corporate headquarters. Clearly these men knew how to present an air of elegance. Their initial idea was to develop ten-acre estates in Bloomington for people interested in an equestrian lifestyle, complete with stables and gardens. They would attract people from northern Utah seeking second homes in a luxury resort setting. To convince them, they built a huge horse barn and brought some good race horses to the site.

In their many visits to St. George, the men often played golf at the new Red Hills Golf Course which St. George City had opened in 1965. They began to think of golf as a more attractive magnet than horses. Golf could appeal to a wider constituency of California and Utah prospects with disposable income. Even more appealing was the fact that a golf course would provide the possibility of subdividing the lots adjacent to the fairways into much smaller pieces — half-acre and quarter-acre plots instead of ten acres. This would greatly multipiy possible sales. Again they took a high-tone approach by inviting Bill Neff, a well-known golf-course designer, to design a quality golf course. Their idea of a planned community evolved into a major attraction, gaining wide publicity.

The success of Terracor's Bloomington depended on several crucial elements, not the least of which was obtaining water. The logical source was St. George City, but city officials were cautious about making a permanent commitment to an "outsider" project beyond the city limits. Rudger McArthur who headed the city water office wanted to "guard the seed corn," knowing that water was a limited resource. Mayor Marion Bowler and the city council were basically receptive but cautious. Fortunately, the city had recently completed the Gunlock Reservoir. Jay Bingham of Bingham Engineering from Salt Lake City was the engineer for the reservoir, and now he was a vice- president of Terracor. That tie helped the city council welcome Terracor. An agreement was reached to sell two million gallons of water per day to the Bloomington promoters, even though the land was not within city limits.

The next step was to gain the support of the Washington County Commission because Bloomington was part of the unincorporated area of the county. Truman Bowler was chairman of the Washington County Commission, with Floyd Ence and Emil J. Graff as commissioners. They proved to be cordial to the developers though they were demanding in setting restrictions on the project concerning storm sewers, water lines, signs, and roads. Roads were a particular issue; most county roads were gravel, and the county preferred not to maintain oiled roads, but the developers wanted asphalt. County officials required a four-inch gravel base and a two-inch layer of asphalt with an agreement that the developer would replace any failures in the roads for five years. The roads were designed to give a countryside appearance — they curved through the development California-style and did not have sidewalks. This arrangement certainly was a contrast to the checkerboard layout of the Mormon villages; gone were the easy addresses and the generic street names — First South, Second East, etc.

On 4 March 1968, the county commission approved a fifty-eight lot subdivision along Sugar Leo Road and Swaps Drive and Terracor began sales. The lots sold fast at the $3,000 price which led to applications for subdivisions two and three, as well as the Bloomington Country Club subdivisions, which were approved on 22 July. Prices were then pegged at a higher rate — $6,000. On the same day, the commission attended the groundbreaking for the golf course on the site and heard golf champion Billy Casper talk about the plans for the Bloomington Golf Course.

Mayor Bowler recently confided in an interview that he went to the opening ceremony, watched Billy Casper hit some golf balls, and saw the drawings of an elegant country club, but in his heart he didn't really believe it would materialize.[14] Another sidelight to that day: Casper was delayed on his way and called to beg off. The promoters would hear none of it. They hired a plane to fly to Denver and bring

Casper to St. George. Casper's status as a Mormon golf celebrity was crucial to their plans.

Bowler, one of the local citizens more favorable to the plan, was hesitant to accept the sales pitch of the young promoters. In the St. George community, Terracor practices were somewhat controversial, a jolt to the local frugality. The company's upscale sales style was a shock to locals — meeting people at the airport with a limousine, providing houseboats on Lake Powell, having purebred race horses on site, hosting elegant dinners, providing a private security force on the premises. It was a country club image that overshot the local folks, but county leaders saw the potential, even if they had doubts.

For the next several years, there were other proposals from Terracor that came before the Washington County Commission. In August 1968, plans were submitted for the Bloomington Ranches subdivision. Then a service district was set up to serve as the government until the area was either incorporated or annexed. The district took on the responsibility of building and maintaining roads and sewers as well as providing for garbage collection, police and fire protection, and other regular municipal functions because the county was not able to provide such services in a residential area. The agreement included the intention to turn over these functions to the homeowners association when it was of sufficient size to manage them. That agreement would later become the bone of much contention.

The company worked swiftly to set up the infrastructure — water, electricity, sewers, and roads — to keep ahead of sales. Instead of doing a little at a time, they worked broadly throughout the 1,300 lots (which would later cause them financial woes). As other areas across the river were approved, those were developed, too, in order that prospective buyers could be attracted and not have to wait to begin home construction. That necessitated a major investment — a bridge over the Virgin River, the Man of War Bridge (the names of streets were often taken from horseracing terminology). Carl Nelson remembers that on his first visit, he had to wade across the river, so the bridge was welcome, but it was costly.

All this activity required a staff. Roger Boyer oversaw the construction and Ellis Ivory focused on sales. Frank Johnson was the chief executive officer of Terracor. In 1971 the company sent Jim Kimball to St. George to live and be the general manager of Bloomington with

Lonnie Adams working on sales. Lynn Ellsworth was in marketing and traveled throughout the nation seeking potential buyers from among people with Utah ties. Jeff Morby came in 1972 as property manager; John and Keith Romney worked on financing and sales. Jim Ward was the project engineer and manager. The initial problem they faced was that many people bought lots, but not many built homes. The project didn't seem to have momentum. The lots attracted speculators who hoped to resell when success inflated the prices.

Together this crew adopted yet another idea: condominiums. In Salt Lake City they conferred with Alan Coombs who had done some condominium financing. Keith Romney took this idea and became an expert in the legal aspects of condominium title design and financing. This was a breakthrough, a product and a financing scheme that fit many customers' needs. Buyers did not need to engage a contractor or architect or seek a financing package. All was provided by the seller, even the furniture and a property management system. People could buy wonderful vacation homes at lower prices than if they had built the home, and the venture was virtually worry free. Soon Terracor had built sixty condos, designed by Les Stoker, around the golf course; they sold fast. Next, thirty-one condos were built across the street. Two years later came twenty-six more on the golf course, then forty-one more across the street. That was the kind of action Terracor wanted.

The Bloomington undertaking required a massive sales effort and a rushed construction schedule. Advertisements were aimed initially at northern Utahns who could afford second homes. Lots were priced at a range from $3,000 to $8,000. Salesmen soon learned that there was a broader market — Mormons who lived all over the nation, especially in the West. Many of these people were nearing retirement and were interested in returning to Utah but didn't want to be back in snow. Bloomington provided a Utah location with mild winters.

Retirement homes, not just second homes, soon became another focus of the sales staff. The same strategy worked for affluent retirees — focus on northern Utah but start working through California and even the east coast where people with Utah connections were employed in the corporate world. Sales then could be directed to people who had no connection to Mormonism or Utah but who liked the southwestern lifestyle.

Terracor's portfolio featured a mix of condominiums for second-home seekers or for those who did not want to do yardwork and building lots for those seeking a permanent home for retirement or for a winter retreat. The developers were especially anxious to get people to build. It was therefore important to provide financing packages to help customers begin home construction. The new homes gave a feeling of momentum and provided the tax base required to finance the utilities.

The product found a ready market, fulfilling the dream so many county residents had shared since 1930, even if the dream was not focused. It took Terracor to package the dream; the scenery and weather had been available all along. Air conditioning, freeways, and retirement financing plans that developed after World War II created the atmosphere to make it possible. The catalyst was the entrepreneurial skills of the Terracor officials — Ivory, Johnson, and Boyer. The response to Terracor demonstrated that Dixie's time of growth had come.

By the mid-1970s, there were so many people buying and building in Bloomington that Terracor designed a second Bloomington. They called it Bloomington Hills, located on the opposite side of the freeway and over the low hills. In 1972 Terracor built another golf course and laid out over 1,000 lots. This concept was limited to homes. The prices were below the Bloomington level, and the lots sold rapidly.

Bloomington was a major success that virtually transformed Dixie. Longtime residents could hardly catch their breath. Some invested in lots; some built homes and moved to the new setting. Most held back, feeling that the Terracor "boys" had greatly overpriced the tamarack bushes in Bloomington where only two old stone houses stood in silent reminder of the pioneer broom factory that was once located there. Some later wished they had invested at the initial prices which soon appreciated. More than one worried about all the newcomers with their lavish lifestyle, but the people who moved in created no problem. On the contrary, they brought civic talents to share, and they gradually found acceptance.

The success of Bloomington did not protect Terracor from financial difficulty. The problems began in Texas. Their financing source was consolidated in a complicated bankruptcy which included scores of financial institutions. The new coalition sent Ian Cumming from New York to protect their interests by being a corporate officer in Terracor. That encouraged Roger Boyer and Ellis Ivory to leave and form their own construction company. Frank Johnson stayed a year longer, then he also left, as did Jay Bingham.

Ian Cumming became the president of Terracor and was the major figure in policies dealing with Bloomington. As early as 1975, he could see insolvency coming; bills in St. George were overdue, conditions at Stansbury Park, Utah, and in Minnesota, other Terracor developments, were more serious. He negotiated with the parent company to carry them and attend to other bankruptcies of their merger first. That gave Terracor six more years, but in 1982 it filed for reorganization. Reportedly the bankruptcy was due more to the difficulties the firm faced in its other projects; Bloomington was healthy but developments in Colorado and northern Utah were in the red.

The Bloomington managers found that providing utilities, security, roads, water, and fire protection were costly. The Man of War Bridge was a major expense; the Bloomington County Club was costly to maintain. These burdens raised the option of either incorporating as a city or annexing to St. George and greatly concerned the residents who had built homes and moved into the development.

In 1973 seventy-one residents formed the Bloomington Community Council to keep a watchful eye on Terracor and to press the firm to abide by its various agreements with Bloomington residents. The officers included Ray Taylor, chair, Byron McLeese, vice chair, Elmer Thacker, second vice-chair, and Carl Nelson, secretary/treasurer. In 1977 club members in Bloomington took up their option to assume the ownership of the Bloomington Country Club, an agreement that had been written into the early Terracor documents. Club officers, Carlyle Stout and Ray Taylor, took on the responsibility of managing the facility.

After many complicated procedures, Ian Cumming purchased the assets of Terracor from the holding banks. This change brought some disagreements between the community council and what remained of Terracor. New council leaders, including Dr. Carl Nelson, Ernest Oates, and Dick Ball, pressed for guarantees that the bankruptcy proceedings would provide funds to complete the electric utility lines for both Bloomington and Bloomington Hills. They spent hundreds of hours inspecting utility lines and streets to amass solid data for claims against Terracor. Attorney Ralph Atkin represented the Bloomington home owners and Ron Thompson the Bloomington Hills residents; they succeeded in obtaining about $1 million to ensure that the resi-

Contemporary home in Bloomington, 1996. (Gene Butera)

dents would receive a completed utility and road program as promised in their purchase agreements.

Carl Nelson developed a long-range plan outlining the need for sewers, electrical power, roads, churches, and schools. His projections showed how the population would grow over ten years. He facilitated the acquisition of the ten-acre horse-barn area by the Washington County School District for a future elementary school. The plan convinced the LDS church to acquire property for a stake center. Nelson's autobiography includes accounts of developing the fire and police facilities for Bloomington, improving the sewers and roads, mosquito abatement, garbage collection, television reception, and the story of the Rural Electric Association. The debate over annexation to St. George is also outlined.[15]

Bankruptcy did not halt the growth of Bloomington. Jeff Morby represented Ian Cumming's Leucadia Corporation that still owned much of the land in the two Bloomingtons.[16] Sales continued through him and other realtors. The developments had become too successful to be stopped by the bankruptcy, nonetheless, there were major problems that had to be solved. Either the Bloomington residents had to incorporate and take on the heavy burden of managing utilities and completing roads or they had to annex to St. George City.

The 1982 debate among the homeowners over annexation was intense. In a controversial decision, the owners (including all non-resident landowners, who could vote by mail) accepted annexation. Feelings were frayed between the advocates of annexation and those who urged a different policy. Many of those who had already built homes and were living in Bloomington were cautious, willing to wait. They did not see as much advantage to annexation as the condominium owners who only visited St. George seasonally. Those who lived on the Wasatch Front, in California, or elsewhere favored annexation, perhaps because they could then let St. George City worry about roads and utilities. The final tally was 70 percent (including both lot and home owners) in favor of annexation, but the majority of those who had actually built homes (not condominiums) opposed it.

St. George City took in Bloomington and Bloomington Hills somewhat reluctantly, refusing to do so unless a third party leased the ill-kept golf course in Bloomington Hills. There were other stipulations too, indicating the view that the annexations would likely be a burden. Quite the reverse has become the case, even to the point that the city has taken over the golf course in Bloomington Hills and annexed all the land to the Arizona border. There were some down-sides to annexation, however. For example, the roads in Bloomington were built to be country style and did not meet the city subdivision standard, thus residents would later press the city for an upgrade.

Gradually Bloomington and Bloomington Hills became two of the nation's fine planned communities, far removed from the original thoughts of a carrot farm or equestrian center. They continue to expand. Like many real estate promotions all over the nation, Bloomington went through a bankruptcy and there were losers, but the project has survived, even flourished. Several fortunes were made and lost in the process. One would hardly realize this when inspecting the elegant subdivisions today. The risk-taking spirit of the entrepreneurs who created the two Bloomingtons still engenders amazement and respect from many.

Residents of the two Bloomingtons act as boosters for their communities. Many have become actively involved in St. George and Washington County, serving on boards and committees, on the city council and county commission, and on cultural and recreational boards. There are still discussions about the pros and cons of annexation, but a more recent debate centered on whether to allow a shopping mall to locate at the Bloomingon 1-15 exit. That reopened a question in which the city and county both originally took a negative position with the Terracor officials who also wanted commercial zoning. It was again turned down in 1991, keeping Bloomington residential.

Green Valley

Alan Coombs was the Salt Lake City attorney who advised Terracor on condominiums. He pointed Keith Romney in the direction of a new financing mechanism that made the concept of condominiums work both legally and financially, but his name is tied to the recreation/resort community of Green Valley. From its beginning to the present day, Coombs has been the central figure.[17] Through financial ups and downs, he has weathered the times and is still building.

While still a student in law school at the University of Utah, Coombs invested in home construction and real estate in the Salt Lake Valley. He entered a law practice in Salt Lake City but was enticed into the St. George market by his classmates Jim Kimball, Keith Romney, and Frank Johnson. His first personal investment was the Georgetown apartments, adjacent to Dixie College. He then built a motel, now known as the South Side, partly to complement his Georgetown venture.

Next came the idea of a convention center. He and his partners, brothers Derrill, Dale, and Grey Larkin, reasoned that if people could be enticed to Washington County for a convention, they would look around and decide that having a winter home in the warm sunshine would be a good idea, so they built the Four Seasons Motel and Convention Center. The oil embargo came just after the project opened in 1973, cutting tourist traffic severely; but Coombs and his associates held on and weathered the down time until business picked up.

Ron and William Snow approached Coombs with a proposal to buy their 600 acres on the west side of the airport hill in the mid-1970s. Coombs resisted for a while but finally struck a deal, becoming their partner. Coombs had been traveling in southern California, looking at high-quality planned communities such as Mission Viejo. He was intrigued by the challenge of implementing such a concept in Dixie.

As had been the case at Bloomington, one big challenge for Coombs was developing the utilities in cooperation with St. George City. At that time, the city was looking for a piece of land to accommodate the Moore Business Forms company plant. The city and Coombs worked out a mutually beneficial arrangement. Coombs gave up twenty acres of land for the plant, and the city installed water and sewer to the area and improved the road, making it possible for Coombs to extend the utilities beyond the Moore plant to his proposed subdivisions. The area was also annexed by the city at that time.

The next element that was key to Coombs was finding a financing partner. This he was able to do in Pennsylvania, just before interest rates soared in the 1970s. His first subdivision went well but did not have the level of elegance he had hoped for. His next project, The Park, took on a more planned dimension; this included a clubhouse, palm trees, tile-roofed models — the tone of a southwest resort. He advertised widely with the theme, "the other Palm Springs," promoting St. George as much as The Park. The project was a major success, but times were changing as inflation sent interest rates up.

Conditions required another strategy which led Coombs to design Sports Village. Instead of semi-detached homes as in The Park, Sports Village appealed to buyers who wanted to invest less money and watch their investment inflate. The units were much smaller and were incorporated in a building with several apartments. This venture sold 280 units in two years, a big success. Times were heady. In 1980 Coombs announced Las Palmas, a recreation community as elegant as anything in southern California and very much in that tile-roof-and-palm-tree style. There were to be 1,000 units with multiple swimming pools and a large tennis complex with a Vic Braden Tennis School. A property management system was set up to allow buyers to put their condos in a rental pool when they were not using the rooms. Coombs was confident that the quality of The Park and Sports Village would sell Las Palmas.

In the pre-sale 100 units were sold in one weekend with a 10 percent down payment required. That success allowed Coombs to receive a $10 million line of credit. In the next two and a half years, his company completed 160 units, 130 of them pre-sold, but the nation's economy was shaky. Oil-dependent cities like Houston went into a nosedive. Interest rates skyrocketed, reaching as high as 17 percent. Savings-and-loan institutions came under suspicion for being overextended and involved in very soft ventures.

Green Valley appeared to be safe because there were firm contracts for the units. By 1983 just as Coombs was completing his condominiums, the Federal government, through the Federal Savings and Loan Insurance Corporation (FSLIC), issued new guidelines forbidding savings-and-loan institutions from issuing mortgages on condominiums and second homes. Almost overnight Green Valley went into default. Coombs had to give the 10 percent deposits back to the buyers. The Pennsylvania Savings and Loan had bigger problems than Green Valley, so it decided to be patient. Over the next few months, the Federal government relaxed its regulations somewhat and some of the units were transferred to buyers. Coombs essentially operated the undertaking for the bank and continues to do so.

That set of circumstances caused Coombs to return to the drawing board and come up with yet another concept. He had 130 completed units, many of them sold but others remained empty. How could he utilize them? The superstructure of the indoor sports facility was finished but not the interior. The pools and some of the tennis courts were completed. Out of that challenge came Coombs's next idea, a spa. With his own money, he finished the athletic facilities in style and began a major advertising campaign. It worked. He brought visitors to Green Valley for week-long resort stays featuring health-and-fitness training. Virtually every week sees the arrival of a new group of health-and-recreation-conscious people.

That is the status of Green Valley in 1996. Strewn with palm trees, it looks like it is in California. Coombs is starting a new phase of condos as the economy again looks positive. Clearly, entrepreneurial creativity is still saying boldly that there is a new Dixie — Dixie as destination.

Silver Reef Reborn

A more modest but also upscale real estate venture has occurred on the site of the old Silver Reef mining area. Unlike Green Valley, this residential project fit into a location where the ruins of a previous effort still existed. Old mine shafts, rigs, mounds of tailings, remnants of mill buildings, and cemeteries were standing where the thriving mining town had been seventy years before.

Several attempts had been made to rework the tailings, starting with Alex Colbath's efforts in 1916 and continuing into the 1960s with the Western Gold and Uranium Company. During part of that time, Wilma and Glenn Beal lived in the old Wells Fargo building as caretakers for Colbath's properties. Colbath had rebuilt much of the interior of the station building to use as an office and a residence while keeping the structure close to what the original had been.

The new approach in the 1970s was to locate expensive homes in the area. Loyal Frandsen, Lindon Frandsen, and Paul McNutt built fine homes in what came to be called Silver Reef Estates. As the elegant subdivision developed, one-acre lots were laid out for some forty homes. Originally the project had serious difficulties with land titles and water rights. The establishment of a special service district led by June Macfarlane Forshaw in 1974 helped resolve the water needs in cooperation with Leeds citizens. Gradually this project has seen the construction of some of the county's most spacious homes.

A further dimension of the new Silver Reef was a series of historical restoration projects. Joy Henderlider was effective in spearheading a drive to restore the old Wells Fargo Stage station. With the help of many Dixie citizens, Henderlider directed her energies to this project. She obtained leases to the land, the support of the county commission, and especially a grant from the state Department of Community and Economic Development. An alliance with artist Jerry Anderson, who maintains his studio and home in Silver Reef, was another advantage, leading to the successful restoration. That project, in turn, encouraged the restoration of three other structures — Rice Bank, a powder house, and a restaurant. These now draw scores of tourists every day to the new Silver Reef. Like other efforts in the county in the 1980s, this development occurred because individuals extended themselves for profit or more often for community service.18

Airline

In 1960 Bonanza Airlines gave up service to St. George and moved its operations to Cedar City after only a short stay. There they became AirWest. The move left Washington County without commercial air service. Thereafter Bruce Stucki took over management of the airport, which was the home of the Dixie Flying Club and some limited charter flights. Stucki took on the city lease and provided the gasoline and the flight school. Dixie College agreed to join his efforts and take charge of the ground school. At the same time, the college initiated its flight-attendant program and engine and airframe maintenance programs.

Stucki operated several charter flights, especially serving the movie industry. That led to the formation of Dixie Aviation Corporation, a modest undertaking by Stucki, Jerry Fackrell, and others. They began a scheduled air service called Dixie Airlines, with daily service to and from Salt Lake City. The operation expanded rapidly, adding Las Vegas connections and acquiring fourteen aircraft including trainers, rentals, and commercial planes. Stucki then decided to sell the airline, which was acquired by J. D. Air Service of Ogden, Utah.

In 1972 the organization of what became SkyWest Airlines was initiated by Ralph Atkin, who purchased the Dixie Airlines certificate. Jerry Fackrell, Garn Huntington, Scott McGregor, and B. Glen Crawford joined Atkin, mostly for the enjoyment of flying. Their initial fleet included four single-pilot-single-engine planes seating two, four, or six passengers. Their idea was to provide a round-trip commuter service to Salt Lake City three times a week, along with flights to Las Vegas, Page, Moab, Bullfrog Basin, Cedar City, and Provo.

The story of the next twenty years is one of those American tales of success drawn from the sure jaws of defeat — major risks, near bankruptcy, continual reinvestment, employees staying with the venture through dark times, many fortunate decisions, mergers, and expansion. Out of all this emerged a successful company with services in many states and hundreds of employees.

On 19 June 1972 the company's first flight left St. George for Cedar City, Salt Lake City, and return. The fare was $32 one-way and $59 round-trip ($28 and $51 from Cedar City). With this minimal operation, the airline had to patch things together to keep afloat. Pilots sold tickets, de-iced the planes, and worked for five dollars an hour. One ally was Dixie College, partially because Jerry Fackrell, master mechanic, had been an airflight instructor there. Dixie students were employed and allowed to use the facilities for their aerotechnology classes. Another strategy was to open a rental car agency in Cedar City to serve tourists who wanted to drive through the national parks after landing in Cedar City. This subsidiary was a good profit-maker for some time.

For a variety of reasons, the venture was soon in financial difficulty, however. It was under-capitalized, under-experienced, and under-equipped. Attempts were made to sell the enterprise, even give it away, but there were no takers. The time had come to quit or expand. Rudger Atkin, his sons Sidney, Lee, Ralph, and Clayton, and Clayton's son Jerry, were most anxious to avoid bankruptcy. The family had a good name in several Dixie businesses. In 1974 they decided to invest more of their resources and reorganize the company. Jerry Atkin was moved from accountant to president. A $15,000 grant from the state of Utah was received, providing a big boost. The first major turning point had been passed.

Then came a series of important stepping stones: extending flights to Page, Arizona; reaching an interairline agreement with American Airlines in 1977; obtaining Federal certification in 1978; leasing their first Fairchild Metroliner; and receiving a Federal subsidy of $160,000. After acquiring SkyWest Page, they expanded from Page to Phoenix via Flagstaff in 1979. Next came an expansion into Las Vegas and Pocatello markets which led to the acquisition of ten Metro airliners by 1984. An $8 million loan from Zions Bank facilitated the addition of routes to Palm Springs and Carson City/Reno, and acquiring Sun Aire in Southern California. Joining Western Airlines' code sharing system and purchasing Brasilia airliners were highlights from 1985-87.[19]

All this development was directed out of the company's St. George headquarters, embracing a wide network of California destinations including Fresno, Bakersfield, Burbank, Ontario, Santa Maria, Santa Barbara, Los Angeles, San Diego, Borrego Springs, and Imperial County. Only a small part of the traffic originated in or even passed through St. George. The board of SkyWest by this time included Ralph, Sid, Lee, Brent, and Jerry Atkin as well as Dell Stout, Frank Chew, Merv Cox, Steven Udver-Hazy, and Ian Cumming. For several years, they had considered the pros and cons of going public. Their initial visits to Wall Street were not exactly warm, but as the airline expanded to become the eleventh largest regional airline in the country, investors began to look again. When another effort was made to prepare documentation and gain Federal approval for issuing stock, permission and interest moved fast. On 26 June 1986, 1.5 million shares were put on the market. The sale was brisk, raising nearly $12 million. This enabled SkyWest to pay off its debt to Zions Bank and Heritage Savings, improve some ground facilities, buy airplanes and put money in the bank.

When Delta Airlines bought Western Airlines and SkyWest realized that Delta serviced the cities where SkyWest landed in the inter-mountain West, board members could see that a linkage with Delta was essential. That new affiliation encouraged the addition of fifty-passenger Canadair aircraft and the opening of flights to Boise, Twin Falls, and Idaho Falls, Idaho; Grand Junction, Colorado; Rapid City, and Sioux Falls, South Dakota; Casper, Wyoming; and Butte, Missoula, Bozeman, and Billings, Montana. The airline has continued to acquire larger planes.

There were many pressures to move SkyWest's corporate headquarters to Salt Lake City, Delta's hub. A thorough discussion of alternatives in 1990 led the SkyWest board of directors to choose to build a corporate headquarters building in St. George. In some ways this was a bow to electronic communications which allows companies to have instantaneous contact with their far-flung agents. In another way it was an expression that the company's leaders wanted to live in St. George. The next question was where to build. After considering downtown options, the board chose a site on River Road, near the I-15 off-ramp instead of in the city center. Both decisions had a major influence on the future of St. George. In August 1995, SkyWest reorganized its board, retiring three local veterans, Lee and Brent Atkin and Dell Stout, and replacing them with Hyrum Smith of the Franklin Institute and Henry Eyring, a Salt Lake City business consultant. Marty Braham, vice president of customer relations for Delta Airlines, replaced Frank Chew who previously had represented Delta.

This expansion has not happened without difficulty. There have been reorganizations that trimmed the workforce or changed assignments. The servicing headquarters was moved to Salt Lake City from St. George, disrupting several people's lives. There were times when the company's stock prices dropped dramatically, scaring away investors. A tragic mid-air accident near the Salt Lake City airport on 15 January 1987 killed the pilot, co-pilot and eight passengers. Although SkyWest was exonerated in the Federal investigation, the collision exacted an enormous human toll. Another accident occurred at the Los Angeles airport when a USAir plane landed on top of a SkyWest plane, killing all aboard the eighteen-passenger plane. Again Skywest was not blamed.

Dixie is thus the home to a significant airline. Its existence is an example of Utah's economic development. The state has discov-

Skywest commuter plane at St. George Airport, 1996. (Gene Butera)

ered that supporting home-grown industries can be more productive than courting outside industries to come to the state (SkyWest Airlines started as a small project in Dixie and has grown to national prominence. SkyWest not only provides employment for 200 people in Washington County but is also a lifeline, bringing business people and visitors into the area. Many people reside in Dixie and commute to work in California on SkyWest. The airline brings the county's communities into easy contact with the whole world.

Dixie College Moves to a New Campus

The campus of Dixie College in downtown St. George had become completely crowded with buildings by 1950. When the college received an appropriation for a new gymnasium, college president Ellvert Himes was faced with a problem. He was convinced that erecting new buildings in the cramped area of the campus in downtown St. George was unwise. During his presidency (1951-54), he and several other college officials and community leaders chose a site for a new campus. The Dixie Education Association, an effective citizen lobby in the past, came forward once again. They had collected funds to support the college and donated $30,000 to the purchase of six blocks on the eastern edge of St. George. State senator Orval Hafen, a member of the association, helped obtain permission from the Utah Legislature to put the building on the new site. The land was donated to the state by the community and was given to start plans for a new campus. In 1957 the cornerstone was laid and the new gymnasium was soon completed.

For some time, students had to rotate between the two campuses for physical education classes and intercollegiate games. The community responded positively to the new gym which has been kept in fine condition even though it has hosted hundreds of athletic meets and has been the site of hard-fought contests with athletic figures such as Arlyn Hafen, Lionel Hollings, Nolan Archibald, Jeff Holland, Ken Belka, Chris McMullin, Avarian Parrish, Brent Stephenson, and many more. In 1985 Coach Neil Roberts' basketball team won the national NJCAA championship with a record of thirty-five wins and one loss.

Under the direction of the state building board and its director, Glen Swenson, plans were drawn for a new campus featuring a desert-oasis look. The second major structure was a Fine Arts Center. With its completion, the college moved to the new campus under the presidency of Arthur Bruhn. Other buildings were also finished: the science and home economics buildings, a snack bar, a heating plant, and the Shiloh dormitory. Bruhn, a science teacher, succeeded Himes in 1954 and brought great energy to his calling. He had a clear vision of what Dixie College should be — a quality academic institution that would train leaders for further higher education. He hoped the college would maintain its small size so that faculty could work closely with students. His view was that the new campus would be a locus for that cordial learning atmosphere.

In 1963 Bruhn faced the task of dividing the college when the new campus was ready. The model of having high school and college students together on one campus had not caught on nationally. For that and other reasons, the system was abandoned; therefore only the collegiate division moved to the new campus. The high school remained in the downtown facilities. Determining which faculty members would remain at the high school and which would move to the new campus was a tough call; feelings were tense about the matter.

Bruhn was a leader who had helped instill devotion of both faculty and students to the college. His critics, however, argued that his view was too limited, both in size and breadth. They had experienced Governor J. Bracken Lee's assault and felt the college must grow substantially from its 360 students to fend off further efforts to close it. They also wanted a larger vocational curriculum. Arthur

Bruhn's untimely death from cancer in 1964 brought in a new leader who agreed with the expansionist view. Ferron Losee came from Los Angeles where he had seen the impact of vocational training on young people and communities. He felt that Dixie College needed to expand its vocational offerings. The new campus was already attracting more students — something he encouraged. He undertook a program to wine and dine decision-makers in the north to overcome the attitude that Dixie was dispensable.

Many buildings were started on the campus during the 1960s and 1970s. President Losee was successful in obtaining Federal funds to match those from the legislature for several projects. He appointed Bill Barlocker as business manager. Barlocker was the colorful St. George mayor who had made and lost a fortune in the turkey business and had been a candidate for governor. Barlocker helped attract Federal monies. During President Losee's term (1964-76) the student center, Shenandoah dormitories, library, administration building, liberal arts, business building, auto lab, and the Zion Amphitheater (in Springdale) were constructed. Losee was a controversial figure — an entrepreneur and a strong-willed decision-maker. Some faculty members challenged his leadership style. The controversy led to an extended confrontation which brought on a court case and an investigation from the state board of education which recommended a more participatory governance system.

William Rolfe Kerr became president of the college in 1976 and served four years. He initiated a council form of governance that addressed many faculty and staff concerns, and his personable style won many friends. Enrollment was 1,343 when he began and reached 1,589 by 1980 when he left to take an administrative position at Brigham Young University. (He later became Utah Commissioner of Higher Education.) The trades and industries building was completed during his term, but his major contribution in physical planning was to generate the idea for the Dixie Center — a convention complex to be located on the campus and shared by the college and the community. His successor, Alton Wade, had to make the tough decision about attracting countywide citizen support for a bond election.

President Wade, Gary Esplin (St. George City manager), and Mayor Karl Brooks went forward with the effort to create a special service district. The bond passed in many communities although it was opposed in some. Several friends of the project, including Governor Norman Bangerter, were then called upon to help in a legislative lobby effort. The legislature, after a controversial debate, appropriated $4 million over two years. Karl Brooks, Grey Larkin, and others lobbied state officials who granted a Community Impact Board loan of $2 million. The college then had to raise $4 million in private funding to complete the financing — a task which took several years to accomplish. Donors rallied to the effort; some donations were large and donor names were placed on each of the four buildings; others were in smaller amounts for seats in the arena or auditorium. Many of the donations were facilitated by the Spirit of Dixie Committee which came together from the community to voluntarily do the landscaping and surface the parking lots. The final financing was completed by a generous anonymous donor.

Once completed, the Dixie Center became a symbol of the new Dixie. It is a center for conventions and celebrations as well as culture and recreation. The college derives benefit from it, as does the community. It is the home of Dixie College basketball, the Southwest Symphony, the Celebrity Concert Series, and scores of special events. Numerous conventions are drawn to the county because the Dixie Center is available.

One of the first events in the Dixie Center was the inauguration of yet another Dixie College president, Douglas D. Alder, a professor of history from Utah State University. He replaced Alton Wade, who was appointed president of Brigham Young University-Hawaii in 1986. Known as an academician, Alder placed emphasis on academic quality, and his years at the helm saw the enrollment continue its gradual ascent. The creation of an honors program, the Dixie Invitational Art Show, and several academic conferences and forums supported the academic emphasis. The building program accelerated with an addition to the science building and library; the construction of the Val A. Browning Building, and the Kenneth N. Gardner Student Center. The creation of a national advisory council and completion of an ambitious $17 million capital campaign occurred during those years.

Robert Huddleston succeeded Alder in 1993. A proven administrator, Huddleston reorganized the campus academically and administratively. Major projects continued during his years; they included the Bruce Hurst Baseball/Softball complex and the Udvar-Hazy Busi-

The Dixie Center, 1996. (Mark Petersen)

ness Building. Huddleston's major proposal has been for the college to acquire the Dixie Center in conjunction with a community plan to build a new convention center near exit 6 of the freeway. Expansion is still part of Dixie College; considerable citizen discussion has been devoted to proposals for turning the institution into a four-year college. The state board of regents has been cautious about such ideas, favoring instead cooperative efforts between Dixie and Southern Utah University (SUU) in Cedar City to provide four-year degrees and masters programs on the St. George campus from universities in the state. The University Center, founded earlier, was turned over to SUU to administer on the Dixie campus.

When the 1996 Utah centennial began, Dixie College could look back to 1963 and see some dramatic changes that had occurred in the three decades since the opening of the new campus. The college's main achievement has been to improve the lives of its students. Heber Jones, local historian, recalls that for him as a youth in Veyo, Dixie College provided a career opportunity he otherwise would not have had. He claims that scores, even hundreds of students, did not have the resources to go away to college. The opportunities to make a living in agriculture were limited in the 1950s. Dixie College was his opportunity, and the chance for many others to move into the professional world.

The Udvar-Hazy School of Business, Dixie College, 1996. (Mark Petersen)

Enrollment had multiplied, from 363 when the new campus opened, to well over ten times that many in 1996, with even more part-time students. The school that largely catered to young people in 1963 is attracting many re-entry students in the 1990s. Thousands of retirees and community members attend non-credit programs, including some 2,000 Elderhostel students over age fifty-five who come from all over the nation each year to spend a week in classes at Dixie College.

The cultural role of the college still thrives: theater, symphony, choirs, concerts, art shows, forums, as well as a continuing athletic program in superior facilities. Citizen audiences remain enthusiastic supporters. The campus has expanded to double its 1957 size when the state of Utah accepted the Dixie Education Association's gift of six city blocks. Governor Scott Matheson later was helpful in acquiring the southern portion of the campus, some thirty-five acres. That space is now fully occupied and administrators are looking for new land. The campus is designed to accommodate a maximum of 10,000 students. If the growth rate of the last thirty years is maintained, that many students could well be enrolled in another decade or two.

ENDNOTES

1. M. Truman Bowler, Interview, Washington County Centennial History Committee, 7 July 1994, Dixie College Archives.

2. Orval Hafen, Journal, II, 16 December 1958, manuscript in possession of Bruce Hafen.

3. Ibid., I, 31 March 1935, 25.

4. Ibid., II, 27 September 1952, 10.

5. Ibid., I, 8 October 1935, 69.

6. Ibid., III, 17 May 1961, 31. (The letter was written 25 years before this entry.)

7. Ibid., II, 17 March 1957, 69.

8. Ibid., II, 1 January 1958, 102.

9. Ibid., II, 16 December 1958, 156.

10. Ibid., III, 24 May 1961, 34.

11. Ibid., III, 14 April 1961, 24.

12. J. L. Crawford, "The Boy Who'd Never Seen a Train," *St. George Magazine*, September 1995, 26.

13. *Washington County News*, 16 April 1931, 2.

14. Marion Bowler, Interview, Washington County Centennial History Committee, 7 October 1994, Dixie College Archives.

15. Carl Nelson, *Autobiography of Carl Erwin "Star" Nelson* (St George, privately published, 1995), vol. II: 847-94; Dixie College Archives. See also Carolyn Reinbold, "History of Bloomington, Utah," typescript, Dixie College Archives.

16. Jeff Morby, Interview, Washington County Centennial History Committee, 23 November 1992, Dixie College Archives.

17. Alan Coombs, Interview with Douglas D. Alder, 9 September 1994, Dixie College Archives.

18. Paul Dean Proctor and Morris A. Shirts, *Silver, Sinners and Saints* (Provo: Paulmar, 1991), 193-202. See also Wilma Beal, *My Story of Silver Reef* (n.p.: privately published, 1987).

19. Kathryn B. Creedy, *Time Flies, The History of SkyWest Airlines* (San Antonio: Loflin and Associates, 1992); See also Michael V. Orchard, "Historical Research on St. George ~tion, 1929 to 1973,"; Kathy Cottam, "The St. George Airport: Past, Present, and Future," 1981; Nada Prisbrey, "A Brief History of SkyWest Airlines," 1983, manuscripts, Gregerson Collection, Dixie College Archives; Sidney J. Atkin, "History of Aviation in St. George," Legacy (St. George: St. George Art Museum, 1996).

11

MODERNIZATION

Professional Medicine

In the twentieth century, like elsewhere in the nation, county health-care providers increasingly were trained in medical colleges, and the dependence on herbal medicine was replaced. J. D. Affleck, who came initially to Silver Reef, moved to St. George and is said to have studied medicine at the same Pennsylvania medical school attended by Salt Lake City's Dr. Ellis Shipp. In conjunction with Walter Keate and Robert Michols, Affleck also opened a drug store.

The next generation of doctors in St. George included Frederick Cliff and Frank J. Woodbury. They were men with considerable professional training. Woodbury invited his brother-in-law, Dr. Donald McGregor, to move to St. George. McGregor had been practicing in Beaver since 1910 but moved to St. George in 1913. He was a surgeon who soon constructed what was known as the McGregor Hospital in the city center. This brought a whole new level of medical practice to Dixie. Dr. Woodbury's son, Clare, and Dr. McGregor's two sons, Alpine and Lorenzo, went to medical school at the University of Maryland and returned to practice in St. George.

Dr. Clare Woodbury moved to Las Vegas and was replaced by Dr. Wilford Reichmann who practiced in St. George from 1925 to 1975. Clark McIntire practiced in Hurricane but took his patients to the Cedar City hospital rather than to McGregor's. George Westin is said to have practiced medicine on the Arizona Strip. The McGregors were known for their surgery, Dr. Reichmann for his bedside manner. People still verify that Dr. Reichmann never sent anyone a bill; he felt that the people were honorable and would pay if they could. If they couldn't, they needed his service anyway. Reichmann's generosity endeared him to the local people who saw him as a leader as much as a doctor. He was the embodiment of the family practitioner. The McGregors were more specialized. Dr. Reichmann often referred his patients who needed surgery to the McGregors, who developed a sizable facility with their own pharmacy and even a dentist located in the hospital. There was no ambulance available; local mortician Henry Pickett and his son Elmer adapted their hearse to double as an ambulance to bring accident victims to the hospital. Sometimes the doctors went to the site of an accident.

In 1952-53 Washington County built the Dixie Pioneer Memorial Hospital for $500,000. The new hospital was an imposing structure but within two decades it required expansion and was renamed the Dixie Medical Center. When it opened, the McGregor Hospital closed, and the McGregors opened a new clinic. Dr. M. K. McGregor had come to Dixie by this time.

Dixie Pioneer Memorial Hospital was the result of a community effort led by county commissioners Murray Webb, Truman Bowler, and Emil Graff. They and the hospital medical staff came to the conclusion that a new hospital was necessary. The Pioneer Memorial Hospital had been a good step forward when it was constructed, but it served mostly family practice and surgery. The time of medical specialization had come to Dixie, requiring highly specialized equipment.

Commissioner Webb negotiated with the governor, the state Department of Health, and the LDS church to contribute a portion of the cost. It then was necessary to pass a bond election for the majority of the funding. The election was called for 2 May 1972, and it passed comfortably. Clearly the citizens intended that health care in Washington County should be maintained at a high level.

When the $4 million addition opened in 1975 with fifty-four beds plus an intensive-care unit, there were six doctors practicing in St.

Dixie Regional Medical Center, 1996. (Gene Butera)

George and one in Hurricane. By 1983 the hospital had been expanded to 106 beds, having been purchased by Intermountain Health Care
of Salt Lake City in 1976. It was the first purchase by the IHC system
following its takeover of Salt Lake City's LDS Hospital. By 1990 the
St. George hospital was again updated, this time with Intermountain
Health Care funding, to become a regional hospital, meaning that patients were referred to it from other hospitals, particularly in southern
Utah. Dixie Regional Medical Center became the major hospital between Provo and Las Vegas.

    Steve Wilson had become the administrator in 1986, replacing
Gordon Storrs, who served from 1975 to 1986. Facilities were set
up to allow patients to be life-flighted to Dixie Regional Medical
Center. The number of doctors had increased from seven in 1973 to
eighty-three plus twenty-one consulting doctors in 1994. The hospital employs 700 people and has 138 beds available at this writing. Its
out-patient services now exceed the in-patient care in numbers served.
Already a new medical facility is being planned to supplement it, perhaps eventually to replace it.

    Perhaps the most renowned part of the hospital is the cancer cen-
ter. In the 1960s the hospital invested in a radiation detection machine,
in part in response to the nuclear fallout the area had experienced dur-

ing the 1950s. Barbara Watson, chair of the board, and Gordon Storrs, hospital administrator, worked with Senator Orrin Hatch and the National Cancer Institute to create a detection center in conjunction with the St. George hospital. The funding provided staffing and reduced screening costs for over a decade. Now that funding has concluded, but the Dixie Regional Medical Center has its own qualified experts and is continuing to provide service.

Recently Rhanee Ballard recalled names of many of the nurses who served in the Pioneer Memorial Hospital. She mentioned Eda Hafen and a Mrs. Rankin among the first certified nurses. Others included Francis Crawford Hepworth, Alice Whipple, Agnes Hunt, Beulah Cottam, Mary Holt, Roxa McAllister, and Nina Green. Marie Cottam was a head nurse. Hettie Burgess Hunt was Dr. Reichman's well-known nurse. Mary Whitehurst and Roma Reber worked for Dr. McGregor at the old hospital and at the newer clinic. Ballard points out that the nurses not only cared for patients but also initiated a fund-raising campaign to pay for a coronary-care unit. Their "Coronary Care Ball" raised $6,000 which was matched with a grant from the Intermountain Regional Medical District, enabling them to open a two-bed care unit.

Another vital function conducted largely by nurses was the county nurse service. These nurses conducted clinics to give children immunizations. They promoted pre-natal and post-natal services. For many the most memorable work of the county nurses was their visits to homes to diagnose children with mumps, measles, and chicken-pox. They brought quarantine signs to be placed in windows of homes when children had communicable diseases. For many families, these county nurses provided their primary health care.

Dentists in Dixie included Alma Dunford, Jed Gates and W. C. Cox. Dunford was trained as an apprentice in Salt Lake City and came to St. George during Brigham Young's lifetime. He married Young's daughter, Susa, and they had two children while he practiced in Dixie. He was called on a mission to England, and upon his return, the couple divorced, whereupon he moved to Salt Lake City. Dr. Gates practiced in his home which had previously belonged to Brigham Young. He had an office in the upper story to which Donald F. Kraack remembers being sent by his grandmother. "He had a treadle drilling machine, with a large wheel and belts which operated in much the same manner as an old-time sewing machine. He pumped it by using his foot on a pedal affair."[1]

In 1911 Dr. Wilford Charles Cox established a practice after receiving a doctor of dental surgery degree from Northwestern University. The young doctor returned to southern Utah near where he had been raised in Iron County and opened a dental practice in St. George. His daughter Carol Cox Watkins reports that he agreed to help his professor continue research. He was especially observant of a condition in Nevada's Moapa Valley and "concluded that fluorine in the water from mineral springs was responsible for the mottling and resultant lack of decay. These observations predated the fluoride work in dental hygiene."[2]

Mary Phoenix reported that Bonita Pendleton Ashby was sent to Dr. Cox to have a tooth pulled. Her father had given her a dollar to cover the costs. She discovered that the charge was a dollar if the doctor "froze" the tooth but only fifty cents without the freezing. She chose the latter and spent the remainder on herself. Dr. Cox's daughter Carol remembers that many of his patients paid with bartered goods such as peaches, pears, gooseberries, firewood, or coal. Dr. Cox even remodeled his house on the barter system during the Depression when people could pay with little else than labor. At the same time, he contracted for the dental work for the CCC boys, receiving a dollar per patient. Doctor Cox continued practicing until 1953. By that time, there was an infusion of new dentists. Mike Hutchings had a dental practice in the McGregor Hospital and moved with the McGregors to their new clinic. A. I. Hutchings was also practicing dentistry in the 1940s and 1950s in St. George. Walter Snow, son of Harold Snow and grandson of Erastus Beman Snow, arrived in St. George to practice dentistry after graduating from the University of Southern California. Several other local men went away to dental school, graduated, and returned: Lee Atkin, Jay Blake, Mervyn Cox, Richard Whitehead, and Wayne Christian. Joe Hamilton and George Sanford moved to the area during the 1960s.

In the 1950s Richard Jennings was in the city a short time, as were Merrill Woodbury and Carlson Terry. ElMyrrh Cox was killed in an airplane crash while searching as a volunteer for a downed jetliner over the Grand Canyon. Later in the 1950s, Alpine Prince was electrocuted the night before he and others were to have moved into a new dental facility. Larry Staples joined Atkin in 1971, focusing on preventive dentistry. The same year Dr. Richard Whitehead was admitted to the full-time medical staff of the Dixie Pioneer Memorial Hospital as an oral surgeon. He reports that he planned to open his office on a Monday, but it was county fair weekend and a man whose jaw was broken in a fight became Dr. Whitehead's first patient on the Sunday before his planned opening.

During the 1960s people began coming from Las Vegas to St. George for dental work. The quality of the dentists and the comparative lower prices attracted many. In 1974 the first dental implants were done. Dr. Jennings had returned to St. George and along with Dr. Whitehead introduced this special treatment. Currently there are two periodontists, two endodontists, four orthodontists, and five who perform oral surgery among the fifty practicing dentists in the county. There are dentists practicing in Enterprise (Craig DeHart), Washington (Kent Heideman), La Verkin (Hugh Howard), and Hurricane (Ken Heaton and David Mason).

Law Enforcement

The transformation of Dixie is illustrated in the activities of the county sheriff and the marshal of St. George. For nearly a century there was one town marshal. The jail was in the basement of the courthouse, with two cells shared by the city and county. In 1880 it was moved to a building right behind the courthouse that had three cells and a drunk tank. The county sheriff sometimes had a deputy. The sheriff and the marshal shared the same desk and often held other community responsibilities such as poundkeeper or sexton.

During the county's first century, infringements of the law were generally confined to public intoxication, robbery, cattle rustling, horse thievery, and fighting (particularly at Silver Reef). Homicides were rare but notable. In 1881 a man named Forest killed a mine overseer in Silver Reef. The murderer was arrested and jailed in St. George, but before a trial could be arranged, a mob lynched Forest. Two other men killed each other in a Silver Reef shootout. In Pine Valley, a father killed the lover of his daughter but was himself killed in doing it. Two cattle rustlers were captured by Bill Pulsipher, who had been deputized by Sheriff Jim Pearson in Pioche. They were placed in jail in St. George until the sheriff came to get them. On the trip back to

Pioche to stand trial, the two cattle thieves were executed near the Black Ridge at Dammeron Valley by masked vigilantes. Royal Hunt was killed at his ranch by a vagabond he had befriended. In 1964 a husband killed his wife and in 1975 a police officer killed a man who was found with his wife. As the population has expanded, homicides have become more frequent; from a dozen in the first century, another dozen have occurred in the last two decades.[3]

Bank robberies also have been memorable. In 1919 two men entered the office of the Bank of St. George late on a Saturday night. They broke the lock to the cash drawer where $1,500 was deposited; however, they could not break the safe. Arthur Miles, the bank's cashier, discovered the robbery and alerted the police when he went to the post office on Sunday morning to collect the Saturday mail. The thieves made their escape from St. George by way of Enterprise, whose town marshall Arthur Huntsman, had received a tip that they were headed in his direction. He discovered freshly made tire tracks heading for the state line. Near Acoma, Nevada, two miles from a railroad stop, Huntsman found the robbers and the money in their Model-T Ford mired in the mud. Nevada officials agreed Huntsman could return the robbers to St. George where they were tried and convicted and sent to the Utah State Prison. Thereafter, the bank hired two young men, Leslie and Clair Morris, to guard the bank for a dollar a night. That continued for six months until the door was fixed and reinforced.

In the early 1930s, another dramatic burglary occurred at the Bank of St. George. The perpetrators were never apprehended. They used a railroad jack to lift the entire back roof off the small building. They entered on a Sunday, took several thousand dollars, and escaped. The bank's insurance company restored the loss. The Hurricane Bank also was burglarized once; its thieves were never apprehended.[4]

The reminiscences of county sheriff Will Brooks capture the homey nature of his office in the 1930s. Many of his efforts dealt with thievery or youngsters involved in rebellion toward parents. He took many of them to his home where his wife fed them and bedded them down to keep them out of the jail environment.[5]

More serious crimes tended to involve professional criminals on the move. The sheriff was often called to set up roadblocks or cooperate with police from northern towns or Nevada officials. The case of Jack Weston, a sophisticated thief, was one. Weston stole throughout

Washington County, Iron County, and the Arizona Strip over several years. Weston and his mistress were apprehended by Sheriff Lew Fife of Iron County, but they were able to overpower Fife, handcuff him with his hands backwards around a tree, steal his car, and escape. In the melee Fife shot Weston. For revenge, Weston wanted to pour gasoline over Fife and set him on fire, but his girlfriend persuaded him to leave. Instead he left Fife to die, tied to the cedar tree in the remote desert between Newcastle and Pioche. In a heroic twenty-hour feat, Fife cut tree limbs and climbed up until he got his arms over the top, then he resumed the chase. The sheriff knew the tire tracks and was able to follow Weston and his female companion onto the Arizona Strip, enlisting the aid of Washington County and Arizona sheriffs along the way. While on the run, Weston died of his gunshot wounds; his female companion and his brother buried him. She was soon captured and led Fife to Weston's grave. Fingerprints of the corpse were taken to make a positive identification of Weston.[6]

Washington County experienced relative domestic peace following World War II and the Korean War. During the 1950s and 1960s Sheriff Evan Whitehead and a deputy patrolled the county, Whitehead serving St. George and the west end of the county, his deputy in charge of the east end.[7] During the same two decades, the St. George police department consisted of three officers. Law enforcement problems began to steadily increase at about the same time as the completion of Interstate 15. Two additional St. George police officers were hired in 1966 with the increase of population and the annexation of Bloomington and Bloomington Hills. The police force in the 1970s grew to nineteen officers. In 1994 there were forty-three police officers serving the rapidly growing population of St. George. Today (1996), according to St. George Police Chief Jon Pollei, the city has about 1.3 officers per thousand residents, well under the state average of about two officers per thousand residents and the national average of slightly more than three officers per thousand.[8] The low number of law-enforcement officers suggests that St. George is still relatively free of crime problems.

According to former sheriff Evan Whitehead and Ken Campbell, who served with him, problems associated with illegal drug use escalated beginning in the early 1970s. Illegal drug use in the county included marijuana, cocaine, and amphetamines. Interstate 15 and the proximity of Las Vegas make illegal drugs easily accessible. Equally disturbing for law enforcement officials in the county is the rise of alcohol abuse. More recently, Dixie has experienced the urban related problem of organized gangs.

Law-enforcement statistics kept by the St. George police chief beginning in 1986 provide a clearer picture of problems in the city. Instances of spouse abuse increased from eighteen in 1989 to 144 in 1993. Burglary cases rose from 157 in 1989 to 251 in 1993. Thefts also increased from 905 in 1989 to 1,503 in 1993, and vehicle thefts increased from 67 to 96 for the same four-year period. Forgery, narcotic violations, and driving under the influence of alcohol also increased. Only the more violent crimes of rape, homicide, and arson remained low.[9] More recently the county installed the emergency 911 telephone system to enable citizens to seek immediate police assistance. In 1993 the county 911 system handled 12,091 emergency calls.

Dixie experiences problems plaguing the rest of the nation. In 1995 the Washington County School District stationed a law enforcement officer in each of the high schools in the county, mainly for crime prevention. The availability of drugs and alcohol in the county and family crises take up the majority of the time of county law enforcement officers.

Clearly the growth of the county from 10,000 people to over 60,000 has its challenges. Isolation once insulated Dixie from most crimes, but no longer. The office of county attorney that Lang Foremaster filled with a part-time contract for two decades has now increased to three full-time attorneys. The story is similar for St. George City with three attorneys. Other communities in the county currently are getting by with part-time attorneys.

The county is also facing other socio-legal issues. One such issue was the lighting at night of the St. George LDS Temple. In 1942 the St. George City Council decided that since the temple was a major landmark, it should be illuminated at night. An agreement between the city council and officials of the temple was made that the city-owned electric utility should give the temple a credit on its electric bill if the church would keep it lit all night. The credit was set at a fixed dollar value which amounted to about two percent of the total electricity used on the temple block.[10] In 1985 local attorney Phillip Foremaster filed suit in the United States District Court in Salt Lake City, arguing violation of the First Amendment dealing with separation of church and state. The city argued that it wanted the temple lit as an historic monument and city symbol. The Federal district court dismissed the suit; however, on appeal to the Tenth Circuit Court of Appeals in Denver, the lower-court ruling was reversed. In October 1989 the city appealed to the U.S. Supreme Court which refused to hear the matter. In the meantime, the LDS church decided to turn off the lights between 11 p.m. and 4 a.m. and assume the costs of electricity for lighting the temple.

St. George City faced another issue over its logo. For many years, the St. George temple was included in the city's logo. City officials decided not to include the temple in a new logo. Coming on the heels of the temple lighting controversy, the change created considerable community discussion and extensive news coverage.

Activities of the extreme right fringe of already politically conservative southern Utah occurred in the late 1970s. Two residents of St. George, Walter P. Mann III and Richard D. Cooper, were ousted from the local John Birch Society for being too radical. A legal notice published in the Washington County News on 13 March 1980 signed by fifteen followers of Cooper and Mann warned that anyone who attempted to oppress, threaten, or interfere with their activities would be subject to prosecution and fines of $1 million per day for each right violated. This was served upon the United States Attorney General, the attorney general and governor of Utah, and most local officials.

Cooper and Mann pushed for the establishment of small townships governed by the common law, recognizing the sheriff as the highest legally constituted authority. Mann created Zion's Township in Washington County. A militia was formed and trained with prescribed uniforms and armaments. Cooper was named chief justice of the township's supreme court, and members of the Zion Township were exhorted not to obey laws considered to be unconstitutional, such as zoning ordinances, speed limits, driver-license laws, and concealed-weapon permits. In an administrative hearing, "Sheriff" Eugene Jones was asked to arrest an IRS agent seeking to question Mann. A high point in their challenges of the legal system was to conduct their own trial against "the world" on the steps of the county courthouse in February 1983 when the courthouse was closed.

The government slowly reacted. Cooper was hauled into circuit court for zoning and building permit violations and was ultimately jailed three times within a ninety-day period. This penalty was imposed for being in contempt. Mann was incarcerated in Federal prison as a result of his activities in the sale of advice on how to defy the Internal Revenue Service. By 1988 Cooper had relocated to the sparsely populated Arizona Strip where the inattention of a distant Arizona government was more appealing than was increasingly intolerant St. George. Cooper formed the Desert Springs Township and soon began challenges to the Arizona government.

The Mountain Meadows Massacre Revisited

In the fall of 1990 a unique event occurred in Washington and Iron counties. It took the form of a joint family reunion between the descendants of John D. Lee and the descendants of the eighteen survivors of the Mountain Meadows Massacre. That tragic event, described in chapter 2, has scarred the history of the region for over a century. Certainly the most noted trial and the most noted violence in the county's history revolved around the Mountain Meadows Massacre. In July 1875 a trial of John D. Lee resulted in a hung jury. Lee was retried in September 1876 and found guilty of participating in the massacre, the only one so charged and convicted. On 23 March 1877, Lee was executed at the Mountain Meadows.

The causes of this event were never fully clear, but an extensive study by Juanita Brooks brought some clarity.[11] Still, the incident continued to bother people of the region. In an attempt to bring about a reconciliation, some regional leaders promoted a formal public event to deal with the remaining agony. The reunion activities included a luncheon in Parowan for monument committee members who met together for the first time, a trip to the site of the massacre, and a barbecue at the Dixie Center in St. George with descendants of the immigrant group as guests. After the meal, a joint family reunion of 400 people was held in the M. K. Cox Auditorium. The following day, 15 September 1990, in Cedar City, a large public program was held to dedicate a new monument erected to honor those who lost their lives in the massacre.

Schools

The county's nineteen school districts were consolidated to one in June 1915. The educational needs of the east and west sides of the county were now addressed together. Residents from all communities in the county share in the financial support and the administration of the schools through a county wide elected school board. The county school district is stable, providing educational opportunities for the children. School district superintendents have provided, in part, the foundation for the stability of the school system. Mathew Bentley, financial administrator of Dixie College, served as superintendent from 1915 to 1929. Milton Moody then served nearly thirty years from 1 July 1929 to 11 April 1958. T. Lavoy Esplin directed schools from 1958 to 1979 when business and almost everything else was booming. Jack F. Burr served from 1979 to 1985, and Steven H. Peterson served to July 1996. At this writing, Kolene Granger is the present superintendent.

The main issue facing schools since 1915 has been finance. The county has always been below most of the state in per capita income, particularly until the 1980s. At one point, the Washington County School District was the third poorest in the state. When the state adopted an equalization law which diverted additional appropriations from the legislature to poorer school districts, Washington County was able to construct many new buildings.[12]

Enrollment remained rather steady, growing gradually from 2,059 students in 1915 to 3,379 in 1964. Then, like everything else in Washington County, there was a boom — the 1972 enumeration showed 4,215 students, 1982 listed 6,782, and 1992 saw a doubling to 13,363, with 17,391 in 1996. These statistics make one essential point very clear: the population explosion in Dixie was not made up only of retirees and second-home owners — many young families also were attracted to the county following 1965.

The explosive growth of enrollment required the construction of some twenty new buildings since 1955, the purchase of a fleet of buses, and the hiring of hundreds of new teachers. In 1932 the district had only two buses, in 1952 nine, in 1972 seventeen, and in 1992 a total of sixty-four. Per capita expenditures have also increased from $341 per student in 1964 to $2,567 in 1992. Because of the population growth, the school district has been able to use the additional revenue from local taxes to hire teachers and purchase supplies. The building of new schools has been funded by various school bonds approved by the citizens. County residents have approved every school bond that has been presented to them. The most recent, in 1994, was for $33.1 million. The school board is preparing for a $50 million bond election in 1996.

This kind of community support has allowed the expansion of school facilities to keep up with the growth of the student population.[13]

During much of the last two decades, Washington County schools have had the highest percentage of enrollment growth in the state. Enrollment has doubled in the years of Superintendent Peterson's administration (1984-1996). Almost all students attend public schools; only 2.12 percent are being home taught. The dropout rate is low (51 students out of 15,769 in 1993) partly because of the establishment of an alternative high school, Millcreek, located in the old school building in Washington City.

The school district has a joint relationship with Dixie College to sponsor an area vocational school which allows students from both systems to use the facilities of each for training in vocational preparation programs. This is a most innovative vocational program because it utilizes existing campuses and faculties. It is the pride of both the college and the school district. Another innovation has been adopting a year-round calendar for elementary schools. Parents accepted the plan partly because the district conducted many meetings where all could comment and partly because there was really no other alternative with such rapid growth. Student achievement scores in 1993 were slightly above the national average in all academic categories.

Banking

Banking as such was not really established in Dixie until after the turn of the century. Before that time, most commerce was by barter or through the bishop's tithing office or Woolley, Lund and Judd, merchandisers. In 1906 Edward H. Snow and James Andrus founded the Bank of St. George, capitalized at $12,000. Bennett Bracken and John Hafen were directors and Arthur F. Miles was treasurer. Miles was county clerk at the time, and the bank operated from his desk in the county courthouse. The bankers deposited their capital in Zions Bank in Salt Lake City which was their correspondence bank. When Miles's term at the county commission ended, the Bank of St. George moved to a small adobe building on Tabernacle Street. They moved periodically in the following years. By 1932 David H. Morris had become president (Arthur E. Miles continued as cashier) and the bank's capital and surplus account had reached $100,000, a strong position that helped it cope successfully with the Depression.

By the end of World War II, Clair Terry became the cashier and later board member. In 1955 Bill Barlocker took over the bank. He also obtained control of the bank in Hurricane. Barlocker's style led the bank into overextending itself, and his huge turkey business also suffered reverses. Finally, the Federal Deposit Insurance Corporation intervened and completely reorganized the bank which was then sold to Zions First National Bank in 1970.

In 1922 a competing organization, the Dixie Stockgrowers Bank, opened in St. George. Joe Atkin, A. L. Woodhouse, and Joe Prince started this organization and were aggressive at loaning money. Gordon Whitehead was cashier. When the Depression hit, they found themselves overextended in loans and the bank was liquidated by the state. The Bank of St. George took over the building and operated from there.

Another early financial institution was the St. George Building Society, founded in 1917 and based on the British idea of a mutual-aid society. The society was chartered with the intention of helping people build homes. Edward H. Snow was president, Hugh M. Woodward, vice president, Leo Snow, secretary, and Wilford W. McArthur, treasurer. Woodruff W. Cannon, Guy Hafen, Wallace B. Mathis, and Thomas P. Cottam were directors. Initially the society simply functioned from a desk in the Snow Furniture Store. In 1930 its name was changed to the St. George Savings and Loan. In 1960 Richard Mathis, grandson of Wallace B. Mathis, one of the founders, joined the company and later became its president. Mathis said that when he joined St. George Savings and Loan, it had assets of $1.25 million which had been achieved in its first 40 years; by 1993 the assets were $168 million.[14]

In 1917 Claude Hirschi established the State Bank of Hurricane with his father, David Hirschi, as president. The bank remained independent until 1957 when Bill Barlocker bought it and made it a branch of the Bank of St. George. When Zions Bank bought Barlocker's interests, it became part of Zions Bank.

The financial turmoil at the Bank of St. George was one factor in motivating a group of local citizens to found the Dixie State Bank in 1970 to support the building boom occurring in the county at that time. Bill Hickman served as executive vice-president and cashier. Among the founding directors were Jim Lundberg, J. C. Snow, Dexter Snow, H. R. Miles, Clayton Atkin, Floyd Ence, S. Rex Lewis, and M. Truman Bowler. Leo Reeve of Hurricane was an advisor and later a board member.

Dixie State Bank began humbly in a house trailer but soon moved into the old Snow Furniture Store, remaining there from 1970 until it moved into a handsome new building constructed for it across the street in 1980. Dixie State Bank opened its first branch in Hurricane and in 1987 acquired the assets and liabilities of the Bank of Iron County under a FDIC receivership. The La Verkin office of the Bank of Iron County was closed while the Parowan and Escalante branches remained open as Dixie State Bank branches. In 1993 Dixie State was acquired by First Security Bank.

The establishment of Sun Capital Bank resulted from another local initiative. Dan Schmutz, Ken Metcalf, Doyle Sampson, and Dean Terry founded the bank on a state charter in 1974. Sun Capital Bank quickly developed a loyal clientele, and once Dixie State Bank was sold to First Security, Sun Capital advertised the fact that it was the county's only home-owned bank. The bank supported local projects such as the restoration of the Pioneer Center for the Arts in downtown St. George. In 1995 Dan Schmutz retired as president and John Allen succeeded him.

The Village Bank opened in 1996, terminating Sun Capital Bank's claim to be the only home-owned bank in the county. Douglas Bringhurst became the president with James Grey Larkin as chairman of the board. There have been and are other financial institutions in Dixie. First Interstate Bank operates currently in St. George. Williamsburg Bank existed during the 1980s but closed when its national headquarters had trouble. American Savings and Loan built a handsome building on the Boulevard, but closed in 1990. Recently, the State Bank of Southern Utah, headquartered in Cedar City, opened a branch in the building vacated by American Savings.

Merchandising

Merchandising in Washington County was clustered in the center of the various communities in the county. The arrival of the 1-15 freeway helped alter that concentration. Other influences for change were the increasing use of automobiles which allowed store owners to locate their businesses outside the downtown and attract people by including parking lots, and the arrival of franchises which required the building of new facilities that looked like their counterparts in national chains.

For example, two blocks of stores marked the Hurricane city center until the 1970s. The connecting highway to 1-15 changed the commercial pattern. New stores began fronting a several block strip, and the old stores downtown became vacant and remained so for a decade until they were taken over by Chums, a manufacturing company. Drive-ins, gas stations, and other stores have stretched the Hurricane shopping area westward. That trend is likely to continue because the Gateway project is re-drawing the configuration of the community ever westward toward the freeway.

In contrast, Washington City's core of stores has remained concentrated in the city center on Telegraph Street instead of moving toward the freeway exit. The interstate has taken most of the traffic off that street which is no longer the highway into St. George, but growth of Washington as a St. George suburb has secured business for the few stores which now serve those residents.

Santa Clara's shopping district has nearly disappeared as the freeway has diverted traffic away from old Highway 91. Only one fruit stand and one small grocery store remain from the many which benefited from U.S. 91 traffic. Santa Clara has attempted to prevent businesses or multiple-unit dwellings in the city limits, preferring to remain residential. Santa Clara, like Washington, has become mainly a suburb of St. George. The trucking business that was once the lifeblood of the town has moved to the St. George Industrial Park.

A few stores still remain in Leeds. There is no merchandising in Virgin. Rockville has consciously banned stores, whereas Springdale has become a strip town with tourist-oriented stores multiplying and thriving on the highway to Zion Canyon. This development stems almost wholly from the ever-increasing number of visitors to Zion National Park. Commerce there has not been directly impacted by the arrival of 1-15. Enterprise has always had its own locally-owned stores. The town is far from both St. George or Cedar City, so having services available there is necessary.

Veyo has been the site of a well-known swimming pool, with roller skating and a dance hall that have drawn fun lovers for decades. It has been a spot where drinking often accompanied high-spirited fun.

The town has gas stations, a motel, trailer park, laundry, cafe, stores, another roller rink, and a pizza parlor.

Ivins, until recently, had only a convenience store. The Ivins now emerging is quite a different place. Located in the town of Ivins, the National Institute of Fitness, an internationally-recognized health spa, brings many outsiders each week and a considerable payroll. Development of Tuacahn, a major performance center attracting tourists, will only hasten growth of the town. Ivins also features new housing developments which are changing the tone of the town from one of low-cost housing to elegant neighborhoods. Nearby Kayenta, one mile to the west, also sets a tone of elegance with its strict building regulations that require Santa Fe style architecture, native landscaping, and large lots. There are two dining establishments in Pine Valley and one in Dammeron Valley, but the towns have remained free of other commerce. Home building has mushroomed in both in the 1990s.

Merchandising in downtown St. George has been revolutionized since the 1950s and 1960s. Up to that period, commerce was almost totally concentrated in three downtown blocks. People were comfortable with Snow's, OK, and Mathis grocery markets, while the J. C. Penney, Sprouse Reitz, and Center department stores attracted shoppers. Three drug stores — Fenton's, Bateman's, and Dixie Drug — and three gas stations were found in those three blocks. The Liberty Hotel and its well-patronized cafe was on the Boulevard; Dick's Cafe was just up the street. The Big Hand Cafe and later the Sugar Loaf were nearby. J and J Mill and Lumber Company was north and east, Pickett Lumber was near the courthouse and Pickett Mortuary was on the block to the east of the Liberty Hotel. Across from the Tabernacle was the telephone company, with Snow's Furniture on the opposite side of the street. Other establishments included the Arrowhead Hotel and the St. George Bank.

The Dixie College campus occupied the southeast part of the tabernacle block and much of the block to the east of the Dixie College administration building. Other buildings on the tabernacle block were the Woodward School and the Recreation Hall. College structures included the Science Building, Industrial Arts Building, LDS seminary/institute, and a World War II barracks for lunchroom and other purposes.

Other downtown commercial establishments in the 1950s included Milne Truck Line, the Sun Bowl Club, McArthur Bakery, Wadsworth

Fountain, and Wadsworth Theater (now Dixie Theater), a Firestone store, Bleak's Jewelry, Whitehead's Ice Cream, and the Whiteway. On Tabernacle Street were the Gaiety Theater, Bill Baker's pool hall, the College Cove, and Dixie Drug. Judd's Store, across the street north from the Tabernacle, was serving as a candy and treats store, as it still is. Motels occupied the blocks immediately east and west of the city center on Boulevard. Until the interstate freeway opened in 1973, these captured the tourist business because St. George was the half-way point between Salt Lake City and Los Angeles. Highway 91 routed traffic directly through town.

St. George commerce was concentrated and owned mostly by local families who raised their children to work in the family business and to pass it on to each generation. This pattern has gone through a nearly complete transformation since the 1970s. Some of it has paralleled the coming of the freeway; some of it was changed because national firms came to Dixie. Several local business owners foresaw the changes in the commercial pattern the freeway would bring. They sensed that the center of the city would decline as a commercial location. The changes were unstoppable. The automobile particularly changed people's shopping habits, requiring large parking lots and allowing stores to be spread out over a wider area.

The new freeway exchanges deliver tourists to two specific locations in St. George. In addition there is also one exit at Washington and one to the Hurricane highway. The existing businesses in St. George were not located at those exits. This meant that the property adjacent to the exits became valuable and new businesses, generally national franchises, have taken up that prime land. New motels, fast-food outlets, and gas stations have been built on the east end of St. George Boulevard in the mid-1990s. This happened over a decade earlier at the exit south of town.

As national companies considered opening stores, they chose locations outside the three-block town center. In 1959 Safeway opened a grocery store with a large parking lot; that was a turning point. There was both anxiety and excitement connected with Safeway's arrival. To some it seemed to threaten generations of sacrifice and community building by local merchants. Brent Snow recalls the revolution in the grocery business. The coming of Safeway challenged the concept that grocery stores would be downtown.[15] He consulted with Gibson Discount Stores and visited larger stores throughout the country. Eventually the Snows decided to take a huge leap — they built a 35,000 — square foot store on the eastern edge of town. On opening day, the store did more business than the old store had ever done in a week, even more than in some months. The new methods of merchandising were so attractive and the discounts so appealing that people changed their habits and adopted the supermarket concept.

The building of the first mall, the Commercial Center in 1983, was as big a change as the arrival of the supermarkets. It was a twenty-store facility. Today the visitor who takes either 1-15 exit into St. George is greeted by businesses with names seen in almost any American town: Denny's, Taco Time, Wendy's, McDonalds, Sizzler, Holiday Inn, Shoney's, Hilton Inn, Best Western, Arby's, and so on. The franchising system has come to Washington County. Real estate agencies, travel bureaus, and banks have linked with larger systems. It seems that little of local origin is left; but that is really an illusion. Many of the franchises are leased to local people, and the majority of the 4,500 businesses presently licensed by the City of St. George are not franchises.

Other developments furthered the commercial growth of the county. Mountain Fuel Supply completed a natural gas line to the county in 1990. Its availability helps attract industries to Dixie. The City of St. George solved its occasional power shortages by completing new lines to bring additional electricity purchased from Utah Power and Light and other sources.

Two recent developments have increased competition and the volume of merchandising in St. George. John Price, with support of Bruce Stucki, developed the Red Cliffs Mall. Yet another merchandising undertaking has developed, Zion Factory Stores. Located at the north I-15 exit, this complex of thirty stores attracts tourists from the freeway. The emergence of several small neighborhood shopping plazas is also of interest. Another important facility was a Wal-Mart distribution center built in 1992. Located near the exit to Hurricane, it is said to be the largest one-story building in the state, some twenty-three acres under one roof, employing over 300 people. Scores of semi-trailers arrive each day, bringing dry goods to the huge warehouse and then delivering materials from the distribution center to Wal-Mart stores throughout the West.

Zion Factory Stores, 1996. (Gene Butera)

The National Institute of Fitness in Ivins is a nationally-known health spa that attracts clients from outside the city who come to the "live in" center to improve their health. Located at the mouth of Snow Canyon, the awesome scenery and the spa's isolation help attract patrons. A new group arrives weekly and stays for a few days to a few weeks; people follow a strict diet and an exacting exercise regime. Its founders Marc and Vicki Sorenson recently sold their enterprise to Hyrum Smith of the Franklin Institute but remain as directors. A second elegant spa created by Alan Coombs at Green Valley brings clients to St. George every week. Both advertise across the nation in health and fitness publications.

St. George has promoted the organization of an historic district and a downtown redevelopment agency. These have succeeded in helping the area change from a merchandising emphasis to a financial/professional center. Office complexes have been developed in the downtown area and more are planned. The new Zions Bank at Main and Boulevard is a handsome addition to the city center with an adjacent city-sponsored historic plaza. Ancestor Square, diagonally across from the bank, is an attractive novelty area with five restaurants, three art galleries, several offices and tourist shops.

Historical restoration advocates have urged the city to spend funds emphasizing tourist attractions. The city government organized a downtown historical district that helped many businesses finance the restoration of the historic facades on their buildings. The restoration of the pioneer opera house, adobe house, and adjacent St. George Art Museum also testify to the appeal of historical renovation. Private funds are responsible for the Greene Gate Village — a handsome restoration of seven historic homes and Judd's Store; the Seven Wives Inn; the Olde Penny Farthing Inn; and other bed and breakfast facilities and commercial establishments that use historic buildings. In 1993 the LDS church completed an extensive restoration of the St. George Tabernacle and reopened it to visitors and civic events. All of these elements have combined to bring renewed life to historic downtown.

Art

Art has become an increasingly important dimension of cultural life in the county. Artists have congregated in Kayenta, Ivins, Santa Clara, and as far east as Apple Valley on the road to Colorado City. Since 1979 St. George has sponsored an annual art festival on Easter weekend which draws 150 artists who sell their creations to the throngs of tourists who come south for the weekend. Dixie College sponsors the Dixie Invitational Art Show that brings paintings of fifty to seventy-five well-known artists to the community for a month beginning on Presidents Day in February.

Among the widely exhibited artists who currently live in the county are Greg Abbott, Jerry Anderson, Lynn Berryhill, Floyd Breinholt, Farrell Collett, Milton Goldstein, Jim Jones, Roland Lee, Gaell Lindstrom, Del Parson, David Pettit, Frank Riggs, Maynard Sorenson, L'Deane Trueblood, Lyman Whittaker, and Erla Young. Robert Shepherd, who died in 1993, was a guiding inspiration to the art community for nearly twenty years. Several commercial galleries have been opened, three in St. George's Ancestor Square, one at Silver Reef, another at Leeds, two more in St. George, two in Springdale. The Artists' Coop Gallery in Ancestor Square is an association of twenty-four local artists.

Dixie College faculty members have influenced art in the county. S. Ralph Huntsman, who died in 1995 at age 99, was a pioneer in this endeavor. He was a regionalist, bucking the tide of impressionism dominant in his day. Beginning in the 1930s, he proclaimed the beauty of the desert his theme for sixty years. He helped people in Dixie look at the desert with new appreciation, to see it not as oppressive but exotic. Huntsman began an annual invitational art exhibit. Gerald Olson, Roger Adams, Ross Johnson, Gene Karl Riggs, Roland Lee, and Max Bunnell have each taught at the college. Glen Blakley, Dennis Martinez, and Del Parson are the current faculty. The public schools are also promoters of the creative process. Viola Cornwall was an art teacher who had great influence on young people in the public schools.

In 1989 the City of St. George converted some space in the basement of city hall into a small but nicely appointed art museum. The museum staff began a series of presentations of Utah artists and theme shows. One of the promoters of the new art scene has been the St. George Magazine. Issues feature artists, galleries, and art shows. Construction of a permanent city art museum is underway at the Pioneer Center for the Arts in downtown St. George. The building is slated to be finished in 1996 as part of the statehood centennial.

Reflections about Living in Dixie Today

As citizens in Washington County celebrate the Utah statehood centennial, they can look back on the county's history with considerable appreciation. The first century of white settlement in Dixie saw people working the land for a sparse yield but spurred on by frugality and commitment to a common mission. Isolated from the American mainstream and to a degree from the rest of the state, they possessed a sense of mission.

The transformation into a recreation destination, a commercial crossroads, and a highly desired southwestern retirement center has occurred in the last four decades. It is a story of moving from isolation to destination. Since the 1960s the number of retirees moving into Washington County has outpaced that in the rest of the state two-fold.[16] Others live in Dixie because they always have, but they are not likely to be sustained by agriculture as were their ancestors. They most likely have sold land at a profit for residential uses and found a way to turn that money into a business or other means of sustenance. Many also keep a hand in either farming or ranching but make sure their offspring go to college and qualify for some other profession.

Other people work in the service sector, supporting tourism and retirement — restaurants, motels, commercial stores — and creatively try to make modest salaries support a family. Still others teach school or college; education is clearly the largest single undertaking in the county and the largest payroll. Often those families hold two service sector jobs. A favored few work in professions or in industrial parks, construction, high-tech, transportation, or Federal and state government positions which provide salaries comparable to the Wasatch Front.[17]

The employment services, despite many low salaries, are crowded with job applicants. Unemployment is lower in the county than in the rest of the state, which is lower than the nation. Professional positions in the county usually draw scores of applicants, an indication that many people prefer living in the Dixie environment at a lower income to seeking opportunities elsewhere. Some of these people have roots in Dixie, have taken advanced education outside the state, and have returned. Others come with no ties to the area but have a desire to live in the American southwest. They have read of St. George in one of many magazine articles that have rated it among the top retirement places in the nation or have heard of Dixie from friends who have been there. More likely they have visited the area for a convention or for recreation and decided to seek residence there.

Because so many visitors come to Dixie, people who live in Washington County sometimes feel they are running a "bed and breakfast." Visiting was a favorite pioneer pastime; it is still a high priority today. Relatives and friends come to Dixie for business or pleasure. Hosting guests is a regular part of the Dixie lifestyle. Most visitors, however, come to Dixie for more than a casual stay. St. George, particularly, has become a significant convention site. The Dixie Center hosts up to 4,000 people at a time. More modest meetings bring other groups. Community celebrations bring visitors in large numbers, often crowding motel space. The annual St. George Marathon in October now brings over 3,000 runners and their families. The World Senior Games, also in October, attract even more. The Dixie Roundup (rodeo) is a popular event for several days in September. The Dixie Art Festival comes on Easter weekend, while three other art exhibits throughout the year also draw large crowds. Easter weekend attracts thousands of high school students who come for spring break. The Rotary Bowl, a national invitational football bowl for community college teams, draws crowds and press attention the first week in December. Softball tournaments draw as many as seventy-two teams for weekend competition in winter and summer.

The restored Pioneer Opera House, 1996. (Gene Butera)

The Dixie Center hosts the Celebrity Concert Series, Southwest Symphony, and major concerts. The Burns Arena at the Dixie Center has various sporting events. The 125 events in 1993 ranged from the elegant Jubilee of Trees to the Air Force Band. All of this is in addition to a full schedule of Dixie College athletics, music instruction, swimming classes, fitness, dance courses, and student activities.

The Washington County School District, St. George Leisure Services Department, and Dixie College publish a combined calendar and support a joint promotion of continuing education. This includes a series of team competitions, craft courses, language instruction, and courses for retirees.

Volunteerism and Philanthropy

Volunteerism thrives in Washington County. Perhaps because of the many retired people settling in the region or because of the community ethic that has always emphasized cooperation and mutual support, many Dixie residents are engaged in volunteer service. This includes visiting patients in nursing homes, teaching preschoolers, serving in scouting programs, being docents at art shows, picking up litter on the highways, being a volunteer firefighter, functioning on one of the community boards — library, hospital, zoning, town council, historic preservation, historical society — working with illness support groups, or serving in the Dixie Regional Medical Center Auxiliary, among others.

Another measure of community vigor is the vitality of service clubs in the county. Chambers of commerce are active in St. George, Hurricane Valley, Enterprise, Washington, and Zion Canyon (including Springdale and Rockville). The Lions Club is active in both St. George and Washington. The Elks, American Legion, Veterans of Foreign Wars, Rotary, Kiwanis, and Exchange Clubs in St. George join with them in undertaking projects such as raising scholarship funds, supporting international students, helping the disadvantaged, and promoting parks and events.

Donating to public causes is also a vital dimension of Dixie life, as it has been since pioneer times. A recent major project includes the Dixie Center. Citizens were solicited to buy seats in the Burns Arena and the Cox Auditorium to make furnishing those facilities possible. Citizens were also asked to buy seats in the Hansen Stadium on the Dixie College campus.

ENDNOTES

1. Donald F. Kraak, "Dentists and Dirt in Early Dixie," *Senior Sampler IV* (7 August 1992), 1.

2. Carol Watkins to author, 11 December 1994.

3. Kelly Larson and Kerry Larson, "History of the St. George Police Department," 1981, Dixie College Archives.

4. Clair Terry, 14 December 1994, Dixie College Archives.

5. Juanita Brooks, ed., *Uncle Will Tells His Own Story* (Salt Lake City: Taggart & Co., 1970), 32.

6. Ibid., Chapter 15.

7. Evan Whitehead and Ken Campbell, interview 24 October 1994.

8. Jon Pollei, "Annual Report of the St. George City Police, 1993," Dixie College Archives.

9. Ibid.

10. Ted Shumway, interview. See also *Washington County News*, 13 March 1980.

11. Juanita Brooks, *The Mountain Meadows Massacre* (Palo Alto: Stanford University Press, 1950). See also *John D. Lee: Pioneer Builder, Zealot, Scapegoat* (Glendale, CA: The Arthur Clark Company, 1962).

12. Robert Hafen Moss, "An Historical Study of the Factors Influencing the Organization of Education in Washington County, 1852-1915." Master's thesis, Brigham Young University, 1961, 183. See also T. Lavoy Esplin, interview 18 February 1994, Dixie College Archives.

13. "Your Washington County Schools Today," *Spectrum*, 28 May 1995, supplement.

14. Richard Mathis, interview, 28 November 1994, Dixie College Archives.

15. Brent Snow, interview, 6 January 1995, Dixie College Archives.

16. James A. Wood, "The Changing Demographic and Economic Structure of Washington County, Utah 1970—1993," *Utah Economic and Business Review 54* (1).

17. Ibid.

18. Boyd L. Fjelsted, "Personal Incomes in Utah Counties, 1992," *Utah Economic and Business Review* (September 1994): 13. Per capita income in Washington County in 1992 was $12,660 compared to Weber County at $16,616, Utah County, $13,052, Salt Lake County, $17,408, Cache County, $13,610, and Iron County, $12,154.

In Washington County, total personal income was $700,516,000 in 1992; farm income was $2,051,000; agricultural services were $4,191,000; mining was $4,752,000; construction was $46,624,000; manufacturing was $33,872,000; transportation and public utilities were $25,372,000; wholesale trade was $17,766,000; retail trade was $70,433,000; finance, insurance and real estate were $24,832,000; services were $127,471,000; Federal government was $9,833,000; military was $2,696,000; and state and local government were $53,199,000.

12

THE DEBATE OVER
THE FUTURE OF
WASHINGTON COUNTY

The Growth Issue

For the first half of the twentieth century Washington County could be said to need population growth. However, by 1970 the flow of newcomers was substantial, and by 1990 the growth rate became a concern. The question of how many people the area can sustain has stimulated intense political debate. The ecological, economic, and aesthetic dimensions of the question were sufficient to entice many into the discussion. The subject is one of pressing political interest. The economic vitality of the region has become dependent on the growth that draws business, particularly construction, to the area. Many enterprises have come to depend on a steady influx of people and resources.

In 1994 an advocacy group — Citizens for Moderate Growth (CMG) — was organized by Alison Bowcutt, Robert Owens, Frank Fair, and Nephi Evenson. It petitioned the St. George City Council to set a three-percent growth limit and gradually reduce building permits from 1,100 that year to approximately 300 annually. The lifestyle they so highly prize will be destroyed, the group reasons, if communities are allowed to continue growing so rapidly. Failing to get satisfaction from the city council, the CMG circulated initiative petitions and succeeded in getting the issue placed on the ballot for the 1995 general election. The election engendered wide debate including a series of position papers from both sides running nightly in the *Spectrum* for a week, extensive door-to-door campaigning, voter surveys, advertisements and candidate meetings. The growth-limitation proposition was rejected by 63 percent of the voters.[1]

The heated controversy leading up to the election illustrated that controlling future growth will undoubtedly be a lively issue for the next decade. An overview of this matter, published in the *St. George Magazine,* explored some of the issues. It began by providing basic data:

> As late as 1970, Washington County had just under 14,000 people. St. George accounted for half of that. Washington City had 750 and Santa Clara had 271. Hurricane had a substantial 1,408....By 1980 the county population was 26,065 which then rose to 48,560 in 1990. It is estimated that in 1994, St. George had a population of about 33,000 with the county reaching 61,657. Official state forecasts project 46,444 people in St. George by the year 2000, 68,176 in 2010 and 84,986 in 2020. The Utah Office of Planning and Budget forecasts that Washington County will have 81,845 people in the year 2000, 118,934 in 2010 and 150,034 in 2020.[2]

The increase in tourism also reveals a concern about growth putting additional pressure on the resources of the county. In 1970, 903,340 visitors entered Zion National Park. In 1980, 1,233,686 came. In 1990 there were 2,342,614; by 1993 the figure reached 2,873,300, a 250-percent increase in two decades. The increase of visitors has park managers considering a limitation on the number of tourists or the number of automobiles admitted, or both.

The Washington County Travel and Convention Bureau reported that in 1983 the county had 1,382 motel rooms; by 1993 the number had risen to 2,758, again more than double. In 1996 the number exceeded 3,000. The bureau also reported that transient room taxes collected in 1972 amounted to $23,737; in 1994 the total was $818,664.

The *St. George Magazine* article listed nine arguments for and against continued growth. The first argument suggests that growth provides advantageous "economies of scale" that bring opportunities for the community. Better libraries, new commercial centers, expanded housing developments, an enlarged college, improved entertainment, new ballparks and golf courses, a fine civic center and convention facilities, improved roads and inter-city highways, an updated sewer system, many new schools, an expanded airport and an airline, a symphony orchestra, classical and popular concerts by nationally known performers, and many other projects have resulted at lower costs per person because of growth.

A second pro-growth argument is that people who are finding new homes in Dixie bring benefits. Many come with years of professional experience which they offer, often on a volunteer basis. They are not a burden to schools or police. They bring their income with them and either buy a home or build one. Young married newcomers often work in the service sector and provide a strong work force as well as a vital group of children.

Third, young people come to Dixie to work in the construction, tourist, or service industries. This is a reversal of the lack of employment opportunity that dominated the past.

A fourth benefit of growth occurs in the improved health care sector. In the last three decades Dixie's growth has justified building a regional medical center and several allied health facilities.

Business expansion is a fifth result of growth. The creation of three malls and several neighborhood shopping centers, two industrial parks, and the Wal-Mart Distribution Center in Hurricane are examples of the favorable business climate in the county.

Sixth is the diversity of people who come to Dixie. People of varied religions, professions, and age groups can find a welcome atmosphere. A Spanish-speaking minority is growing, attracted by construction and service jobs. Public schools are having to meet the needs of Latinos and Native Americans, mostly Navajos, who do not speak English.

A seventh reason to allow continued growth is that people want to come to Dixie. It is an enjoyable place to live. Some growth comes from offspring of current residents who choose to stay.

Market demands are an eighth reason. Many believe that the market is the best regulator, and it has brought growth to Washington County since Dixie became a destination. If we meddle with the market, growth proponents argue, we will likely cause unanticipated chain reactions that are undesirable. The market also says growth comes in cycles. Such cycles will occur without artificial regulation.

Finally, the ninth point is that consideration should be given to "momentum." Dixie definitely has momentum, but if the people of Washington County send a message that is unwelcoming to new-comers, or opposed to new business, then people will look elsewhere — perhaps Kanab, Mesquite, or Las Vegas — for a future home. Mo-mentum is fragile; once gone it is difficult to regain. Casting it aside could have unexpected or unwanted consequences.

Nine arguments were offered in opposition to unbridled growth. The first is that growth is consuming resources at an alarming rate. Dixie is fast becoming a luxury community where consumption of resources is high. Life in Dixie should be developed in the context of a desert, where such consumption is resisted.

The impact of high-consumption living on the fragile desert land-scape is a second concern of those who would limit growth. Automo-bile exhaust pollutes clear desert air and mars scenic beauty. Housing developments scar the landscape. Unsightly excavation on the black hill west of St. George's business district is an example. New housing units can also damage plant and animal life. Seven species of animal life in the county are officially listed as endangered and more are be-ing considered. One result of this is that some 60,000 acres above St. George and extending into Washington and Hurricane have been des-ignated as a tortoise habitat preserve.

A third argument: bigness is a problem in itself. Growth creates situations that police, social workers, courts, and political leaders can't keep up with. Greater dependence on welfare, increasing family dis-integration, higher rates of child abuse, homelessness, and crime can overwhelm officials and upset community balance.

Access to water is another element central to the growth-limita-tion arguments. Water is a limited resource, particularly in Washing-ton County. People in the county use 374 gallons of water per day in contrast to a state average of 284. Water diverted to an urban center must be taken from somewhere else; it can't be manufactured.

A fifth argument maintains that future generations deserve a vote in this debate. Will scenery still be pristine for them? Will air still be as clean as it is today or will resources have been used up and replaced with sprawling waste, polluted water, and urban blight? Should the present generation not be stewards of the land as Brigham Young taught? Should this generation preserve it for the unborn?

A sixth consideration involves transportation and traffic. All areas are of concern, but downtown St. George is especially worrisome. How will these already congested streets handle even more cars as growth continues?

A seventh issue is that conservation is an ethic which requires an extraordinary amount of community wide agreement and investment. Few seem to be addressing conservation. Why not look to water-conservation techniques? Couldn't we reduce the number of cars per person? How about using desert landscaping instead of lawns? Could we limit the use of wood-burning stoves? Shouldn't we establish pricing incentives for people to conserve water and electricity and recycle their waste? Are these not the rational things to do in a desert?

The eighth issue is the disappearance of farming land and open space as many farms are turned into subdivisions. Should the Washington Fields, for example, really become residential housing?

Finally, some ask this question: will we lose our sense of community and neighborly relationships as urbanism arrives? Will we be forced always to lock our doors? Will we no longer know people who live nearby?

These nine points on each side of the growth question illustrate how complex the problems are that growth already has brought to Dixie.

Three recent studies provide examples of planning efforts to address the growth. The first considered the physical limitations of expansion (e.g., hillsides, floodplains, differing altitudes, and undeveloped acreage). One focused on available land. It presented three scenarios — low growth, moderate growth, and high growth. Scenario one forecasted a population of 140,435; scenario two estimated 323,078, and scenario three predicted that 690,665 people could fill the county if the land were utilized as that scenario suggested. The report neither predicted nor advocated any of these options. Rather, the study examined land availability and population distribution under differing land utilization and development proposals. The report generalized, "the availability of unconstrained land resources should not be a limiting factor to human population growth in Washington County until well into the next century if ever."[3]

A second study focused on the availability of water instead of land. It saw much more constraint on growth, saying: "This means by the year 2040 the population of Washington County would increase to about 261,000 and the basin population would increase to about 275,000."[4]

A third recent study led to the adoption of St. George's long-range plan prepared in 1994 with the assistance of Winston Associates of Boulder, Colorado, and input from several community hearings. The St. George general plan provides a vision for the city's future. It foresees a community with an uncrowded feeling, plenty of shade trees, protected hillsides, neighborhood parks, and an efficient transportation system. The plan calls for ties to pioneer heritage, low crime rates, a diverse tax base, and well-managed growth. Good shopping, recreation opportunities, health care, entertainment resources, and stable government are valued in this plan. The plan's vision seems ambitious, but the existing community has already made some positive beginnings in each of the categories.[5]

What Will the Future Bring?

Though some people may be nostalgic about small village life without traffic congestion, that life has long disappeared in most of Washington County. Not all people are thriving, but many, if not most, benefit from the high employment rate in the county. Job creation is notably high. County retail sales increased from $132.5 million in 1980 to $528.8 million in 1992. In 1992 tourists spent $22 million for lodging, from which $650,000 was collected in transient room taxes. The airport has expanded and increased enplanements from 11,115 in 1987 to 18,750 in 1993, with another 18,000 passengers passing through. The Utah Department of Transportation spent $50 million on highways in the county during the last seven years. Personal income has risen steadily as have population, construction, tourist visitation, and almost any indicator used to measure the economy of the county.[6]

To anticipate the future of Washington County, one can reasonably surmise that the "graying of America" will continue, even accelerate. Retirement-related business must be closely examined since it likely will become Washington County's most important economic factor.

Washington County's desirable weather most likely will continue to draw retirees, tourists, families, and college students. Dixie's sunshine is an unlimited resource. Though it burdened pioneers, it is a boon to-day. Also, the desert scenery of Washington County will continue to be a major magnet. Many people of all ages, tourists and local residents alike, are attracted to the red sand and the sandstone mesas.

Though retirement is increasingly an economic and cultural influence, tourism is the industry which ended Dixie's isolation and transformed its economy. Tourism still receives much of the community's promotional and economic efforts. A central issue in the county's future is protection of its world-class landscape. This will be the most serious concern of the next fifty years. It will be central to most political conflicts and decisions.

The "Mormon factor" has been and will continue to be a significant influence. Dixie is often the retirement choice for many Mormons living in Utah, Idaho, and Wyoming. This group chooses Dixie because it is more culturally compatible to them. Some younger people are attracted to Dixie for the same reasons. Interestingly, people of other convictions find life in Dixie desirable despite (or maybe because of) the Mormon majority. Clearly the number of non-Mormons will increase as in Utah's other urban areas. Nonetheless, numbers of LDS people will also increase in the county as Mormons move to Dixie. The percentage of LDS people in the county remains high, 79.5 percent in 1992.[7]

Dixie has an appealing formula — sunshine, scenery, golf and other recreation, cultural amenities, moderate size, relatively clean air, and a peaceful, stable atmosphere that appeals to large numbers of tourists, retirees, and families. The big question facing Washington County is whether the appealing formula can be sustained as growth continues. How it is to be answered will certainly be the subject of heated debate in the near future as Washington County prepares to enter the twenty-first century.

Because the Federal government owns the largest portion of the county's 1.5 million acres, Federal regulations could modify growth expectations. About 40 percent of the land is under the jurisdiction of the Bureau of Land Management. Some is controlled by the U.S. Forest Service, some by the Bureau of Indian Affairs, and some by the National Park Service. In addition, the State of Utah owns major sections of school-trust lands. Only 18 percent of county land is owned privately.

Federal legislation and agency regulations directly impact Washington County resources. The Taylor Grazing Act of 1934 cut grazing permits for sheep and cattle herds in the county as much as two-thirds. The Endangered Species Act (ESA) provides a more recent example of Federal regulatory impact. St. George City abandoned plans to develop on the red hill, north of the Sugar Loaf, as a result of ESA regulations. A golf course planned for the area was not developed. One motive of the city and county was to reach a settlement so other areas could be developed. Such negotiations appear to be a significant part of the political reality for the future.

Environmental advocacy groups such as the Southern Utah Wilderness Alliance have impacted policies of government agencies and have also become increasingly vocal among citizens in the county who are sympathetic to the environmental movement. Two groups of other local people have become active in the county — the Grand Canyon Trust and the Virgin River Land Preservation Association. These two are less confrontational, more into promoting dialogue and purchasing scenic lands and wetlands for preservation. Linkages are developing between these liberal advocates of environmental protection and conservative anti-growth advocates who worry about crime and growth and traffic. An alliance of these groups could influence policies that would limit growth.

Another critical future issue will be Virgin River water distribution. Since this tributary of the Colorado River was not included in the Colorado River Compact, its flow is still mostly negotiable. Utah's Virgin River communities currently are not fully utilizing the river's winter flow. The towns hope to meet expected water demands by diverting future winter flows by means of additional reclamation projects. Las Vegas, on the other hand, has immediate need for more water. Were Nevada able to arrange the redistribution of the Virgin River water because of its political clout, Washington County could be in serious difficulty. The Dixie communities have historical claim to the river's water and they have clear expectations of growth. Nonetheless, the river's distribution is a problem.

So what can one conclude about Washington County, its past, present, and future? Certainly standing at this state centennial point allows many people more confidence than looking at the area through Paiute eyes between 1800 and 1850 or through European immigrant eyes between 1850 and 1900. Even as late as 1950, life for most county residents was marginal. The advent of air conditioning, tourism, retirement, freeways, airlines, and consumerism have wrought dramatic changes in the county.

The graves of those earlier people, both Native Americans and European immigrants, were dug in parched soil following lives that knew no luxury. The awesome beauty of the landscape was the same then as now; the views of Zion Canyon from atop Kolob have not changed. However, the meaning of human lives before 1950 was attached more to people's values than to their possessions. Since then human life in Dixie has been somewhat recast. It is ironic that, in contrast to the past austerity, living in Washington County for many people has become so desirable that the most urgent current issue is limiting the influx of people who are drawn to that lifestyle. If the graves of the pioneers could speak, they would likely warn about luxury, about overburdening the land, about being diverted from values. It is to be hoped that Washington County is one of those places where history and landscape and values will provide the best guide for the future.

ENDNOTES

1.   *Spectrum*, 8 November 1995, 1.

2.   Douglas D. Alder, "The Growth/Limited Growth Debate," *St. George Magazine* (July-August 1994): 14-23.

3.   Keith J. Maas and Ken D. Teis, "Population Buildout Study, Washington County Utah," (Logan, Utah: GEO/Graphics, 1994). This study was commissioned by the Washington County Conservancy District.

4.   *Utah State Water Plan, Kanab Creek/Virgin River Basin*, (Salt Lake City: Utah Board of Water Resources, August 1993).

5.   "City of St. George General Plan," draft, Department of Community Development, 27 September 1994, 6.

6.   James A. Wood, "The Changing Demographic and Economic Structure of Washington County, Utah 1970-1993," *Utah Economic and Business Review 54* (January-February 1994).

7.   *Historical Atlas of Mormonism*, ed. S. Kent Brown et al. (New York: Simon & Schuster, 1994), 149.

13

GROWTH EXPECTATIONS FULFILLED
1996-2006

The decade from the Utah statehood centennial in 1996 to 2006 in Washington County has been dominated by the word "growth" — growth in population, in job creation, in home building, in school enrollments, in industrial development, in water projects, in medical care facilities, in cultural offerings, in virtually everything including concerns about growth. In 2005, for example, St. George was listed by the U.S. Census as the second fastest growing community in the United States. And then it became number one in 2007.[1]

Why this growth? Why now? What are the consequences?

Many communities in the state and nation would gladly trade places with Utah's Dixie. Does the credit (or blame) for this growth go to officials and residents of Washington County or was it outside forces that brought about this expansion? If the latter, is this a bubble that will burst? If not, is continued growth likely and how can it be supported or controlled?

In 1996 the county's population was 77,500. By the time this book's second edition appeared in 2007, estimates were that more than 145,000 people would be living in Washington County. This is an acceleration of a trend that began in 1965 when the population was 10,400. From that date forward there has never been a year without a population increase. Sometimes it was only 2% but in the years 1985-6 it rose to 10%. That meant a few hundred new people per year but by the 1990s and beyond there was a steady growth of 6% or more, resulting in more than a thousand per year. Since the year 2000 more than 5,000 a year have arrived and by 2005 it was 10,000.[2]

Population Influx

How did this come about? The same sunshine and the same arid climate controlled this area in 1965 as in 2007. What changed?

Shortly after World War II ended in 1945 a dynamic group of the new generation in Dixie talked of transforming the economy of the county — from concentrating on self-sustaining agriculture to making Dixie a destination site. They envisioned a location for golfers, for tourists, for second homeowners, for industries, for conventions. This was their vision. Gradually their efforts and such national breakthroughs as air conditioning and the interstate highway system laid the groundwork for today's economy with industrial parks, an airport and airline, golf courses, condominium complexes, parks and trails, motels and restaurants, movie theaters, convention centers — amenities to sunshine. Dixie became desirable year-round. Their formula has worked even though some did not live to see it and they did not have the capital then to bring it about.

What has motivated people to come to Dixie? Was it the efforts of entrepreneurs or were other forces working upon Dixie? Obviously it is a mix. The five national parks and five national monuments within four hour's drive continue to draw people. Two-and-a-half million visitors come to Zion National Park each year, more to Grand Canyon National Park. This introduces many people to the idea of living in the U.S. Southwest. Some people decide to escape the urbanism in Los Angeles or Phoenix or Las Vegas and consider a smaller place in the Southwest.

The biggest factor is likely retirement and the services it attracts, retirement of people all over the United States who consider relocating to a warm climate in the winter and one air conditioned in the summer. In 1945 the concept of retirement was hardly known. By 1996 the financing framework was firmly in place nationally and most people planned on retirement. Thus one component of the in-migration was retirees headed to Washington County, seeking warm weather, dry climate, great scenery, compatible community.

Interestingly only 17% of Washington County's permanent residents are over age 65 (compared to 9% statewide). Estimates indicate that retirees are slightly more than that percentage. Another contingent of retirees visit about three months in the winter. St. George is not mainly retirees like Sun City, Arizona but the retirement cohort is a vital economic force. They drive the construction industry, retail merchandising, restaurants, theaters, concerts, parks and particularly the health care industry. This in turn employs service sector people, school teachers and medical professionals. The result is a healthy mix of age groups, children (31 % of the county are under age 19), parenting adults and retirees.3

Industry

Retirement obviously is only one element in the growth. Industry is another. The Wal-Mart Distribution Center and its neighbors (Orgill Inc., Pace American Inc., Pepsi, SAST and DATS Trucking) in the Gateway Industrial Park, near the 1-15 turn off to Hurricane, are a new draw, as is the Fort Pierce Industrial Park complex south of Bloomington Hills where the Blue Bunny ice cream factory is located. Also in that area are Bomatics (plastics), Sunroc (concrete), The Spectrum (printing), Les Olson Company, and many others, totaling 54 firms.

Deseret Laboratories, in that park, is just one of the examples of a new horizon for the county. In 1983 Scott Gubler and his colleagues renewed a claim to gypsum deposits near the Arizona border. They knew of the possibility of using gypsum for nutrition. Since then they have conducted advanced research and found ways to utilize it in calcium carbonate and other nutraceuticals. Since 1996 their research in high tech biology has moved on to many pharmaceutical options and branched into research in other countries. They currently employ 230 people, with future expansion expected. This is an example of linking with scientific and technological research that holds great promise in the county.

These two new industrial parks have added investment and employment opportunities to the county, doubling the options that the

Dixie Development Corporation and St. George City had initiated in two earlier parks, the first located on what later came to be called Industrial Road west of Middleton in 1961, hosting the Rocky Mountain Company and Kellwood corporation and others. The second in 1983 was called the Millcreek Industrial Park near Pine View High School where Ram Company, Andrus Trucking, Quality Park Products, American Linen, as well as truss and cabinet and printing companies are located (see chapter 10).

Another economic development in the county during this decade has been the increase of high technology firms. Some like Strata, LearnKey, Ramco and Infowest began before 1996. Newer ones include Steton Corporation, Facilities Maintenance Engineering, Stonefly Technology, Online Web Marketing, Internet Effects, Interlinx, Unsanity LLC, ClearVision-Southernutah.com, Schooltree, AreaTravelinc, SyncZ, Moki Systems, KimballJones.com, Dixie Direct-241Dining, Eclipse, Lasko Media, Nutel, SkyView, The Studio, Spiral Studios, Proseedure Productions, Canyon Media, West Rim Digital Arts, Strategic Media, and Xpea Corporation. These firms are involved in many phases of high technology from travel reservations to software production to data tracking to web development and more. Some have been spin offs from Dixie College. Others are the brainchild of young entrepreneurs. All of them suggest that high technology will be an increasing element of the county's economy.[4]

High technology is a driving force throughout the nation and is likewise in Washington County. One of the earliest firms was Infowest, now titled Infowest Global Internet Services. Its story is somewhat legendary. Kelly Nyberg and Randy Cosby were students of Eric Pedersen at Dixie College and participated with him in the college's Center for Excellence. One of their projects was to link all the buildings and offices of the campus. While they were pulling those wires they dreamt up creating their own firm to do the same throughout the local area. They did so, establishing the first internet service in the county in 1994. They later expanded the service to Iron County. Since that beginning, their company has grown to be the major internet provider. Their inexperience was offset by establishing a board of seasoned leaders including Eric Pedersen, John Clemons (LearnKey), David Grant (Metalcraft Technologies in Cedar City), Gary Koeven, later dean of Information Services at Dixie

State College, and Aaron Gifford. They now have 23 employees and provide services to 9,000 homes and businesses.

In 1993 Qwest, Utah's provider of electricity, built a fiberoptic cable linking the state from Logan to St. George. This major development guaranteed that technology in Washington County could link into advanced computer technology from all over the world. Several firms agreed to locate in the county because of that availability. That seemed to be a great foundation for the future but three times in the last decade that cable has been accidentally cut by backhoes on construction projects, one near Provo and two near Richfield. That interrupted service for a full day and was a serious setback for several firms which lost their ability to serve their customers all over the nation.

The need to end such dangers to high tech firms in Washington County motivated Gene Morris, Chris Chandler, Kay Traveller and Lowry Snow to create a redundant alternative for fiberoptic service. They created a new firm called Interlinx and worked with Williams Communications to bring a branch line from their Portland-to-Los Angeles cable. They established a link via Lund, Nevada through Gunlock and the Shivwits Indian Reservation to St. George.

In May 2005 Utah Interlinx president Gene Morris announced that a redundant fiber line was nearing completion. It is an above ground fiberoptic link to Washington County, entering through Ivins and then into the Main Street Plaza at Tabernacle Street and Main Street and terminating at the new Tonaquint Center Hi-Tech Business Park. It provides voice, data and video services to government, health care, businesses and homes throughout the St. George metro area and insures that fiberoptic service will survive any further interruptions. The new Tonaquint Hi-tech Center on Dixie Drive and 1600 South (across from Tonaquint Park) has been developed by Kay Traveller and his colleagues to host high technology firms as well as government and businesses. It is one more evidence that the county is friendly to economic development. Even existing servers such as Infowest use this line as a redundant service.

Employment

The Washington County Demographic and Economic Profile prepared by the Utah Department of Workforce Services (August 2005) provides some data to explain the economy of the county. It begins by noting that since 1980 the number of jobs in Washington County has grown by more than 500 percent. That can only be understood by considering the enormous population increase since then. Nonetheless, economic growth in the county has been ahead of the state for several years and job creation is hot. In 2004 there was an increase of 3,700 jobs, a 10 percent increase. The job growth came heavily in construction. Next was in education and health and social services followed by manufacturing, trade/transportation/utilities, professional/business services and then leisure/hospitality, each generating between 300 and 500 new jobs. This healthy employment is reflected in retail sales which outstrip the general population and growth rates.

The report points out that the unemployment rate in the county is 3.8%, well below both the state and national rate. As appealing as that seems, the report also announces the well-known fact that the pay scale is lower in Washington County than in the nation or even the state, being 77 % of the state average. Probable reasons for that lower figure include the considerable number of people working in lower paying jobs such as tourism and retail. There is a large college-age workforce, many of whom work part-time. Nonetheless salaries for people such as teachers are dramatically lower than nearby Nevada. So the median family income is below the state and national average, being $41,845 in contrast to the state average of $51,022 and the national average of $50,046. About 50% of eligible females in the county are employed.[5]

Education

Linked to all this growth is Dixie State College. Fall enrollment for 2006 was 5,967 (3,982 FTE).[6] A branch campus in Hurricane was serving 331 students (92 FTE) and property was being sought for an eventual branch in the Ivins area. Courses were also being taught in Kanab. Several four-year degrees had been added to the curriculum, including computer and information systems, business, elementary education, medical radiography, nursing, communication and new media, English, biology, and dental hygiene. More are in the planning stage. These baccalaureate degrees led to a change of the college's name in December 1999 to indicate the four-year status from Dixie College to Dixie State College of Utah. They also caused the college athletic program to move from the NJCAA to NCAA Division II in 2006, opening a whole new era and changing the traditional opponents; even the mascot changed from Rodney Rebel to Red Hawk.

Campus expansion was a necessity to accommodate the growing enrollment. Early in the decade the college acquired the convention meeting room portion of the Dixie Center before its move to a new facility near the 1-15 exit 6. That enabled the college to change the name to the Avenna Center and install an up-to-date computer facility in the Smith's Building. A new Eccles Fine Arts Center was opened in 2004 and in 2005 a nursing building was authorized on the new IHC campus at River Road. Other expansions included acquiring and modifying two buildings north of the campus, the former LDS Institute and Harmon's Shopping Center. The first became the North Instructional Building to house the mathematics classes and other programs. The second became the North Plaza and includes the Art Department and the home for the Dixie Applied Technology College (DXATC), the Washington County branch of the new state-wide technical college. An addition to the Kenneth Gardner Student Center provided a needed new kitchen and food court.

Parking lots were expanded to accommodate the increasing enrollment. Fire lanes and handicapped access was improved all around campus. Remodeling also improved the College Inn, the downtown center for the successful Elderhostel Program. One of the most noticed improvements was a handsome railing with landscaping placed on 100 South from 700 East to 1000 East. This was to accommodate St. George City's change of First South into a four-lane road. The college had to prevent students from walking across that street except at designated pedestrian zones. They did it creatively with the well-designed landscaping which is also a pleasant view to the drivers on that heavy traffic road. The same landscaping design was extended south on 700 East and on 1000 East.

The Washington County School District faced major challenges to accommodate the new public school student enrollment. There were 17,915 students in 24 schools in 1996. Kolene Granger was the new superintendent who inherited a thorny issue. The district had adopted a year-round calendar to conserve on fuel and construction costs. After several years of its implementation, parents were convinced they did not like the system. They found it most frustrating to have their children spread in three levels of schools, elementary, middle and high school, which were on different calendars. Employed parents found it difficult to adjust their work schedules to the children's unusual hours. Families could never find a time when they could be together to travel, among other disadvantages. The school board responded to citizen urging and set a date to terminate the year-round schedule. That necessitated building four more elementary schools between 1995 and 1997: Bloomington Hills, Three Falls, Diamond Valley and Coral Cliffs. The next project was to replace the old Enterprise Elementary, which was done in 1996.

Natural growth by the year 2000 had led to an enrollment of 18,323 students. Planning and construction continued so that Red Mountain Elementary was completed in 1998, then Sandstone Elementary in 2000 and Desert Hills Intermediate the same year. In 2001 the alternative Millcreek High School moved from its temporary location in the old school in the center of Washington to its new facility on Riverside Drive.

The school district knew such growth would continue. The retirement image of the county masks the reality of the fast-growing children's portion of the population. It was essential that the district have long-range plans. In June 2002 the school board went to the citizens with a bond election proposal for $74 million. That passed with a solid majority. A new superintendent, Dr. Max Rose, was appointed upon the retirement of Dr. Granger. The construction of new schools continued. Lava Ridge Intermediate was finished that year, then Riverside Elementary in 2004 and Fossil Ridge Intermediate in the same year. Little Valley Elementary is under construction.

Considerable land was purchased for many other schools throughout the county and a new administration building was built on Tabernacle Street, next door to the remodeled Woodward School, which became the district's media and technology center. In 2005 Arrowhead Elementary was completed. Replacing the buildings on the Dixie High School campus was finished, essentially creating a whole new facility. Pine View High School was also remodeled.

The district had its next step ready for the longer range and they put a $99 million bond to the voters. The Utah Taxpayers Association endorsed the proposal, something they had not done before. They liked the long-range planning. The bond also passed but its funds were reserved to be used beginning in 2006. Now a decade after 1996 there are 23,160 students between the ages of 5 and 18 (about 1/6 of the county population) and 13 new schools, including three new intermediate centers. A charter school was also authorized to be located at the Tuacahn Center for the Arts. Its curriculum focuses on the fine arts and involves 200 students.[7] A new charter school, Little Valley School, opened in 2006 serving students in Bloomington Hills.

One more educational development has been the establishment of several youth correctional schools. These included Cinnamon Hills and Red Rock Canyon School across the street from each other on St. George Boulevard, Sun Hawk Academy on 1300 West, Cross Creek Manor on State Street in La Verkin, Diamond Ranch Academy in Hurricane, Liahona Academy in Virgin, Falcon Ridge Ranch in Springdale, and Red Cliff Ascent in Enterprise. Citizens in the county often wonder why so many of these detention facilities congregate in Dixie. There has even been some anxiety about having so many troubled youth in these facilities. So far there have been very few difficulties and many jobs have been created. Undoubtedly the semi-rural atmosphere and the relative peacefulness add to the appeal for these schools.

Funding

To support the expansion of public facilities, city and county governments have had to raise revenues to build the infrastructure of roads, water facilities, libraries and schools. Much of that revenue has been generated through property taxes paid by the increasing population and through sales taxes from both residents and the many visitors. Considerable money was raised in St. George City by charging impact fees on new home construction. Those were raised from $5,700 in 1996 to $10,000 in 2006. In addition, there are modest hook-up fees and substantial building permit fees based on the value of the proposed structure, plus a $4,500 Washington County Water Conservancy District pipeline fee for the entire county.[8]

A 1% tourist tax was approved in the county in 1982 to support the promotion of tourism and continued in the next decade. The growth of tourism saw new hotels and motels built, increasing the number of beds available to 4,000. These were often full when the major events occurred, the St. George Marathon, the Huntsman World Senior Games, the Parade of Homes, the many baseball/softball tournaments, Spring Break/St. George Arts Festival, as well as the regular holidays and conventions.

A new Dixie Center was constructed near 1-15 at the exit 6 interchange to house conventions. In 1998 it moved from its site on the Dixie College campus where it had been administered by a council of representatives from county communities. The expanded facility near the freeway is now administered by an eight-person board and chairperson representing St. George City and Washington County only, not the individual communities. By 2005 it was necessary to begin a major expansion. In 2005 some 60 conventions were held there, averaging 400 people each, but by the time such meetings were included at all of the hotels and other facilities in the county, there were 3000 conventions and meetings with an average attendance of 40 people.[9]

One of the important public funding developments in St. George in this decade was the initiation of a bus transit system. In 2000 a grant was received from the Five County Association of Governments and the Utah Department of Transportation. After two years that ran out and St. George City assumed the costs and obtained some other grants for a reduced program and shortened routes. Beginning in 2002 a system of three routes called SunTran was regularized, one to the Red Cliffs Mall, one traveling through downtown St. George to Riverside Drive and back to the Dixie College Campus where all three routes met, and one on Sunset Drive to Dixie Drive along Valley View Drive to the city center and the college campus.[10]

Residents of the city are now used to seeing the bronze buses and know where the many bus stops are located. The present system has increased ridership from 500 a month (when DARTS ended its service) to 1,500 a month currently. The busses are handicapped accessible and include bike racks. They serve as an alternate transportation for residents who have no access to automobiles. They even connect with the trail systems so bicyclists can enjoy extended rides.

Even with increased revenues from growth, it was necessary to go to the public with bond proposals. The citizens of the county have been supportive of bond elections during this decade. This says a lot about the people of the Dixie communities. Even though many residents are earning wages below the state average and others are stretching a retirement income, they obviously feel that children should have adequate schools and citizens need parks and libraries.

A bond passed in 1996 for the construction of parks in St. George included trails, athletic fields, neighborhood parks and an aquatic center. Today there are 38 parks in the community, plus 18 trails and 20 other facilities such as swimming pools, a recreation center, tennis courts and a new cemetery. The trails, have been a great attraction and the ball diamonds have supported the tourism industry by bringing hundreds of youth and adult ball teams to compete and incidentally to occupy the motels and hotels with their parents and coaches. [11]

A county bond was approved in the November election of 2001, a more modest one for $23 million. This bond enabled the construction of a new Senior Citizen Center in St. George and several branches of the county library system. Since the bond passed, new libraries have been completed in Santa Clara, Springdale, New Harmony, St. George and also an expansion of the Hurricane library. A branch will be built in Washington City and an addition in Enterprise.

In 1996 Washington County approved plans for a $12 million prison to be located in Hurricane at Purgatory Flats on highway 9. They received 40 acres from the Bureau of Land Management and constructed the secured facility by 1998. It had 430 beds and 50 more were added since then. Both county and state prisoners occupy the facility; the Sheriff's Office is headquartered there as well as a new Juvenile Justice Center.

Hospital

One of the most dramatic developments during the 1996-2006 decade came in the area of health care. Washington County completed construction of a new hospital in 1975 replacing the Pioneer Memorial Hospital. Intermountain Health Care (IHC) assumed ownership and management of the regional medical center on 400 East in St. George in 1976. From that time until 1996 there were five major remodeling projects and additions, including the Cancer Center in 1985. The hospital gradually became a 137-bed facility by expanding onto the 5th floor.

Even before that last expansion, the local hospital administrators called for a long-range plan to consider the future needs of the region. Local and Salt Lake City planners considered expanding at the existing 400 East site. It was paid for and located in the central city, both important advantages. The planners expected continuing population growth but also realized that improving technology would change the profession. Same-day surgery was increasing because of new equipment and methods; that would limit patient stays in the hospital. The community would grow, but patient stays would be shorter. They thought one more expansion on the old site might work.

As planning progressed, the idea of staying on the 400 East campus was brought into question. The planners agreed that changes brought by outpatient service would have an impact on facilities but they suggested that the time had come to expand the hospital's offerings to include open heart surgery and other services that had previously been available only by life-flighting or referring patients to Salt Lake City or Las Vegas. These procedures should now be made available to growing Washington County and adjacent counties.

They suggested a 100-year plan: a completely new campus, enabling a major expansion of services. Soon thereafter such a location was found on River Road and 700 South, near Foremaster Ridge. The first step was construction of an Instacare facility on River Road in 1998 where patients could go without appointment and be served by IHC doctors and nurses.

Plans eventually called for a new $100 million hospital. The completion of that structure in November 2003 opened a new era for health care in Utah's Dixie. A new wing was included with nearly 40 professionals to perform open-heart surgery. The emergency wing was tripled in size. A fourth floor was included but left vacant for later development. The 400 East campus was retained and remodeled, housing women's and children's services, newborn intensive care, psychiatric care, several testing services, the cancer center and acute rehabilitation. By 2005 it was completely remodeled and occupied. A portion of the reserved fourth floor at the River Road facility had to be completed one year after the new hospital opened to accommodate orthopedic and geriatric surgery and care. Together the two hospitals provide 245 beds.

The new facilities paralleled a major expansion of specialties; the professional staff was expanded to include 206 physicians plus an extensive nursing and support staff. This medical practice and hospital service has become a cornerstone to the decision of many people to move to St. George and has caused others to travel to St. George for medical services they had previously sought either in Las Vegas, Provo or Salt Lake City. The hospital is clearly a central element in the growth and economic development scenario of Washington County. It is the largest employer in Washington County with more than 2,000 employees.[12]

Airport

The story of the St. George Airport resembles that of the hospital. There were a few attempts to use the present airport site between 1920 and 1930 and then it was used often from that time forward. St. George City acquired the airport in 1941 and extended the runway to 3500 feet by 100 feet wide. In 1946 Challenger Airlines began service and urged the city to expand the runway, which they did to 5100 feet in 1958. Bonanza Airlines took over from Challenger, beginning service in 1959, but soon moved their operation to Cedar City. Dixie Airlines then began service under the leadership of Bruce Stucki. It was purchased in 1972 by a new local airline, SkyWest, when their important era began. The city obliged by expanding the airport to 6100 feet in 1978 and building a new terminal in 1980. In 1985 Dixie College, which had been conducting pilot training, built a new hangar at the airport on the west side of the runway. In 1990 SkyWest began using Brasilia aircraft, which allowed several daily flights of 30-passenger planes. The city of St. George expanded the terminal building in 1991.

By this time the economic expansion of Washington County was well fueled and the airport had become a limiting factor. There was no more land on the west black ridge to allow further expansion so city planners were forced to consider a new site. In 1997, when SkyWest celebrated its 25th anniversary, the city identified the old Federal aviation emergency site near the Arizona border, southeast of Washington Fields, as the most desirable location for a much-expanded new airport. The pressure for the change was considerable. It had been an emergency landing area during World War II and then became a favorite flying spot for serious model airplane hobbyists.

SkyWest had become a large commuter airline with connections serving Delta, Continental and United Airlines and was flying to the U.S. Northwest, California, Texas, the Midwest and gradually to the East Coast. In 2005 SkyWest purchased Atlantic Southeast Airlines with many more connections along the Atlantic Coast and inland. They had already become the nation's largest commuter airline but this acquisition made them a dominant part of the industry and reportedly the largest independently owned commuter airline in the world.

The St. George airline already had the potential of bringing larger airplanes to the city but was limited by the length and width of the runway. The airline had been under pressure to move its headquarters to the Delta hub in Salt Lake City but after long consideration, chose to remain in St. George. They did move their service facilities to Salt Lake, however. In 1993 they completed an impressive corporate head-quarters on River Road, confirming their decision. Seven years later they expanded that facility. In October of 2005 they employed 9,066 people nationally, not counting Atlantic Southwest; 517 of them are in Washington County.[13]

Opposition soon arose to the proposed new $100 million airport. Grand Canyon Trust represented the environmental protection commu-nity by bringing a lawsuit against the Federal Aviation Administration (FAA). They were concerned about the cumulative noise impact over Zion National Park. The designers tried to avoid having planes fly over population areas, especially Washington City and the Washington Fields. The lawsuit caused a judge to require a full environmental impact state-ment review, not just an environmental assessment, and postponed the construction for several years. In 2007 the matter was resolved.

One major reason for choosing the new site is its safety and jet capability as well as expansion potential. Another major advantage is that the area around the runway can be developed as an industrial park, providing a much-needed area for new industry. The site will require an I-15 freeway exit near the Arizona border and it (exit 2) is already being planned. This exit is part of a larger belt route, a 50-mile high-way beginning at the exit and going in a circle past the new airport and on to Hurricane. This portion will begin construction in 2007. From Hurricane the belt route will complete a large circle over the I-15 free-way and create a northern belt across the mountains, past highway 18 below Veyo and on above the Shivwits Indian Reservation to the old Highway 91, into Santa Clara and St. George and then back onto the I-15 freeway at St. George.

The decision to build the new airport was not as easily obtained as the corporate approval that got the new hospital underway. Govern-ment agencies at several levels were involved as well as citizens with varying opinions. Democracy is not an efficient decision process but it has gradually found a resolution because the present airport cannot accommodate larger airplanes, which means that many airlines do not link to Washington County. Future economic development has a plug in its artery that needs to be opened.

Fine Arts

During the recent decade the fine arts have also thrived. For example, the Pioneer Center for the Arts, opened in 1996 and 1997, has been an important addition to St. George. Located at Main Street and Second North, it includes a restoration of the pioneer Opera House, a replica of the St. George Hall, now called the Social Hall, an authentic one-room pioneer adobe house and the conversion of an old warehouse into the St. George Art Museum. Art shows, concerts, conferences, receptions, and a variety of performances occur there as well as the Historic St. George LIVE tours. Visitors to the Pioneer Center for the Arts are impressed with its beauty, especially the plaza between the buildings. The interior of the museum is an architectural delight.

The Tuacahn Performing Arts Center in Ivins opened in 1992, another example of a major leap forward for the cultural arts. The center, funded by Hyrum Smith and others, includes a 2000-seat outdoor amphitheater. An indoor theater is named in honor of Orval and Ruth Hafen, who owned the site in the 1950s and initiated its development. Tuacahn Charter School, a performing arts high school, also uses the center for its instruction. The summer season of Broadway musicals draws large crowds to the outdoor theater with its architectural and natural beauty in the red rock canyon.

The O. C. Tanner Amphitheater, on the opposite side of the county in Springdale, continues its summer weekend performances of popular music in the setting surrounded by the cliffs of Zion National Park. Also in Springdale there are three photography galleries, a theater and the Z-Arts concert series that establish an "artsy" tone at the gateway to Zion National Park. In 2006 a new community center was constructed next to the city hall on Zion Boulevard. It includes a branch of the Washington County Library as well as a community meeting/ performance room.

The new Eccles Fine Arts Center at Dixie State College was opened in 2004 and is another major addition to the county's cultural life with its Sears Art Gallery, a small concert hall, two theaters, symphony rehearsal hall and several instructional facilities. The vitality of the Southwest Symphony, the Celebrity Concert Series, the Heritage Choir, the Tabernacle Dixie History and Music Series, the various community choirs, the art shows at the St. George Art Museum and commercial art galleries, the St. George Musical Theater, the Dixie

College Theater and the outstanding high school theater and musical productions provide a vibrant cultural atmosphere, many based on local talent and instructional programs. One of the additional secrets of the cultural vitality is the available audience. Retirees as well as long-time residents are avid attendees at these productions but so are parents, siblings and grandparents for the school events.

Recreation

The image of "Come play in the sun" has been linked to Washington County for several decades. In the 1950s the St. George Chamber of Commerce adopted a slogan: "Where the summer sun spends the winter." For a time motels even offered a free accommodation if the sun did not shine during a visitor's stay. (Patrons would receive a free second night.) Then, with the addition of golf and second homes, the image of a recreation destination grew.

Leaders in Dixie quickly realized that packaging the county could be helped with the recreation image. John and Daisy Morgan, owners of the St. George Hilton, placed enticing footage on northern Utah television showing people golfing; that became the image of St. George in the minds of many northern Utahns. Also, Alan Coombs heavily promoted his Green Valley resort and thereby St. George in the 1980s. In the 1996-2006 decade he advertised the Green Valley Spa nationally and drew a regular clientele for week-long stays. The Red Mountain Resort and Spa in Ivins also draws people from all over the nation for health retreats at their scenic facility near Snow Canyon. A new destination spa, The Body Shop, also broke ground in 2005. It is a residential exercise program located on highway 91 at 400 East in Ivins.

The St. George City Leisure Services Department adopted a strategy to promote recreational events in the city. One of the best known is the St. George Marathon. In 2005 there were 6800 people registered for the 26-mile run from Central to St. George on the first Saturday of October. The whole community was impacted and delighted with this 29th running of the marathon. It is one of the prime marathons in the U.S. and is a qualifier for the Boston Marathon.

Another major event which has grown since its beginning in 1987 is the Huntsman World Senior Games. In 2005 some 9700 contestants participated in the two-week event, including people from all over the world. They competed in 22 different sports, from horse-shoes to ping pong, bicycling to swimming, basketball to track, even pickleball and bridge.[15]

Softball/baseball competitions for young and older players are held many weekends during the winter and spring, attracting hundreds of teams and their families to compete on the many community ball dia-monds. This is probably the biggest single visitor attraction to the city. For a short time it appeared that the community would be the location of a professional baseball team; the Zion Pioneerzz took up residence at Bruce Hurst Field on the Dixie State College campus. They were able to sustain two professional seasons at the independent league lev-el. The facilities were excellent, built under the guidance of Dixie's own former major league pitcher, Bruce Hurst, in 1995, but the owners were unable to generate the funding and following to sustain it after 2000. They were followed by the Road Runners in 2007.

Both visitors and county residents travel to Springdale and Zion National Park for many forms of recreation. This decade has seen several major developments in that community including the building and expansion of hotels and restaurants and shops. One of the most noticeable changes has been the introduction of the shuttle bus system for the national park. On Memorial Day 2000 the park began limit-ing automobile access to the Zion Canyon Scenic Drive. It provided a shuttle bus service during the summer, which picked up visitors at parking lots and bus stops throughout Springdale every 15 minutes and then drove them through the park. The service is free and very popular. One side benefit is that the National Park Service built hand-some bus stops at several places in the community and the whole ap-pearance of the main business district improved.

Recreation is not limited to visitors. Locals find many options avail-able, some of them enabled by the construction of parks and recreational facilities such as the new Sand Hollow Aquatic Center. The Recreation Center on 400 East in downtown St. George, established in this decade, offers handball, ping pong, basketball and other options year-round. The 18 trails entice runners and bicyclists. The high schools and col-lege have stadiums and tracks. There are runners out every day all over the county, and bicyclists too. Hiking is big in Dixie, especially in Zion National Park, Snow Canyon and the Red Cliffs Desert Reserve — for all levels from beginners to professionals.

One of Washington County's new, attractive recreation areas is Red Cliffs Desert Reserve. It contains 62,000 acres of desert tortoise habitat conservation land. The establishment of this reserve was the result of a long negotiation between the environmental community and the agricultural/developer interests as well as the State of Utah and the Bureau of Land Management. An agreement was implemented in February 1996 to reserve the large tract of land immediately north of St. George, Washington, Hurricane, Santa Clara, and Ivins to protect the desert tortoise. Formerly one-third of that land belonged to the State Trust Lands, another third to the Federal government through the BLM and the remaining third was private property. The private owners were allowed to exchange their property for government lands elsewhere and could develop those lands with fewer restrictions. Many citizens were critical of this effort, arguing that the tortoise is not native to the county.

In the decade since the agreement the Reserve Administration has initiated recreation options on the land. They established miles of trails available for hikers and horse riders and bicyclists. There are now sixty-one trails and thirty trailheads where citizens can enter the extensive trail system. There are a few designated campsites. The Red Cliffs Desert Reserve also opened a small visitor's center at Tabernacle Street and First East in downtown St. George where people can get literature, make reservations and view live desert tortoises and other animals that live on the reserve. It is a favorite spot for children.

At Green Valley the Vic Braden Tennis School has ten outdoor courts and four indoor ones. There are other courts at several community parks and at Dixie State College. The Summit Athletic Club also teaches tennis.

Four-wheelers are a favorite with many people and there are several designated areas for them. Similarly, camping is popular and fishing too. Boating is active at several reservoirs — Quail, Sand Hollow and Gunlock. The big boating attractions are Lake Powell and Lake Mead, a comfortable drive away. The long drought between 1998 and 2004 caused the lake level at Powell to drop by 50%, exposing geological and historical sites that had long been covered up. That drew visitors to view them.

Washington County built a Regional Park and Equestrian Center on the Purgatory Flat (formerly BLM land) adjacent to the new prison. The county officials purchased a racetrack in Wichita, Kansas in May 1996. The seats and fences and rail were shipped to St. George in September 1996 and the construction was finished in time for the county fair to be there in 1997. The park is also home of an equestrian center, replacing the one at Dixie Downs, which had been constructed in the 1970s. Home construction in Dixie Downs was expanding and the decision was taken to move the horse facilities to the new regional park. There are 2000 seats at the race track and 6000 seats at the outdoor arena with 3000 seats in the indoor arena, a barn with 280 stalls and racing stalls for 300. It is now the center of many meets and activities, including car shows and high school rodeos.[16]

One of the unique places in Washington County is the St. George Dinosaur Discovery Site at Johnson Farm. In 2005 a museum was opened which is essentially a big protective open space covering the site where dinosaur tracks were found on the farm of Sheldon and La Verna Johnson. They were discovered in 2001 when Dr. Johnson attempted to level the rocky ridge. It is located just east of Foremaster Ridge on Riverside Drive. When some of the large stones were up-ended he noticed what were obviously pre-historic animal tracks. He showed them to his wife's son, Kelly Bringhurst, a geologist at Dixie State College. Bringhurst helped them contact specialists who determined that the large tracks were Dilophosauraus dinosaurs and the smaller ones were called Megaphosaurus. There are many other specimens as well.

The Johnsons approached St. George city officials who agreed to provide fencing and other services which were needed because so many people wanted to inspect the site and its hundreds of tracks. Gradually the city and the Johnsons established more permanent plans. The city purchased the site and applied for grants with both the state and the Federal government and were able to create a museum with a professional staff. The public now visit the site in large numbers and the staff is continuing in its scientific work, uncovering fossils nearby.

Some people say that the four-letter word in Dixie is "Golf." People of all ages are involved, if not addicted to this outdoor sport. Young people engage in community-sponsored competitions. High schools and the college have active teams. Adults of all ages adopt golf as their major hobby.

Currently there are twelve golf courses in the county, five of them owned by city governments. Several are part of a real estate development such as Sun River, Bloomington, Sky Mountain, Coral Canyon, Entrada and a new one at The Ledges near Winchester Hills. Only Bloomington is private. Several more are being planned. Coral Canyon, Entrada and Sun River are the most recently built. Dixie Red Hills was built in 1965; Bloomington, Southgate and St. George in the 1970s. Green Springs, Sky Mountain and Sunbrook are over a decade old but Sunbrook added a third nine holes within the decade. There is a refinished 3-par course called Twin Lakes in Middleton. A golf course is being planned near Hurricane in the Sand Hollow area. In Dixie, golf is big and for all ages, both men and women.

Merchandising

The most noticeable change in the decade has been the emergence of a new merchandising megaplex along River Road and Red Cliffs Drive. It has become the county's Main Street, drawing people from as far away as Hildale and Kanab on the east, Enterprise on the west and Mesquite on the south and certainly the communities in the middle of the county. Virtually all of it is the result of the population growth. It seems that when the county population neared 100,000 there was an automatic bell that rang in the planning rooms of national chain stores.

The first big change came with the development of the Red Cliffs Mall. The initiative for it came from John Price in Salt Lake City and Bruce Stucki in St. George. It was necessary to modify exit 8 on 1-15 to access the mall. The original freeway construction in 1970 only included an exit to the west (onto St. George Boulevard). It had to be changed to add an option to turn east, allowing traffic to reach the new Red Cliffs Drive built to bring traffic to the Red Cliffs Mall where Wal-Mart, ZCMI and Penney's were the anchor stores. By 2005 Dillard's replaced ZCMI and Sears occupied an addition to the mall.

Red Cliffs Mall opened in 1990 and began the transformation of the county's merchandising. Soon after the mall proved itself, the Zion Factory Stores was planned and built right at the new road from exit 8, next to the Ramada Inn in 1991. Then it expanded across the street as the Promenade at Red Cliffs in 1998, building larger stores and attracting major chains such as Old Navy, Staples, Hollywood Video, Chili's, Red Lobster, Chuck-a-Rama and others.

South of the exit 8 off ramp Red Cliffs Drive received the name of River Road. Harmon's opened a superstore at 700 South and River Road and in 1997 SkyWest built its headquarters a block north, expanding it in 2002. In 2004 the new Dixie Regional Medical Center was completed across the street, becoming a magnet for the whole region. North of the hospital, Lowe's built their big home center. North of them came a Target store and several smaller outlets including Ross Dress for Less and Pier I. In 2005 a Marriott Hotel was constructed north of Target, set back against the bluff. The same year and across the street west another small mall was constructed including the Golden Corral smorgasbord, T. J. Maxx, Great Rooms, Sandstone Village, Bruce's Rent to Own, South Central Communications and other outlets. All of these facilities included large parking lots adjacent to the street, causing the stores to be set way back.

A shock to the system was a decision by Wal-Mart. They abandoned their footage in the Red Cliffs Mall and moved to Washington City to build a superstore on Telegraph Road in 2001. Home Depot built a major outlet next door and Albertsons opened a grocery store with accompanying stores across the street south. A year earlier Costco built its huge outlet on 3050 East, two blocks behind Albertsons. In 2005 another complex of stores was constructed, this one across the road from Home Depot hosting Best Buy, Bed, Bath and Beyond, Ethan Allen, Honeybaked Ham, Gandolfos and others. The old Redlands R V Park was sold and another department store, Kohl's, has been built there. Boulevard Home Furnishings built one of the nation's largest furniture stores with amazing decor across the street north from the Red Cliffs Mall. The merchandising boom seemed to have no end.

The reconstruction of the 1-15 Washington exit 10 helped attract customers to these new merchandising facilities. This improvement linked the new frontage road to the St. George Industrial Park, without going through Middleton as it had done in the past. Yet another major highway improvement was the construction of an interchange at exit 13 on the north end of Washington City. Both were completed in 2005. The exit 13 completion has now opened the possibility for many new commercial developments adjacent to the off-ramps.

From Wal-Mart on the north to Harmon's on the south, Red Cliffs Drive and River Road became one extended merchandising complex. Most of the firms were national chains and looked like similar developments in the suburbs all over America. Certainly a new Main Street had been built, this one for cars, not pedestrians.

On the western side of St. George another merchandising complex developed. At the junction of Bluff Street and Sunset Boulevard the Jennings family initiated Sunset Corner where their old concrete dispatching plant had been located. Once the J & J enterprises were sold to Sunroc Corporation in 1996, they created a commercial site they describe as a "lifestyle center." A movie megaplex, a bank, restaurants and other shops are included in the project that began in 1999 and is still underway.

The Orton brothers, Rod, Roy and Sterling, moved their grocery store, Lin's Market, to Sunset and Dixie Downs Road in 1995. This was somewhat of a gamble, abandoning their downtown site and locating a larger store on the west side of town. The location turned out to be well chosen. People from Ivins, Santa Clara, Green Valley and Dixie Downs identified with the store and many of their previous customers choose to drive out to their sales. The location proved so successful that Albertsons built a store across the street on the Sunset and Dixie Drive corner and several other smaller outlets were included.

The initial plans for Bloomington in 1970 foresaw a commercial park adjacent to the exit 4 off ramp. A gas station and some offices were constructed early on. Then a complex was developed to house small commercial outlets. It struggled but in 2002 Wal-Mart opened a second superstore, this one in Bloomington. That necessitated a complete restructuring of exit 4 to include two roundabouts. It was controversial and received considerable criticism from Bloomington residents. Nonetheless the city went ahead with the plans and the Wal-Mart store opened. That led to other commercial outlets nearby, including two banks. The latest and more controversial decision was the city council's approval for the construction of a hotel at that site in 2005. On the east side of the freeway at exit 4 is a truck stop. The owners originally asked to build one twice as big but were limited and it is now not large enough for the demand. Adjacent are a fitness academy, a performing arts studio and a trailer sales and service.

Revitalizing Town Centers

The amazing growth of merchandising on Red Cliffs Drive/River Road, Sunset Boulevard, Bloomington and Washington put major pressure on businesses elsewhere, in Hurricane and in downtown St. George. This was not a new issue. Ever since Safeway built a grocery store with a parking lot on the Boulevard in 1959 and since Kemp Korner was built at 700 East and Tabernacle and Snows moved their grocery store to 800 East and 100 South with a big parking lot, the commercial viability of downtown St. George was under pressure. A few years later, in 1983, the Commercial Center was built on South Bluff, housing Albertson's and Christensen's and Kmart and other stores; it was another blow to downtown St. George.

Since then the St. George city government has been trying to prevent the decline of the city center. Similar efforts have been attempted in Provo, Ogden and Salt Lake City. During the 1996-2006 decade a major revitalization of downtown has occurred. Using Downtown Redevelopment District funds, the city created the Pioneer Center for the Arts at Main and 200 North. The city also used redevelopment funds to help landlords restore the facades dating from 1900 on the downtown businesses and to build a small park at the intersection of Main Street and St. George Boulevard. Recently the city has adopted an ambitious beautification project with a water feature running through the three central blocks and placing a series of sculptures along Main Street, called "Art Around the Corner." Local sculptor L'Deane Trueblood and Sara Urquhart have been the sparkplugs for this effort and have involved sculptors from around the state. A major change has been the recently completed redesign of St. George Boulevard with landscaped medians. The construction interrupted business for several months but the result has extended the tone of a pleasant downtown.

A private venture, the Main Street Plaza, was completed in 2005. This has been a big factor in the revitalization of downtown, bringing a Blue Bunny Ice Cream retail outlet to the city center. The city government joined the developers, the Jennings and Gardners, in constructing a parking ramp garage adjacent to the office building. Suites on the upper floors have attracted significant business to the city crossroad of Main Street and Tabernacle. In 2007 there were nine art galleries on Main Street.

The city adopted a major plan for the redesign of the town square, including a new library and a major water feature. Local citizens joined the Washington County Board of Education in restoring the Woodward School. The school board also built a new headquarters office building next to the square on Tabernacle Street. The city restored the Arts and Community building (The Old Dixie College) to become the host of community educational and cultural activities and redesigned the plaza. These together made the downtown square a gathering place for the whole community. Despite the influx of the national "box stores" on River Road, the downtown of St. George has been revitalized.

Other communities in the county wrestled with the same challenges. Hurricane has seen major commercial developments, including Lin's Market, Coral Cliffs Cinema, Stout Home Furnishing, a medical clinic (with the Dixie State College building next door) and several other new additions. The Hurricane Chapter of the Sons of the Utah Pioneers continued its efforts to maintain the town square there with its museum and the Bradshaw Hotel Museum across the street. They help identify the town center and the community identity. The chapter is also working to preserve the Hurricane Canal, which virtually created the community around 1900.

Washington City experienced a major reinvention of its city center during this period. In 1996 a restoration of the Old Relief Society Hall was completed on Telegraph Street, across from the post office. The handsome restoration now provides a place for public meetings. A statue honoring pioneer women is on the grounds as well as the names of 340 pioneer women. On those grounds is also the original corn cracking stone used by Thomas W. Smith in 1857. This emphasizes the fact that Washington City was the site of eight mills on Mill Creek (sometimes called Machine Creek). The old town school has been transformed into a community museum and is the site of four large statues of historic pioneers. Many busts of pioneers are also included in the museum, which was completed in 2003-4. The Washington City Historical Society members, particularly Harold and Priscilla Cahoon, promoted most of this restoration work. Before moving into the Relief Society Hall for its meetings, the Washington City Historical Society refinished the pioneer Smithson home on the comer of First East and Telegraph. They met there for a few years. Later it was a store to sell baked goods and then became an art gallery. Today it is empty and the city government is torn over what to do with it. The site is valuable for development, being right next to a small park and the city offices. The contest between destroying and preserving historical structures is embodied in this building.

The adaptation of the Cotton Factory in Washington to commercial use is another success story. The building was restored in the 1990s but failed to attract a permanent sponsor. Finally it was sold to the owners of Star Nursery. They have adapted it to use as a store for plants and trees and garden materials but they have retained the historic work that was so well done before they became the owners. Next door to the Cotton Factory, Washington City built a handsome city park with the financial support of the Nisson family who have been so crucial to the community in the last century. Across the street from these two developments, the Staheli family created several buildings in pioneer style to house their catering kitchen and dining spaces. They attract a steady stream of customers, mainly groups, to use their barn and other buildings for dances and dinners. All of these buildings together — the Relief Society Hall, the Cotton Factory, the museum and the Staheli facilities — have created an impressive city center which also includes a new city hall.

Santa Clara residents have also worked with their historical society to do the same. They began annual Swiss Days celebrations in 1990, initially to raise funds for the restoration of the pioneer Relief Society Hall in the town center. That was dedicated in 1993. Then they went on to restore the Hug/Gubler house next door, which they completed in 1998. That project gives the old part of Santa Clara a central focus. Most of the fruit stands are gone that once identified Santa Clara with tourists driving on the Highway 91 route to California but the restored pioneer buildings such as the Jacob Hamblin home keep the pioneer town identity alive. What was once a village has now expanded to be a very large suburban neighborhood but that is up on the hill above the old town.

Leeds undertook a similar project through the initiative of their historical society. They restored the Civilian Conservation Corps (CCC) campsite. Two buildings were refinished on the south end of town and the location of the barracks was identified. A sign directs visitors to the site near the southern entrance to the town. Nearby Toquerville has also completed a restoration of the old church to be a community center and park.

Rockville did a similar thing by obtaining the old LDS church and remodeling it into a useful town hall. They also built a pleasant community park right behind it. This gives the historic town a continuing community center. Even more ambitious was the restoration of pioneer Grafton, now a part of Rockville. An independent group, the Grafton Heritage Partnership, undertook that challenge. With the help of the Grand Canyon Trust, they raised funds to purchase much of the land in Grafton and restore the old church/school and the nearby Russell House. They continue to manage that project.

In St. George the Historical Society, with the leadership of Dr. Mark Greene, took on the challenge of restoring the Old Courthouse located at Boulevard and 1st East. With the aid of the St. George City Planning Office, they remodeled the upstairs courtroom and repaired much of the exterior. It serves today as the headquarters of the St. George Chamber of Commerce and a site for Historic St. George LIVE Tours.

Dr. Mark and Barbara Greene undertook historic restoration projects on their own in the heart of St. George. They restored about a dozen pioneer homes, eight of which became the Greene Gate Village, located directly across the street from the Woodward School on Tabernacle Street. They spent over a decade doing this historical restoration and added much to the attraction of downtown St. George. They proved that historical restoration is one of the ways of revitalizing a community center.

The Flood of 2005

Beginning in 1999 Washington County experienced a drought. Each year following, the lack of rain severely damaged the area, causing real anxieties. The expectation of continued growth came into question. The Washington County Water Conservancy District posted warnings, then alerts. They made pleas for water conservation, urging people to water their lawns only every third or fourth night (not in the day). It became clear that lawn watering was the biggest consumer of water but people were also asked to reduce their use for car washing, sidewalk cleaning, showers, baths, and even tooth brushing. Prayers and fasts for rain became standard procedures in churches, public meetings and homes as each succeeding year brought no relief.

The impact on agriculture was severe. The six years of drought forced cutbacks in cattle grazing as the range became increasingly dry. Similarly, alfalfa yields declined. Most severe, however, was the parched situation in the mountains and on the Arizona Strip. This led to wildfires caused by both humans and lightning. Wildfires were not new to the county. Since 1996 there had been fires covering as many as 25,000 acres in that year to as few as 784 acres in 2001. But in 2003 there were 138 fires over 29,000 acres and in 2004 there were more fires, 317, covering another 23,000 acres. Fire crews worked throughout the summer of 2004 and often around the clock to extinguish fires that often spread in the western half of the county. They found themselves fighting a new enemy — cheatgrass. That plant had been imported and spread for several decades to get the ground covered with foliage. Later people discovered that this new plant was particularly susceptible to lightning, burning quickly and spreading fires widely. The drought exacerbated the danger. In 2005 (after the flood) there were fewer fires but they burned many more acres, 184,850.

The drought extended year after year. Informed people thought about the Anasazi Indians who faced an extended (25 year) drought leading to their exodus from the region around 1300 A.D. Would this 21st century drought cause a halt to the issuing of building permits? What would be the consequence of that? Had the county come to the end of its growth potential? Would residents find it necessary to move?

Growth advocates had been anxious to further plans for the construction of a water pipeline from Lake Powell to St. George. The drought seemed to justify their idea but tough questions arose as the water level of that reservoir sank drastically, to below 50% of capacity. Some people wondered if it was wise to stake the county's water future on the importation of water — a supply that could disappear.

Then in the fall of 2004 the rains came, all over the state of Utah. It was the beginning of a water year that more than doubled the annual rainfall, the most plentiful rain year in two decades. Enterprise and Gunlock reservoirs filled in October as a result of a big snowfall above the Enterprise reservoir; groundwater packed the whole watershed. The most dangerous areas in Washington County were the mountains that feed the Moody and Magotsu creeks, which flow into the Santa Clara River. The hills around those upper creeks had been denuded by wildfires and could not hold back water after their soils were waterlogged.

Normally it was the Virgin River with its tributaries, reaching high into the mountains around Zion National Park, which were the source of flood danger. The citizens of Washington County had become used to flooding on the Virgin. This time it was different; it was the upper system of the Santa Clara, not mainly in Pine Valley but above Enterprise, where the majority of the flood began. Nonetheless, the Virgin also rose, causing considerable flooding in Bloomington.

After a very wet fall and early winter, an extended series of rain and snow storms began the first week of January 2005. Children in St. George danced among the snowflakes but in the mountains the snowfall became dangerous. Lyman Hafen recounts the story:

"On the night of Sunday, January 9th, 2005, and in the early morning hours of Monday, the Santa Clara River began to swell. The stream, known as a creek to locals, is little more than a trickle most of the year. Since the dam was built at Gunlock Reservoir in the 1960s, its flow has been controlled, for the most part, and it can often be crossed with little more than a hop or a couple of steps on well-placed stones. It is no secret to anyone who has lived along the stream over the past several decades that it is capable of swelling significantly when water runs in the drainages below the dam, and even flood when the Gunlock Reservoir overflows. The potential for a devastating flood has always existed. But hardly anyone, in their wildest dreams, could have imagined the volume of water, the magnitude of power, or the intensity of horror that would be generated by this serene little stream when all the right elements aligned to transform it into a monster.

"Just after mid-day on Tuesday, January 11th, the raging Santa Clara finished undercutting the bank beneath a new home in Santa Clara, then swallowed it up and swept it downstream in the heartless act that would be repeated many times over the next several hours. By Wednesday, more than 50 families in the St. George-Santa Clara area had either seen their homes disappear in the muddy torrent, or were displaced because their home had been rendered uninhabitable. Losses of public infrastructure and private property would mount to nearly $200 million. Downstream, at Beaver Dam and Littlefield, Arizona, and Mesquite, Nevada, the volume of devastation grew.

"Many of the homes lost in St. George neighborhoods, like Creekside, Shadow Creek and Riverwood, had two days earlier stood more than a football field away from the meager trickle of the Santa Clara River. The stream's normal average January flow of five cubic feet per second had multiplied exponentially in a matter of hours to more than 6,500 cubic feet per second. This horrific hydraulic equation translated the river into a deep, wide, demonic snake that jumped its established channel and capriciously whipped from bank to bank, cutting away at the landscape as if it were sugar. Giant cottonwood trees heaved over and crashed into the water. The trees and other debris lodged in this place and that, causing the channel to shoot off in new directions. Key bridges and roads connecting the area's neighborhoods washed out. In Bloomington and Sun River, below the confluence of the Santa Clara and Virgin Rivers, the usually serene Virgin transformed into a twin of the mighty Colorado, rising over the magnificent Man 0' War Bridge and threatening homes hundreds of yards from the traditional channel. In the end, more than 25 homes along the Santa Clara were either swept away completely or declared uninhabitable due to their dangerous condition."17

The response of the community to the flood was immediate. Local LDS and other congregations in Santa Clara, Green Valley, Bloomington and Gunlock marshaled hundreds of volunteers to evacuate residents and store their possessions and house the victims temporarily. Police and fire officials quickly arrived to protect and help residents and volunteers. The construction industry immediately volunteered workers and heavy equipment to extract debris and bring in boulders to protect the banks. Students and athletic teams came to carry sandbags. Women and children brought food to feed victims and workers. Helicopter pilots flew in supplies to land-locked Gunlock where the flood impact was intense. The Red Cross provided temporary housing for flood victims. All this went on around the clock.

Many victims of the flood were later interviewed and their recollections appeared in the book *Portraits Of Loss-Stories Of Hope*. Some of their ideas include:

- The flood was unexpected; many were in denial until nearly too late.
- They felt their homes were built well away from the river.
- The debris, especially fallen trees, diverted the river from

its channel, causing the undercutting of the nearby hills where the houses were. The volunteers were a godsend.

- Most victims had no worry about being looted or abused.
- Their losses were traumatic. They were grateful for public help and later philanthropy. One death resulted from the flood.

Long-term the city and county and Federal government devoted millions of dollars to reconstruction of infrastructure and redesign of the river channel. Armoring the riverbanks to hopefully avoid a reoccurrence continued into 2006. A local fundraising committee chaired by David Watson, including several banks, raised resources to help the victims establish new residences. They reached their goal of raising $3 million. This enabled 65 % of the mortgage losses to be paid.

The flood of 2005 was the disaster of a century but it was also the best opportunity for community response in recent memory.

Water Development

The drought and flood in this decade dramatized the centrality of water. That is just the continuation of the same concern since the 1850s when the Mormons arrived and set up permanent village homes, began agricultural irrigation and cattle grazing. Now, a century and a half later, all of the growth and development in Washington county hinges on the same central issue — water. The pioneers initially diverted the Virgin and Santa Clara Rivers and their tributaries to sustain their villages and farms. They also captured spring waters. This use of surface waters stressed their lives as well as sustained them because flash floods continually washed out their dams and silted their canals. It was a never-ending struggle (see chapter 7).

The story of building one reclamation project after another has been central to Dixie's history every period since. In the most recent decade that story has accelerated as thousands of homes and condominium developments have appeared. The Washington County Water Conservancy District expanded the Quail Creek Reservoir with a capacity of 40,000 acre feet (built in 1985) by adding Sand Hollow Reservoir in 2003, containing a 50,000 acre feet capacity. Like Quail Creek Reservoir, it also diverts Virgin River water into a storage reservoir. It then diverts the water by gravity flow to Quail Lake where it is fed into the water processing plant below the Quail Dike and enters into the St. George water system. In 2006 the city completed an addition to the plant, doubling its production from 20 million gallons of water per day to 40 million gallons.

The Water District has undertaken several other projects in this decade. The Sand Hollow Reservoir was designed to recharge the aquifer below the dam, allowing wells to be drilled. Seven wells are producing water and another ten can be drilled later. A new well has been drilled in Leeds, the Sullivan Well. On Kolob, the Crystal Creek has been piped to Kolob Lake to support irrigation, allowing other irrigation water to be used for culinary purposes. At Anderson Junction, well water has been delivered to supplement La Verkin and Toquerville. A pipeline is being installed to put the open Santa Clara ditch waters from the Shivwits, Ivins and Santa Clara canal companies into a delivery system that will prevent evaporation and be more efficient.

The next big project is linking all the water systems in the county — Ivins, Santa Clara, St. George, Washington, Hurricane, La Verkin, Toquerville, Leeds, even the upper Virgin — so that water can be shifted from one area to the other to balance the ups and downs of each community's supply. This has not been possible in the past; sometimes one town was very short while others had surpluses and then the situation reversed. A connected system will be more effective and more economically stable. It takes considerable political will to do this but the 1998-2004 drought argues that it be done. That is the immediate task and it is underway.

The longer-range plan is to bring a pipeline from Lake Powell to produce 70,000 additional acre feet of water per year, nearly as much water as can be held in Quail Creek and Sand Hollow together. Its projected cost is $500 million in today's dollars and that will demand a lot of political will. It is apparently do-able but it creates considerable debate. Proponents argue that there is no real alternative. Critics say that serious conservation could provide notable water savings. The counter argument points out that such attempts to halt growth have been seriously flawed elsewhere and that the economics of growth should govern reality. Both sides cite Las Vegas, Phoenix and Los Angeles as examples of communities that exist on imported water. Advocates say they prove that it is possible. Critics say that they don't want Washington County to be another Las Vegas. They also argue that, in a time of terrorism, a pipeline could be vulnerable. Providing water for some

300,000 more people, they say, will assure that such hordes do in fact come. The Washington County Water Conservancy District responds that their role is to develop a reliable water supply, as generations before have done, and not to regulate life. The argument will likely continue for the next decade but a decision will have to be made about construction of the pipeline within the next five to eight years.

The Washington County Water Conservancy District has been working on feasibility studies since 1995, expecting it to be implemented by 2020. They have held dialogue with Kane and Iron Counties that show interest in participating. These will need an additional 10,000 acre feet for Kane County and 20,000 acre feet for Iron County. The likely alignment of the pipeline would be from Lake Powell to Kanab, into Arizona along Highway 389, returning to Utah and ending at Sand Hollow Reservoir. This would be 127 miles, using two pump stations. Extending the line to Cedar City would cost an additional $114 million with pumps at Quail Creek, Pintura and New Harmony. All of these costs will rise.[18] In 2007 an "Envision Dixie" project has involved citizens from throughout the county in a planning process to capture the desires of people and to influence living in Dixie.

Public Safety

One way to measure growth is to examine the crime rate and the size of the police force. It is also a way to consider if the challenges of urbanism have damaged community spirit. Statistics from the St. George Police Department show that there were 100 police personnel in 1996 and 160 in 2004 with 58 sworn officers serving 43,000 people in 1996 and 94 serving 70,000 in 2007.

In 1996 there were 28,574 crimes reported in St. George, including runaways, DUI, public intoxication, disorderly conduct, theft, burglary, robbery, rape. In that same year there were 7,254 arrests. In 2004 there were 56,843 reported crimes including all categories from loitering to homicide and there were 11,378 arrests.

Does all this mean that St. George is calm and relatively safe or violent and dangerous? Consider homicides. Between 1996 and 2004 there were four homicides, one in 2000, one in 2001 and two in 2002. Rapes went from four in 1996 to 14 in 2004 but there were 15 in 2000, 17 in 2002 and 2003 and 21 in 2004. Forgery rose from 25 in 1996 to 168 in 2004. In 1996 there were 1,205 liquor law abuses and in 2004 there were 940. DUI was similar with 217 in 1996 and 207 in 2004 but vandalism went from 185 arrests in 1996 to 298 in 2004. Narcotics arrests went from 705 in 1996 to 1210 in 2004. Sex offenses ranged from 28 in 1996 to 95 in 1997 to 96 in 2002 to 74 in 2004.[19]

St. George has an image of being a relatively safe place but it is clear that it has most problems of urban centers. Graffiti is rare and gangs are rather limited. There are policemen on bicycles riding about the city as well as patrol cars; one officer is stationed in each high school and middle school.

The Washington County Sheriff's office reported the following: In 1996 they had 48 employees. By 1999 there were 109; in 2005 there were 160 employees. In 1999 there were 1124 arrests based on 3742 criminal reports. By mid-November of 2005 there were 1070 arrests and 5879 criminal reports. Comparing those figures one can see that the arrests in 2005 were about the same as in 1999 but the criminal reports had increased by 2000.[20]

Housing

The most noticeable trend in Washington County since 1996 has been the explosion of home construction, a natural result of the population increase. The year 1991 was the first time that more than 1000 building permits were issued in the county. In 1993 just over 2000 permits were issued. Then 1996 saw the number at 1929; permits remained under 2000 until 2003 when 2678 building permits were issued, followed the next year at over 3500. Home sales are another indicator of the boom. In 1998 there were 3968 home sales in the county. By 2004 that had climbed to 10,337, only to be surpassed in 2005 by about 12,000 sales.[21]

Concrete provides another glimpse at this building boom. In 1995 Sunroc Corporation produced 90,000 yards of concrete. By 2000 that had increased to 100,000 yards. In 2005 they made and delivered 200,000 yards. Since concrete is used in almost all construction, it is apparent that the building boom has been formidable. There are two other concrete companies, Western Rock, which produced about the same as Sunroc, and Interstate, that made about half that amount. Sunroc reported that by 2005 the demand for sand exceeded the amount that their factory produced and they had to import sand from outside the county.[22]

In some ways the availability of desirable homes also caused the influx. Each year the Southern Utah Home Builders Association sponsors the Parade of Homes, attracting as many as 35,000 visitors to view a wide array of home models from modest to very pricey. People seem interested in inspecting what Utah's Dixie has to offer.

What did designers and developers and contractors and realtors offer these people? Many of the basic ideas for contractors were already set by the two Bloomingtons built in the 1970s. Both were promotional designs with golf courses as their centerpieces. The first Bloomington included single family homes near the course, condominiums and larger lots with equestrian possibilities farther out. Bloomington Hills focused on more moderate family homes and originally had no condos but did have a golf course. The success of these planned communities set the tone for many others. They are developer-initiated, designer-constructed and agent-sold.

The 1996-2006 decade saw more use this developer mode. One includes several projects surrounding Sunbrook Golf Course owned by St. George City. This is upscale and very successful, producing Crystal Lake, River's Edge and Sunbrook communities. Several developers have worked on these projects as the course expanded to 27 holes.

In Washington, the city-sponsored Green Springs Golf Course had the same result with upscale projects near the course and more modest ones nearby, even to neighboring Buena Vista. Again, most of these were developer-initiated.

Southgate Golf Course was purchased by St. George City in 1992 and already included condominiums and homes. Elegant large homes have been built in this decade, especially in the Fairway Hills area overlooking the Southgate Golf Course and the roads above it linking to the Legacy Homes built by Kay Traveller.

Hurricane's Sky Mountain Golf Course created a whole new section of the city west of the old town near highway 9. Many homes surround the scenic course and more are nearby. Some 500 homes have been constructed there since it began in 1997.

Kayenta is one of the best-known developments because of its desert tone homes nestled at the foot of the dramatic vermillion cliffs of Snow Canyon. The entrance is on highway 91 west of Santa Clara and the Ivins junction. It has been under construction for 20 years, using a slightly different model and no golf course. The land is all developed by Terry Martin but a lot purchaser authorizes each home. Owners must abide by strict design standards which prescribe a Santa Fe one-story design, with desert landscaping and no lawns, placed on large lots with the approval of Martin, so it will not obstruct any views, and built by a Kayenta-approved contractor. The project has grown gradually and steadily and has become a major scenic achievement, currently including 450 homes with space for that many more.

Entrada is an upscale community on the northwest edge of St. George city, placed among the outcroppings of lava rock. Innovative entrepreneurs took advantage of these black rocks that seemed to obstruct development and turned them into a design advantage. The artful layout of the golf course meanders among the lava rock piles and challenges the golfers to keep their golf balls on the green. A variety of designs have been created; some homes stand alone and some are cluster units, all in a harmonious architectural design. An adjacent gated neighborhood, Entrada Trail, has been built across Snow Canyon Boulevard north with similar designs and water features. A clubhouse was added in 2005.

Sun River is located south of Bloomington near the Arizona border. The current approach requires residents and visitors to drive three miles through Bloomington from the 1-15 exit 4 but an exit from the freeway at milepost 2 is being planned in conjunction with the new airport that will need to use the same exit but turn east instead of west. Sun River, a golf community limited to senior adults, began in 1998, in the most southern part of St. George City. By 2005 there were 700 homes completed and occupied by retired adults. Construction is proceeding to the goal of 2900 units.

At the junction of highway 9 and 1-15, the turnoff to Hurricane, is Coral Canyon, yet another golf course designed community. Constructed by SunCor out of Phoenix, in cooperation with SITLA (School Institutional Trust Lands Administration), this development is also tightly controlled by architectural unity, with 700 homes finished by 2005 and a potential of 2400. Compared to other golf communities, this one includes a small business center with a Harley-Davidson outlet, a Holiday Inn, and several shops and offices. An elementary school will be finished in 2006, emphasizing that the community is not only for retirees.

Another major real estate development is The Ledges, five miles north of downtown St. George on state highway 18. This area, just south of Winchester Hills, was annexed to St. George in 2001. Homes have been built nearby for nearly 20 years, particularly some with larger acreage, including horse stables. In 2005 a major development was begun to include a golf course with lots surrounding it and a plan for 1000 new homes.

On state route 9 in Hurricane City between 4300 West and 2200 West another development is underway. It occupies the land on the south side of the highway toward Sand Hollow Reservoir. Roland Walter owns it with Gene Sturzenegger as a local representative. They began the roads and layout in early 2006 with commercial sites near the highway and internally. They call their approach "new urbanism" which will include housing of mixed prices and even some in the upper stories of the commercial buildings. Everything from work force housing to luxury homes will be included with a build out between 7000 to 10,000 units, virtually a new city. Consultant Robert Trent Jones is planning one golf course. Another may come later.

It may appear from the above description that the county is linked to golf. Actually most of the home construction follows other models, some the developer controlled, and much the result of individual buyers.

Ivins is growing rapidly. The town that was once a low cost haven has now become quite the opposite. The completion of Snow Canyon Parkway allows residents to drive directly to Ivins along the less congested route from St. George or they can use the Red Hills Parkway from the Washington City 1-15 exit 10 to avoid congested St. George Boulevard.

The area on Snow Canyon Parkway from Ivins to highway 18 (extension of Bluff Street) is also surrounded by new neighborhoods of single homes built since 2003, most of them the products of developers. They are architecturally harmonious; most have tile roofs.

Dixie Downs is a big neighborhood between Sunset Boulevard and Snow Canyon Parkway. It has been the location of many mobile homes and condominiums as well as single family homes. Recently the land that had long been the home of the Dixie Downs horse race track has been transformed into housing developments, mostly single-family homes. A Baptist Church, an elementary school and a large seven-field ball park enhance this new upper area of Dixie Downs.

South of Santa Clara to the Santa Clara River along Dixie Drive and Valley View Drive is an area called Green Valley. The name was adopted by the Green Valley Resort across the Santa Clara River on the adjacent hill. Many condominium communities are located in this area, some modest and some plush. It is also the location of lower cost rental units, including many built since 2004. In the last 10 years substantial homes have been constructed along the west base of the Black Hill. At the south end of the airport hill is a desirable area served by Indian Hills Drive, overlooking the Santa Clara River concourse. Several condominium developments have been established there: Creekside, Riverwood, Shadow Creek, Pinebrook and Gubler's. This was where the most extensive damage occurred in the flood of 2005. A score of homes were destroyed from those developments and much land was damaged.

The Pine View area of St. George, adjacent to Washington City, is growing, particularly the Mall Drive section with many contractor planned single family homes. New schools and churches have been built there. The area below the Mill Creek Industrial Park has seen rapid development of rental housing on the road connecting to Foremaster Ridge and Riverside Drive, around the south ridge along the Virgin River connecting to River Road.

On the way to Bloomington Hills along River Road are the Boulders and St. James Place. This area is new in this decade, suggesting that there is a considerable market for very nice homes. East of River Road after the bridge over the Virgin River, one can drive left out to Stone Cliff, a gated community built in the last five years on Schmutz Hill. Further on comes the Washington Fields which is growing rapidly, mostly large family homes. New churches are being built there and an LDS Stake has been organized. Little Valley, east of Bloomington Hills, is an area where many single family homes are being constructed.

Condominiums are an important part of the residential housing in the county. The first condominium project was Sunstone, next to the Red Hills Golf Course, in the 1970s. Shortly after their construction, condos were built in connection with the Bloomington project and the same at Green Valley. Many people who wanted to have a second home found the condominium arrangement convenient. These attached units were places they could live for a few weeks or months and then lock them up while they were away. The owners' association took care of the grounds and other amenities during their absence.

Some people also found them acceptable as a permanent residence, particularly the elderly who did not need a lot of space and wanted to avoid laborious upkeep. Once those condos were successful, other developers began projects in the inner city. Many downtown blocks in St. George had inner land that had long been used as gardens. These could be put together from several lots and make condo space available inside the block.

Dozens of similar projects were built and sold. The city favored such housing because it did not require new streets and was close to available utilities and yet still brought many owners into the community. The condominium arrangement proved to be desirable for retirees and the projects multiplied rapidly. In the 1996-2006 decade scores of condo projects have been constructed. The Association of PUDs and Condominiums reports that there are over 115 condominium projects in their association. Several others have not chosen to join. AOPC estimates that there are 15,000 units in the county.[23]

The Legacy on Tonaquint Drive to Bloomington is one such condominium community. Another is The Vintage on Bloomington Drive near the entrance from the Legacy area. In the area along Dixie Drive in Green Valley and close by, several condominium developments have been constructed. Many condos have also been built in the Pine View area as well as the 700 South to 900 South neighborhood between 900 East and River Road. For example, in the area along 900 East are the following: Meadow Creek, River Breeze, River Cove, Palm Meadow, Country Meadows South, Southfield Estates, Heritage Lane and Pine Meadow. Most of them include a clubhouse with a swimming pool, exercise machines and a park. This concentration of condominiums in one neighborhood is not unusual. For example, there are many condominiums in the St. George city center and around the St. George Temple.

Care centers, rest homes and assisted living facilities have existed in the county for several decades. One thinks of Porter's in downtown St. George and the Hurricane Rehabilitation Center and the St. George Care Center east of Dixie State College campus as well as The Meadows near Snow Park in the Dixie High School neighborhood. The current decade has seen the doubling of such services. These include an expansion of The Meadows and the building of the Ridge View Gardens and Kolob Care Center, both on 1200 East in St. George. Cliff View overlooks the 1-15 freeway near the Southgate community and Sterling Court is behind the Red Cliffs Mall. There are a score of smaller care facilities. All of these serve the aging community of the county and link with the increased medical care.

Religion

A natural question that is often posed by visitors regards religion. Is Washington County still dominantly LDS? Has all this in-migration changed the religious makeup of the county? The answer to both questions is yes. In 2005 there were 180 LDS (Mormon) congregations (22 Stakes). LDS stakes include: Hurricane, Hurricane West, Ivins, La Verkin, Santa Clara, Bloomington, Bloomington Hills, St. George, St. George East, St. George College First, St. George College Second, Green Valley, Morningside, Pine View, Snow Canyon, Sunset, St. George West, Washington Fields, Washington Buena Vista, Washington, Little Valley, Enterprise. Recent estimates of 84,663 members (65%) are very close to the state percentage which is 62 % LDS.

At the same time membership in Protestant, Catholic and Jewish congregations has also grown. There are now 37 congregations in those religions, with many new church buildings constructed in the 1996-2006 decade. The new Catholic center at 200 North between 200 and 300 West is impressive. Others include Presbyterian, Episcopal, Jehovah's Witness, Lutheran, Methodist, Baptist, Seventh-day Adventist, Christian Science, a Jewish Congregation and others such as Oasis Community, True Life Center, Living Faith Community, Living Word, Christian Fellowship, New Covenant Christian Center, The Lighthouse, and Calvary Chapel.

Other dimensions of diversity in the county include the immigration of Polynesians and Hispanic people in this decade. The Polynesians are few in comparison to the Hispanics but they are a conscious group, as is evidenced by the activities of the Polynesian Choir. Many of the islanders are LDS and they are employed in blue-collar jobs. The Spanish-speaking immigration has risen dramatically in the last five years and impacted the Roman Catholic parish. About 5000 of these people now reside in the county, though figures are difficult to establish because many are illegal immigrants. Again, most of them are employed, being active in the building trades. Many are males without families and may return to Mexico and elsewhere; they often mail funds back to their families. This continuing increase of Spanish speakers is likely to be substantial.

Polygamy

The practice of polygamy in Washington County remains the major local enigma. Hildale, Utah, and Colorado City, Arizona, immediately to the south across the state line, are gathering spots for people who openly practice plural marriage in defiance of official LDS Church doctrine as well as the state constitution and Federal courts. The LDS Church abandoned the practice between 1890 and 1904, but some resisted the change. This resistance was largely carried out by certain families located in the Salt Lake City area who considered it their mandate to quietly continue that practice based upon a special calling from John Taylor, president of the LDS Church, immediately before his death in 1887.

One such family was that of John Y. Barlow, who along with a modest following, moved to the picturesque Short Creek area in the early 1930s. Barlow linked up with the family of LeRoy Johnson, and soon the town of Colorado City, Arizona was established. The location on the border was convenient for evading state lawmen and especially process servers.

In the early 1960s, the group became more organized into a loose legal structure for ownership and control of property known as the United Effort Plan Trust. By the 1980s, a more formal organization had been established, known as the Fundamentalist LDS Church, now the largest of the various polygamist sects in the western United States. Its adherents can be found in enclaves in northern Utah, Texas, and also in Alberta and British Columbia, Canada.

There have been four prophets since the move to Washington County, namely, John Y. Barlow, LeRoy Johnson, Rulon Jeffs, and Warren Jeffs, the latter two being a father and son from the Salt Lake City area.

The attempt to evade notoriety vanished in 1953 when an effort was undertaken by both the state of Utah and Arizona to eradicate the practice by swarming into Short Creek and arresting all of the polygamist men and, further, removing children from polygamist homes. The "53 raid," as it is known, failed miserably and in time gave strength to the polygamist cause, partially because national public opinion boomeranged, sympathizing with the wives and children.

After the fateful raid on Short Creek by the state of Arizona in 1953, the town regrouped and changed its name to Colorado City. In 1958 Fred Jessop established Hildale in Utah, adjacent to Colorado City. The U. S. Census for 2000 listed 1,968 people in Hildale. Colorado City had nearly 4,000. Local county officials consider those numbers to be low because so much of the communities is secretive and resistant to census takers. Both the Daily Spectrum newspaper in St. George and the Salt Lake Tribune consistently estimate the combined population to be over 10,000.[24]

As mentioned in Chapter 9, the two communities have become economically stable by focusing on blue-collar employment in community-owned industries. This has the effect of keeping their youth working in the town instead of moving away or seeking careers through higher education. Separation and isolation appear to be their goal. Their form of United Order living is thereby promoted.

During the 1980s actions were taken to accommodate somewhat to the outside society. An agreement was reached with Washington County to build an elementary school in Hildale, thus sending the children to a secular setting. The same was done in Colorado City, where the state of Arizona accepted the request to take over the high school and support it with state tax funds. Alvin Barlow became the principal of the high school and his brother, Dan, became the mayor of Hildale, both polygamists. They favored a policy of co-existence with the state governments of Utah and Arizona. The same thing happened with the police and court systems.

This co-existence strategy was brought into question when the fundamentalist prophet, LeRoy Johnson, died in 1986. Rulon Jeffs succeeded him. By 1996 there was a major rift in the community over several issues: schools, under-age brides, non-conforming boys, the impact of Mohave Community College and management of the United Effort Plan Trust. Some polygamist leaders became increasingly suspicious of the accommodation with secularism.

In 2000 Rulon Jeffs instructed all residents to withdraw their children from public schools and teach them at home. This returned to the policy of separatism, assuring that the children would be less able to leave and would be more tied to community-owned businesses. Since that time, Warren Jeffs, who succeeded his father in 2002, has become even more assertive against accommodation. A group of people in the community purchased the Hildale Phelps Elementary School and opened their own private school there.

One of Jeffs' most amazing acts was excommunicating scores of young men and expelling them from the community. These were teen-agers who incurred the wrath of the prophet for their actions in dress or TV viewing or other rebellious behaviors. The youths were ex-pelled from the community with nowhere to go. Newspapers claimed there were 400 of these "lost boys" expelled. No one can really know the number since such actions are secret.[25]

A splinter group from the Jeff's leadership is called the "Second Ward." They broke away some fifteen years ago and moved across the highway south from Colorado City, establishing their own academy school. They do not dress in the same manner as the Colorado City/ Hildale polygamists but they practice plural marriage. They have been very successful in their building businesses but have avoided the controversies that are plaguing those under Jeffs.

The state governments in Utah and Arizona had long chosen to avoid the head-to-head legal clash that had been a disaster in the 1953 polygamy raid by Arizona.[26] The Washington County and Mohave County attorneys and the Attorney Generals of both states maintained that they did not have the resources to prosecute all those practicing polygamy. In the 1996-2006 decade a different strategy emerged, lead-ing to a major rift in the communities. The Attorneys General of Utah and Arizona decided to pursue legal action against polygamy. They were under pressure from citizens and legislators who were frustrated with polygamists. The excessive use of the welfare system by po-lygamists and their refusal to educate their children in formal schools led to the wide public criticism. At base was the open flaunting of the constitutions of both states which outlawed plural marriage.

Newspapers provided data about what appeared to be misuse of public welfare. The enrollees in Medicaid in Hildale in 2002 were 1,410, 65% of the official population. In 2003 there were 4,138 in Colorado City, more than the total official census. The newspapers went on to point out that family size in Hildale was 8.1 persons per household in contrast to 3.21 in St. George. It contrasted the per capita income, citing the 1999 figure of $17,022 for St. George and $4,782 for Hildale. These figures provide a picture of people in the polygamous communities living at a very modest level, often dividing a father's income among several families and many children. Naturally this motivates people to qualify for welfare support.[27]

The stable, industrious behavior of the residents in the two communities muted the criticism for a long time but finally the state of Utah decided to nip away at polygamy by prosecuting any possible cases of child abuse and particularly arresting anyone they could charge with forcing underage girls into polygamous marriages.

Either this campaign or Warren Jeffs' arbitrary leadership caused a rift in the community. Some people determined to break with the FLDS Church but claimed the right to take their property with them. Others were expelled by the FLDS leaders such as the Barlow brothers, Dan and Alvin. The homes and land legally belonged to the United Effort Trust so that led to a court challenge by Ross Chatwin. A police officer in the community, Rodney Holm, was prosecuted for marrying an underage wife, the sister of his other wife. Justice Court Judge Walter Steed of Hildale, who had served for 24 years, was decertified for having three wives. He appealed his case to the Utah Supreme Court.[28]

Jeffs became increasingly secretive and eventually left for Eldorado, Texas where he and others built a new community, including a temple.[29] That action led to charges that Jeffs was diverting sizable sums from the $100 million United Effort Trust account to the Texas project. A court decision to remove Jeffs and his colleagues from the Board of the Trust was announced in 2004.[30] In 2005 a warrant was issued for Jeffs' arrest on the charge of arranging marriages between underage girls and polygamist men and eventually lead to his arrest. His pre-trial hearings in 2007 have been widely publicized.

The conflict that had been avoided for five decades after the Arizona raid was underway again, fed by wide television and press coverage. The courts are dealing with continuous litigation, which hinge largely on the belief versus conduct distinction first enunciated in the 1879 polygamy test case, Reynolds vs. the United States, which upheld the outlawing of the practice of polygamy. Thus far, the court decisions have largely run against any relaxation of the laws banning polygamy and bigamy despite the more liberal views favoring other nonconforming lifestyles, such as gay and lesbian relationships.

Volunteerism

One of the most interesting aspects of life in Washington County is the high level of volunteerism that permeates the society. Many people find volunteering a way to make their life meaningful. Others do it to be involved with the community. Some feel it is a way to repay society for their good life. Some just see a need. Volunteers are visible and conduct a considerable part of the community's activity. One sees them as greeters and helpers in the hospitals and as sales people and producers for the thrift and gift shops. The Doctor's Free Clinic is another volunteer service. Volunteers pervade the schools; they usher at concerts and are docents at the art museums. The Historic St. George LIVE tours are conducted entirely by some 125 volunteers. People serve in several LDS assignments — Deseret Industries, the Cannery, Social Services, Visitor Center, Name Locator Mission. For example, there are 1500 people serving in the St. George Temple. Members in all denominations visit families, teach classes and run offices.

Volunteers visit prisoners and teach youth in the Detention Center. They serve at the Dove House and at Dixie Care and Share. They shelve books at libraries and run the used book sales there. The St. George Area Chamber of Commerce has 45 volunteers each week as greeters and telephone operators. The Daughters of the Utah Pioneers Museum's entire staff is volunteers. Nursing homes depend heavily on volunteers to visit patients, greet them, conduct entertainment and classes. The St. George Marathon requires 1,700 volunteers to make the event possible. The Huntsman Senior Games uses some 2,000.

The Volunteer Center of Washington County has been coordinating some of the volunteering for a decade, directed by Linda Sappington and her able staff. They receive requests for volunteer service and they also accept the offers of many who wish to volunteer. In 2005 the Center was conducting several programs — RSVP (Retired and Senior Volunteer Program), Seniors in Schools, Senior Companions, Foster Grandparents, Health Insurance Information Program, Court Ordered Community Service, and the Youth Volunteer Corps. More than 4,000 people are involved in these activities.[31]

In addition to these volunteers, there are scores of people who serve the various towns on councils and zoning boards and numerous other appointed committees. Then there are guilds which support such groups as the Celebrity Concerts, DRMC, the Heritage Choir, St. George Musical Theater and many more. There are fund-raising committees to help community services. Thousands of people sing in community choirs and perform in orchestras and bands and quartets. This is a county driven by citizen effort, and it thrives.

Waste Management

The communities in Washington County have had to respond to the growth with much improved systems for dealing with waste. For decades towns had their own garbage dumps. For example, St. George had a dump on the hill above the old tunnel entrance into the city. At least two other dumps preceded that one, the dump located where the Red Hills Golf Course now is and one before that on the west side of the black hill which today overlooks Valley View Drive. All the other towns had sites and collected their own garbage.

In the 1970s the Washington County Solid Waste District #1 came into existence, uniting the various community garbage collections. It is directed by a board of 21 members with each city having a vote and St. George allowed five. For a few years the district ran its own service but they soon came to the conclusion that they wanted to bid out the work to a commercial company. Laidlaw Company from Canada won the bid. A few years later the bid was awarded to an eastern firm, Red Rock Waste Management, affiliated with Allied Corporation.

In 1978 the Solid Waste District obtained land where the current dump is located between Washington City and Coral Canyon on Landfill Road. They implemented a modern land fill technique whereby they dig a large trough. A rubber base is placed in the bottom to prevent seepage into ground water and then layers of garbage are laid in the long trough. A layer of dirt is placed on top and is compacted, then another layer of garbage is laid out, covered and compacted. The county board operated that system until 1998 and then contracted the process to Red Rock Waste Services that had only been collecting the garbage. By 2006 the first large trough had been filled and a second was dug and prepared for another decade of compacting. The volume of garbage has increased but so has the technology of compacting. The district plans call for the system to expand on the present site for many more decades.

The district charges each household $9.70 per month and actually reduced the price 50 cents a few years ago. Increasing fuel costs will likely require them to raise the price back by 50 cents. They are presently making 40,000 weekly pickups. Red Rock's contract will end in 2008 and the district will have to decide whether to accept new bids or attempt their own management.

In addition to providing for garbage, the Solid Waste District had undertaken a service to accept garden clippings, including tree branches. Citizens can drop these off at a re-use station on Brigham Road in Bloomington Hills. There the branches are run through a chipping machine. The chips are taken to the dump on Landfill Road where they are further processed into a finer sawdust. The resulting pile is then mixed with purified sewer sludge and cooked and made into mulch that is made available to citizens to buy for their gardens at $15 a ton. The entire endeavor is up-to-date and vital to community growth.[32]

Concluding Thoughts

What does all this mean, all this growth, vitality, space expansion, water consumption, opulence, waste, industry, infrastructure, high culture and population? It is breathtaking. Should it be a concern? Is it evidence of the vitality of the American economy and the vibrancy of good development? Or is it tenuous? Is it a bubble about to burst?

On the positive side, one can say that it is the steady continuation of a 40-year sustained trend. It is not sudden; the growth has varied between 2% and 11% in various years but has been positive every year since 1965. It is linked to the aging of America, a trend that will continue. It is set in desert beauty that will continue to exist. It is located on a good pathway to many places. Its economy is increasingly diverse, including tourism, retirement, industry, transportation and service sector dimensions but very little agriculture. Its geography is away from tornados and most natural disasters but floods and earthquakes are occasional realities. It is close to many national parks and monuments. The cohort of people who live in the county are a very desirable rnix — many youth, lots of young parents, and plenty of grandparents, most well educated. Unemployment is low, almost always below the state and national rate. People feel safe.

On the questionable side is its vulnerability to gasoline prices and dependence on automobile, truck freight and air travel. The fragility of its landscape is of particular concern as is the limited supply of water that impacts the landscape and the population. Its link to retirement incomes seems safe but could be tenuous if the national economy should decline, endangering their investment income. Increasing population means more pollution, a real danger.

One of the most concerning recent developments is the spiraling inflation of land costs. Building lots have become scarce in many communities; much of the home construction is on newly acquired lands where contractors are developing projects in such places as the Washington Fields. Land prices have been skyrocketing. Some lots sell for $100,000 or more and homes in the established neighborhoods are being sold for greatly increased prices. The result is that service sector people are being priced out of the market — nurses, schoolteachers, city workers, etc. This is becoming a very serious problem.

A far out crisis that seems possible after the world and national disasters of 2005 (Indonesia tsunami, Gulf of Mexico hurricane, Midwest tornados, Pakistan earthquake) would occur if a major earthquake hit southern California (as has long been predicted). Conceivably a million refugees could flee to Washington County within a few hours, completely overloading the water, food, energy and housing possibilities of the Dixie communities. Similar nightmares could occur if global warming continued to increase and droughts extended.

It is not uncommon to walk around the communities and the trails and the parks and marvel — marvel at the great air, the beautiful sky, the stunning red hills, the orderly society — and feel a genuine tingling of just being here. Then immediately comes the hope that this can be preserved as so much change comes tumbling in upon us.

ENDNOTES

1. *Spectrum*, St. George, Utah, 22 September 2005, A1. A more specific statement is that in the decade 1990-2000 the St. George Metropolitan Statistical Area was the fastest growing area in the nation, measured as a percentage of growth — 86.1%. Scott Hirschi at Washington County Economic Development Office.

2. These data are based on the research of the late Conrad Jamison. Also see "The County Grows by 8.4 percent," *Spectrum*, 16 November 2005, A1; "This is the place for growth," *The Salt Lake Tribune*, 15 November 2005, A1.

3. *Washington County Demographic and Economic Profile*, Utah Department of Workforce Services, August 2005, 9.

4. Interview with Eric Pedersen, 17 November 2005.

5. *Washington County Demographic and Economic Profile*, Utah Department of Workforce Services, August 2005; 9, 10, 27, 31.

6. Enrollment data provided by Dixie State College Registrar, David Roos, July 2007.

7. Data for the section on public schools were provided by the Washington County School District Superintendent's Office, October 2005.

8. St. George City Planning Office, October 2005.

9. Washington County Travel Council, October 2005.

10. St. George City, SunTran Office, Ryan Marshall, November 2005.

11. St. George City, Leisure Services Department, November 2005.

12. Data for the section on the hospitals were provided by Terri Draper and Steve Wilson of the Dixie Regional Medical Center administration and in Douglas D. Alder, History Of Health Care In Utah's Dixie, St. George, Utah, IHC, 2003.

13. Data provided by SkyWest Airlines administration office.

14. *Salt Lake Tribune*, Friday, November 4, 2005, B4-5. Data provided by Huntsman World Senior Games office in St. George.

15. Data provided by Huntsman World Senior Games office in St. George.

16. Data provided by John Willie, Washington County Planning Office.

17. *Portraits Of Loss, Story Of Hope*, St. George, Stories of Hope Volunteer Committee, 2005; 7, 9.

18. Some data in this section was provided by Julie Breckenridge at the Washington County Water Conservancy District, also WCWCD reports. See also *Spectrum*, 7 November 2005, A6.

19. Public safety information on St. George City was provided by Kelly Larson, retired city police officer, October 2005.

20. Public safety information on Washington County Sheriff's Office was provided by that office, November 2005.

21. John Willie, Washington County Planner, October 2005.

22. Interview with Frank Mathis, SunRoc concrete dispatcher, October 2005.

23. Gary Bedingfield and Gary Campbell, officers of the AOPC, October 2005.

24. *Salt Lake Tribune,* 21 August 2005, A1, A6; *Spectrum,* 25 March 2004, 1, 27 March 2005, 1.

25. *Salt Lake Tribune*, "The Lost Boys," 4 August 2004, A14. See also 1 August 2004, Bl and 14 March 2004, 6.

26. *Salt Lake Tribune*, "State of Siege" by Brooke Adams and Pamela Manson, 21 August 2005, A1, A6.

27. *Spectrum*, 4 May 2003.

28. *Spectrum*, 3 November 2005.

29. *Spectrum*, 25 March 2004, 1.

30. *Spectrum*, 19 Feb 2005, 1; 8 Nov 2005, 1; 28 May 2005, 1; 23 June 2005, 1.

31. Linda Sappington at RSVP, October 2005.

32. Interview with Walter Cox, chair of Washington County Solid Waste District #1, 21 November 2005.

The author wishes to express gratitude to colleagues who served as readers and critics: Elaine Reiser Alder, J. L. Crawford, Heber and La-Ree Jones, Paul Crosby, Rob Snyder, Lyman Hafen, Scott Hirschi, Bob Nicholson, Steve Wilson, Lee Caldwell, John Willie, Lorri Kocinski-Puchlik, and Tim Anderson.

Appendix A

Washington County Commissioners

Feb. 1856 to	Nov. 1856	Lorenzo W. Roundy
Dec. 1856 to	Aug. 1862	Jacob Hamblin
Sep. 1857 to	Aug. 1859	William Slade
Sep. 1859 to	Aug. 1863	Joshua T. Willis
Sep. 1859 to	Dec. 1859	Harrison Pearce
Jan. 1860 to	Dec. 1860	John L. Harris
Jun. 1861 to	Aug. 1864	Robert D. Covington
Sep. 1862 to	Aug. 1871	Jacob Gates
Sep. 1863 to	Aug. 1864	Anson P. Winsor
Sep. 1864 to	Aug. 1866	Marius E. Ensign
Sep. 1864 to	Aug. 1872	James Lewis
Sep. 1866 to	Aug. 1870	William Snow
Aug. 1870 to	Jun. 1873	Henry W. Miller
Sep. 1871 to	Aug. 1874	Marius Ensign (Santa Clara)
Sep. 1872 to	Aug. 1875	Robert D. Covington
Sep. 1873 to	Aug. 1879	Nathaniel Ashby
Sep. 1874 to	Aug. 1880	Henry W. Miller
Sep. 1875 to	Aug. 1878	James Pace
Sep. 1878 to	Aug. 1881	Thomas Jefferson Jones
Sep. 1879 to	30 Mar. 1882	George H. Crosby (resigned)
Sep. 1880 to	30 Mar. 1882	David H. Cannon (resigned)
Sep. 1880 to	30 Mar. 1882	Henry W. Miller (resigned)
Apr. 1882 to	Aug. 1883	Thomas Judd

Apr. 1882 to	Aug. 1883..............	Richard Bently
Apr. 1882 to	Aug. 1889..............	Moroni M. Snow
Sep. 1883 to	Aug. 1885..............	James P. Terry (Rockville)
Sep. 1883 to	Aug. 1887..............	Richard Ashby
Sep. 1885 to	Aug. 1888..............	Neil D. Forsyth
Sep. 1887 to	Dec. 1896..............	R.C. Lund
Sep. 1888 to	Aug. 1890..............	Martin Slack (Toquerville)
Sep. 1889 to	Dec. 1892..............	John A. Gardner
Sep. 1890 to	Dec. 1894..............	James G. Duffin

Terms begin on January 1

Year	Commissioner	Commissioner	Commissioner
1893	James G. Rencher	R.C. Lund	R.C. Lund
1895	Orrin H. Snow	R.C. Lund	John F. Langston
1897	Isaac Macfarlane	Chas. Westover, Jr.	George A. Holt
	James Andrus *(appointed July 1897 on I. Macfarlane's resignation)*		
1899	James Andrus	James Jepson	Edward R. Frei
1901	James Andrus	Edward Frie	Wm. Stirling
1903	Edward M. Brown	John Wood, Jr.	Neil D. Forsyth
1905	Edward M. Brown	Franics Prince	G.M. Spilsbury
1907	Francis L. Daggart	Francis Prince	Samuel Isom
1909	Francis L. Daggart	Samuel Isom	Reuben Gardner
1911	George T. Cottam	Samuel Isom	Reuben Gardner
1913	George T. Cottam	Samuel Isom	James A. Holt
1915	Alex B. Andrus	Samuel Isom	James A. Holt
1917	Alex B. Andrus	James Judd	Alma Nelson
1919	Alma Nelson	James Judd	Geo. F. Whitehead
1921	Geo. F. Whitehead	Herman Hafen	Henry W. Gubler
1923	Henry T. Atkin	HenryW. Gubler	William Lund
1925	Henry T. Atkin	William Lund	James Judd
1927	Henry T. Atkin	James Judd	Francis J. Bowler
1929	Henry T. Atkin	James Judd	Francis J. Bowler
1931	Henry T. Atkin	Francis J. Bowler *(elected Nov. 1930)*	Morris Wilson, Jr. *(elected Nov. 1930)*

1933	Morris Wilson, Jr.	Henry T. Atkin	William Lund
1935	George H. Lytle	Morris Wilson, Jr.	Rex Gardner
1937	George H. Lytle	Morris Wilson, Jr.	Rex Gardner
1939	Newell R. Frei	George H. Lytle	Finley M. Judd
1941	George H. Lytle	Finley M. Judd	Newell R. Frei
1943	Newell R. Frei	Evan J. Woodbury	D. Waldon Ballard
1945	Evan J. Woodbury	D. Waldon Ballard	Roland H. Bowler
1947	Evan J. Woodbury	D. Waldon Ballard	Arthur Barlocker
1949	Arthur J. Barlocker	Evan J. Woodbury	J. Linden 1-leaton
1951	Arthur J. Barlocker	Evan J. Woodbury	Ervil Sanders
1953	Ervil Sanders	Evan J. Woodbury	Arthur J.Woodbury
1955	Arthur J. Barlocker	Ervil Sanders	Rudger C. Atkin
1957	Rudger C. Atkin	Ervil Sanders	Arthur J. Barlocker
1959	Rudger C. Atkin	Ervil Sanders	M. Truman Bowler
1961	Evan J. Woodbury	M. Truman Bowler	Wayne Wilson
1963	Evan J. Woodbury	Wayne Wilson	Irvin E. Barlow
1965	M. Truman Bowler	Wayne Wilson	Floyd G. Ence
1967	M. Truman Bowler	Floyd G. Ence	Emil J. Graff
1969	M. Truman Bowler	Floyd G. Ence	Emil J. Graff
1971	M. Truman Bowler	G. Murray Webb	Emil J. Graff
1973	M. Truman Bowler	G. Murray Webb	Vernon Church
1975	M. Truman Bowler	G. Murray Webb	Vernon Church
1977	G. Murray Webb	Jerry B. Lewis	Vernon Church
			Howard Smith *(appointed Mar. 1978 on V. Church's death)*
1979	G. Murray Webb	Jerry B. Lewis	Lyman W. Gubler
1981	Jerry B. Lewis	Kurt L. Young	John F. Whitney
1983	Jerry B. Lewis	Kurt L Young	John F. Whitney
1985	Jerry B. Lewis	Kurt L. Young	John F. Whitney
		Dr. Garth B. Last *(appointed Sep. 1986 on K. Young's resignation)*	
1987	Jerry B. Lewis	John F. Whitney	Garth B. Last
			David L. Watson *(appointed Jun. 1988 on G. Last's resignation)*

1989	Jerry B. Lewis	Gayle M. Aldred	Scott Hirschi
1991	Jerry B. Lewis	Scott Hirschi	Gayle M. Aldred
1993	Gayle M. Aldred	Jerry B. Lewis	Russell J. Gallian
1995	Gayle M. Aldred	Jerry B. Lewis	Russell J. Gallian
1997	Gayle M. Aldred	Jerry B. Lewis	Alan D. Gardner
1999	Gayle M. Aldred	Alan D. Gardner	James J. Eardley
2001	Gayle M. Aldred	Alan D. Gardner	James J. Eardley
2003	Alan D. Gardner	James J. Eardley	Jay Ence
2005	James J. Eardley	Alan D. Gardner	Jay Ence
2007	James J. Eardley	Alan D. Gardner	Denny Drake

Appendix B

Sheriffs of Washington County

Apr. 1856 to	Apr. 1857	Charles Wakeman Dalton
Sep. 1857 to	Mar. 1859	Evan Edwards
Mar. 1859 to	Aug. 1859	Harrison Pearce
Sep. 1859 to	Aug. 1863	Albert Washington Collins
Sep. 1863 to	Mar. 1864	Andrew Smith Gibbons
Mar. 1864 to	Aug. 1867	David Henry Cannon, Sr.
Sep. 1867 to	Aug. 1869	George Henry Crosby
Sep. 1869 to	Nov. 1877	Daniel Seegmiller
Nov. 1877 to	Aug. 1883	Augustus P. Hardy
Sep. 1884 to	Aug. 1888	Samuel Judd, Jr.
Sep. 1888 to	Dec. 1900	George Brooks, Sr.
Jan. 1901 to	Dec. 1904	Alex Y. Milne
Jan. 1905 to	Dec. 1906	Frank Richard Bentley
Jan. 1907 to	Dec. 1908	William Thomas Perkins
Jan. 1909 to	Dec. 1920	Charles R. Worthen
Jan. 1921 to	Dec. 1922	W. W. Cannon
Jan. 1923 to	Dec. 1926	Wilford Goff
Jan. 1927 to	Dec. 1934	William Brooks
Jan. 1935 to	Dec. 1936	John H. Cottam
Jan. 1937 to	Dec. 1958	Antone Prince
Jan. 1959 to	Dec. 1962	Roy Ralph Renouf
Jan. 1963 to	Dec. 1978	Evan Whitehead
Jan. 1979 to	Dec. 1982	Eugene S. Jones

Jan. 1983 to   Dec. 1986....................Kenneth Campbell
Jan. 1987 to   Dec. 1998....................Glenwood Humphries
Jan. 1999 to   present.........................Kirk Smith

Appendix C

Mayors of St. George

Erastus Snow (Camp Council)..............1861 to 1862

Angus M. Cannon ....1862 to 1866

Jacob M. Gates......................................1866 to 1870

Joseph W Young....................................1870 to 1872

Robert Gardner......................................1872 to 1876

Alexander F. McDonald........................1876 to 1878

Richard I. Bentley ....1878 to 1882,
1888 to 1890

Henry Eyring...1882 to 1884

Robert Lund ....1884 to 1888

Anthony W. Ivins ....1890 to 1894

Isaac C. Macfarlane ....1894 to 1896,
1904 to 1906

Edward M. Brown.................................1896 to 1900

Thomas P. Cottam ....1900 to 1904

F. L. Daggett...1906 to 1910

George F. Whitehead.............................1910 to 1912

Thomas Judd ....1912 to 1914

John T. Woodbury ....1914 to 1916

James McArthur....................................1916 to 1918

Albert E. Miller.....................................1918 to 1920,
1922 to 1924,
1936 to 1940

A. B. Andrus .... 1920 to 1922

Henry T. Atkin...................................... 1924 to 1932

John T. Woodbury, Jr............................. 1932 to 1936

D. Clark Watson .... 1940 to 1946

E. Eric Snow .... 1946 to 1948

Joseph T. Atkin.................................... 1948 to 1954

J. Clinton Snow .... 1954 to 1958

William A. Barlocker .... 1958 to 1966

Marion H. Bowler .... 1966 to 1974

Neal M. Lundberg................................ 1974 to 1978

James Grey Larkin .... 1978 to 1982

Karl Brooks.. 1982 to 1994

Daniel D. McArthur .... 1994 to present

Appendix D

Irrigation Systems in Washington County

In 1904 the U.S. Department of Agriculture published a study on irrigation in the United States chaired by Elwood Mead. A volume was devoted to Utah, and within that, a chapter written by Frank Adams focused on the Virgin River Basin. Adams's study includes an examination of each community, even each irrigation ditch. This enables us to perceive the scarcity of watered land and the intensity of work demanded to provide crops to sustain the people in the county. This is his listing of irrigated lands:

Bloomington .... 190 acres, average holding 12 acres

Price .... 140 acres, average holding 11.5 acres

Atkinville .... 120 acres, private holding of William Atkin

Santa Clara .... 455 acres, average holding 10.5 acres, 6 ditches

Gunlock .... 105 acres, average holding 10 acres, 9 ditches

Pine Valley .... 623 acres, average holding 20 acres, 7 ditches

Shebits .... 80 acres, 3 ditches

Magotsa .... 78 acres, 6 ditches

Hunt's, Chadburn's
and Foster's Farms ... 46 acres, 3 ditches

Grass Valley .... 103 acres, average holding 25.75 acres, 4 ditches

Middleton .... 35 acres, average holding 8.75 acres

Washington .... 325 acres, 6 ditches

Harrisburg .... 30 acres

Leeds .... 230 acres, 3 ditches

Anderson .... 150 acres (depending on water supply), 1 ditch

Harmony .... 305 acres, average holding 16 acres, 9 ditches

Kanarraville .... 350 acres, average holding 12 acres, often short

Bellevue .... 75 acres, average holding 19 acres

Toquerville .... 350 acres, average holding 6.5 acres, 6 ditches

Virgin .... 277 acres, average holding 12 acres, 12 ditches

Mt. Dell .... 137 acres, average holding 12 acres, 12 ditches

Duncan's retreat .... 4 acres

Grafton .... 154 acres, averge holding 8.5 acres, 2 ditches

Rockville .... 293 acres, average holding 9 acres, 3 ditches

Springdale .... 160 acres, average holding 8 acres, 2 ditches

Shunesburg............... 35 acres

Subtotal ...... 4,844 acres

St. George 1,660 acres and Washington Fields,

Subtotal ...... 6,504 acres

Kanab and Muddy bring the GRAND TOTAL to,

Total .... 13,700 acres[1]

1. Elwood Mead, *Report of Irrigation Investigations in Utah*, Washington, D.C., Government Printing Office, Document 720, 58th Congress, 2d Session, 1904. Frank Adams "Agriculture Under Irrigation in the Basin of Virgin River."

Selected Bibliography

Addy, Caroline S. "James Godson Bleak: Pioneer Historian of Southern Utah." Master's thesis, Brigham Young University, 1953.

Alder, Douglas D. "The Growth/Limited Growth Debate." St. George Magazine (July-August 1994): 14-23.

Alder, Elaine R. "The Heartbeat of St. George," *St. George Magazine* (July August 1993) 67.

Alexander, Thomas G. Utah, *The Right Place*. Layton, Utah: Gibbs Smith, 1995.

Anderson, Nels. *Desert Saints*. Chicago: University of Chicago Press, 1942, 1966.

Arrington, Leonard J. *Great Basin Kingdom*. Cambridge: Harvard University Press, 1958.

------."The Mormon Cotton Mission in Southern Utah." *Pacific Historical Quarterly*, 25 (August 1966):22 1-38.

Ashton, Katherine. "Whatever Happened to Maurine Whipple?" *Sunstone 14* (April 1990): 36-41.

Bailey, Paul. *Jacob Hamblin, Buckskin Apostle*. Los Angeles: Westernlore Press, 1948.

Banfield, Edward C. "Rural Rehabilitation in Washington County, Utah" *Journal of Land and Public Utility Economics 23* (August 1947): 261-270.

Bate, Kerry. "John Steele: Medicine Man, Magician, Mormon Patriarch." *Utah Historical Quarterly 62* (Winter 1994): 71-90.

Beckstrom, Elizabeth Snow and Bessie Snow. *Oh Ye Mountains High: History of Pine Valley, Utah*. St. George: Heritage Press, 1980.

Bennion, Lowell C. "The Incidence of Mormon Polygamy in 1880: 'Dixie' vs. Davis Stake." *Journal of Mormon History 11* (1984): 22-47.

Bennion, Lowell C. and Merrill K. Ridd, "Utah's Dynamic Dixi Satellite of Salt Lake, Las Vegas, or Los Angeles?" *Utah Historical Quarterly 47*, (Summer 1979) 311-27.

Bracy, Maryruth and Linda Lambert. "Maurine Whipple's Story of The Giant Joshua." *Dialogue 6* (Autumn-Winter 1971): 55-62.

Bradley, Martha Sonntag. *Kidnapped From That Land: The Government Raids on the Polygamists of Short Creek*. Salt Lake City: University of Utah Press, 1993.

------."The Women of Fundamentalism: Short Creek, 1953." *Dialogue 23* (Summer 1990): 15-57.

Bradshaw, Bernice, ed. *Under the Dixie Sun*. Washington County Daughters of Utah Pioneers, 1950.

Brooks, Juanita. "The Arizona Strip." *The Pacific Spectator 3* (Summer 1949): 290-301.

------."The Cotton Mission." *Utah Historical Quarterly 29* (Summer 1961): 201-222.

------.*Emma Lee*. Logan: Utah State University Press, 1975.

------."Indian Relations on the Mormon Frontier." *Utah Historical Quarterly* (January-April 1944): 1-48.

------."Indian Sketches from the Journals of Thomas D. Brown and Jacob Hamblin." *Utah Historical Quarterly 29* (Fall 1969): 347-60.

------.*Jacob Hamblin: Mormon Apostle to the Indians*. Salt Lake City: Westwater Press, 1980.

------."Jest a copyin' — word fir word." *Utah Historical Quarterly 26* (Summer 1958): 375-95.

------.*John Doyle Lee: Zealot, Pioneer Builder, Scapegoat*. Glendale, CA: Arthur H. Clark Company, 1962.

------."The Land That God Forgot." *Utah Historical Quarterly 26* (Summer 1958): 207-19.

------."Memories of a Mormon Girlhood." *Journal of American Folklore 77* (July-September 1964): 195-2 19.

------."The Mountain Meadows: Historic Stopping Place on the Spanish Trail." *Utah Historical Quarterly 35* (Spring 1967): 137-46.

------.*Mountain Meadows Massacre*. Palo Alto, CA: Stanford University Press, 1950.

------.*On the Ragged Edge: The Life and Times of Dudley Leavitt*. Salt Lake City: Utah Historical Society, 1973.

------.*Quicksand and Cactus: A Memoir of the Southern Mormon Frontier.* Salt Lake City: University of Utah Press, 1988.

------."Silver Reef." *Utah Historical Quarterly 29* (Summer 1961): 281-87.

------."Silver Reef: Fact and Folklore." In *Essays on the American West,* edited by Thomas G. Alexander. Provo: Brigham Young University Press, 1974.

Brooks, William. *Uncle Will Tells His Story.* Edited by Juanita Brooks. Salt Lake City: Taggart & Co., 1970.

Brown, Thomas D. *Journal of the Southern Indian Mission: Diary of Thomas D. Brown,* Edited by Juanita Brooks. Logan: Utah State University Press, 1972.

Burt, Olive W. "Wine-making in Utah's Dixie." In *Lore of Faith and Folly,* edited by Thomas E. Cheney. Salt Lake City: University of Utah Press, 1971.

Corbett, Pearson. "A History of the Muddy Mission." Master's thesis, Brigham Young University, 1968.

------.*Jacob Hamblin, the Peacemaker.* Salt Lake City: Deseret News Press, 1952.

Greedy, Kathryn B. *Time Flies, The History of Skywest Airlines.* San Antonio: Loflin, 1992.

Crawford, J. L. "The Boy Who'd Never Seen a Train" *St. George Magazine* (August-September 1995): 26-27.

Dellenbaugh, Frederick Samuel. "A New Valley of Wonders." *Scribner's Magazine 35* (January 1944): 1-18.

De Mille, Janice Force. *Portraits of the Hurricane Pioneers.* St. George: Homestead Publishers, 1976.

Driggs, Ken. "After the Manifesto: Modern Polygamy and Fundamentalist Mormons." *Journal of Church and State 323* (Spring 1990): 367-89.

------."Fundamentalist Attitudes Toward the Church: The Sermons of LeRoy S. Johnson." *Dialogue 23* (Summer 1990): 38-60.

England, Eugene. "The Dawning of a Brighter Day: Mormon Literature After 150 Years." *Brigham Young University Studies 22* (Spring 1982): 13 1-160.

Fife, Austin and Alta. "Folkways of the Mormons from the Journals of John D. Lee." *Western Folklore 21* (October 1962): 229-46.

Fish, Joseph. *History of Enterprise, Utah, and Its Surroundings.* n.p., 1967.

------.*The Life and Times of Joseph Fish, Mormon Pioneer.* edited by John H. Kenkel, Danville, Illinois: Interstate Printer and Publisher, 1970.

Gregerson, Edna J. *Dixie College, Monument to the Industry of a Dedicated People*. Salt Lake City: Franidin Quest, 1993.

Hafen, Arthur K. *Beneath Vermillion Cliffs*. St. George: n.p., 1967.

------.*Dixie Folklore and Pioneer Memoirs*. St. George: Privately published, 1961.

------.*Devoted Empire Builders*. St. George: Privately published, 1969.

Hafen, Lyman. *Over the Joshua Slope*. New York: Bradbury Press, 1994.

------.*Roping the Wind*. Logan: Utah State University Press, 1995.

------.*Making the Desert Bloom: The Story of Water and Power in St. George*. St. George: Publishers Place, 1991.

Hafen, Mary Ann Stucki. *Recollections of a Handcart Pioneer of 1860*. Denver: Privately published, 1938, 1980.

Hansen, Jennifer Moulton. *Letters of Catharine Cottam Romney, Plural Wife*. Urbana: University of Illinois Press, 1992.

Hardy, B. Carman. *Solemn Covenant, The Mormon Polygamous Passage*. Urbana: University of Illinois Press, 1992.

Harline, Osmond L. "Utah's Black Gold: the Petroleum Industry." *Utah Historical Quarterly 31* (Summer, 1963): 294.

Harman, George. *Diary of George Harman, 1826-1891*. Provo: Brigham Young University, 1942.

Haskell, Thales Hastings. "Journal of Thales H. Haskell." Edited by Juanita Brooks. *Utah Historical Quarterly 12* (January-April 1944): 69-89.

Heywood, Martha Spence. *Not By Bread Alone, The Journal of Martha Spence Heywood, 1850-56*. Edited by Juanita Brooks. Salt Lake City: Utah State Historical Society, 1978.

Hinton, Wayne H. "Soil and Water Conservation in Washington County." Master's thesis, University of Utah, 1961.

Jackson, Richard H. "Utah's Harsh Lands, Hearth of Greatness." *Utah Historical Quarterly 49* (Winter 1981): 4-25.

Jarvis, Zora Smith. *Sketches from the Lives of Brigham Jarvis, Sr. and Mary Forsythe Jarvis*. Provo: Gendex Press, 1967.

Jones, York F. and Evelyn K. Jones. *Lehi Willard Jones, 1854-1947*. Cedar City: Privately published, 1972.

Judd, Zadok Knapp. *Autobiography of Zadok Knapp Judd*. Ogden: n.p., 1937.

Kane, Elizabeth Wood. *A Gentile Account of Life in Utah's Dixie, 1872-1873: Elizabeth Kane's St. George Journal*, edited by Norman R. Bower. Salt Lake City: Tanner Trust Fund, University of Utah Library, 1995.

------.*Twelve Mormon Homes Visited in Succession on a Journey Through Utah to Arizona.* Salt Lake City: Tanner Trust, 1974.

Kraack, Donald F. "Dentists and Dirt in Early Dixie." *Senior Sampler IV* (August 1992): 1.

Lancaster, Dennis. "Dixie Wine." *Sunstone I* (Summer 1976): 74-84.

------."Dixie Wine." Master's thesis, Brigham Young University, 1972.

Larson, Andrew Karl. *Erastus Snow.* Salt Lake City: University of Utah Press, 1971.

------.*I Was Called To Dixie.* Reprint, St. George: Dixie College Foundation, 1993.

------.*The Red Hills of November.* Reprint, St. George: Dixie College Foundation, 1993.

Larsen, Wesley. *A History of Toquerville.* 2 vols. Cedar City: n.p., 1985.

Lee, John D. A Mormon Chronicle. *The Diaries of John D. Lee 1848-1876*, edited by Robert Class Cleland and Juanita Brooks. 6 vol. San Marino, California: Huntington Library, 1955.

Little, Jesse C. *Jacob Hamblin.* Salt Lake City: Deseret News Press, 1881.

Logue, Larry M. *Sermon in the Desert: Belief and Behavior in Early St. George, Utah.* Urbana: University of Illinois Press, 1988.

Macfarlane, John M. *Yours Sincerely, John M. Macfarlane.* Salt Lake City: L. W. Macfarlane, 1980.

Manger, Marietta M. *Saga of Three Towns: Harrisburg, Leeds, Silver Reef.* Panguitch, Utah: Garfield County News, 1952.

Meeks, Lenora Atkin. "John Nock Hinton. The Reconstructed Life of an English Born Mormon Convert of Virgin City, Utah." Master's thesis, Brigham Young University, 1987.

Meeks, Priddy. "Journal of Priddy Meeks." Edited by Juanita Brooks. *Utah Historical Quarterly 10* (1942): 145-223.

Miller, Albert E. *The Immortal Pioneers. Founders of the City of St. George, Utah.* n.p: Albert E. Miller. 1946.

Mitchell, Albert O. "Dramatics in Southern Utah — Parowan, Cedar City, Beaver, St. George — from 1850 to the Coming of the Moving Picture." Master's thesis, University of Utah, 1935.

Mooney, Bernice. *Salt of the Earth.* Salt Lake City: Catholic Diocese of Salt Lake City, 1987.

Moss, Robert Hafen, "An Historical Study of the Factors Influencing the Organization of Education in Washington County, 1852-1915." Master's thesis, Brigham Young University, 1961.

Nelson, Carl. *Autobiography of Carl Erwin "Star" Nelson*. St. George: Privately published, 1992.

Pendleton, Mark A. "Memories of Silver Reef." *Utah Historical Quarterly 3* (1930): 99-118.

Peterson, Charles S. "A Utah Moon: Perceptions of Southern Utah." Juanita Brooks Lecture Series. St. George: Dixie College, 1984.

------."Book A — Levi Mathers Savage: The Look of Utah in 1873." *Utah Historical Quarterly 41* (Winter 1973): 4-22.

------."Jacob Hamblin, Apostle to the Lamanites and the Indian Mission." *Journal of Mormon History 2* (1975): 21-34.

------."Life in the Village Society, 1877-1920." *Utah Historical Quarterly 49* (Winter 1981): 78-96.

------.*Take Up Your Mission, Mormon ColonizingAlong the Little Colorado River, 1879-1900*. Tucson: University of Arizona Press, 1973.

Peterson, Levi. *Juanita Brooks, Mormon, Woman, Historian*. Salt Lake City: University of Utah Press, 1988.

Powell, Allan Kent. *Utah Remembers World War II*. Logan: Utah State University Press, 1991.

Proctor, Paul Dean. *Geology of the Silver Reef-Harrisburg Mining District*. Utah Geological and Mineralogical Survey Bulletin no. 44 (1953): 70-77.

Proctor, Paul Dean and Morris A. Shirts. *Silver, Sinners and Saints: A History of Old Silver Reef*. Paulmar, Ind.: n.p., 1991.

Reeve, W. Paul. "A Little Oasis in the Desert: Hurricane, Utah, 1860-1920." *Utah Historical Quarterly 62* (Summer 1994): 222-45.

------.*Century of Enterprise, a History of Enterprise, Utah, 1896-1996*. Springville, Ut.: City of Enterprise, 1996.

Reid, H. Lorenzo. *Brigham Young's Dixie of the Desert*. Zion Natural History Association, 1964.

Reinbold, Carolyn. "History of Bloomington, Utah." 1994.

Savage, Levi. *Diary of Levi Savage, 1852-53, 1877-99*. Provo: Brigham Young University Library, 1956.

Smith, Melvin T. "Forces That Shaped Utah's Dixie: Another Look." *Utah Historical Quarterly 47* (Spring 1979): 110-29.

Steele, John. "Extracts from the Journal of John Steele." Edited by Juanita Brooks. *Utah Historical Quarterly 6* (January 1933): 2-28.

Stratton, Alice Gubler. *The Story of the Hurricane Canal*. La Verkin, Utah: Rio Virgin Press, 1985.

Thompson, Reed Paul. "Eighty Years of Music in St. George, Utah 1861-1941." Master's thesis, Brigham Young University, 1952.

Tobler, Douglas. "Heinrich Hug and Jacob Tobler: From Switzerland to Santa Clara, 1854-1880." *Dialogue 26* (Winter 1993): 104-28.

Walker, Charles Lowell. *Diary of Charles Lowell Walker.* Edited by Andrew Karl Larson and Katherine Miles Larson. 2 vols. Logan: Utah State University Press, 1980.

Washburn, Lorraine T. "Culture in Dixie," *Utah Historical Quarterly 29* (Summer 1961): 255-67.

Webb, Ruby. *A Brief History of the La Verkin Hot Springs and the La Verkin Canal.* 1986.

Whipple, Maureen. *The Giant Joshua.* Boston: Houghton Muffin, Co., 1942.

Wood, James A. "The Changing Demographic and Economic Structure of Washington County, Utah 1970-1993." *Utah Economic and Business Review 54* (January/February 1994): 1-18.

Woodbury, Angus M. "A History of Southern Utah and Its National Parks." *Utah Historical Quarterly 12* (July-October 1944): 112-209.

Woodbury, Grace Atkin, and Angus Munn Woodbury. *The Story of Atkinville, A One-family Village.* Salt Lake City: n.p., 1957.

Woodbury, John T. *Vermillion Cliffs: Reminiscences of Utah's Dixie.* St. George: n.p., 1932.

Index

A

Abbott, Greg, 344
Adair, Samuel, 27, 47, 62
Adams, Don, 264
Adams, Duane, 264
Adams, Eleanor, 160
Adams, Emma, 160
Adams, Frank, 185, 187, 196, 267, 417-18
Adams, Lonnie, 305
Adams, Roger, 345
Adams, Walt, 166
Adams River, 7, 187, 417
Affleck, J. T., 100
Agarapoots, 21-22
Airlines, 222-223, 313-317, 323, 358, 371-72, 406, 421
Airport, xviii, 58, 222-223, 229, 246, 255, 258, 275, 290, 304, 310, 313, 316-17, 323, 352, 355, 360, 371-72, 393, 395
AirWest, 313
Albright, Horace, 205, 246
Alder, Douglas D., 199-200, 281, 320, 323, 358, 406, 419
Alder, Elaine, xi, 248, 407, 419
Alder, Lin, xi
Alder, Nate, xi
Aldred, Gayle, ix, 412
Alfalfa, 28, 90-92, 103, 178, 186, 385
Allen, John, x, 338
Allen, Rufus, 19

Allred, John A., 218
Alsop, Charles, 245
American Savings and Loan, 338
Ammon, Chris, 178, 180
Amphitheater, 319, 373
Anasazi, xv, 4-5, 385
Ancestor Square, 101, 221, 343-344
Anderson, Anna, 94
Anderson, E. L., 222
Anderson, Jerry, 313, 344
Anderson, Nancy Pearce, 62
Anderson, Nels, 48, 122, 226, 419
Anderson, Peter, 94
Anderson's Ranch, 41, 95, 121, 152, 214-15, 252, 267
Andrus, A. B., 244, 416
Andrus, Alex, 166, 410
Andrus, Blame, 220
Andrus, Calvin, 259
Andrus, James, 92, 106, 129, 178, 238, 255, 336, 410
Andrus, Milo, 58
Andrus, Tom, 166
Angell, Truman O., 58
Apex Mine, 109, 224, 244, 284
Archibald, Nolan, 318

Arizona, 2, 9, 13, 18, 36-37, 45, 57, 59, 70, 72, 76, 78, 91, 94, 107, 109, 118, 120, 143, 151, 158, 173, 182, 207, 211, 222, 232, 240-41, 244, 247, 265-66, 272-74, 277, 282-83, 301, 309, 315, 325, 331, 334, 361, 371-72, 385-86, 390, 393, 398-401, 420, 423-24

Arizona Strip, 2, 9, 13, 45, 59, 72, 91, 94, 107, 118, 182, 222, 244, 265-66, 301, 325, 331, 334, 385, 420

Armstrong, Ellis, 196

Arrowhead Hotel, 211, 246, 340

Arrowhead Petroleum Corp, 244-245

Arrowhead Trail, 211, 214-216, 299

Arrowhead Trail Automobile, 211

Art, x, 5, 56, 148, 162, 246, 264, 320, 322-23, 343-47, 365, 373, 381, 383, 402

"Art Around the Corner," 381

Artists' Coop Gallery, 344

Ash Creek, xvi, 6, 9, 12, 18, 26-28

Ashby, Bonita Pendleton, 328

Ashby, By, 166

Ashby, Nathaniel, 92, 409

Ashby, Richard, 91, 410

Ashton, William, 32

Ashworth, William B., 149

Assembly of God Church, 280

Association[s], 120, 154, 157, 162, 165, 195-196, 209-11, 236-37, 240, 248, 264, 304, 308, 317, 322, 344, 357, 366, 368, 392, 396

Atkin, Anthony W., 220, 255, 265

Atkin, Brent, 315-316

Atkin, Clayton, x, 298, 338

Atkin, Jerry, 315

Atkin, Joe, 297, 337

Atkin, Lee, 315-316, 328

Atkin, Ralph, 307, 314

Atkin, Rudger, 265, 290, 315, 411

Atkin, Sidney, x, 220, 246, 285, 297, 315, 323

Atkin, William, 410-411, 417

Atkinville, 44, 48, 71, 94, 417, 425

Automobiles, 208, 210-12, 215, 217, 221, 245, 257, 283, 338, 351, 368

Avenna Center, 365

Averett, C. G., 32

Averett, Clinton, 159

Averett, Elijah, 64

Averett, George Washington Gill, 85

Aviation, 222, 246, 314, 323, 371-72

B

Backman, Tom, 164, 170

Bailey, Paul, 252, 419

Baker, Bill, 191, 341

Baldwin, Nathaniel, 273

Baldwin Radio Plant, 273

Ball, Dick, 307

Ballard, J. Monroe, 194

Ballard, James M., 183

Ballard, Rhanee, x, 327

Band, Thompson, 160

Bangerter, Norman, 197, 320

Bank of Hurricane, 224, 337

Bank of Iron County, 338

Bank of St. George, 224, 330, 336-37

Bank Robberies, 330

Banking, 336

Baptist, 280, 395, 397

Baptist Churches, 280

Barbee, William Tecumseh, 106

Barlocker, William, 194, 298, 416

Barlow, Dan, 275, 401

Barlow, Israel, 273

Barlow, John Y., 273-74, 398

Barron, Byron, 159

Bass, Nell, 280

Beal, Glenn, 313

Beal, Wilma, x, 109, 122, 313, 323

Beard, Jack, 173

Beaver Dam, 3, 7, 79, 105, 176, 213, 265-66, 286, 291, 386

Beaver Dam Mountains, 3, 105

Behunin, Isaac, 32, 205

Belka, Ken, 318

Bell, E. Jay, 70

Bennett, Helen, 242

Bennion, John, 40, 79

Bennion, Lowell C., x, 11, 419-20
Bentley, Joseph, 156
Bentley, Mathew M., 191
Bentley, Richard I., 106, 415
Bentley, W. O., 233-234
Berry, Isabella, 273
Berry, Joseph 273
Berry, Robert, 273
Berryhill, Lynn, 344
Big Hand Cafe, 221, 340
Big Plain, 268
Bingham, Jay, 192, 199, 303, 307
Birch, Joseph, 172
Black, Joseph, 79
Black, William, 32
Black Ridge, xvi, 12, 26-27, 33, 40, 61,
    95, 115, 118, 201-202, 212-13, 267,
    330, 371
Blackburn, Jehu, 29
Blackburn, Nellie, 278
Blake, Jay, 328
Blake, Joseph, 290
Blakley, Glen, 345
Bleak, Earl J., 161, 250-251
Bleak, James G., 18, 37, 46, 52, 69, 82,
    113, 119-20, 134, 156-57, 165, 167
Bleak, Stella Christian, 161
Bliggensdorfer, Gottlieb, 159
Blood, Henry, 233
Bloomington, xviii, 71, 169, 192, 196-97,
    241, 244, 288, 300-10, 323, 331, 361,
    366-67, 378, 380-81, 386-87, 392-93,
    395-97, 404, 417, 424
Bloomington Community Council, 307
Bloomington Country Club, 303, 307, 309
Bloomington Hills, 197, 241, 306-07,
    309, 331, 361, 366-67, 378, 392, 395,
    397, 404
Bloomington Irrigation Company, 192
Bluff Street, 380, 394
Bonanza Airlines, 223, 313, 371
Bonanza City, 107
Bonneli, Daniel, 38
Booth, Craig, x, 192

Bosshard, Herman, 159
Bosshard, Jacob, 159
Bowcutt, Alison, 350
Bowler, Ed, 267
Bowler, Erinn, 225, 246
Bowler, Francis Joseph, 235
Bowler, Joseph, 235
Bowler, Kip, 267
Bowler, Laura, ix
Bowler, Leon, 240-41
Bowler, Lewis, 194, 338
Bowler, Marion, x, 11, 246, 298, 302,
    323, 416
Bowler, Truman, x, 194, 235, 247, 300,
    303, 323, 325, 338, 411
Boyer, Roger, 301, 304, 306
Bracken, Bennett, 336
Bradshaw, Hazel, 46, 100, 122
Bradshaw Hotel, 218, 382
Braham, Marty, 316
Branch, William A., 157
Breinholt, Floyd, 344
Brigham City, 47, 110, 120-121
Brimhall, George H., 185
Bringhurst, Douglas, 338
Bringhurst, W. A., 183
Broadbent, Leslie, 273
Brooks, George, 52, 70, 156, 413, 424
Brooks, Juanita, 1, 46-47, 70, 121, 152,
    170, 209, 226, 253-54, 281, 289, 334,
    348, 420-24
Brooks, Karl, 200, 319-20, 416
Brooks, Wil, 52
Brown, Charles, 69, 180
Brown, Newman, 32
Brown, Robert, 32, 46
Brown, Thomas D., 19, 46-47, 124, 152,
    168, 420-21
Browning, Val A., ix, 320
Bruce Hurst Field, 375
Bruhn, Arthur, 209, 236, 318-19
Bryce, Ebenezer, 66
Bryner, Ulrich, 102
Bunker, Edward, 117

Bunker, Jimmie, 194

Bunker, Steven A., 190-91

Bunkerville, xvi, 9-10, 45, 80, 232, 241, 266

Bunnell, Max, 345

Bureau of Land Management, 291, 356, 369, 376

Burgess, Abraham, 140

Burgess, George M., 178

Burgon, George A., 152, 154, 156, 169

Burke, Charles, 79

Burke, Fannie, 137, 278

Burns Arena, 347-348

Burr, David H., 83

Burr, Jack F., 335

Burt, John, 60

Burt, Olive, 148, 153, 421

Burt, William, 65

Burton, Laurence J., 195

Bush, George, 271

C

Caanan Livestock Company, 88

Cahoon, Harold, 47, 382

Cahoon, Priscilla, 382

Calkins, Mariette, 134

Call's Landing, 35, 72

Calvary Chapel, 397

Campbell, Ken, x, 331, 348

Canals, (see irrigation)

Cancer, 269-270, 319, 326-27, 369-70

Canning Centers, 227

Cannon, Angus M., 113, 165, 415

Cannon, David H., 23, 53, 104, 409

Cannon, Howard, 251, 259

Cannon, Walter, 240

Cannon, Wilhemina, 1, 73

Cannon, Woodruff W., 337

Care Centers, 396-397

Carling, Isaac, 273

Carnegie Foundation, 165

Carpenter, Joseph, 163, 169

Carpenter, W. H., 32

Carter, William, 172

Casper, Billy, 303

Catholic Church, 34, 107-08, 160, 277, 279-80, 282, 397, 423

Cedars Hotel, 216

Celebrity Concert Series, 320, 347, 373

Census Insights, 80

Challenger Airlines, 371

Chamber of Commerce, 215, 221, 230, 233-34, 244

Chew, Frank, 315-316

Chidester, John Peck, 64

Chidester, John R., 172

Christensen, C. L., 59, 150

Christian, Wayne, 328

Christian Fellowship, 397

Christian Science Church, 280

Christmas, 43, 93, 160-61, 225, 239, 242

Chums, 339

Citizen Call, 270

Citizens for Moderate Growth (CMG), 350

Civic Clubs, 234, 237, 255, 298

Civil War, xvii, 35, 62, 83, 88, 167

Civilian Conservation Corps (CCC), 228-30, 328, 383

Clark, Alonzo, 166, 173

Clark, Sarah, 134, 154, 156, 279

Clark Theatrical Company, 156

Cliff, Frederick, 100, 324

Cliff View, 397

Climate, 1, 4, 8-10, 13, 21, 27-28, 61, 79, 89, 102, 117, 178, 221, 289, 352, 360-61

Clinton, Bill, 271

Clinton, Zina, 134

Clyde, George Dewey, 192, 199

Coache, William, 129

Cochrane, D. U., 164, 169

Colbath, Alex, 312

Colbert, Jim, 297

Coleman, Ray C., 223

Collett, Farrell, 344

Color Country Spectrum, 164

Colorado, xv-xvi, 3, 7, 16, 20, 24, 35-36, 49, 61, 72, 75, 78, 86, 118, 120, 138, 171, 189, 202-04, 247, 272, 274-76, 301, 307, 316, 344, 355, 357, 387, 398-400, 424

Colorado City, 272, 274-276, 316, 344, 398-400

Colorado River, 3, 7, 20, 24, 35-36, 61, 72, 75, 78, 118, 120, 138, 171, 202-03, 357, 424

Commercial Center, 342, 381

Condominiums, 287-288, 290, 305-306, 309-310, 312, 392, 394-396

Conklin, Sarah Louisa, 279-280

Connor, Patrick, 83

Construction of Dams, xvi, 20-21, 27, 42, 50, 64-65, 84-85, 88, 138, 171, 178, 197-198, 230, 388

Convict Labor, 214

Coombs, Alan, x, 305, 310, 323, 343, 374

Cooper, James, 159

Cooper, Richard D., 333

Coral Canyon, 378, 393, 403

Corbett, Pearson, 127, 152, 421

Cordova, Robert, 193

Corn Fest Days, 101

Cornwall, Viola, 345

Cort, A. B., 137, 278

Cosby, Randy, 362

Cottam, Arthur, 238

Cottam, Beulah, 327

Cottam, Leah, 245

Cottam, Lester, 222

Cottam, Marie, 327

Cottam, Melbourne, 194

Cottam, Thomas P., 179, 337, 415

Cotton, xvi, 8-9, 11, 21, 26-28, 35-36, 38-39, 53, 57, 61-65, 72, 88-89, 95-96, 100-01, 104, 128, 131, 138, 147-48, 150-151, 166, 173-174, 181, 383, 419-20

Cotton Days, 101

Cotton Factory, 53, 57, 61, 63-65, 72, 88, 138, 150, 181, 383

Cotton Mission, xvi, 26, 38, 174, 419-20

Cottonwood Project, 173, 189

County, Millard, 76-77, 79

Covington, Bert, 220

Covington, Robert, 27, 47, 409

Cox, Boots, 264

Cox, ElMyrrh, 298, 328

Cox, LeRoy H., 191, 193

Cox, Malm, 195

Cox, Martha Cragun, 129, 132, 134, 152, 168

Cox, Mervyn, 328

Cox, Retta, 134

Cox, Warren, 211-212

Cox, Wilford Charles, 328

Coyne, James, 278

Crane, Thomas, 157

Crawford, B. Glen, 314

Crawford, Fern, xi, 260, 281

Crawford, J. L., ix, 5, 31, 67, 73-74, 85, 101, 204, 206, 208, 215-216, 218, 229, 246, 260, 265, 294, 323, 407, 421

Crawford, John R., 265

Crawford, Sam, 184

Crawford, William L., 206, 218

Crawford, William R., 32

Crime, 331-332, 353, 355, 357, 390

Crimes, 330, 332, 390

Crosby, Paul, xi, 258-259, 281, 407

Crosby, Samuel O., 133

Crystal Lake, 392

Cultural Activities, 232, 382

Cumming, Ian, 306-308, 315

Cutler, Van Blaine, 222

D

Daggett, F. L., 101, 415

Daily Spectrum, 10, 121, 164, 170, 399

Dalton, Charles, 18, 29, 413

Dams, xvi, 3, 7, 20-22, 27, 30, 42, 50-51, 62, 64-65, 71, 79, 84-88, 105, 118-19, 138, 171-73, 176, 178-83, 185, 189-98, 213, 228, 230, 239-40, 265-66, 286-87, 291, 386, 388-89

Dancing, 144-145, 251

Daniel, Q. Dennett, 32
DARTS, 368
Davich, George, 278
Davidson, James, 64
Davis, William R., 18
Day, Wilford, 234
Declaration of United Trust, 274
DeFriez, E. G., 155
DeHart, Craig, 329
Dellenbaugh, Frederick, 203, 421
DeMille, Oliver, 33
DeMille, Raymond, 193
Dennett, Woodrow, 258
Deseret Laboratories, 361
Desert Land Act, 87
Desert Springs Township, 334
Dick's Cafe, 220-221, 291, 293, 340
Dickey, Virginia, 137, 278
Dinosaur Discovery Site, 377
Dinosaurs, 377
Dixiana Dormitory, 237
Dixie, ix-x, xvi-xviii, 2, 8-13, 18, 21, 27,
    34-40, 45-49, 53, 56-58, 60-63, 65,
    68-71, 73-75, 77-82, 84, 86, 88-89,
    91, 95, 97-100, 102, 104, 108-09, 112,
    117-23, 128, 134, 136, 139, 143-45,
    147-64, 166-71, 175-76, 181-82, 185-
    86, 192, 194-203, 209-10, 212-13,
    222-26, 228-41, 244, 246-59, 261-62,
    264, 274, 277-93, 295-96, 299-301,
    306, 310, 312-27, 329, 332, 334-38,
    340-42, 344-49, 352-60, 362-68,
    370-71, 373-80, 382, 388, 390, 392,
    394-96, 402, 405-06, 419-25
Dixie, definition of, 8
Dixie Academy, 161, 231, 251
Dixie Advocate, 164, 169
Dixie Airlines, 314, 371
Dixie Apex Mine, 244
Dixie Applied Technology College, 365
Dixie Arts Festival, 367
Dixie Aviation Corporation, 314
Dixie Care and Share, 402

Dixie Center, 10, 155, 319-21, 325-27,
    334, 346-48, 363, 365, 368, 373, 379,
    396, 406
  photograph, 321
Dixie Cooperative Produce Co., 104
Dixie Development Corp., 295-96, 362
Dixie Downs, 377, 380, 394-95
Dixie Education Association, 236-37,
    317, 322
Dixie Falcon, 164, 169
Dixie Flying Club, 313
Dixie High School, 10, 366, 396
Dixie Invitational Art Show, 320, 344
Dixie Mission, 35, 40, 46, 57, 75, 79,
    86, 88, 235
Dixie Pioneer Memorial Hosp., 325, 329
Dixie Project, 192, 194-96, 198-200,
    256, 317, 348, 390
Dixie Regional Medical Center, 10, 325-
    27, 348, 379, 403, 406
  photograph, 326
Dixie Roundup Rodeo, 256, 346
Dixie Rural Electric Assoc., 196, 240
Dixie [State] College, ix, xviii, 9-10,
    46-48, 69-70, 121-22, 136, 152-53,
    156, 161, 169, 199-200, 222-23,
    226, 228, 230-36, 239, 246-48, 252,
    254-55, 257-59, 261, 274, 277, 280-
    82, 310, 313-14, 317-23, 335-36,
    340-41, 344, 347-49, 355, 362-65,
    368, 371, 373, 375-77, 382, 396,
    406, 422-24
Doctors, Thompsonian, 98
Dodge, W. E., 113
Dominguez, Francisco Atanasio, 6
Doolittle, Henry, 244
Downwinders, 269-71, 282
Drought, 3, 34, 39, 46, 82, 90, 118, 195,
    225, 376, 384-85, 388-89
Drugs, 332
"Drums Along the Mohawk," 249
Dry Farming, 268
Duncan, Chapman, 110
Duncan's Retreat, 75-77, 121, 418
Dunford, Alma, 327

Dutton, Clarence, 203, 246
DXATC, 365

E

Eardley, John, 159
Earthquake, 58, 118, 178, 199, 405
Earthquakes, 404
Eccles Fine Arts Center, 365, 373
Electric Power, 194, 237, 240
Electric Theater, 249-50
Ellsworth, Lynn, 305
Emmett, Simpson, 29
Empey, Clark, 255
Empey, Joseph, 245
Empey, Lynne, 192, 220, 297
Ence, Floyd, 303, 338, 411
Ence, Jay, 297, 412
Endangered Species Act, 357
Enterprise, x, xvi, 10, 28, 45-46, 51, 62,
    67, 71, 77, 79, 82, 88, 101, 103-04,
    111, 118-19, 164, 168-69, 175-80,
    182, 189, 191, 201, 213, 223, 230,
    234, 238, 241, 256, 286, 292, 315,
    329-30, 339, 343, 348, 366-67, 369,
    378, 385-86, 397, 421, 424
Enterprise Reservoir, xvi, 77, 119, 168,
    175, 178-80, 182, 191, 385
Entrada [Golf Course], 378, 393
Entrada Trail, 393
Episcopalian Church, 280, 397
Escalante, Silvestre Velez de, 6
Escalante Rural Electric Assoc., 240
Escalante [Oil] Wells, 244-45
Esplin, Gary, 319
Esplin, T. Lavoy, x, 335, 349
Evening Telegram, 163, 169
Evenson, Nephi, 350
Everett, Addison, 172
Everett, Orpha, 134
Ewell, Bill, 229
Excell, Austin, 195
Eyring, Henry, 78, 316, 415

F

Fabian, Harold, 290
Fackrell, Jerry, 314
Fair, Frank, 350
Fairs, 100-101
Fames, Joe, 184
Fancher/Baker Wagon Train, 24, 47
"Far, Far Away on Judea's Plains," 161
Farming, 12, 16, 19-20, 23, 26, 28-30,
    39, 77, 81-82, 88-89, 91-92, 94, 104,
    176, 180, 182, 203, 205, 225, 261,
    268, 276, 284, 286, 345, 354
Fawcett, Albert, 238
Fawcett, Ruth, 134
Fawcett, William, 113, 172
Federal, Joseph Lennox, 277
Federal Emergency Recovery Adminis-
    tration, 227
Federal Reclamation Act, 189
Federal Reconstruction Finance Corpo-
    ration, 175
Felter, George C., 223
Ferris, John, 106
Fife, Lew, 331
Fifth Avenue Girl, 249
Fiore, Roene di, 11
Fire, 1, 38, 43, 67, 130, 140, 146, 242,
    297, 304, 307-08, 331, 365, 385, 387
First Interstate Bank, 338
First Security Bank, 338
Fish, Joseph, 168, 421
Fisher, Vardis, 252
Five County Assoc. of Governments, 368
Flanigan, David, 205-206
Flickenger, C. M., 245
Floods, 18, 21, 27-28, 31-32, 34, 38-39,
    42-44, 53, 57, 71, 76-77, 79, 82, 84,
    86, 90, 105, 119, 171-73, 182, 193,
    230, 384-88, 395, 404
Fluorine, 328
Force, Clarence, 220
Foremaster, Lang, x, 332
Foremaster, Philip, 194
Forlorn River, 295

Forshaw, June Macfarlane, 313

Fort Harmony, 18-19, 21, 26-27, 37, 43, 47, 61, 168

Four Seasons Motel and Convention Center, 220, 310

Francis, Joseph, xiv, 235

Frandsen, Lindon, 313

Frandsen, Loyal, 313

Freeman, John Woodruff, 66

Freeway, xviii, 33, 220, 263, 296, 299-01, 306, 321, 338-39, 341-42, 368, 372, 378, 380, 393, 397

Frei, Bill, 222

Frei, Claude, 194

Frei, Don C., 263

Frei, Newell, 238, 411

Fremont, John C., 7-8

Friends of Kolob, 210

Frodsham, Edward, 32

Fruit Growing, 101-02, 104, 163

Fuller, Craig, x, xiv

Fuller, Elijah K., 54

Fuller, Revilo, 54, 69

Fuller, Walter, 221

Fuller, Wid, 54

Fundamentalists, 271, 273-75

Funk, Marcus, 86, 172

G

Gaiety Electric Theater, 249

Gallian, Russell, ix, 412

Gangs, 332, 391

Gardner, Dorothy, ix

Gardner, Kenneth N., 320

Gardner, Lenora Cannon, 140, 153, 168

Gardner, Reid, 238

Gardner, Robert, 40-41, 48, 415

Gardener's Club, 100-01

Gates, Jacob, 35, 113, 115, 155, 165, 409, 415

Gates, Jed, 327

Gates, Susa Young, 134, 155

Gentry, Harry S., 264

Gentry, Jamie, 210

Geography, 1, 136, 404

Geology, 1, 122, 193, 424

George O'Brien, 249, 292

Gibbons, Andrew, 47, 80, 413

Gibbons, Richard, 29

Gibson, D. W., 194

Gibson Discount Stores, 341-342

Gifford, Aaron, 363

Goldstein, Milton, 344

Golf [Course], xviii, 52, 220-22, 277, 283, 285, 287-88, 290, 296-99, 302-06, 309, 352, 356-57, 360, 374, 377-78, 392-95, 403

Goode, Harry, 193

Goold, Robert F., 110

Gordon, Janet, 270

Graff, Emil J., 194, 268, 303, 411

Graffiti, 391

Grafton, 26, 31-32, 43, 48, 62, 66-67, 71, 75-77, 121, 144, 153, 182, 213, 244, 292, 384, 418

Grafton Heritage Partnership, 384

Graham, Maurice, 222

Graman, Wallea Baker, 277

Grand Canyon Trust, 357, 372, 384

Granger, Kolene, 335, 365

Grant, Heber J., 205, 257, 285, 296

Grapevine Pass, 27

Graves, Elisha H., 18

Gray, Wallace, 223

Great Depression, 207-208, 224, 230, 237, 246

Green, Nina, 327

Green Valley, xviii, 187, 196, 310, 312, 343, 374, 376, 380, 387, 395-97

Greene Gate Village, 344, 384

Greenwell, James, 277-78

Greenwell, James M., 277

Gregerson, Andrew, 87

Gregory, Herbert E., 209

Growth, 4, 196, 198, 248, 275, 278, 306, 308, 322, 332, 335-336, 339, 342, 350-361, 363-71, 373, 375, 377-79, 381, 383-85, 387-91, 393, 395, 397, 399, 401, 403-07, 419

Gubler, Donworth, 258

Gubler, Emil, 263

Gubler, Ensign, 263

Gubler, Glen, 193

Gubler, Henry, 172, 194, 410

Gubler, Nellie McArthur, 38, 48

Gubler, Norman, 263

Gunlock, x, 7, 26, 28, 33, 66, 72, 76-77, 79-80, 82, 91, 100, 114, 116-17, 121, 132, 136, 168, 192, 194-96, 213, 225-26, 230, 238, 241, 256, 265-67, 303, 363, 376, 385-87, 417

Gunlock Reservoir, 192, 195-96, 303, 386

H

Hafen, Arlyn, 318

Hafen, Arthur K., 147, 153, 422

Hafen, Charles, 159, 273

Hafen, Eda, 327

Hafen, Grant, x, 266, 281

Hafen, Guy, 337

Hafen, John, 159, 286, 336

Hafen, John G., 159

Hafen, Keith, 222

Hafen, Lyman, ix, xi, 174, 199, 386, 407, 422

Hafen, Mary Ann, 96, 121, 152, 168, 422

Hafen, Orval, 195, 234, 237, 239, 248, 254-55, 285-86, 290, 317, 323, 373

Haight, Isaac C., 27

Hail, Brown, 192, 220, 291-92

Hail, George W., 246

Hale, George, 244, 281

Hall, Jennie Nelson, 241

Hall, John C., 32

Hall, Mary Bertha Wood, 144, 153

Hall, Thomas, 32

Hamblin, Jacob, 15, 20-22, 26, 28-29, 43, 46-47, 80, 93, 124, 127, 138, 151-52, 168, 182, 273, 383, 409, 419-21, 423-424

photograph, 15

Hamblin, Oscar, 47

Hamilton, Joe, 328

Hammer, Dick, x, 291-93

Hancock, Cyrus, 129

Hansen, Katy, 280

Hansen, Roger, 280

Hansen Stadium, 348

Harding, Warren G., 95

Hardy, Augustus, 46-47, 62, 124, 413

Hardy, Caroline Baker Rogers, 99

Hardy, Eva, 180

Hardy, G. M., 119

Hardy, Galen, 137, 278

Harman, Everett, 278

Harmon, Appleton, 63

Harmon, Elmer, 264

Harmon, Levi N., 152

Harmony, x, xix, 12, 18-21, 26-27, 33, 35, 37, 40, 43, 47, 56, 61, 72, 112-13, 168, 187, 202, 212, 250, 252, 268, 369, 390, 418

Harradence, Mary A., 100

Harriman, Henry, 35, 110

Harris, Moses, 33

Harris Comedy Company, 157

Harrisburg, 33-34, 71, 74, 99, 106-08, 118, 122, 215, 417, 423

Harrisburg Mining District, 106-07, 122

Haskell, Maria, 22

Haskell, Thales, 22, 46-47, 124, 422

Haslam, Joseph, 266

Hatch, Ira, 46-47, 124

Hatch, Orrin, 327

Hawthorne Company, 295

Hayes, Gabby, 293

Health, 97, 99, 138, 142, 260, 269, 325-27, 340, 343, 352, 355, 361, 363-64, 369-70, 374, 402, 406

Heaton, Daniel H., 240

Heaton, Ken, 329

Hebron, 28-30, 71, 77, 91, 111-12, 118, 122, 132, 138, 153, 176-80

Hebron LDS Ward, 112, 138

Heep, William, 73

Heideman, Kent, 329

Henderlider, Joy, x, 313

Hennefer, William, 21

Hepworth, Francis Crawford, 327

Hernia Dam, 189-190

Hess, Harold, 295

Heywood, Martha Spence, 97, 121, 422

Hiatt, Alton, 223

Hickman, Bill, x, 337

Hicks, George, 9

Hidden Power, 249

Higbee, John M., 28

Higgins, Francis, 119

Higgins, Louisa C., 100

Higgins, Silas, 99

Higgins Brothers Theatrical Co., 156

Hildale, 94, 219, 271-72, 274-76, 378, 398-401

Hildebrandt, Charles, 159

Himes, Ellvert, 237, 317

Hinckley, 77, 79, 247

Hinton, Emma, 96

Hinton, John Nock, 30, 47, 96, 121, 423

Hinton, Wayne, x, 194, 422

Hirschi, Claude, 194, 337

Hirschi, David, 182, 194, 224, 234, 337

Hirschi, John, 184, 194

Hodges, James, 110

Holland, Alice, 242

Holland, Frank, 229, 255

Holland, Jeff, 318

Hollings, Lionel, 318

Holt, George A., 178, 410

Holt, Mary, 327

Home, Joseph, 62

Horne, Richard, 134

Homestead Act of 1862, 83

Honeymoon Trail, 203

Horn, Don, 229

Hospice, 270

Hospice of Southwestern Utah, 270

Hospital, McGregor, 324-325, 327-328

Housing, xviii, 57, 207, 232, 277, 296, 340, 352-354, 370, 381, 387, 391, 394-96, 405

Howard, Hugh, 329

Huber, Albert, 32

Huber, Edward, 32

Huddleston, Robert, 320

Huff, Max, 229

Hug, Heinrich, 78, 80, 117, 122, 425

Hunt, Agnes, 327

Hunt, James W., 136

Hunt, Jefferson, 8, 13

Hunt, Orpha, 54, 69

Hunt, Royal, 188, 330

Huntington, Garn, 314

Huntsman, Arthur, 330

Huntsman, Joseph S., 136

Huntsman, Orson, 78, 111, 122, 168, 176, 178, 180, 199

Huntsman, S. Ralph, 344

Hurley, Robert, 256

Hurricane, x, xvi-xvii, 2-3, 6, 10, 26, 28, 30, 48, 66, 76-77, 79, 82, 88, 101, 119-20, 153, 169, 180-82, 184-85, 187, 191, 193-94, 199, 208, 212-16, 218-19, 224, 228-29, 234, 238, 242, 252, 255-56, 265, 267-68, 274, 280, 289, 296, 299-300, 325-26, 329-30, 337-39, 341-42, 348, 351-53, 361, 364, 367, 369, 372, 376, 378, 381-82, 389, 392-94, 396-97, 405, 421, 424

Hurricane Canal, xvi, 76-77, 79, 181-82, 184-85, 187, 191, 193, 199, 382, 424

Hurricane Canal Company, 184, 193

Hurricane Cliffs, 2-3, 182, 212-13

Hurricane Mesa, 182

Hurst, Bruce, 320, 375

Hurst, Ross, 192

Hutchings, A. I., 328

Hutchings, Joe, 292

Hutchings, Karl, 292

Hutchings, Mike, 328
Hutson, Kenneth Medford, 280

I

I-15, xviii, 316, 342, 372
Impact fees, 367
Indian Mission, 18-22, 26, 46-47, 124,
    152, 168, 421, 424
Indian-White Relations, 19, 420
Industrial Park, 295-96, 339, 361-362,
    372, 379, 395
Industrial Parks, xviii, 285, 295, 346,
    352, 360-61
Infowest, 362-363
Intermountain Health Care (IHC), 326,
    369, 326, 365, 369-70, 406
Interstate 15, 212, 219, 267, 331
Irrigation, 13-14, 19-21, 27, 33, 42-43,
    49-51, 62, 65, 71-72, 82, 84, 88, 104,
    117, 139, 164, 171, 182, 185-86,
    188-89, 192-194, 199, 240, 388-89,
    417-18
Isom, Alice Parker, 96, 121
Isom, Clinton, 269
Isom, Ellen, 96
Isom, George, 74, 121, 410
Isom, John W., 183
Isom, Lizzie Ballard, 42
Isom, Sarah Laverna, 96
Itten, John R., 159
Iverson, Wallace, 240
Ivins, x, 38, 99, 113, 134, 152, 155-157,
    166, 172-74, 177-80, 193-94, 233, 257,
    276, 285, 340, 343-44, 363-64, 373-74,
    376, 380, 389, 392, 394, 397, 415
Ivins, Anthony W., 157, 174, 178, 233,
    257, 285, 415
Ivins, Edith, 152, 166
Ivins, Israel, 38, 99, 113
Ivins, McKean Caddie, 134
Ivins, Tony, 156
Ivory, Clark, 301-302
Ivory, Ellis, 301, 304, 306
Ivory and Boyer Co., 301-02, 304, 306

J

J & J Enterprises, 380
J. D. Air Service, 314
J and J Mill and Lumber Company, 340
Jackson, Victor, 209
Japanese workers, 190, 258
Jarvis, Brigham, 156, 172, 174, 422
Jarvis, Brigham Jr., 156
Jarvis, Eleanor, 134, 160
Jarvis, George, 172, 174
Jarvis, Maggie, 160
Jarvis Ditch, 172
Jeffs, Rulon, 398-399
Jeffs, Warren, 398, 400-01
Jehovah's Witness, 280, 397
Jennings, Henry, 32
Jennings, J. H., 144, 153
Jennings, Leon, 295
Jennings, Mansfield, 296
Jenson, Andrew, 69, 118, 122
Jenson, Richard, 220
Jepson, James, 182-83, 185, 199, 410
Jessop, Lyman, 273
John Birch Society, 333
John S. Lindsay Company, 156
John Y. Barlow University, 274
Johnson, C. E., 155-156
Johnson, Clifton, 302
Johnson, Frank, 304, 307, 310
Johnson, Franklin, 302
Johnson, Glendon, 302
Johnson, Grant, 298
Johnson, Joseph E., 99, 101, 152, 169
Johnson, LeRoy, 275, 398-99, 421
Johnson, Nephi, 30, 32, 47, 205
Johnson, Price, 274
Johnson, Ross, 345
Johnson, Sixtus, 91
Johnson Land Company, 302
Johnson's Twist, 30
Johnston, Albert Sidney, 24
Jolley, Donal, 5
Jolley, LaFayette, 159

Jolley, W. L., 110
Jones, Alfred, 184
Jones, Eugene, 333, 413
Jones, Heber, ix, 57, 70, 122, 179,
    321, 407
Jones, Jim, 344
Jones, Thomas J., 66
Jones, Willard, 189, 199, 422
Jones, William Ellis, 40-41, 48, 79, 100,
    122, 132, 168
Journal Writing, 166
Judd, Mary Lund, 161
Judd, Samuel, 65, 180, 413
Judd, Thomas, 88, 165, 177-78, 180-81,
    409, 415
July 24th, 145, 147, 257
July 4th, 145

K

Kanarraville, 77, 267, 418
Kane, Elizabeth Wood, 139, 153, 422
Kane, Thomas, 139
Kane County, 2, 31, 66, 72, 77, 267, 390
Kayenta, 340, 344, 392
Keat, Martha, 119
Keate, Daniel Lester, 223
Keate, Martha Snow, 156
Keate, Walter, 156, 324
Keck, Ellis, 280
Keller, John, 159
Kellwood, 295, 362
Kellwood Corporation, 295, 362
Kelsey, Easton, 113
Kemp, Elias, 166
Kemp, Kate, 152, 166
Kemp, William, 160
Kemple, John, 106
Kenner, Samuel, 32
Kerr, Rolfe, 319
Kerry William Bate, 99, 121
Keyes, Grant, 194
Kimball, Jim, 304, 310
Kitterman, Joseph, 245
Kleinman, Conrad, 102, 148

Kleinman, Moroni, 223
Klingonsmith, Philip, 32
Kolob, 9, 90-91, 193, 210, 266, 268,
    358, 389, 397
Kolob Lake, 389
Kolob Plateau, 91
Kolob Reservoir, 193
Kraack, Donald F., 327, 423
Kuhn, Henry, 159
Kunz, Francis, 278
Kuzy, Paul, 278

L

La Verkin Canal, xvi, 77, 180, 184, 199,
    424-25
La Verkin Fruit and Nursery Co., 180
Lake, Veronica, 292
Lake Powell, 287, 304, 376, 385, 389-90
Lane, George F., 201
Langston, Issac H., 223
Langston, J. F., 183
Langston, John, 32, 183, 410
Langston, Rulon, 194
Larkin, Dale, 310
Larkin, Derrill, 310
Larkin, Grey, 296, 310, 320, 338, 416
Larkin, James Grey, 338, 416
Larsen, A. L., 161
Larson, Alvin, 194
Larson, Andrew H., 172
Larson, Andrew Karl, 48, 56, 69, 120,
    122, 166, 170, 199, 248, 254, 423, 425
Larson, George, 301
Larson, John, 172
Larson, Melvin, 220
Las Palmas, 311
Las Vegas, 7, 10-11, 35, 104-05, 185,
    194, 215, 257, 263-64, 282-85, 287,
    289, 314-15, 325-26, 329, 332, 353,
    357, 360, 370, 389, 420
Lassiter, William, 298

Latter-day Saints, xv-xvi, 44-45, 48, 52, 57, 61, 63, 65, 71-72, 83, 98-99, 106, 108, 110, 112-13, 116-18, 140, 170, 173, 188, 213, 242-243, 247, 282

Lauritzen, Jacob, 273

Law Enforcement, 274, 329, 331-32

"Law of the Pampas," 249

Leavitt, Dixie, 194-195

Leavitt, Dudley, 21, 28, 30, 47, 151, 420

Leavitt, Ether, 194

Leavitt, Jeremiah, 28, 47, 136

Leavitt, Lavoid, xi

Leavitt, Lee, 194

LeBaron, David, 134

Lee, Evan, 194

Lee, Frank, 185

Lee, George A., 43

Lee, J. Bracken, 236, 318

Lee, John D., 17-19, 26-27, 29, 35, 37, 46-47, 61-62, 122, 167-68, 170, 253, 289, 334, 348, 421, 423
photograph, 17

Lee, Margaret Ann, 43

Lee, Roland, 344-345

Lee, Sarah Caroline, 43

Leeds, 33-34, 41, 71, 73, 79, 82, 104, 107-108, 118, 148, 157, 213, 230, 237, 313, 339, 344, 383, 389, 418, 423

Leigh, Reed, 256

Lemmon, James, 32

Lemmon, Jess, 184

Leucadia Corporation, 308

Leukemia, 269

Lewis, Jerry, ix, 411-12

Lewis, S. Rex, 338

Liberty Hotel, 211, 220, 246, 291, 340

Lin's Market, 380, 382

Lincoln Automobile Club, 211

Lindsay, John S., 156

Lindstrom, Gaell, 344

Lions Club, 256, 292, 348

Little Colorado River Settlements, 120, 203

Littlefield, 240-241, 244, 266, 301, 386

Littlefield Rural Electric Assoc., 240

Livestock, 88, 91-92, 94, 100, 197, 225, 287, 292

Living Faith Community, 397

Living Word, 397

Location, 10, 27-28, 30-32, 57, 95, 109, 218, 221-22, 237, 244, 250, 256, 263, 274, 293, 295-96, 299-300, 305, 312, 340-41, 360, 366, 370-71, 375, 380, 383, 394-95, 398

Long Valley, 18, 72, 99, 121, 213

Look Magazine, 253

Losee, Ferron, 319

Lost Boys, 400, 407

Lucerne, 39, 89-91, 146

Lund, George, 152, 166, 411

Lund, Lizzie, 166

Lund, R. C., 154, 156, 410

Lundberg, Jim, 290, 295, 337

Lundberg, Neal, 255-56, 285, 295, 297-98, 416

Lutheran, 280, 397

Lutheran Church, 280

Lyceum Dramatic Company, 156

Lytle, Andy, 292

Lytle, Cornelia, 134

Lytle, George P., 238

M

Macfarlane, Isaac C., 86, 176, 178, 180, 415

Macfarlane, John Menzies, 108

Mackelprang, August, 64

Madsen, J. R., 210

Maggart, Skylar, 229

Mahon, John, 280, 282

Main Street Plaza, 363, 381

Maloney, Billy, 245

Man of War Bridge, 304, 307

Manifesto, 151, 272-73, 421

Mann, Walter P. III, 333

Mansfield, Mary, 134

Mansfield, Mathew, 172

Manti LDS Temple, 58

Martin, Allyson, ix
Martin, Terry, 393
Martinez, Dennis, 345
Mason, David, 329
Mather, Stephen T., 205, 216
Matheson, Scott M., 270
Mathis, Barbara, 134, 160
Mathis, Richard, x, 337, 349
Mathis, Wallace B., 337
Mathis, William, 173
May, Dean, 80, 120
McAllister, John D. T., 108, 113
McAllister, Joseph W., 119, 161
McAllister, Roxa, 327
McAllister, William, 160-161
McArthur, Andrew, 69, 238
McArthur, Daniel D., 91, 113, 115, 119,
    145, 177, 416
McArthur, James A., 68-69
McArthur, Rudger, x, 23, 192-93, 302
McArthur, Wayne, 192
McArthur, Wilford W., 337
McConkie, Wayne, xi, 236
McCullough, James D., 47, 64, 115
McDonald, Don, 221
McFate, James, 32
McGregor, Alpine, 324
McGregor, Donald, 324
McGregor, Lorenzo, 11
McGregor, M. K., x, 325
McGregor, Scott, 314
McKee, Robert, 217
McLeese, Byron, 307
McIntire, Clark, 325
McIntire, William P., 172
McIntyre, Robert, 273
McMillan, Duncan, 137
McMullin, Chris, 318
McMullin, Leone Russel, 146
McNeil, David L., 223
McNutt, Paul, 313
McQuarrie, Annie, 134, 160
McQuarrie, Hector, 180
McQuarrie, John G., 119

McQuarrie, Robert G., 180
Mead, Elwood, 185, 187, 199, 417-18
Medicine, 5, 21-22, 98-99, 121, 126-27,
    324-25, 419
Meeks, Athe, 129
Meeks, Lenora Atkin, 47, 96, 423
Meeks, Priddy, 99, 118, 423
Meetinghouses, 66
Merrill, Joseph F., 233
Mesquite, xvi, 5, 9-10, 45, 146, 241,
    264, 266, 280, 353, 378, 386
Metcalf, Ken, 338
Methodist Church, 397
Michols, Robert, 324
Midwives, 97, 99-100, 122
Miles, Arthur F., 156, 234-35, 330, 336
Miles, H. R., 338
Miles, Josephine J., 134, 152
Miles, Louie, 166
Miles, M. J., 239
Miles, Samuel, 134
Miles, William G., 52, 166
Miles, William O., 160
Miller, Albert E., 69, 238, 244, 415, 423
Millett, Joseph, 32
Milne, Anna Hess, 99-100
Milne, Bert, 220
Milne, David, 99
Milne, Merlin, 222
Milne Trucking Line, 103
Milne, Arvel, x, 262-63, 281
Milne, Joseph J., 262
Mining, 16, 34, 80, 83-84, 96, 104-10,
    122, 148, 163, 173, 201, 224, 242-44,
    284, 289, 312, 349, 424
Mix, Tom, 294-95
    photograph, 294
Mo-ke-ak, 93
Mojave Community College, 274
Moody, Milton, 335
Morby, Jeff, x, 305, 308, 323
Morgan, Daisy, 220, 374
Morgan, John, 220, 374
Mormon Battalion, 8, 13, 70

Mormon Village, 84, 93, 112, 120, 138, 186
Morris, Clair, 330
Morris, David H., 234, 336
Morris, Gene, 251, 363
Morris, Hyrum, 32
Morris, Leslie, 330
Morris, Mary, 166
Morris, Vella Ruth, 251
Moses, Sam, 280
Moss, Clarence, 259
Moss, David, 52
Moss, Frank E., 195
Motel, 218-20, 291-92, 300, 310, 340, 346, 351
Motels, 219-20, 285, 290, 300, 341, 345, 360, 367, 369, 374
Motion Pictures, 156, 249
Mount Trumbull, 53, 58, 107
Mountain Fuel Supply, 342
Mountain Meadows, xviii, 7, 24-26, 29, 35, 47, 91, 93-94, 151, 167, 213, 253, 281, 289, 334, 348, 420
Mountain Meadows Massacre, xviii, 24, 26, 35, 47, 167, 253, 281, 289, 334, 348, 420
Mountain States Telephone and Tele-graph Company, 242
Movies, 31, 36, 249-50, 281, 291-92, 294
Moyle, Parley, 240
Mt. Carmel Junction, 78, 207
Muddy Mission, 72, 79, 421
Mukuntuweap National Monument, xvii, 203-05
Music, 11, 109, 119, 144, 147, 154, 158-161, 169, 183, 232, 252, 347, 373, 425

N

Naegle, Bob, 149
Naegle, John C., 66, 102
National Institute of Fitness, 340, 343
Native Americans, 4-5, 24, 39, 81, 92, 124, 352, 358
Navajo Indians, 277

Neff, Andrew, 252
Neff, Bill, 302
Neilson, Ina, 159
Neilson, Israel, 159
Nelson, Aaron, 110
Nelson, Alma, 166, 241, 410
Nelson, Carl, x, 304, 307-08, 323, 424
Nelson, Ray, 245
Nelson, W. A., 156
Nevada, xviii, 2-3, 9-10, 18, 35-37, 45, 53, 57, 72, 79-80, 87, 102, 106-07, 119, 133-34, 143, 148, 158, 178, 197, 215, 232, 259, 263, 265, 268-70, 282-283, 301, 328, 330, 357, 363-64, 386
New Covenant Christian Center, 281, 397
New Deal, xvii, 175, 194, 226-28, 230, 284
New Harmony, x, 12, 250, 252, 268, 369, 390
Newcastle, 189-91, 199, 240-241, 331
Newcastle Reclamation Company, 189
Newspapers, xvii, 49, 80, 162-65, 168-70, 257, 400
Nicholes, Joseph K., 231, 233, 239, 247
Nicholson, Cail, 245
Nielsen, Peter, 53-54
Nielson, Mary Ann Hunt, 99
Nisson, Della, 159
Nisson, Edward, 159
Nisson, Willard O., 152, 159, 383
Nixon, James W., 265
Nuclear Testing, 269-270, 282
Nutter, Preston, 265
Nyberg, Kelly, 362

O

O. C. Tanner Amphitheater, 319, 373
Oakley, John, 113
Oasis Community, 280, 397
Oasis Community Church, 280
Oates, Ernest, 307
Office of Price Administration, 260, 281
Oil [Wells], 21, 96, 134, 151, 203, 215, 242-245, 262-63, 284, 289, 310

Old Spanish Trail, 7-8, 13, 25, 28

Old Virgin Ditch, 172

Olde Penny Farthing Inn, 344

Olsen Tourist Camp, 218

Olson, Gerald, 345

Orderville, 72, 78, 118, 222-223

Orson Pratt, Jr., 78, 113, 134, 156, 162, 165, 169

Orton, Joseph, 134, 152, 154-156, 160, 162, 169

Orton, Rulon, 258

Otti, Henry, 161

Our Dixie Times, 9, 163, 169

Owens, Lee, 222

Owens, Robert, 350

P

Pace, Andrew, 255

Pace, Andy, 220, 292

Pace, George, 221, 292

Pace, John E., 110

Paiute, 4, 7, 29-30, 92, 125, 276, 357

Paiutes, xv-xvi, 5, 20, 27, 92, 123-24, 128-29, 276

Palmer, John, 296

Paolasso, Julio, 220

Parrish, Avarian, 318

Parkinson, Ken, 239, 241

Parrusits, 5-6

Parry, Chauncey, 216

Parry, Gronway, 216

Parry, Whitney, 216

Parson, Del, 344-45

Pattie, James Ohio, 8

Peach Days, 101

Pearce, Jim, 54

Pearce, Tom, 54

Pearson, Jim, 329

Peddling, 102-04, 108, 210

Pedersen, Eric, 362, 406

Pendleton, Benjamin F., 113

People's Progressive Telephone and Telegraph Company, 241

Perkins, Ute, 113

Peter's Leap, 41

Peterson, Charles S., 424

Peterson, Clifford, 240

Peterson, Levi, 254, 281, 424

Peterson, Steven H., 335

Pettit, David, 344

Petty, Albert, 32-33

Petty, Charles B., 152

Petty, George, 32

Phoenix, Mary, 328

Photograph, 204, 208, 218, 229, 268

Pickens, Slim, 293

Pickett, Elmer, x, 258-59, 281, 325

Pickett, Evan, 259

Pickett, Henry, 227, 325

Pickett, Horatio, 155, 160-161, 173

Pickett Lumber Company, 340

Pickett Mortuary, 340

Pine Nuts, 146

Pine Valley, x, 2-3, 9, 22, 26, 28-29, 47, 53, 65-66, 72, 76-77, 79-81, 86, 91, 94, 107, 114, 129, 132, 137, 140-41, 168, 174, 177-78, 188, 190, 213, 230, 241, 257, 264-65, 287, 290, 329, 340, 386, 397, 417, 419

Pine Valley chapel [Meetinghouse], 66

Pine Valley Mountain, 2-3, 22, 86, 94, 174, 287

Pine Valley School District, 137

Pioche, 53, 102, 104, 106-08, 119, 148, 244, 329-31

Pioneer Center for the Arts, 338, 345, 373, 381

Pioneer Day, 147, 257

Pioneer Lodge and Restaurant, 218

Pioneer Opera House, 344, 347, 373

Pipe Spring, 9, 91-93, 99, 213, 265, 273

Pitchforth, Shirl H., 192-93, 200

Platt, Rowland, 229

Pocket Farms, xvi, 88

Pocketville, 30

Police, 242, 304, 308, 330-32, 348, 352-53, 387, 390, 399, 401, 406

Pollei, Jon, x, 331, 348

Pollock, Samuel, 28
Polygamy, xix, 78-79, 81, 86, 93, 99, 120, 137, 142, 148, 150-51, 168, 252-53, 271-73, 276, 278, 398, 400-01, 419, 421
Powell, Dick, 293
Powell, Kent, x, xiv, 281, 424
Pratt, Orson, 32, 35, 37, 48, 53, 78, 113-115, 134, 156, 162, 165, 169, 272
Pratt, Parley P., 1, 8, 12, 19
Presbyterian Church, 119, 137, 278-82, 397
Price, Andy, 297
Price, John, 47, 342, 378
Prince, Alpine, 328
Prince, Bill, 220
Prince, Joseph, 244
Prince, Lida, 220
Prisbrey, Arlo, 255, 263
Prisbrey, Scott, x, 259
Prison, 168, 213, 330, 334, 369, 377
Proctor, Paul Dean, 106, 122, 323, 424
Prohibition, 235
Pulsipher, Bill, 329
Pulsipher, Charles, 29
Pulsipher, John, 29, 112, 138
Punch Bowl [Oil] Well, 244
Purgatory Flats, 369
Pymm, John, 53, 113, 265
Pymm, Seth A., 134

Q

Quail Creek Reservoir, 195, 388
Quail Lake, 198, 388
Qwest, 363

R

Radiation Exposure Compensation Act, 271
Radio, 239, 250, 273
Railroad, xvii-xviii, 35, 87-88, 91, 110, 154, 164, 201-02, 207, 209-10, 216-17, 223, 260, 262, 266-67, 281, 284, 299, 330

Ramco, 296, 362
Rampton, Calvin, 301
Ranching, 16, 29, 91-92, 94, 176, 264-65, 267, 345
Rationing, 258, 260-61, 281
Ray, Stan, 263
Reber, Afton, 240
Reber, F. A., 244
Reber, Glen J., 223
Reber, Louis, 240
Reber, Roma, 327
Reber, Rumell, 240
Reber, Spencer, 104-05, 122
Reber, Spencer Jr., 105
Recreation Center, 369, 375
Red Cliffs Mall, 342, 368, 378-79, 397
Red Cliffs Reserve, 375-76
Red Cross, 223, 226, 387
Red Desert Digest, 165, 170
Red Hills Golf Course, 52, 296, 299, 302, 395, 403
Redford, Robert, 291
Reeve, Brian, x
Reeve, Leo, 338
Reeve, Paul, 79-80, 120, 424
Reeves, Josiah, 28
Reichmann, Helen, 239
Reichmann, Howard, 255
Reichmann, Wilford, 255, 325
Reid, H. L., 254
Religion, xvii, 138-139, 141, 143, 272, 278, 280, 397
Religious Science Church, 281
Rice, Clayton, 138, 279
Richards, Lanthus, 96
Richards, Willard, 99
Richey, Robert, 29, 46-47
Ricketts, Jack, 255
Riddle, Isaac, 28, 47, 124
Riggs, Frank, 344
Riggs, Gene Karl, 345
Rio Virgin Times, 163, 169
River's Edge, 392

Roads, xvii, 53, 61, 90, 94, 114, 154,
166, 178, 202, 204, 207, 210-14, 230,
246, 257, 303-04, 307-09, 352, 367,
387, 392, 394
Roberts, Neil, 318
Robson, Thayne, xi
Rockville, x, 5, 26, 32-33, 43-44, 66-
67, 72, 75-77, 79, 82, 89, 115, 129,
144, 182-183, 203, 207-08, 213-14,
218-19, 222, 252, 268, 339, 348, 384,
410, 418
Rockwell, Orrin Porter, 8
Rocky Mountain Company, 103, 263,
295, 362
Rocky Mountain Produce Co., 103, 263
Rogers, Art, 264
Romney, Catharine Cottam, 120, 150, 422
Romney, John, 305
Romney, Keith, 305, 310
Romney, Mary, 152, 154, 156
Romney, Miles, 54, 65, 78, 120, 134,
150, 152, 154, 156
Roosevelt, Franklin Delano, 226
Rotary Bowl, 346
Rotary International, 255
Roundy, Lorenzo, 29, 46, 409
Rowe, Charles H., 180
Rozencrans, C. Y., 206
RSVP, 402, 407
Ruesch, Walter, 205
Russell, Jane, 293
Russell, Lorenzo, 146
Russell, Sterling, 223

S

Safeway Store, 341, 381
"St. George and the Dragon," 145
St. George, 2-3, 6, 10-11, 34-38, 43, 202
St. George Airport, 222, 246, 258, 317,
323, 371
St. George Art Museum, 246, 323,
344, 373
St. George Bank, 224, 298, 330, 336-
338, 340
St. George Baptist Church, 280, 395, 397

St. George Boulevard, 220-221, 256,
299, 341, 367, 378, 381, 394
St. George Building Society, 337
St. George Chamber of Commerce, 215,
221, 230, 233-34, 244
St. George Dramatic Assoc., 154, 157
St. George First Ward School, 133
photograph, 133
St. George founding, 51
St. George geography, 1, 136, 404
St. George LIVE, 304, 316, 373, 384, 402
St. George location, 221, 263
St. George Marathon, 346, 367, 374, 402
St. George Police Department, 331,
348, 390
St. George Hall and Opera House, 34, 69,
101, 155-56, 161, 344, 373
photograph, 155, 347
St. George Literary Society, 166
St. George Magazine, 199, 248, 323,
345, 351, 358, 419, 421
St. George merchandising, 340, 342, 380
St. George post office, 50, 228
St. George Savings and Loan, 337
St. George Stake Academy, 9, 161, 165
St. George Tabernacle, 51, 55-56, 69,
91, 100, 108, 119, 160, 234, 242, 344
St. George Tabernacle Choir, 119, 160
St. George Temple, 10, 57, 59, 70-71,
91, 203, 332-33, 396, 402
St. George Tithing Office, 68-69
St. George Water and Power Board,
192, 197
St. George-Santa Clara Canal Company,
187, 192
St. George-Washington Canal Company,
193
Salt Lake City Commercial Club, 211
Sammons, Jimmie, 229
Sampson, Doyle, 259, 295-96, 338
San Bernardino, 28, 33, 35, 75, 90
Sand Hollow, 375-76, 378, 388-90, 394
Sand Hollow Aquatic Center, 375
Sand Hollow Reservoir, 388-90, 394

Sandberg, Chauncey, 194

Sanford, George, 328

Sangiovanni, G. R. R., 134, 162-63, 169

Sanitation Improvements, 142, 227

Sant Corporation, 296

Santa Clara, x, xvi, 5, 7, 9, 11, 13, 20-
21, 26-28, 33, 35-36, 38, 42-43, 47-
48, 62, 66, 72, 75, 77, 79-82, 91-94,
101-105, 108, 114, 117, 122, 124-25,
128, 132, 145, 147-48, 151, 159, 166,
168, 171, 178, 187, 189-90, 192-95,
222-223, 230, 241, 250, 252, 262-63,
265-66, 273, 276, 286, 300, 339, 344,
351, 369, 372, 376, 380, 383, 385-89,
392, 395, 397, 409, 417, 425

Santa Clara Irrigation Company, 194

Santa Clara River, 7, 26, 28, 33, 77, 91,
94, 114, 187, 189, 385-87, 395

Saunders, B. E., 265

Savage, Levi, 89, 121, 168, 424

Scanlan, Lawrence, 108, 160, 277

Scannel, Charles E., 223

Schaize, Fred, 220

Schlappi, Henry, 173

Schmutz, Dan, 338

Schmutz, Ray, 193-194

Schmutz, Wilford, 238

Schneiter, Ernie, 297, 299

Schneiter, Gene, 298

Schools, xvii, 10, 41, 49-50, 65-67,
71, 84, 93-94, 124, 131-32, 134-38,
140-42, 144-45, 152, 156, 161-63,
166, 168, 225-26, 230-35, 257, 259,
273-74, 276-80, 296, 308, 310-13,
322, 324, 328, 332, 334-36, 340, 345-
47, 349, 352, 359, 361-62, 365-68,
373-75, 376-77, 382, 384, 391, 393,
395-96, 399-400, 402, 406

Scroggins, William, 32

Searles, Kenny, 264

Sears, Robert N., 210

Sears Art Gallery, 373

Second Manifesto, 273

Seegmiller, Artemisia Snow, 155-56

Seegmiller, Charles W., 86

Seegmiller, Dan, 155

Seegmiller, George H., 240

Seegmiller, Ida, 100

Seegmiller, Paul, 238

Seep Ditch Company, 192

Sego Lilies, 74

Senior Citizen Center, 280, 369

Seniors in Schools, 402

Seven Wives Inn, 344

Seventh-day Adventist, 281, 397

Seventh-day Adventist Church, 281

Sex offenses, 391

Shakespeare Festival, 289

Shepherd, Robert, 344

Shipp, Ellis, 100, 324

Shirts, Morris, 106, 122, 323, 424

Shirts, Peter, 41

Shivwits Indians, 20, 22, 276-77

Shoal Creek, 29, 118, 168, 176-79, 191

Short Creek, 91, 272-74, 276, 398-99, 420

Shumway, Audrey, ix

Shunesburg, 9, 30, 32-33, 66, 72, 75-76,
143, 182, 213, 418

Silver Reef, x, 34, 66, 80, 83-84, 88-91,
102-04, 106-09, 116, 119, 122, 148,
157-158, 160, 163, 168-69, 202, 242,
244, 277, 312-13, 323-24, 329, 344,
421, 423-24

Silver Reef Estates, 313

SkyWest Airlines, 314-317, 323, 371,
379, 406, 421

Slack, L. J., 183

Slack, Martin, 183, 410

Slavery, 23, 125, 272

Smith, B. Glen, 222

Smith, Charles N., 145

Smith, George A., 25, 34, 38, 40, 59, 72,
110, 159

Smith, Hyrum, 316, 343, 373

Smith, Jedediah Strong, 6

Smith, John W., 47, 110

Smith, Joseph, 24, 47, 49, 183, 272-73

Smith, Joseph F., 183, 273

Smith, Melvin T., xvi, 7, 11, 424

Smith, Thomas "Pegleg", 8
Smith's Mesa, 268
Smoot, Reed, 205
Snow, Angus, x, 165, 277, 282
Snow, Artemisia, 155-56, 160
Snow, Ashby, 92, 119, 156, 166
Snow, Brent, x, 341, 349
Snow, Clinton, 299, 416
Snow, Dexter, 295
Snow, Donnitta, x, 277
Snow, E. Eric, 238, 416
Snow, Edward H., 152, 179, 241, 336-37
Snow, Elizabeth, 47, 152, 160, 419
Snow, Erastus, 10, 16, 29-30, 35-38, 44-
    45, 48, 50-53, 57, 63-64, 66, 68, 72,
    78, 91, 93, 104, 106, 108, 110, 115-
    17, 122, 139, 141-42, 156, 160, 165,
    182, 242, 252, 290, 328, 415, 423
    photograph, 16
Snow, Frank, 156
Snow, George, 36, 38, 50, 56-57, 156,
    194, 215, 234, 238, 299, 328, 397, 415
Snow, Glen, 236-37
Snow, Harold, 191, 328
Snow, J. C., 337
Snow, Joseph S., 234
Snow, Leo, 204, 246, 337
Snow, Lorenzo, 56, 70, 110
Snow, Maud, 166
Snow, Moroni, 152, 410
Snow, Olive Bleak, 245
Snow, Rob, ix
Snow, Ron, 310
Snow, Walter, 156, 328
Snow, Wendell, 255
Snow, William, 160, 194, 290, 310,
    409, 416
Snow Canyon Parkway, 394
Snow Canyon State Park, 288, 290
Snow Furniture Company, 340
Snow's Hotel, 246
Soldier, Dollie Big, 277, 282
Sorensen, Neils, 110
Sorenson, Ray, 222

Sorenson, Andrew, 265
Sorenson, Marc, 343
Sorenson, Maynard, 344
Sorenson, Vicki, 343
Southern Baptist Church, 280
Southern Indian Mission, 18-19, 46-47,
    124, 152, 168, 421
Southern Star, 164, 169
Southern Utah Free Press, 164, 169
Southern Utah Mission, 18-19, 34, 46-48,
    71, 75, 82, 102, 117, 120, 167, 419
Southern Utah News-Advertiser, 164, 169
Southern Utah Paiutes, 276
Southern Utah Power Company, 238-40
Southern Utah Telephone Co., 241-42
Southern Utah University, ix-x, 274, 321
Southern Utah Wilderness Alliance, 357
Southgate, 297-298, 378, 392, 397
Southgate Golf Course, 392
Southland Bible Church, 280
Southwest Symphony, 320, 347, 373
Spencer, Emily, 134
Spencer, George, 47, 134
Spencer, I. Carling, 274
Spendlove, Winfred, 193-94
Spendlove, Winford, 193
Sports Village, 311
Springdale, x, 26, 32-33, 66-67, 72,
    75-77, 82, 121, 182, 203, 205, 210,
    213, 218-19, 223, 238, 252, 268,
    319, 339, 344, 348, 367, 369, 373,
    375, 418
Springdale Church and School, 67
Sproul, Andrew, 173
Sproul, Angus, 159
Sproul, Emmeline, 159
Sproul, Mazel, 159
Spry, William, 205
Squiers, Ray, 229
Squire, Lorin D., 195
Squire, Phil, 259
Staheli, Frank, 159
Staheli, George, 159
Staheli, George Jr., 159

Staheli, John, 159
Staheli, William, 161
Staheli, Woodrow, 193
Stahle, Gail, 164, 169
Stambaugh, Samuel C., 83
Staples, George, 32
Stapley, Charles, 28
State Bank of Southern Utah, 338
State of Utah v. Royal Hunt, 188, 330
Steele, John, 99, 121, 182, 419, 424
Stephenson, Brent, 318
Stevens, George, 194
Stevenson, Anna, 278
Stewart, Dave, 280
Stockgrower's Bank, 224
Stocks, Henry, 32
Stocks, Moroni, 32
Stoker, Les, 305
Storrs, Gordon, 326-27
Stout, Carlyle, 307
Stout, Dell, 315-16
Stout, Hosea, 113-14
Strausser, Bastian, 159
Strickland, Bill, 229
Strong, Hyrum, 32
Stucki, Bruce, x, 192, 263, 295-98, 313,
    342, 371, 378
Stucki, H. Bruce, 192, 263
Stucki, Harvey, 263
Stucki, John S., 147, 153
Stucki, Rulon, 263
Sturzenegger, Clare, 240
Sturzenegger, Romain, 301
Sullivan, Charles R., 240
Sullivan, Mary Ann, 160
Sun Bowl, 255, 340
Sun Capital Bank, 338
Sun River, 378, 387, 393
Sunbrook, 378, 392
Sunbrook Golf Course, 392
Sunroc Corporation, 380, 391
Sunset Boulevard, 380-81, 394
Sunset Corner, 380
SunTran, 368, 406

Swiss Colony and Settlers, 38
Syphus, Alfred, 178

T

Taft, William Howard, 203-05
Tanner, Annie Atkin, 89, 121
Taylor, Byron, 238, 307
Taylor, Ray, 307
Taylor Grazing Act, 264, 267, 357
Telephones, 241-42
Tenney, Marvelous "Marve" Flood, 43
Tenney, Nathan, 31, 43
Terracor, 302-307, 310
Terry, Carlson, 328
Terry, Clair, x, 191, 337, 348
Terry, Dean, 338
Terry, Fenton, 221
Terry, Jacob, 32, 145
Terry, James P., 91, 410
Terry, Lowell, 222
Terry, Thomas, 176
Terry, Tommy, 68
Terry, Zera, 133
Terry, Zora P., 178
The Cactus, 163, 169
The Deadwood Coach, 294-95
The Electric Horseman, 291
The Fighting Gringo, 249
The Giant Joshua, 252-54, 281, 420, 425
The Ledges, 378, 394
The Lighthouse Ministry, 397
The Mineral Cactus, 163, 169
The Vanishing Pioneer, 295
The Vepricula, 162-63, 169
The Windows of Heaven, 70
Theater, xvii, 65, 126, 138, 143, 154-58,
    161-162, 210, 232, 249-50, 322, 341,
    373-74, 403
This is the Place: Utah, 253
Thomas, Charles J., 157
Thomas, Elijah, 106
Thomas, Erma, 270
Thomas, George, 47, 179, 188, 199
Thomas, Hy, 295

Thompson, Agnes Calkins, 100
Thompson, Ron, 196-197, 307
Thompson, Samuel, 99
Thompson, William, 159
Thurston, Harry, 166
Thurston, Morgan, 166
Tietjen, Maurice, 260
Tobler, Merl, 269
Tonaquint, 13, 26-27, 35-36, 114, 363, 396
Tonaquint Center, 363
Toquer, 27-28, 66, 125
Toquer Hall, 66
Toquerville, x, 5, 27-28, 30, 62, 65-66,
    72, 74, 76-77, 89, 91, 94, 99, 101-04,
    108, 117, 125, 137, 143, 148, 168,
    182-83, 202, 212-13, 223, 241-42,
    266, 268, 278, 300, 383, 389, 410,
    418, 423
Tortoise Habitat, 353, 376
Tourism, xviii, 203, 207, 211-12, 215,
    218-19, 246, 261, 298-99, 345, 351,
    356, 358, 364, 367, 369, 404
Tri-State Advertiser, 164
Trucking, 103, 210, 223-24, 261-63,
    339, 361-62
True Life Center, 397
Trueblood, L'Deane, 344, 381
Truman, Jacob, 29
Truman, Preston, 270
Truman, Spence, 259
Tuacahn, 290, 340, 367, 373
Tut-se-gab-its, 21
Tyler, Albert, 113
Tyler, D. M., 113

U

Udvar-Hazy Business Building, 320-21
    photograph, 322
Union, 83, 106, 119, 143, 163, 169, 207,
    209, 217, 267, 289
Union and Village Echo, 163, 169
Union Mining District, 106
Union Pacific Railroad, 207, 209, 217, 267
United Effort Plan Trust, 274-75, 398-99

United Order, 110-12, 274, 399
Utah Hill, 105, 118, 300
Utah Parks Co., 207-08, 214, 217, 251
Utah Pomologist and Gardener, 102,
    163, 169
Utah Power and Light Company, 196, 342
Utah War, 33, 35, 139, 215, 257, 281,
    284, 424
Vaughn, Dinah, 132
Vermillion Cliffs, 392, 422, 425
Veyo, 194-95, 230, 238, 241, 256, 321,
    339, 372

V

Vic Braden Tennis, 311, 376
Vic Braden Tennis School, 311, 376
Village Bank, 338
Village System, 13, 84, 93, 95, 180, 186
Virgen, Thomas, 8
Virgin, x, xvi-xvii, 3, 5-10, 12-13, 18,
    25-27, 29-36, 41-44, 47, 62, 65-66,
    71-72, 74, 76-77, 79, 84-85, 87, 89,
    91, 94, 96, 114-15, 118, 121, 163-64,
    169, 171-73, 180, 182, 185-187, 189,
    193-97, 200, 203, 207-08, 213-14,
    219, 230, 243-44, 252, 266-69, 300-
    01, 304, 339, 357-58, 367, 386-89,
    395, 417-18, 423-24
Virgin River, xvi-xvii, 3, 6-10, 12-13,
    18, 25-27, 30-34, 36, 41, 44, 66, 74,
    76-77, 84-85, 87, 114-115, 118, 180,
    182, 185-87, 189, 193-94, 196-97,
    200, 203, 207-08, 213-14, 219, 230,
    300-01, 304, 357-58, 386, 388, 395,
    417-18
Virgin River Gorge, 9, 13, 118, 300-01
Virgin River Land Preservation Assoc.,
    357
Virgin Valley Enterprise, 164, 169
Volunteerism, 347, 402

W

Wade, Alton, 319-20
Wadsworth, Eugene, 194
Wadsworth Theater, 341

Wal-Mart, 296, 342, 352, 361, 378-80
  Corporation, 296
  Distribution Center, 342, 352, 361
Walker, Charles Lowell, 37, 48, 84,
  119-120, 142, 154, 156, 160, 162,
  167, 425
Walker, Hyrum, 64
Walker, Zaidee, 152, 156
Wallis, John R., 163, 169
Washington City, 9, 27, 47, 61, 63, 66, 75,
  81-82, 84-86, 88, 97, 101, 116, 159,
  172-73, 191, 222, 229-30, 238, 258,
  278, 296, 299, 336, 339, 351, 368-69,
  372, 379, 382-83, 394-95, 403
Washington County, ix, xi, xvi-xviii, 1-3,
  5-10, 14-16, 18, 24, 29, 37, 40, 42,
  45-46, 48-50, 61-62, 64-65, 68-70, 72,
  75, 77, 80-81, 83, 88, 90, 97, 99-101,
  106, 109, 114, 118, 122-24, 130, 133,
  137-38, 140, 143, 151-52, 154, 159,
  161-64, 166, 169, 171, 175-77, 180,
  186-87, 189, 194-95, 197-202, 208-13,
  215, 223-24, 226-30, 232, 235-36,
  238, 242, 244-49, 252, 256-57, 260-
  61, 264, 267-69, 271, 277, 280-82,
  284-85, 290, 292, 296, 299, 303-04,
  308-10, 313, 317, 323, 325, 331-33,
  335-36, 338, 342, 345-59, 361-65,
  367-74, 376-77, 382, 384-86, 388-91,
  397-400, 402-03, 405-07, 409, 413,
  417, 419-20, 422-23, 425
  boundaries, xiv, xvi, xx, 4, 10,
  early descriptions, 1
  geology, 1, 122, 193, 424
  population, 354-355, 358
Washington County Courthouse, 53, 65,
  72, 333, 336
Washington County Historical Society,
  xi, 65
Washington County News, ix, 122, 163-
  64, 169, 200, 210, 215, 224, 228, 244,
  246-48, 252, 256, 281, 285, 296, 323,
  333, 348
Washington County road development
  and maintenance, 213

Washington County School District, 232,
  235, 308, 332, 335, 347, 365, 406
Washington County School District
  superintendents, 152, 335
Washington County Water Conservancy
  District, 195, 197, 358, 367, 384, 388,
  390, 406
Washington Field Dam, 87
  Photograph, 87
Waste Management, 403
Water, xv-xix, 1, 3, 18-22, 28-29, 33-34,
  37, 39, 41-46, 49, 51, 54, 58, 60-64,
  71, 73, 76-77, 82, 84-88, 90, 93-94,
  97-98, 105, 112-15, 117-19, 125-26,
  130-31, 136, 139, 145-47, 164, 166,
  171-200, 204, 217-19, 225, 227-28,
  239-40, 242, 253, 268, 273, 277, 290-
  91, 296-97, 302-04, 307, 311, 313,
  328, 353-55, 357-359, 367, 381-382,
  384-90, 393, 403-06, 418, 422
Water Development, 175, 191, 194, 198,
  359, 388
Watkins, Carol Cox, 328
Watson, Barbara, 327
Watson, D. C., 239
Watson, Dan, xi, 11
Watson, David, 388, 411
Watt, Catherine, 278
Wayne, John, 250, 293-94
Wayne County, 78, 176
Webb, Loren, ix, 169, 248
Webb, Murray, x, 264, 325, 411
Wells, George, 68, 192
Wells, Stephen R., 113
Wells Fargo State Station, 313
Western Airlines, 222, 315-16
Western Gold and Uranium Co., 313
Westin, George, 325
Weston, Jack, 330
Westover, Edwin R., 29
When a Man's a Man, 292
When Tomorrow Comes, 249
Whipple, Alice, 327
Whipple, Charles, 156
Whipple, Maurine, 252, 281, 419-20

Whiskey, 114

White, Douglas, 216

Whitehead, Adolphus R., 152

Whitehead, Evan, x, 331, 348, 413

Whitehead, George F., 165, 173, 179, 415

Whitehead, Gordon, 337

Whitehead, Richard, 328-29

Whitehurst, Mary, 327

Whitehead, E. G., 166

Whitlock, Hardin, 32

Whitmore, James, 99, 273

Whittaker, Lyman, 344

Wiegand, William K., 278

Wildfires, 385-386

Wilkie, Alex, 280

Wilkinson, Randy, 192

William "Gunlock" Hamblin, 28

Williams, Jack, 301

Williams, Kumen D., 244

Williamsburg Bank, 338

Willis, J. C., 183

Willis, Joshua T., 27, 92, 242, 409

Willis, Wesley, 28

Wilson, J. Morris, 194, 410

Wilson, Steve, 326, 406-407

Wilson, Wayne, xi, 192-96, 198, 200, 411

Winchester Hills, 378, 394

Winding River Corporation, 296

Wine [making], 60, 63, 66, 101-02, 104,
    147-50, 153, 190, 319, 423

Winsor, Andrew W., 180

Winsor, Anson P., 92, 409

Winsor, Frank, 180

Winston Associates, 355

Wittwer, Glade, 259

Wittwer, Julius, 264

Wittwer, Lester, 263

Wittwer, Reed, 263

Wolfskill, William, 7

Women, 5, 16, 21, 25, 41, 44, 81, 88-89,
    95-96, 99, 116, 125, 128, 137-38,
    147, 150, 168, 185, 223, 226-27, 236-
    37, 254-55, 278, 282, 370, 378, 382,
    387, 420

Wood, Ether, 43

Wood, Luwayne, xi, 266, 281

Woodbury, Angus, 47-48, 246, 254, 425

Woodbury, Clare, MD, 244, 324-25

Woodbury, Eleanor, 134

Woodbury, Evan, xi, 193, 240, 411

Woodbury, Frank J., 324

Woodbury, John T., 135, 152, 156, 415-
    16, 425

Woodbury, Merrill, 328

Woodhouse, A. L., 238, 337

Woodruff, Wilford, 60, 70, 151, 272, 337

Woodward, Hugh M., 337

Woodward School, 159, 161, 259, 340,
    366, 382, 384

Woolley, E. G., 106, 154

Woolley, Franklin B. G., 157

Woolley, Fred, 166

Woolley, Lorin C., 273

Woolley, Louie, 166

Woolley, Lund and Judd Company, 86,
    88, 109, 336

Workman, A. J., 47, 79

Workman, Carl, 251

Workman, Charles A., 152

Works Progress Administration, 226

World Senior Games, 346, 367, 374, 406

World War I, 207, 223,

World War II, xviii, 207-08, 217-19,
    224, 252, 255-57, 260, 264, 268-69,
    281, 283-84, 306, 331, 337, 340, 360,
    371, 424

Worthen, Joseph, 52

Worthen, Louis, 160

Worthen, Mary, 160

WPA, 152, 226-28

Wright, Elizabeth Bruhn, xi, 270

Wright, Flint, 194

Wylie, William W., 207

Y

Young, Brigham, ix, 8, 14, 18-19, 24, 26-27, 30, 34-36, 44-47, 51, 55, 57-58, 60, 62-64, 68, 71-72, 79, 88, 92, 98-100, 102, 106, 110, 115, 121, 124, 128, 139, 141, 147, 153, 159-160, 167, 169-70, 185, 188, 202, 226, 242, 247, 272, 281, 319-20, 327, 349, 354, 419, 421-25
  photograph, 14
Young, Brigham Jr., 57
Young, Erla, 344
Young, John W., 110, 127
Yount, George C., 7

Z

Z-Arts concert Series, 373
Zion Factory Stores, 342-43, 378
  photograph, 343
Zion Lodge, 204, 207-08
  photograph, 204, 208
Zion National Park, xvii, 2, 5, 9, 85, 95, 203, 205, 207-09, 212, 214-16, 229-30, 243, 251, 254, 261, 265, 267, 285, 294, 299, 339, 351, 360, 372-73, 375, 386
Zion Natural History Assoc., 209, 424
Zion Pioneerzz, 375
Zion's Township, 333
Zion Tunnel, 205, 212
Zion-Mt. Carmel highway, 207
Zions Bank, 315, 336-37, 343
Zitting, David, 275